Ellen B. Basso

A Musical View of the Universe

University of Pennsylvania Publications in Conduct and Communication

Erving Goffman and Dell Hymes, Founding Editors
Dell Hymes, Gillian Sankoff, and Henry Glassie, General Editors

The author is grateful to those listed below for permission to quote from the works indicated:

Sigmund Freud, The Complete Introductory Lectures on Psychoanalysis. Copyright 1966 by W. W. Norton, New York.

Richard Bauman, Verbal Art as Performance. Reprint. Copyright 1984 by Waveland Press, Prospect Heights, Ill.

Claude Lévi-Strauss, The Naked Man. Copyright 1981 by Harper & Row, New York.

Photos by Ellen B. Basso

Design by Tracy Baldwin

Library of Congress Cataloging in Publication Data

Basso, Ellen B.
  A musical view of the universe.

  Bibliography: p.
  Includes index.
  1. Apalakiri Indians—Rites and ceremonies.
2. Apalakiri Indians—Folklore.   3. Apalakiri Indians—
Music.   4. Indians of South America—Brazil—Xingu River
Valley—Rites and ceremonies.   5. Indians of South America
—Brazil—Xingu River Valley—Folklore.   6. Indians of
South America—Brazil—Xingu River Valley—Music.
I. Title.
F2520.1.A63B38   1985   306'.08998   84–5166
ISBN 0–8122–7931–X

Printed in the United States of America

Contents

Appendix 3: Songs Called "Birding" (itolotepe)
            (as sung by Kudyu, Ugaki, and Tsaŋaku)   *321*

Illustrations

Tables

Preface

The Kalapalo are a community of about two hundred Carib-speaking people who live in their settlement called Aifa in a region of central Brazil that is protected as a national reserve, the Parque Nacional do Xingu. Within the southerly region of the park, the Kalapalo together with seven other Indian groups live artificially segregated from national Brazilian society and economy, cultivating fields of manioc, corn and rice, and orchards of piqui fruit, and fishing in the many lakes and streams that cross the region. Although they are considerably less isolated than in the recent past, their protected habitation has made possible their continued survival in the face of increasingly disastrous demographic, social, and economic pressures which on several occasions have threatened the integrity of the reserve. The policy of the agency responsible for administering the park—the Fundacão Nacional do Indio (FUNAI)—has been to isolate and maintain these native populations as curiosities, while ruling and controlling them through authoritarian decrees. The alternative strategy of encouraging the maintenance of a unique identity and intellectual independence while assisting with the development of an effective understanding and set of skills for dealing with the outside world—a world that is less and less "outside" and increasingly one in which they are participants—has yet to be adopted. A few young men have thus taken it on their own to become minimally literate and knowledgeable about Brazilian ways, but this educational process requires lengthy residence in a distant city, which is impractical and distinctly unpleasant for almost every Kalapalo who has tried it. Most people remain monolingual in Kalapalo; a few can speak enough Portuguese to communicate with outsiders, but none are literate in that language.

The Kalapalo language is one of several Carib dialects in the Upper Xingu Basin and is most closely related to what is known as the Southern Carib branch of the Carib family, which also includes the branches called Southeastern Colombia Carib and Southern Guiana Carib. Because these various Carib languages are only now beginning to be compared, almost nothing is known about the prehistoric relationships of the ancestors of the speakers and even less about their geographic origins or early sociotechnical development. It seems certain, however, that the Kalapalo are descendants of people who moved south from the western Guiana region sometime after the Spanish Conquest, probably around three hundred years ago.

The more southerly region of the Upper Xingu Basin in which the Kalapalo live contains a number of linguistically diverse groups whose history and society pose several problems to anthropologists. Despite extreme linguistic diversity (there were speakers of the mutually unintelligible Carib, Ge, Tupian, and Arawakan families, as well as the Trumai isolate) the people currently occupying this area hold a large number of social and cultural features in common, sharing a distinctive system of social classification and status allocation, marriage practices, cosmology, ceremonial organization, and trade specialization of settlements.

My earlier study of the Kalapalo* focused upon a set of concepts that could be used to construct a model of Kalapalo society. I was particularly concerned to describe a system of classification by which the Kalapalo distinguish social relationships, which is manifested in a distinctive behavioral and conceptual complex that distinguishes all the Upper Xingu people of the southerly region of the park from their traditionally surrounding neighbors. Although I have gone far beyond my earlier discussions of mythology and ritual, this earlier study is still useful for its detailed description of the central aspects of Kalapalo world view as it bears upon understanding Kalapalo society.

My hope is that this book will make the reader think seriously of cultural similarities and differences in lowland South America but also of similarities and differences in contemporary life imposed upon native peoples in all of Latin America, with which the situation of the majority of Xinguanos contrasts remarkably though with fearful tenuousness.

*Basso, 1973.

Acknowledgments

Many of the ideas advanced in this book were first presented to my colleagues at various conferences and workshops, and I am exceedingly grateful to them for much lively discussion and good, strong advice. I would like to thank in particular Donald Bahr, Steven Feld, William Hanks, Gilbert Herdt, Charles Keil, Waud Kracke, Bruce Mannheim, Joel Sherzer, Michael Silverstein, and Barbara Tedlock. To Desmond Derbyshire, Steven Feld, Dell Hymes, Robert Netting, Gillian Sankoff, Joel Sherzer, Dennis Tedlock, and Will Wright go my thanks for their helpful comments on portions of earlier drafts of the manuscript. I am also deeply grateful to my friend and colleague Professor Roque de Barros Laraia of the Universidade de Brasilia and to the officials of the Conselho Nacional de Desenvolvimento Científico e Technologico and the Fundacão Nacional do Indio for their considerable assistance in furthering my research in Brazil.

My stay among the Kalapalo during 1978–80 was supported by a National Science Foundation Research Grant (BNS 78-00849) and the University of Arizona. A grant from the Wenner-Gren Foundation for Anthropological Research, Inc., supported my travels during 1982. The Humanities Committee of the University of Arizona provided funds to help defray costs of publication.

In making the collection of Kalapalo myths from which those presented in this book have been drawn, I have been preceded by important work in the Upper Xingu Basin done by Brazilian and French colleagues, as represented by Aurore Monod-Becquelin's comprehensive collection of Trumai mythology (1975), Pedro Agostinho's publication of Kamaiura stories (1978), and Roque de Barros Laraia's study of sun and moon myths (1967). Another worthy study of Xingu mythology is the publication by Orlando and Claudio Villas Boas (1970, 1973), which includes what appear to be compilations of myth variants condensed into single narratives. Several important studies by Brazilian colleagues of native Brazilian ritual and music must also be mentioned: Pedro Agostinho's study (1974) of the *kwarìp* ritual among the Kamaiura; Julio Cezar Melatti's book on Kraho (Ge) ritual (1978); Helza Cemeu's analytic survey of native Brazilian music (1977); and especially the groundbreaking work on Kamaiura concepts of sound and of music by Rafael José de Menezes Bastos (1978).

Because Kalapalo culture is so deeply concerned with images of the natural world of the central Brazilian plateau, the interested reader should consult pictures of as many of the species referred to as possible. I suggest the following relatively available sources: for birds the magnificent *A Guide to the Birds of Venezuela* (Princeton, 1978) by Rodolphe Meyer de Schauensee and William Phelps, Jr.; for mammals and some insects and fish the famous *Dicionário dos animais do Brasil* (São Paulo, 1940) by the late Brazilian naturalist and teacher Rodolphe von Ehring; and for a more comprehensive look at fish (much more difficult) Richard Goulding's *The Fishes and the Forest* (Berkeley, 1980), but any good tropical fish handbook in which many of the major neotropical freshwater groups are illustrated might serve.

This book is dedicated to the Kalapalo, for their constant and sympathetic sharing with me of the good things of their lives and for continuing to allow me the great privilege of learning from them in so many different and lasting ways. To single out individuals would be an injustice, for whatever any one person did, it was with the enthusiasm, interest, and encouragement of many others.

Guide to Pronouncing Kalapalo Words

The following phonetic symbols have been used to write Kalapalo words:

Vowels

a,   as in oper*a* (low front open)

e,   as in b*e*st (middle open)

ë,   as "oe" in French *coeur* (middle closed)

i,   as in s*ee*m (high front open)

ï,   as in sh*ou*ld (middle open)

o,   as in *o*ld (middle rounded)

u,   as in June (high back rounded)

Vowel nasalization is indicated by a tilda (as in ũ). Nasalization usually occurs in a stressed syllable.

Consonants

d,   voiced alveolar stop

f,   voiceless bilabial fricative

g,   voiced glottal fricative

h,   voiceless glottal fricative

dy, voiced alveopalatal fricative (occasionally written "j")

k,   voiceless velar stop

l,   voiced alveolar lateral

m,   voiced bilabial nasal

n,   voiced alveolar nasal

ŋ,   voiced velar nasal

ñ,   voiced palatal nasal

p,   voiced bilabial stop

s,   voiceless alveopalatal fricative

ts, voiceless dental affricate

t, voiceless alveolar stop

w, voiced bilabial semivowel

z, voiced alveolar fricative

ž, voiced alveopalatal fricative

The following rules can be fairly safely followed for syllabic stress in pronouncing Kalapalo words: In words of two syllables, stress is usually on the first syllable. In noncompound words of more than two syllables, the second syllable of the word is normally stressed.

Chapter 1
Introduction: Meaning Constructed Through Performance

Anthropologists concerned with the symbolic expressions of thought that constitute culture have come to recognize the need to focus upon the interpretive and instrumental uses to which people put these forms—their place in action. This focus is the result of an increased understanding of how we construct an awareness of our experiences of life, how they are organized and thereby understood as signs, and how symbolic systems (what Clifford Geertz has called "conceptual structures molding formless talents") give specific, comprehensible meaning to our biologically mediated experiences.[1] As a consequence, in considering the relation of culture to human life we need to study symbols through their creation and use in explanatory and orienting strategies: Under what conditions do certain themes, practices, and strategies arise? How are changes in social and ecological roles and relationships given meaning and integrated into the older forms of knowledge that constitute a peoples' received models of the universe, of the self, and of society? How are these models reaffirmed or made more satisfactory, how are novel solutions to the perennial difficulties of a particular way of life introduced, and how are traditional solutions modified to accommodate new problems? By what means are these new views of the world, reformulated concepts of identity, and new solutions to old difficulties communicated and made acceptable to others? And finally, how do people assert new attributes of their political, social, religious, and artistic selves? These questions focus upon the problems of relatively comprehensive processes of change in cultural systems. However, that focus suggests a way of understanding the relation between cultural symbols and psychodynamic processes that are a consequence of changes in the more inwardly focused, privately felt processes of living. For the use of cultural forms gives meaning to what is happening mentally to a person, thereby assisting in the construction of ideas of feeling and of a sense of self that are developed from both public, social experiences and those of private self-reflection.

These imaginative, transforming, creative characteristics of culture and the rhetorical contexts in which they are most clearly developed and expressed are closely connected to the fact that culture constitutes and contains within itself explanations of human life and thought and of social, psychological, environmental, and cosmological events and processes. By "explanation" I mean the ways knowledge is organized and used—in persuasion, debate, reflection, and especially narrative—to clarify that which is considered problematic or puzzling, thereby effecting a particular orientation toward something in the world. Explanation (an aspect or concretization of epistemological principles) is a process that is embedded in the very general cultural function of interpretation, of making experience intelligible through symbolic codes that are ever subtly shifting to accommodate new insights, new applications, newly available forms, and new contexts of use. Hence the explanatory aspect of culture seems most critical for understanding the efficacy of creative play—a process of experimenting with symbols and concocting new ones that involves extending meaning beyond what is commonly accepted and understood. The relation of explanation and symbolic play is suggested by the fact that what we hold to be true about the world and the meanings given to our experience of it are most often developed and expanded in situations of action—found in all cultures—that are marked or foregrounded by virtue of their performed, artistic, and fantastic attributes. These cultural modes of action give scope and meaning to daily experience through images that reveal both the most deep speculation and concern with the fascinating and mysterious aspects of human life and the role of human beings in a sensory universe of polymorphic entities and problematic events.

Anthropologists see performances as especially heightened forms of cultural expression wherein creative experimentation is appropriate, even often expected, where the performer is responsible to a critical audience and therefore needs to adjust the action to satisfy that audience. Hence the success of symbolic play in performed events is judged by the participants according to criteria specifically suited to the genre and context;[2] in performance, responses to play strongly influence and are thus an integral part of the process, for it is in such situations that the performer becomes an affecting presence (to use Robert Plant Armstrong's expression) eliciting anticipated responses from an audience for whom the performance is both meaningful and interesting.

Not all performance involves the transmission of traditional knowledge, but when it does conditions for consecration of that tradition arise. If judged successful the playful use of symbols to transmit knowledge and to communicate explanatory messages in turn has a strong affirmative, even venerating effect. The essential comprehensibility of the world is assured in the minds of people involved, and the suitability of the models is reconfirmed. Not surprisingly, the suggestion has been made that oral tradition and performance may be inseparable components of the same cultural phenomenon.[3]

But the forceful appeal of newly created symbolic forms in contexts of dramatic social crisis also cannot fail to escape our notice. As many writers concerned with performance have noted, the ability to give meaning to something baffling and threatening, and to make that meaning (however ultimately misleading) understandable and acceptable to others, is the sign of a successful political performer, one who may even have the power to transform society.[4]

Understanding Art as Performance

In our own society, creative symbolic play tends to be closely associated with a class of specialists we call "artists," and the results of their activities are treated as "works of art" having (for better or worse) value as commodities. For the nonartist, the "work" takes precedence over the activity of its making and is evaluated for what it shows, or is known about, or has been learned about the virtuosity of the maker. The works of nonvirtuosos are hardly taken seriously and rarely have commercial value. Though virtuosity is constantly redefined by commerce, the appeal of a "work of art" is (philistinism aside) an indicator of social acceptance of the artist's work—its meaning for the society at large. In both anthropology and Western art historical scholarship even the most insightful studies reflect the general attitudes of our society insofar as they are determined to explicate the particular features of objects that make them "great art" (or to use another label of Robert Plant Armstrong, "affecting works"). These analyses emphasize the social and evaluative contexts of the use of art objects—their effect on those for whom they have determined meaning—which (though important) tend to be emphasized at the expense of the processes through which they were created.[5]

But for the artist, the process of creating art is as significant if not more so than the results. Although it is necessary to understand the processes by means of which those results create a response in others, equal consideration must be given to creative processes. These are, after all, the means by which the aesthetic, sensory, and scientific ingredients of human awareness are integrated in the goal of making experience intelligible, for giving form and meaning to human life. Considered from this perspective, art that is made in situations of performance often results in interpretations that are actually restructured worlds, worlds located in space-time frames different from those of ordinary life, which are not accessible to most people in other circumstances. This restructuring of reality involves the creation of possible worlds, apparitions, or illusory images that seem to exist without any practical or immediate relation to life and that may at first appear doubtful and possibly threatening. Yet such images sometimes eventually come to assume a central and convincing place in rational discourse, constituting primary interpretive possibilities for giving meaning to existence.

Art and Illusion in Performance

Speech becomes artistically important when the particular resources of a language and the forms of discourse available to speakers are used for what are taken to be their intrinsic expressive and structural characteristics, to project distinctive ideas or insights bearing upon conceptualization that cannot be made by other means. Such a "reevaluation" of linguistic resources (a word Roman Jakobson used to describe this poetic process) thus extends the meaningful effects that are given within a performer's medium, including the social consequences of the use of those particular resources. And yet, as Richard Bauman suggests, through performance a communicative event is created "in which speech is not to be interpreted literally."[6] Since the reality of performed cultural events is not literal representation of the day-to-day life of narrator and listeners, these events have a universal quality of truthfulness because they are unbounded by relativistic necessity. Though making reference to carefully observed aspects of the world of experience, performed cultural events actually achieve a nonordinary reality as a consequence of the ability of human beings to create illusory apparitions that seem to exist for themselves without any necessary practical relation to the world. According to Suzanne Langer, while experiencing an artistic form, we cease to be aware of the materials and become involved in the formal illusion created by what is being said.[7] Hence if an illusion is intriguing and vital, we can even forget we are watching a performance and become drawn into it to the extent that it achieves a palpable reality by means of our own active imagining or self-enchantment.

Considering that illusionary expression is a vital component of performance, a situation that unites all the participants in a shared mental experience, we can understand how such activities can be taken seriously or regarded as truthful by a listener and how they can then become useful and meaningful symbols. Furthermore, although it is easiest to understand how the creation of mental apparitions could occur in situations of artistic performance, any cultural process in which an imaginary world is constructed through performative participation can effect this experience.

Performance and Fantasy

Because many elements of a performance do not match everyday life, the listener can interpret them only through reference to "normal" or, more accurately, common and expected experiences. Performances are compellingly convincing just when they play upon a people's most exact knowledge of the substantial world. Because of the way analogies have been built up by the many anonymous artists over the course of a peoples' existence to form the symbolic images used in this mode of action, performances constitute a "clarification of reality" (as Wallace Stevens described it)—developed from the experiences of reality but reconstructing it and thereby illuminating aspects of it that remain hidden elsewhere in the communication of understanding.

What is most distinctive about this "normal life" is that it is governed by perhaps the most verbally explicit and socially pervasive cultural models, taking the expressive form of linguistic etiquette, imperatively stated taboos, and undisguised moral judgments. As a consequence, in the domain of social life many things, but most notably feelings about one's closest associates arising from that association, must often remain concealed or at least deliberately controlled. These emotions are revealed in events for which the participant is not held personally responsible for content, especially when the content is considered part of a group's tradition, or if the participant is a narrator claiming to be reporting an occurrence that another is thought to have experienced. If such expression is characterized by an elaborate tropic process and is communicated within a performative frame, the result will be cultural forms (as diverse as myths, dreaming reports, seances, carnivals, or initiation rituals) that serve for prominent expression of fantasy.

Freud saw fantasy as a conscious waking dreamwork that is most clearly observed in artistic processes; his final words in "The Paths to the Formation of Symptoms" are an eloquent statement on art as performance. He suggests that the artist's work involves a special appreciation, understanding, and playfulness toward the symbols of culture, whose relevance to the products of his own imagination is always apparent.[8] If performance is the appropriate frame of expression in the creation of what we call art, this daydream work becomes especially prominent. Performance thus allows a participant extensive opportunity for imaginative manipulation of content, for describing a sense of the world different from the commonplace, for creating an imaginary world, and for participating in that world in a socially acceptable way. And because some people explicitly see events in their lives as constituting substance for such illusionary expression, the performative frame allows them the opportunity for satisfying this wish, for contributing their own imaginative self-consciousness to a narrative or ritual tradition, for playing with the images that arise from the conditions of their lives. These imagined worlds are actually a performative reevaluation of the conditions of life, often resulting in the resurrection of images that have been imaginatively created by other performers at other times; and performance allows them to be approached with interest and amusement rather than fear, anger, and rejection.

The relation of performed events to substantial understanding of the world allows a special freedom of situational usage in contrast with other forms of discourse. In the course of reflecting upon a performance people can ponder the suitability of its content both in nonperformative discourse contexts and in exceedingly private situations or situations that are new or unfamiliar to them. In such cases, illusions, apparitions, and self-enchantments acquire and subsequently convey propositional truth value, serving important explanatory and orienting functions. Such forms (be they utterances or imagined sensory imagery) then cease to be illusionary (or "mythological") and enter the realm of ordinary discourse, while retaining their appropriateness for private and individual experience. From this perspective, cultural forms created within a performative frame can be regarded as strikingly imaginative sources of variation and adaptation to changing conditions—reservoirs for models of new social relationships, attitudes, and moral-evaluative systems, the materials for new cultural inventions. These symbolic forms may provide people with solutions to hypothetical problems, describing these solutions with respect to imaginary but nonetheless realistic motives. When dramatically sudden changes occur in one's life, or productive forces change, these forms may suggest strategies for engaging in new systems of social integration, productive relations, and the presentation of unusual (but especially meaningful) public selves.

Kalapalo Performed Art

The forms of Kalapalo culture that are the most directly associated by them with performance are storytelling and collective ritual, processes participated in by virtually everyone so often as to be considered familiar but hardly commonplace or trivial in their lives. The relations between Kalapalo myth and ritual are in part a matter of homologies resulting from references to similar themes and personages, but more fundamental is the complementarity between the two symbolic media resulting from the special performative processes typifying them. These processes distinguish myth and ritual as unique expressive events in Kalapalo life that construct and clarify fundamental cosmological ordering principles, the enhanced awareness and understanding of which constitute a special experience for the performers. The heightened form of expression in Kalapalo myth is verbal; in ritual it is musical.

Unlike our own attitude toward art as a professed specialty, the Kalapalo do not restrict artistic activity to specialists or to people exhibiting virtuosity. The Kalapalo understand that everyone has the capacity for creativity and expressiveness. Indeed, the importance of participation in verbal and ritual art indicates that they virtually insist upon people actively developing such capacities from childhood. This is not to say that performative events are not evaluated or that virtuosity is not occasionally significant for identifying some people of unusual accomplishment and for creating distinctive roles and relations for them. The point is that the processes through which various performed events are constructed are integral to social life and are a significant aspect of the ordinary person's means of comprehending reality. Hence both creative performance and nonperformative creativity are of vital significance for understanding the general experiences of Kalapalo life. Yet instances of performance are, if successful, events that are interpreted in special, marked ways by the participants, and hence the experiencing of them, the effects of participation, are multiply and distinctively meaningful in ways that are different from experiencing cultural forms that are not performed.

Kalapalo Narrative Art

The Kalapalo refer to narrative art by the form *akiña*, a transitive verbalization of the noun *akisï*, "(someone's) speech." Although the Kalapalo word subsumes any form of narrative speech (including personal accounts and oral tradition or "ancestral stories"), topic is not as important to their idea of narrative performance as are two elements critical to the narrative process: the speaker's adherence to a set of conventional discourse structuring elements and the participation of a listener-responder, who is responsible for creating the conditions under which a speaker's story can unfold. The Kalapalo do not formally classify categories of narratives, all of which are performed to a certain degree insofar as the manner of adherence to the two conditions described above is closely related to the relatively public or private nature of the event. Because they are deliberately public events and are accessible to virtually anyone who cares to listen, traditional narratives (henceforth called "myths") provide the opportunity for elaborate performance in a way personal accounts, which tend to be narrated in more secretive circumstances, often do not. This is because the telling of traditional stories, which involves both the expression of fantasy and the use of highly refined and consciously structured figurative speech, comes under the critical scrutiny of an audience that is evaluating the speaker's expertise. As verbal art, the Kalapalo use of grammatical categories and discourse features is as crucial to understanding their mythology as are the characters, events, and themes. For a storyteller creates an interpretive and explanatory matrix through poetic and rhetorical organization of these resources of the Kalapalo language, and this matrix mentally engulfs the listeners until they understand, or "see," the point of what is being said.

As a visitor to the Kalapalo, from the first I suffered the gentle but persistent poking and stroking accompanied by close, frank, and long-held stares that constitute these people's confrontation with anything new and strange that intrudes into their world. This is one characteristic suggestion of the nearly microscopic attention to the details of the apparently obvious aspects of life that we also see in Kalapalo mythology. The Kalapalo display a remarkably precise and detailed awareness of the natural world that is revealed in their complex systems of naming and classifying the life forms in their species-rich environment, in their understanding of the processes of life in which they are involved, and in their refusal to succumb to sentimentality. This knowledge and understanding are best revealed in the poetry of their stories but obviously are the basis for their continual adaptational success and their remarkable technological inventions. The result of countless meticulous and patient observations, these mental recordings of natural phenomena and reflections and speculations about the causes, consequences, and implications of natural events could (in the absence of writing) have been preserved, shared, and evaluated through time only in oral tradition. The Kalapalo "thirst for objective understanding"[9] lends remarkable precision of sensory detail to their narratives and is expressed in their quick ability to metaphorize through the imagery of nature. This sensitivity to the world around them also has an extraordinary imaginative effect, for it is through the many metonymic chains of sensory detail that mental apparitions are created in the minds of listeners.

But Kalapalo storytelling is an imaginative activity, high entertainment that involves great attention to form through the creative manipulation of language and the use of tropic imagery, repetition, purposive structuring, and other poetic devices. Kalapalo storytelling should be approached as an extremely efficient means of communication, compressing a great amount of information, interpretation, speculation, and imaginative play. In Kalapalo myths, we meet a fascinating blend of poetry and science, fascinating not only because it forces the mind to focus on esoteric matters, but, more important, upon otherwise hidden, secretive matters that are prohibited expression elsewhere, and upon those things that have been too often taken for granted.

Although the worlds of mythic narrative are in the imaginative sense illusory, the Kalapalo understand the characters in their myths to be real and the events described therein as true. Kalapalo describe their narrative speech as a way of teaching or imparting knowledge (*ikanïgï*) and of explanation (*ifanïgï*). It has been said that myth is true in the sense that our own poetry is true. We can think of Kalapalo mythology more prosaically as a kind of science fiction constructed out of the people's most advanced and learned scientific understanding of their world to convey narratives of very unusual lives. But whereas the writer of science fiction speculates about an imaginary future, the tellers of Kalapalo myths evoke an illusionary past. In so doing, they clarify the conditions of the present world.

Kalapalo Ritual Art

Collective music-making *(aŋ-)* is also directly associated with performance. As with Kalapalo myth, the particular conditions under which collective ritual performances occur permit the expression of meanings that have at best a limited field in nonritual life. But that is the field in which narrative discourse appears. As with Kalapalo narrative art, these special ritual meanings arise from the actual conditions of performance. In Kalapalo collective ritual, sound, especially musical performance, is most salient, although visual images also contribute to the performative whole. As with Kalapalo narrative art, Kalapalo ritual meanings are effected through a redefinition of certain normative boundaries and contexts of operation, establishing new conditions under which a special social experience—another normality and an alternative understanding of life— is effected. As a performed process, Kalapalo ritual involves the creation of a musical experience that effects a condition of personal understanding of and collective response to certain social imperatives that are different from those that accompany nonmusical life. Seen this way, Kalapalo collective rituals are more than ordered sequences of symbolic action. Kalapalo ritual experience forms essential meanings through the significance given to musical performance and the functional consequences of the meaning of musicality to the Kalapalo and how music is performed. Generally, sound in Kalapalo ritual must be understood, as (following John Blacking)[10] a "primary modelling system" rooted in social praxis and environmental understanding.

Kalapalo rituals are shaped by the use of sound as symbol. The manner in which the performance of sound (especially music) emerges from and is related to other ritual conditions (altering their subsequent forms) indicates that it is an enacted symbol that is expressive of the literal physical and mental processes that produce it; it is the bearer of visions of fundamental cosmological, environmental, social, and personal truths.

Because Kalapalo ritual life is essentially musical, Lévi-Strauss's much repeated proposal that an understanding of music might be the key to an understanding of myth seems a particularly useful guide to examining Kalapalo ritual experience.[11] Lévi-Strauss's primary concern was with the profound homologies of transformative semiotic structure between music and myth and with the asymmetric relation between them resulting from their different connections to natural language, but he also writes of the analogies between the unconscious structure of Western music and "primitive" myth. Moreover, until the end of the final volume of *Mythologiques*, when he rejects its pertinence for mythological studies, he is virtually unconcerned with ritual. Lévi-Strauss's rejection of ritual's pertinence for myth[12] is especially misleading because throughout the New World musical performance is crucial to ritual action. Musical ritual therefore represents a third cultural mode that might have assisted understanding the phenomena of thought to which his life's work has been dedicated. For ritual that is musical is meaningful music, not only (or necessarily) in a programmatic sense or through conventional reference (which is the position Lévi-Strauss understandably rejects) but in its significance as a performed event, from which both its structural and semantic links to cosmology and cosmogony arise. As Lévi-Strauss himself points out in a passage equating mythical and musical experience: "Mythology and music have in common the fact that they summon the listener to a concrete form of union, with the difference, however, that myth offers him a pattern coded in images instead of sounds. In both cases, however, it is the listener who puts one or several potential meanings into the pattern, with the result that the real unity of the myth or the musical work is achieved by two participants, in and through a kind of celebration."[13]

For the Kalapalo, mythological narrative, musical ritual, and the "sound rituals" of a person's life crises (especially mourning, which uses all possible human sounds, and puberty, which is soundless) are all symbolic action aimed toward comprehension of the world and of the self through active imagining and performative experience, and sound is the primary symbolic form uniting these processes. The Kalapalo mythological perspective is therefore close to what the philosopher Victor Zuckerkandl calls a "musical view of the universe,"[14] which he suggests is attained not through faith and revelation as in Western culture but through sense perception and observation or, in the words of that most musical of anthropologists, through the "science of the concrete." In Kalapalo myth, this "science" organizes signs into implicit ordering models. In life-crisis rituals, these models take the form of explicit propositional statements effected through sound symbols and *techniques du corps* that serve to orient personal identity and justify and explain the efficacy of the performative process and the general value and understanding of the performed self. Yet Kalapalo myth is the speech genre that most deemphasizes by a compression of categories the boundaries of such cosmological structures. It is performative action striving for a merging of the speaker with the listeners and of both speaker and listeners with what is spoken about. Kalapalo storytelling resembles the experience of performing music, the hearing of tones produced by the self, the experience of something that is at once external and internal, and the merging of the self with what is produced. Musical ritual goes beyond myth, of course, by putting into collective practice what is normally shared verbally and occasionally among only a few persons, thus creating the conditions for total communication, for experiencing power of community that is a consequence of collective understanding. To use Lévi-Strauss's expression, musical ritual moves doubly "right outside language," first because it is a performed process and second because it is musical. Kalapalo myth and ritual are connected not only by thematic homologies but more particularly by their respective ability to create—through a performative frame that is conditioned by a unifying social aesthetic—a distinctive consciousness and to construct complementary visions of a comprehensive reality.

Chapter 2

Narrative Performances and Discourse Structures

Published myths are factitious objects—what we call texts—that are the products of a complex process of recording, transcribing, translating, and ultimately presenting them on the printed page according to a selected plan of arrangement. This process takes one step by step from the original context of a performed, motivated series of utterances that constitute a cultural form with complex meaning for the people involved in its creation and hearing to a distant place and a distant reader; this analytic procedure is inevitable if such utterances are to be preserved and appreciated outside their original setting.[1] Close study of the details of these utterances requires exquisite attention to matters of grammar, prosody, structure, theme, and image, but this focus must occasionally be reset to allow the pertinence of the original context to retain its significance for the meaning of the whole. The original narrative was itself a process, implying not only communicative intent but evocation, interpretation, and an experience of performance before an audience, all set in a historical and social context that needs to be comprehended for the text's richness to be appreciated as an artifact originally created in symbolic action. A myth that is smooth, complex, subtle, and rich complements the human experience from which it has emerged and in its original narrative context is served up in a manner befitting the depth of tradition that has preserved and refined the techniques of its performative manufacture.

Kalapalo narrative art is best considered a complex set of conceptual symbolic processes at once verbal, social, and psychodynamic. Making Kalapalo myths intelligible is a matter, then, of focusing upon particular instances of performance, proceeding in a manner that integrates the analyses of theme, image, performance, and discourse, all of which are necessary for a comprehensive understanding of the cultural significance of the texts, and each of which is necessary for an understanding of the narrative as a textual whole—as a story that is meaningful to both teller and listener.

Kalapalo storytellers are conscious of their participation in an active tradition, of being members of a long and unbroken line of tellers. This is because as oral tradition, myths are associated not only with their contemporary narrators but with those who came before, both ancestors and more recently remembered authorities whose role as conveyors of their tradition to subsequent generations gives that tradition a special authority, validity, and credibility. Furthermore, the teller's self is much less apparent than in Western literature because the narrative conforms to what tradition has defined as interesting and therefore as important for passing on to the next generation, so as to perpetuate an unforgettable vision of reality. Yet if their performances are deemed especially honest in their conformity to tradition, these people become known as *akiñotoi*, "narrative specialists" or "authorities," a title that carries with it a distinct aura of prestige extending well beyond their own settlements. Among the Kalapalo successful performance of traditional knowledge is one of the important things that makes people interesting to each other, and those who are most interesting are called "knowers" and therefore expected willingly to instruct others.

The translations I have prepared for this book are the result of an attempt to convey the feeling of the original narrative performances, following the innovative insights of Dennis Tedlock's presentations of Zuñi myths as dramatic poetry, which have transformed the quality and appearance of textual presentations, and the techniques of discourse analysis and poetic organization developed by anthropological linguists following the program established by Roman Jakobson.[2] Dell Hymes's discovery of an extraordinary field of linguistic devices used to create measured verse in Native American texts is of fundamental importance for our understanding of verbal art, and his work shows how close, even obsessive attention to a text's structural details can reveal the precision and care taken by a narrator to construct a story.[3] Hymes (as well as William Labov[4]) has superbly demonstrated how carefully some narrators use the resources of their languages to fulfill simultaneously poetic and rhetorical ends, as well as to communicate common-sense meanings. Their work shows the extraordinary fruitfulness of combining discourse analysis with a performance-centered approach to the study of verbal art, which is complemented by Tedlock's concern with the translator's characterization in print of the stylistic and paralinguistic aspects of a speaker's original narrative performance. Collectively these insights have revolutionized the understanding and appreciation of oral tradition and the manner of presenting translations of that tradition, and they help us to think about what is distinctive about particular traditions other than the North American cultures they describe.

Hymes's studies of North American narrative art are powerful demonstrations of how both grammatical particles and discourse features above the level of the word are used by verbal artists to effect such patterns as repetition, parallelism, segment-marking, and segment organization into higher-order units. This is clearly the case with Kalapalo verbal artists. It is clear, moreover, that the rhetorical and didactic functions of these patterns are crucial for our understanding of the emergent structures in Kalapalo narratives. In other words, the various and often changing ends to which a narrator addresses listeners can be understood with considerable subtlety through attention to narrative patterning. The distinctively Kalapalo manner in which narrative patterning unfolds is intimately connected to the characteristically Kalapalo rhetorical and explanatory concerns that are themselves but a part of the special Kalapalo vision of their world, their theory of reality. Hence discourse analysis of Kalapalo narrative performances provides a more complex and subtle appreciation of them as narratives than is possible through thematic analysis alone and shows the special importance of narratives for giving meaning to those aspects of experience with which the Kalapalo are most fascinated: human feelings and the problems that people have controlling them so as to engender *ifutisu*—the grace of demeanor necessary for maintaining social roles to which others can comfortably respond. In a Kalapalo story, a thematic configuration is in fact created through symbols that are developed within various linguistic levels. Together these construct an interpretive model that gives meaning to the attitudes, motives, activities, and relations between the characters (the events of a Kalapalo narrative), especially when these contrast markedly with what the Kalapalo take to be correct and therefore anticipated social action. That the processes by means of which Kalapalo narrators construct a text are to an overwhelming extent in the service of didactic and explanatory goals, as well as serving as a prime source of entertainment, makes it imperative that we remember that these narratives are related by people who are paying close attention to their audience and who expect in turn to receive close attention. Hence what they say and how they say it is governed fundamentally by who the members of that audience are and what their response is during the course of the telling. Although I wish to emphasize the formality, the great care with which the Kalapalo narrator uses language to create an art form in which meaning is intimately associated with structure, these structures unfold in a dialogic context involving not only an especially effective use of the resources of the Kalapalo language but also attention to the concerns of the listener. The listener's age, linguistic abilities, and degree of knowledge of exoteric and esoteric matters all influence what will be said. As a consequence, each instance of narration can be said to present its own technical problems. Telling a story well for a Kalapalo means to realize the most successful—that is, psychologically satisfying—narrative relationship between speaker and listener. A successful Kalapalo narrator's presentations remain in the listener's memory for some time, giving pause for reflection and promoting subsequent attempts at replication, refinement, and recontextualization.[5]

Settings for Telling

Kalapalo storytelling occurs most commonly during the times of day when people are relatively idle: in the early afternoon, when visitors walk from house to house to exchange news, plan a collective project, or scrounge food from relatives and friends; and in the early evening, after they have settled into their hammocks, the young men are walking about visiting their lovers, and fires have been built up to ward off the cold of the heavy mists that nightly blanket the central Brazilian plateau. Stories are also told in the ceremonial house (*kuakutu*) located in the center of the settlement, a gathering place for men.

Because a story is a source of knowledge, its sharing is clearly seen as a form of generosity, a gift of the narrator to the listeners, and particularly to the person who has made the request or to whom the story has been offered. Hence storytelling is a particularly apt activity when the giving of material wealth may not be propitious or necessary but some form of generosity is clearly called for. Youths in puberty seclusion frequently ask the best storytellers in their families to visit them in their seclusion chambers after everyone has settled down for the night. At this time many of the more elaborate stories are told, a practice that must have considerable effect on the production of the youths' dreams, which are extremely important during this time of life. I have often heard leaders offer to tell stories or to sing an obscure ritual song for a visiting dignitary from another community. Then, with both men lying side by side in hammocks or sitting together inside the ceremonial house, a performance begins that soon draws the attention of a small crowd of interested onlookers. Senior men who are hereditary leaders (*anetaü*) are also expected to tell stories in the ceremonial house when men gather together. What are called "stories of disgusting Dawn People" are usually told when a group of men and women find themselves together in the absence of their spouses, or when several young men, having begun to joke with an older man, provoke him into telling some of the more pornographic stories. For example, when Makalalu's old father came from the Kuikuru settlement of Ipatsi to visit his daughter, he came into the house in which I was living to visit Ambo and her mother Afualu. It was still early in the day, but these two women had already finished their manioc processing. Tsëfi, the wife of Afualu's son, was still seated before her processing pot. Ambo began to tease the old man into telling a story, even though he persisted in denying he knew any. To encourage him, Afualu began telling about a "disgusting Dawn Person" who had married a Burity Palm Woman, and when she was done Makulalu's father, not to be outdone by the old woman's decorous performance, told two related stories in rapid succession. After he had finished, Ambo took her turn, followed by her sister-in-law Tsëfi. Although all of the stories that were told were certainly well known by everyone present, it was also apparent that each person was carefully listening for variations in the tellings from those they already knew, and particularly when the old man spoke, for he was a Kuikuru, and his versions were known to contain a wealth of unusual detail that many Kalapalo were eager to learn. But even more important was the erotic tone of the event that grew with each telling; that tone could have been generated only in the absence of the participants' spouses, none of whom were anywhere near the house.

Since no two texts are ever exactly alike, listeners can expect to hear new information or gain a somewhat different perspective on a character with each telling. The Kalapalo stress the importance of detail (the naming of place and person; delineation of episodes; clarification of which events led up to those constituting the story being told) as crucial for successful narrative performance. Performances are criticized when the speaker cannot elaborate these details upon request, when too much of the detail is repeated, or when irrelevant matters are included—for example, when one man gave me a fairly detailed description of a certain kind of bamboo knife that was no longer made. It is with respect to these values concerning explication and clarification of detail that even the same speaker will inevitably vary a story to suit the audience, and the listener's idiosyncratic requests for information will inevitably result in a new version with each telling. It is for these reasons—close attention to those aspects of experience most in need of explanation, variety in the tellings, and the emphasis placed upon performance—that Kalapalo rarely seem bored when stories are being told, whether they are myths that are commonly known and remembered or ones they have apparently never heard before.

The Akiñotoi, "Narrative Authorities"

The storytellers from whom I collected the narratives have a number of common characteristics. First, virtually all are (or were, when in their prime) ritual leaders known as *igiñotoi*, "song authorities." They are, in other words, the most musical of the older Kalapalo. Although this trait may be somewhat accidental, resulting from their earlier training by authorities to whom they were related, all Kalapalo have the ability to learn musical ritual from nonrelatives under a system of clientship. It seems that musicality has some relation to a person's interest in verbal performance, and perhaps more important, a person's success in public performance generally encourages the development of the role of "narrative authority."

Second, although some of these *akiñotoi* number among the most elderly members of the community, and hence might be considered knowledgeable by virtue of sheer experience, the ability of each to tell a story well is associated by the Kalapalo with their having learned from a distinguished teacher—such as Taijui and Mugika, who were storymasters many years ago. It is easy to see who will be the next generation of *akiñotoi* among the Kalapalo, for they are the more intelligent of the young adults who are most in daily, intimate contact with the present masters.

The Role of the "What-Sayer"

The telling of a Kalapalo story is an event in which the speaker engages in a special relationship with the listeners and ordinary speech and social conventions are suspended, with important consequences for both teller and listener. A Kalapalo narrative is not fully constructed by the narrator alone; in order for the story to be told at all, it must be received by a responder or "what-sayer" (*tiitsofo*), who is a crucial actor in the situation. The what-sayer may be someone who asked to be given the narrative or the recipient of a story that exemplifies explanatory principles needing clarification during the course of some other discussion; the person serving as what-sayer can change during the course of a telling, particularly when the original what-sayer drops out to attend to something that cannot be left undone, leaving a group of interested listeners who demand that the story continue. The narrator then selects another responder from the group.

As recipient of the story, the what-sayer is responsible for responding to the speaker's utterances. At each pause of the speaker, this person must respond to the previous remark, using expletives such as *eh* ("yes"), *iŋke* (literally meaning "Look!" but implying "I told you so"), *koh* ("Wow!"), *mm* (the most neutral and affectless response, one that simply allows the narrative to continue), *kïtsï* (an expression of disgust), or repeating the focal phrase or clause of a sentence. Minimally these responses signal that attention is being paid and let the narrator know that what is being said is understood, but how the listener replies—casually with boredom or in apparent excitement, awe, amusement, or wonder—is important. It is necessary for the narrator to know that the images being created are not simply understood but are enhancing the listener's appreciation of the story, even though it may be one the listener has heard many times before. A good performance, according to the Kalapalo, not only communicates the story line accurately, avoids extensive repetition, and provides sufficient detail to hold the listener's interest, but it also calls to mind and heightens experience through the constructing of vivid word images (*futofo*, "used for knowing"), which make the listener "see" (that is, think more vividly about) what is happening in the narrative.

The what-sayer (and anyone else who is present) may appropriately ask for information at a major break in the story. The narrator may also break the performance to say, "Ask me their names," or "Ask me where they were," such urging allowing a deviation from the story to provide seemingly insignificant details that nonetheless enrich understanding and appreciation because of their practical connections with contemporary life. The knowledge of such details in a story can be useful in other contexts; place names, for example, not only locate settings in the course of a narrative but give the Kalapalo landscape a special connection to the past. This is most deeply understood when the Kalapalo travel to ancient settlements, for their knowledge of place perpetuates adaptational success in settings that may have been long unused but to which people sometimes return with little but narrative tradition to guide them.

A Kalapalo listener thus has the ability to direct the flow of a narrator's speech into side channels of explication and elaboration, and this aspect of the event helps the speaker to recall incidents and details that might otherwise be omitted. The narrator's own mental images are thereby enhanced or contributed to by the listener, who is in effect a performer as well, aiding the construction of the narrative text. But the listener's understanding and acceptance of crucial pieces of evidence in an explanatory model contained within a narrative (marked by the repetition of a relevant phrase during the speaker's pregnant pauses) serve as affirmation and approval of the separate elements of the explanation. A what-sayer's request for clarification of details, usually framed as a question, indicates that the substance of the argument is not being challenged. (The latter would be signaled by silence or the use of the ambiguity expletive *kooh*.) A conclusion or summing up is also frequently uttered, not by the narrator but by the what-sayer, who thereby lets the speaker know not only that the point has been understood and that the correct inferences have been made from information provided by the narrator but that there is agreement with the speaker's conclusion. In other words (and in marked contrast with our own didactic strategies), among the Kalapalo explanatory principles used in connection with an event or phenomenon needing clarification are not always stated directly by the explainer. Rather, they are represented first by the quoted speech of characters in the narrative and finally in statements made by the listener to signal acceptance of these principles.

How the what-sayer responds to the narrator is crucial to a successful narrative performance, which depends on the competence of both narrator and responder. The Kalapalo find it difficult to use small children as what-sayers because their attention is said to be weak and they do not yet appreciate the significance of the role. So, although many stories are told for the benefit of young children, they are actually told "to" an older what-sayer.

As performance, Kalapalo narrative deemphasizes the boundaries between individuals, perhaps more so than any other Kalapalo speech event. During a mythic narrative, the speaker attempts to create or enhance certain images in the mind of the listener, images that will, with skill, begin to approximate the speaker's own mental apparitions very closely. The speaker's social self is diminished as he or she takes on the voices of characters through manipulation of pitch and degree of rapidity of speech, and through the use of grammatical features such as tense, modality, evidential particles, and focalization markers. The listener's hoped-for responses of wonder, surprise, laughter, and even requests for more information emphasize the sharing of both this imaginative intimacy with a particular story and the narrative event. Because of these processes, the social differences between listener and speaker, which are often considerable, are temporarily ignored. To take an extreme example, in the situation of an older man telling a story to his subservient son-in-law, the usual marking of their respectful relationship (by means of speech avoidance and other highly marked forms of social etiquette) is clearly not manifested. In an even more extreme case, my own success in understanding what was being said when someone told me a story was in large degree measured by my ability to ask questions of the storyteller, thereby responding in the appropriate way. I found myself becoming less peculiar a visitor among people who were particularly interested in narrative art as the inevitable differences between us were temporarily erased by my ability to participate in that imaginative process. In other words, the differences between participants, which are inevitably reinforced in ordinary speech—through the selection of speech forms indicating relative deference, as in the first example, or the relative linguistic competence and cultural knowledge of the what-sayer, as in the second—are in situations of narrative speech considerably weakened, if not extinguished. Both speaker and listener take account of each other, not primarily as social persons but as bearers of implicit knowledge of what is being narrated and how that narrative content should be responded to. Going somewhat further, the images that are produced verbally by the speaker presumably appear both in his or her and the listeners' minds; they are "seen," as both we and the Kalapalo say. Thus they objectify the events and characters at the same time that they assimilate them to the self through the processes of imagination, reflection, and comprehension. Rather than ambiguity, there is a sense of submersion of concrete individuality into a larger whole (the narrative event) accompanied by an experience of concreteness and individuality through heightened cognitive work, by thinking about what is being said in a way that might not occur during casual speech. This experience is much the same as what is actually described in myth—the participation of all animate entities in human language. We shall see later that it also occurs during Kalapalo musical ritual in which there is a distinct weakening of social identity and a heightened emphasis on community of persons.

A Kalapalo performer's rhetorical, didactic, explanatory, and poetic intentions are all consequences of the socially motivated and socially contextualized facts of Kalapalo storytelling. Because of the manner in which Kalapalo narrative performances are achieved, one of my primary concerns has been to understand the performative interaction between narrator and responder, especially to know where in the text and under what conditions the responder responds. This comprehension, together with an analysis of the relations between rhetorical and didactic intent and versification, helped me to understand the communicative as well as poetic ends that the narrative structure serves. The poetry in Kalapalo narrative often serves explanatory and didactic intentions. Kalapalo narrative art is a form of high entertainment and designed to create an illusionary intimacy, but it is at the same time perhaps the most important means of imparting complex forms of knowledge. Yet despite the importance of this didactic function it is often accomplished by means other than explicitly referential statements that we might immediately recognize as explanations. I emphasize here that I am not writing of covert allusions but rather of explanations that are conveyed through linguistic vehicles, which are different from those through which Western scientific explanations are communicated. Most important, the inferences and implications people draw from stories are not necessarily based upon information made superficially explicit in them.

A Narrative Example

To illustrate these points in greater detail, I shall continue my description of narrative structure by using a particular example, a major section of a story about Taũgi (an important trickster), who tries to deceive his friend Kutsafugu. I recorded this story when Ulutsi (the old Kalapalo leader) told it to his older daughter one evening while his grandchildren and I listened from our hammocks slung close by. Ulutsi had finished telling another story that I had asked him for, but then he continued with an apparent favorite of his, asking his daughter to be the what-sayer. The story begins in a relatively slow tempo, but toward the end of the quoted portion it was told with considerable speed. This portion took about eight minutes to tell.

Kutsafugu
Told by Ulutsi at Aifa, July 6, 1982

uletinafa uŋifatanïmi, uletinafa fegey. 1
Now, I really should have told you all about someone else. It really should
have been this other person.

    inenïgïtafale ugefale.
    In fact, had I made the choice myself, I would have begun with it.

    igeafale.   *(eh he)*
    But now, this one.

ñafetsaŋe wahatsifeke ufïgi nitomi.   *(ah)*
"You must urge my ear-piercing companion to bring me my arrows."

        ñafe.   *(ñafe)*   5
        Quickly.

eh he nïgifeke.   *(ah)*
"Very well," the other answered.

ñafetsaŋe iŋinïmiŋoifeke.   *(ah)*
"Urge him and he will bring them."

kaŋaŋatï itsafegey tsufïgïfigey Taugi atanigele kïŋamukegele Taugi atani,
What I'm talking about are burity leaf-rib arrows from a *long* time ago
when Taugi was still a child Taugi was,

    ŋikombealefegey etegatïfïgïpegelefa,
    and even though they were made from wild plants they were still his
weapons.

        ifïgikogele.   *(eh he)*   10
        Still his arrows.

        kaŋaŋatï fegey.   *(eh he)*
    These are *kaŋaŋatï* arrows.

        eh
        Yes.

eh he nïgifeke.   *(eh)*
"Very well," it went.

    ninitanitapetsaŋe.   *(eh)*
    "I will certainly bring them to you just as you wish."

etimbelulefa segati.   *(ah)*   15
"When you arrive there,

    Wahatsifeke einenïgï,
    'It's Wahatsi who called for you,

        afatsitsïfeke.   *(ah)*
        your ear-piercing companion.'"

ñafefetsaŋe ufïgi ïki sitomi,
"Urge him to come bringing my arrows,"

        nïgifeke   *(nïgifeke)*
        he went,

ufïgi ïki. (ah) 20
"Bringing my arrows."
eh he.
"Very well.
utetaniapafetsaŋe.
I'll certainly go right away just as you wish."
lepe kohotsilefa, ah, etelulefa, ah,
Then at dusk, well, the other went on, well,
etelulefa. (ah?)
the other went on.
etelulefa, tuinzage (eh) 25
It went on alone by itself.
ipa ifiña, igeyfuŋu ifiña,
Through a lake, through one like this one,
tuwakagafuŋu (ah)
like the place where water is drawn.
nakagagïfa,
The bathing place,
Taugi nakagagïfa (ah)
Taugi's bathing place
Taugi nakagagïfa. 30
Taugi's bathing place.
tiki tuwakaga, tuwakaga, imïñigena. (ah)
Tiki at the place where water is drawn, at the place where water is
drawn, across toward the other side.
atani (atani)
He was there.
atani tïnakaga. (ah)
He was there at his own bathing place.
lepene, igitalïpeŋine, tētimbe efukuēgï,
Then, from where it was in the middle, after that Canoe Monster came
toward him,
efukuēgï. (efukuēgï) 35
Canoe Monster.
pupupupu agakuni feley (um)
Pupupupu that was *agakuni.*
pupupupupupupupupu laa, tiki igia. (um)
Pupupupupupupupupu tha-at way, *tiki* right here.
Kutsafugu, nïgifeke. (um)
"Kutsafugu," it went.
ketefa nïgifeke. (ketefa)
"Come along," it went,
eytigitafa weta. (ah) 40
"I've come because I must escort you.
Taugifeke ufumipïgïï weta (ah)
I've come because it was Taugi who sent me."

afïtï ugela.   *(ah)*
"Not me."
    afïtï ugela.   *(afïtï ugela)*
    "Not me."
afïtïje nïgifeke,   *(ah)*
"You're wrong to say that," it went.
    eytigitafa weta.   *(ah)*   45
    "I've come because I must escort you."
afïtï ugela nïgifeke.
"Not me," he went.
    afïtï ugela.
    "Not me."
eh he nïgifeke.
"Very well," it went.
    etelïlefa igitati.   *(ah)*
    And it went out to the middle of the lake.
Kutsafugu nïgifeke.   *(ah)*   50
"Kutsafugu," it went.
    igea eïwifolï ufeke, wïnïgïmbele alolatilefa,   *(um!)*
    "Had I brought you out here, I would have sunk down to the
    bottom after that,
        wïnïgïlefa. Eh.   *(um)*
        I would have sunk. Yes."
    ifutiñi feley,
    He knew about it,
    itseke feley gehale,   *(Kutsafugu)*
    he also was a powerful being,
eh, Kutsafugu.   55
Yes, Kutsafugu.
Taugi tagiñokoŋope feley.   *(eh he)*
He was Taugi's friend.
Taugi afatsitokoŋo feley.   *(eh he)*
He was Taugi's ear-piercing companion.
Taugi afatsitokoŋo feley.   *(eh he)*
He was Taugi's ear-piercing companion.
    lañaketï tsitseketu.   *(ah)*
    Because of his own power, I'm told.
lepene, Tafiŋa tsalefale.   60
Then, but this time it was Alligator.
    ñefugufale eley,   *(ah)*
    This time it was his canoe.
        Tafiŋa.   *(ah Tafiŋa)*
        Alligator.
moh hu, igeyfuŋu mbetsafeley.   *(moh)*
moh hu, it was huge, the one I'm talking about was this large.
[*gestures to indicate great width*]

titititi tuwakagalïpeŋine titititi ina.
Titititi from the place where water is drawn *titititi* to him.
   tiki itsaiŋa.   *(ah)*   65
   Tiki. It was beside him.
   Kutsafugu nïgifeke.   *(Kutsafugu)*
   "Kutsafugu," it went.
   ketefa nïgifeke.   *(ah)*
   "Come along," it went.
      eytigi weta.   *(ah)*
      "I've come to escort you."
[*Breathily, as if casting a spell*]
   eyitse eyitse eyitse eyitse eyitsefa, nïgifeke
   "Get in get in get in get in get in now," he said.
      eyitse eyitse eyitse eŋelefa eley.   70
      Get in get in this time, he's the one.
      eyitiñi feley, eyitiñi feley, eyitiñi feley, nïgifeke   *(ah)*
      "He's your escort, he's your escort, he's your escort," he went.
      eh he nïgifeke.
      "All right," Kutsafugu went.
lepene pok, iñïgilefa ugupoŋa.   *(eh he)*
Then *pok*, and he sat on its back.
      pok, aifa.   *(pok)*
      Pok, ready.
Ah, titititititi. egeyfuŋuna.   *(ah)*   75
Now, *titititititi.* Over that way.
   Kutsafugu nïgifeke.   *(ah)*
   "Kutsafugu," it went.
      ai.   *(um)*
      "What?"
tigikumukuila kitse ufeke.   (laughter)
"'What an ugly lumpy head he has,' say it to me.
      tigikumukuila kitse ufeke.
      'What an ugly lumpy head he has,' say it to me."
etembegenila egitïgï.   (laughter)   80
"Oh no, your head's nicer than that.
      etembegenila.
      Oh no, it's nicer than that.
tigipoliñemale wegey,   (laughter)
I thought you had a smooth head,
      tigipoliñe.   (laughter)
      a smooth head."
      augïndajogu fegey.   *(eh)*
      Alligator was lying heartlessly to him.
eh he nïgifeke.   *(um)*   85
"All right," it went.

lepe eteli tititititititi egeyfuna. (ah)

Next it went *titititititi* further on over *that* way.

    Kutsafugu nïgifeke. (ah)

    "Kutsafugu," it went.

    ai nïgifeke. (ah)

    "What," he went.

    tüfeleila ekitse ufeke. (laughter)

    "'How ugly are those things poking out of him,' say it to me.

          tüfelelila ekitse. 90

          'How ugly are those things poking out of him,' say it."

    etembegenila.

    "Oh no, you're nicer than that."

    eteh! aïpïgifuŋuhale eigïi. (laughter)

    "But how nice and straight your teeth seem to me."

    eh he. (um)

    "Very well."

    imbukinetajogusufa ifeke.

It wanted to exterminate him heartlessly the way alligators do.

lepe titititititi, egeyfuna. 95

Next *titititititi*, even *further* on.

    Kutsafugu nïgifeke. (ah)

    "Kutsafugu," it went.

    ai nïgifeke. (ah)

    "What?" he went.

    teŋgïgïtila kitse ufeke. (laughter)

    "'How ugly is that crooked thing of his,' say it to me.

        teŋgïgïtila kitse.

        'How ugly is that crooked thing of his,' say it."

    etehmbegenila eü. (etehmbe) 100

    "Oh no, your tail is nicer than that.

        etehmbegenila.

        On the contrary, it's nicer than that.

        teh! laŋombale eitsïgïi.

        Actually your bones lie beautifully in place.

        eüi, teh, laŋombale eü tJemboliñï. (tse)

        Your tail is *beautiful*. Actually your tail lies straight in place.

        temboliñï.

        It's a straight one."

    eh he. 105

    "Very well."

titititititi, egeta.

Titititititi, up that way.

    Kutsafugu nïgifeke. (um)

    "Kutsafugu," it went.

    ai. (um)

"What?"

tifitseŋekiñela kitse ufeke.

"'What an ugly strong smell he has,' say it to me.

    tifitseŋekiñe.   *(um)*   110

    'What an ugly strong smell he has.'"

atahmbegenila egikegï.   (laughter, *atah*)

"Oh no, your fragrance is nicer than that.

    atah.

    What a nice smell."

eh he nïgifeke.   *(eh)*

"Very well," it went.

ifakilakugulefa,   *(eh)*

When it wasn't very far away at all,

kutsafugu nïgifeke.   *(um)*   115

"Kutsafugu," it went.

ai.   *(um)*

"What?"

tïgimukuila kitse ufeke.

"'What an ugly lumpy head he has,' say it to me."

igeakugulefa tïgikumukuila, puu tiki,

And so, almost there, "What an ugly lumpy head he has!" *puu tiki,*

puu tiki,

puu tiki,

alulefa egeyfuŋuna,   *(ah?)*   120

he flew off toward that place over there,

    alulefa.

    he flew off.

egeyfuŋunafa,

There at that place,

    Kutsafugu nïgifeke.

    "Kutsafugu," it went.

        [*Very rapidly*] *igeasueuifolïufekeeeeh . . . puh!*

        "If I had my way I would have done this to youuuu . . .

        puh!"

etelujogufale!,   125

but anyway IT HEARTLESSLY WENT ON!

    etelulefa.   (laughter, *Tafiŋa*)

    and so it went on.

tafiŋa eley.

That was Alligator.

Eh, Taugi efugu feley.

Yes, that was Taugi's canoe.

    Taugi efugu.   129

    Taugi's canoe.

Segmenting in Kalapalo Narratives

Kalapalo narrators separate their narrative performances from the rest of discourse by utterances that frame the narrative and alert the listener to the need for a special communicative role. Within this frame the listener becomes a what-sayer who must attend to the speaker in a special way. These "keying" devices[6] regulate the manner in which the speaker's discourse is to be interpreted and responded to, transforming the action of unmarked conversational communication into (or out from) action that is performed. The most common keys are the introductory *Tsakefa!* "Listen!" and the concluding *Aifa, apïgïfigey,* "It's finished, that's all there is to it." Sometimes, however (as when Ulutsi began his story), a speaker will omit *tsakefa* and refer to the fact of his performance more directly (see lines 1–3). Yet another strategy is for a speaker both to open and close a performance with *"Tsakefa!"* Whatever the expressions used, together they have a major bracketing function and separate the narrative from other utterances of the speaker, especially the frequently heard introductory story-line brief that is not treated as part of the narrative performance.

In addition to these performance keys, narrators have regular means for separating events from each other and for linking descriptions of events to form a linearly ordered sequence (see Table 1). This is a complex procedure involving the narrator's use of two distinct but related sets of standard discourse devices, which are sometimes complemented by nonverbal markers. The first set includes two words (*lepene; aifa*) whose use results in segments of several types which can be correlated with discourse coherence functions (I consider that function at length further on). The second set, phrases making reference to the experience of time, seem to be keys that shift the interpretive frame of the listener from one topical focus to another. The two sets parallel each other in

Table 1.
Narrative Structuring

Discourse structure units	Discourse devices	Content
line	what-sayer's response	minimally a noun phrase
segment	intonational contours/sentence types; parallelism	description of acts; listing of persons
verse	*lepene/aifa*; counts of 4 or 5	description of complex activities and of significant sets of persons; references to experience of traveling
stanza	*lepene, aifa*; *itsa(ko)lefa*; counts of 4 or 5	references to experiences of time; major shifts in theme (especially new complex activities)

that segments of similar types can be marked in both ways; the discourse devices in effect cross-reference each other.

I call the smallest segment the line (numbered in the text of the story). The Kalapalo line is a unit resulting from a speaker's pauses, which break the intonational contour of a sentence so as to allow for the responses of the what-sayer. These pauses are clearly different from shorter ones taken for breath; if an inexperienced what-sayer should interpret these breath pauses as places for response, the response almost invariably collides with the next words of the speaker (as often happened to me before I became comfortable with the rhythms of the telling). Although the what-sayer does not always respond, the response pauses are the appropriate places for expletives to be used, and if at least one is not forthcoming within a segment, the speaker will repeat a final clause or even the entire line as a way of prompting the what-sayer. Repetition also occurs after the what-sayer repeats a word or entire clause; both the what-sayer and the speaker seem to be marking the word or clause as particularly significant, the what-sayer by repeating it rather than using an expletive, the speaker by once again uttering the word or clause in response to the what-sayer's remarking upon it. In the text of Kutsafugu, this occurs after lines 5, 19, 33, 35, 39, 43, 62, 66, 74, and 100. If the tone of voice adopted by a what-sayer suggests to the speaker that the word or clause in question is confusing or needs clarification, the what-sayer's repetition will result in the speaker's offering the necessary clarification, by means of a definition (an indicative statement) or a confirmation. After line 24, the what-sayer's "*ah?*" (with a rising tone) is a question response, which Ulutsi clarifies by his remark in line 25. Lines 55 and 63 are also examples of the narrator's responses to the what-sayer's succinct requests for clarification. Lines 127–29 follow the what-sayer's summing up in the form of a single word utterance ("*Tafiŋa*").

Some lines are equivalent to whole sentences, while others are equivalent to clauses within complex sentences. The line break may occur within the clause, usually when an important word must be stressed (for example, in lines 18, 19, and 20) or when the speaker measures words for dramatic effect; these are relatively unusual occurrences. When the lines are equivalent to clauses, the clause boundaries may also be marked by vowel lengthening. Vowel lengthening can also be used to surprise the hearer, when it slows down an extremely rapidly spoken clause and leads into description of a sudden or unpredicted action (as in line 124).

Lines are organized into higher-order units I call segments. These are usually equivalent to pieces of conversations (a request or injunction followed by a response) or to descriptions of complex actions. Lines in the segment tend to be ordered into pairs of similar intonational contours. Most commonly, the segment begins with a declarative sentence contour (accompanying either quoted speech or a narrator's comment), broken into lines by pausing, and often a second intonational contour, shorter than the initial one in the segment, is introduced at the end of the first. It is not easy to generalize about this second intonational contour because in some cases a complex sentence will seem to have two of them rather than one, so that it is not always clear whether an

entirely new sentence has begun or whether the earlier sentence is being quali-
fied by a second set of related clauses (see, for example, lines 8–10, where
there is parallelism in use of the continuative modal affix *-gele*, "even so";
"still"; *gele* plus *lefa* become *gelefa* in the last word of line 9). Usually, however, the second intonational contour represents either a repetition of a previous
sentence or a very close paraphrase of it, such paraphrasis closely agreeing with
the earlier sentence morphologically (again, as in lines 9–10). As in lines 8–10,
in complex Kalapalo sentences subordinate clauses are linked to each other and
to the main clauses by verbal and subject/object anaphora, the metonymic
modal suffix *-lefa*, and by agreement or parallelism in other kinds of marked
modality. Paraphrasis in this context is closely related to the speaker's didactic
intent, usually upon recognition that the what-sayer may not fully understand
the meaning of certain words in the preceding sentence. The what-sayer's *eh he*
("all right"; "very well") that follows lines 11 and 12 is a means of indicating
to Ulutsi her understanding of his extended comment.

Following this second intonational contour, a different type of contour occurs, most often in connection with quoted speech that involves the use of a
question or an imperative expression. But even when quoted speech is not involved, the narrator will frequently utter a remark whose intonational contour
is very similar. Most commonly, these utterances are declaratives with strongly
emphasized initial words, such emphasis also being achieved by the intonational
contour associated with question or imperative sentences; in questions the initial
question-marked noun phrase is emphasized, while in imperatives it is the action. The third intonational contour may be repeated in a manner similar to the
repetition of the earlier contour. The result is at least two pairs of repeated
intonational contours, each pair having a distinctive shape, with the possibility
of each contour carrying over into more than one line (in other words, I am not
talking about pairs of lines). Table 2 illustrates the forms Kalapalo intonational
contours take, with examples of contour patterning from the Kutsafugu text.

In addition to indicating line structure (represented by the line breaks occurring from top to bottom of a page), I have characterized the different intonational contours and relative voice tone (loud or soft) by spacing the lines from
left to right. Lines that appear toward the right of the page were uttered in a
relatively soft voice; those appearing at the left (which also mark major segment
breaks in the story) were spoken with a relatively loud voice.

Segments may also correspond to descriptions of incidents that have more
than one component, especially to a series of statements beginning with description of an intended action (often through quoted speech), followed by initiation
of that action (also often accompanied by the quoted speech of an actor or by
the narrator's commentary). Examples are lines 15–22, where Taugi instructs
Canoe Monster (at this point as yet unnamed) about what to say to Kutsafugu.
In the case of segments consisting of a single sentence, the particular act being
described is part of a series of different acts, which together effect a particular
goal. In such cases, each act is introduced by *lepene* (which is best translated
"next" in such cases), and the speaker frequently concludes such segments with
the expression, "*Aifa.*" At this point, the speaker may also do something appar-

Table 2.
Intonational Contours

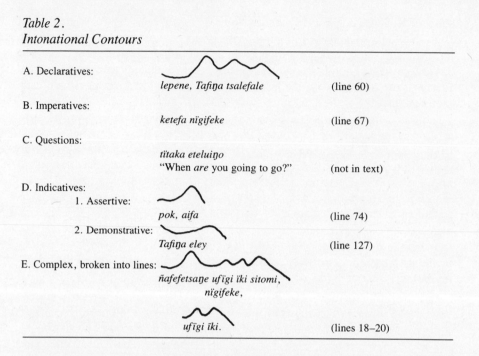

A. Declaratives:	*lepene, Tafiŋa tsalefale*	(line 60)
B. Imperatives:	*ketefa nïgifeke*	(line 67)
C. Questions:	*tïtaka eteluiŋo* "When *are* you going to go?"	(not in text)
D. Indicatives: 1. Assertive:	*pok, aifa*	(line 74)
2. Demonstrative:	*Tafiŋa eley*	(line 127)
E. Complex, broken into lines:	*ñafefetsaŋe ufïgi ïki sitomi, nïgifeke,*	
	ufïgi ïki.	(lines 18–20)

ently trivial and unrelated to the storytelling situation such as swing her hammock, blow on the fire, or scratch himself. These seem to be nonverbal markers of segment breaks.

Above the level of the segment is the verse. Kalapalo verses are composed of segments that are organized according to one or more discourse devices that have coherence functions. These devices may be used in combination. The first is a set of expressions such as *lepene* or its elided form *lepe* ("next," "then"), *aifa* ("finished," "ready"), and *aah* ("why," or "so," or "now") or *uumm* ("well"). The latter two always introduce a declarative sentence, seemingly for the purpose of creating an indicative mood. Second are numerical counts of either four or five. Third is the process of metonymy. Fourth is reference to experiences of traveling.

The expressions given under the first device seem to help connect one segment to another (see lines 23, 34, 60, 74, 86, and 95). Numerical counts are used to develop the description of complex activities and to associate them with specific goals. Descriptions of action constructed from repeated acts are almost invariably organized into four segmented divisions within a verse. A fifth segment presents the conclusive result of the four repeated acts, often accompanied by a summary of the whole. An example of this patterning (or "motivated number") is the hilarious confrontation between Alligator and Kutsafugu as they cross the lake. Alligator's four verbal tests are followed by a fifth, which effects Kutsafugu's goal—to reach the opposite shore safely. Ulutsi concludes his verse by summarizing the entire process in line 124. Elsewhere, this characteristic commentary segment seems to link the events described in myths with the present by expressing either a continuity or discontinuity of some practice. In the story of Kutsafugu, the hero's ability to cross safely on Alligator's back (until he is able to fly to land) is implicitly contrasted with what would have happened had Alligator been carrying a human being and not a powerful being. In other stories, motivated number is used to describe sets of siblings, among whom the fourth or the fifth (that is, the last born) is invariably the most physically and morally beautiful of the group.

Internal organization of verses may also be achieved by means of metonymic relations between segments (the third device), these relations generally having rhetorical functions. (Some of these have already been pointed out in connection with the patterning of intonational contours.) Examples of metonymy are (a) initial statement → clarification or qualification; (b) statement of mood → statement of motive or goal (often by means of quoted speech); (c) statement of action → statement of function of action. Quoted conversations also contain pairs of statements that manifest metonymic relations such as (d) statement → denial or rejection of validity of statement; (e) statement → agreement; (f) question → response. Pairs of these quoted speech segments ordered into groups of four or five often constitute entire verses.

Some speakers separate verses with the statement, *"lepene, aifa"* ("then, finished," or "then, ready"), which concludes the section and distinguishes it from the one to follow. (Ulutsi did not use this device.) Usually the speaker pauses here significantly because it is an appropriate place for the listener to ask a question or otherwise seek clarification of what has just been said. Perhaps for this reason, when stories are told during the day, verses are marked by deliberate eye contact between the speaker and the what-sayer, and at night speakers seem to attempt contact by turning their faces toward the what-sayer. Eye contact occurs at other points in the story but seems less essential. Muluku, a more hesitant and slower speaker than the others, used the phrase *lepene, aifa* more often than any other narrator, seemingly to reassure himself that he had fully completed the previous segment. Other speakers, perhaps more practiced and therefore assured, used it less often, or simply concluded their verse with the phrase, *"itsa(ko) lefa,"* "and so s(he) (they) remained there." *"Aifa"* may also be used with this phrase, or alone, to conclude the verse.

Segmenting through Temporal Reference

At the next segmental level, stanzas are most commonly separated from each other by references to experiences of time, usually in connection with a character's travels. Temporal images serve to break up the narrative flow into discontinuous and topically discrete units, to define events and actions as occurring at different times, and to distinguish different kinds of time. Events in a Kalapalo narrative are separated from each other by changes in the time frame, and they are also connected logically through the persistent imagery of the cyclical successiveness of time conveyed by the words used to refer to movements of the sun, seasonal changes, and day turning to night turning to day. Moreover, these expressions (listed in Table 3) all indicate concrete ways in which temporal changes or natural processes of time are experienced, rather than an objec-

Table 3.
Speaking of Time

A. Times of day: used for arrivals and departures	1. *mitote* ("at dawn") 2. *kohotsi* ("at dusk")
B. Movements of the sun: used for describing a journey or any sequenced event	*inde Giti atani* ("when the sun was here"), accompanied by pointing
C. Reference to light: usually combined with A or B	1. *iŋila* ("at the beginning"; sunrise) 2. *afugutïlï* (as "darkness falls") 3. *koko* ("darkness"; at night)
D. Seasonal periodicity: "a year passed," or some number of years passed	1. *sisoanïgï* "(someone's) dry season" 2. *etuwolï*: "flooding" (i.e., the height of the rainy season)
E. Monthly periodicity: "a month passed," or some number of months passed	*ŋunegï*: "(someone's) moon," e.g., *tilako ŋunegï*, "three of (someone's) moons" (i.e., after three months passed, the character did something)
F. Daily periodicity: "a day passed," or "several days passed"	1. *isïŋïlï*: "(someone) slept"; e.g., *wïŋïluiŋo ñatui*, "I will sleep five days" 2. *ifagutïlï*: "(someone) spent the night"
G. Bodily processes:	1. *imagu*: experiencing childbirth 2. *tefualï*: experiencing pregnancy 3. *apuŋu*: experiencing death

tification of them. These references thus serve to emphasize the way time is experienced differently by different types of characters, which contributes to a sense of different experiential worlds existing side by side in the same story. Thus Canoe Monster's departure at dusk is a sign that Kutsafugu has to deal with an awesome powerful being, a canoe that has a mind of its own, so to speak, for which reason Taugi's ear-piercing companion refuses to get inside.

Here again, a device that serves a poetic end also has important rhetorical and metaphorical functions. In many texts, references to life processes either introduce or conclude major, thematically discrete sections of the story. A shift from one temporal reference to another often conforms to breaks in sections of different orders of magnitude, as well as to shifts in focus, as from a general description of social relations among characters, for example, to a focus upon an individual person. Reference to a character's sleeping is particularly interesting in that it typically seems to prefigure a suddenly narrowed and magnified focus upon the persons of the characters. Sleeping is often associated with a shift from the normal, expected, social "mask" of a character to a hidden, unexpected, antisocial reality of feeling. This use of sleep as a device makes sense when we think of the Kalapalo idea that sleeping may be accompanied by the wandering of the sleeper's *akũa* or "interactive self," during which future goals are fixed upon. Reference to sleeping may also cue the listener to a narrative movement in the direction of goals decidedly different from those pertinent to earlier activities in the story. Sleeping often suggests a major reorientation of the characters because of a significant shift in attitude on the part of the sleeper.

Temporal reference seems to key distinct shifts in thematic reference. First, changes occur from reference to a character's feelings or mood to motive or goal, or from the motive to a realization of it, any of which are correlated with reference to times of day. Shifts from one major psychologically oriented action complex (mood/motive/realization of that motive) to another are accompanied by a change in focalization of a character (discussed later in the chapter). Second, introduction of new characters into a story, or the removal of characters, is associated with references to bodily processes. Finally, reference to seasonality and the lunar cycle seems to be correlated with duration of motive. To summarize, discourse devices at the level of the major segment (the stanza) are especially associated with the rhetorical concern with describing characterological actions, shifts in mood and feeling, the formulation of motives or goals, and attempts to achieve those goals.

Images of Space and of Traveling

Kalapalo notions of time are closely connected to ideas about space, and spatial imagery in Kalapalo myths is complementary to that of time. It is constructed by means of the ubiquitous device of traveling that lends a sense of contrast between qualitatively different experiences while distinguishing between different places or sites as, on the one hand, social, predictable, and ordinary, and on the other, antisocial, magical, dangerous, and liminal. The distinction emerges from the language describing the journey, which is a way of establishing boundaries that are both geographic and psychological and that are treated less as visual objects than as spatial relations experienced through human temporal sensitivity. Traveling modes, involving active experiences of time and the contrasts experienced in different places, thus serve as symbols for different consciousnesses.

Travelers normally leave a socially defined space (a settlement described as if it were one such as human beings now build) and move to a liminal site (the forest or a settlement of powerful and dangerous beings), where strange and unpredictable events occur. These two sites are often contrasted continuously as a character moves back and forth repeatedly between them. The movement from structured space to liminal space and the return trip are always described differently. Usually the former is described by means of conventional verbs that indicate the stage of the trip, for example, "they left," "they went on," "they came," "they arrived." After action within liminal space ends, the focal character is either "miraculously" returned to the social space described at the beginning of the story (a man is shot from the bow of a powerful being or he flies home), or the return is not described. As if awakening from a dream, the character suddenly "arrives home," and the next sentence in the text typically describes an incident that occurs after the protagonist has returned. Sometimes, however, the experiences of traveling are reversed: the trip "out" is sudden and dreamlike, while the return home is arduous and clearly described. In these stories such a reversal of the usual description of traveling seems to indicate that the traveler is moving from an illusory state into a material or substantial one. In "Alamigi," a story I present in Chapter 4, moving through the shallow water of the lake or walking through the wilderness is an iconic image of sensory, material thought, whereas the main character's sudden transport while bespelled is an image of her experience of a twilight state. Such an archaic expression for what we now think of as "alternate states of consciousness" or "waking dreams" is particularly apt for the times of day that such dreamlike traveling occurs because in Kalapalo myths these journeys typically occur at dawn or dusk. Thus traveling is a narrative device for distinguishing between two sites, and the time of day when departure from social space (or a traveler's return to it) occurs is normally liminal in that it is an occasion for one's experience of "timeless light": departure just before dawn (*mitote*) or the very beginning of the day (*iŋila*) and arrival at dusk (*kohotsi*). The reverse is true for monsters, powerful beings in their dangerous mode, who always begin their travels at dusk.

There seems to be a clear connection between the use of temporal images to construct a sense of time as experienced by an individual (times within time and the timelessness or flow of time) and of spatial images to convey a sense of both discrete sites within space and the possibility of space as liminal. These spatial and temporal contrasts are neatly achieved through the use of verbs having to do with experience of movement, traveling in the first case, external and inner movement of time in the other.

Focalization

In addition to these segmenting discourse features, a fifth device for structuring discourse in narratives is a grammatical strategy that is used by Kalapalo speakers to distinguish the focal or nonfocal status of characters in a story. Focalization of a character who is agent in a transitive verb phrase works by means of word-order shifting from the normal declarative object-verb-subject order to subject-object-verb. The character's agentivity is marked by the suffix *-feke*; after being focalized, the pertinent agentive noun returns to its normal place in the word order.[7] If such characters then temporarily drop out of the action of the story, they can be recalled by the use of a special focalization anaphora, the pronoun *ŋele*.

Nonfocal characters in a discourse segment are normally introduced by pronominal prefixes to verbs (in which subject/object relations are marked) and only later (in an indicative mood) by name or through a label establishing their relationship to the focal character. Anaphoric reference to these characters is by means of nonfocalizing demonstrative pronouns that have deictic implications (*ege* referring to a socially, temporally, or spatially close animate being; *ele* referring to a socially, temporally, or spatially distant animate being; *ige* referring in an inanimate being). Finally, new characters or characters who have already been mentioned but who are neither focal nor secondary (they might be called "tertiary") are referred to by the pronoun *ule*. When *ule* introduces a character, it is fronted for emphasis; when named, the character referred to will be focalized. (Ulutsi begins his story with such a sentence.)

Focalization seems to be a means of emphasizing the thematic status of a character, in other words, the person's agentivity relationship to other characters. In the Kutsafugu story, there are several instances of focalization within quoted speech but not in the narrative matrix itself (lines 4, 16–17, and 41).

Many characters in Kalapalo narratives represent an idea of a social dilemma, a form of human feeling, or a way of orienting oneself to the Kalapalo world, but they never move mechanically and predictably through that world (or the restructured world of myths). By means of focalization, the relationships between a character and those engaged with that person are brought to life through subtle shifts in emphasis or revelation of hitherto unexpressed aspects of their being. This device gives the story as a whole a new thrust toward its conclusion, so the characters are never stereotyped objects or mere tokens of personal types but acquire the shapes and complexities of living people.

Verb Categories

The purposeful manipulation of tense, aspect, mood, and mode in Kalapalo myths is a sixth structuring strategy, for these verb categories can be used not only to indicate different temporal relations between events and the manner in which actions are performed, but to indicate a character's attributes as actor in an event and the importance of the event itself for altering those attributes.

Within the verb, relations between the speaker's time and the time of the action are indicated by a class of suffixes that may be considered markers of tense (see Table 4); the tense classes are distant or remote past, recent past, and unmarked. The unmarked tense also obligatorily marks aspectival properties of the action: whether it occurs continuously or as a punctual event. (In addition, the singular or collective status of the subject is also marked in the suffix.) The unmarked tense is further marked for a category of mood, subdivided into the reportive, the conditional, the hypothetical, and the potential. Finally, all but the remote past can be further optionally marked by one or more of at least twenty-six modal suffixes that indicate the quality or status of the event as cause or effect, with reference to either a goal or a past action or event.[8]

To summarize, there are four grammatical levels of action meaning expressed in the Kalapalo verb: (1) tense (remote past, near past, unmarked); (2) aspect (continuous, punctate); (3) mood (reportive, conditional, hypothetical, potential); and (4) mode. There are consequently many Kalapalo words for action processes, in which grammatical categories reify action in terms of *how* and *why*: the circumstances from which events have emerged, their place in an ongoing series of temporal forms, their consequences or effects, and their roles in giving shape to time through a living pulse. Consequently I see a special

Table 4.
Kalapalo Tense Paradigm
Affixes shown are for noncopula verbs in declarative and question sentences.

	Singular subject	Collective subject
Distant past		
Continuous	*-ïgï*	*-ïŋgo*
Punctate	*-isi*	*-isiko*
Recent past		
Continuous	*-ga*	*-gako*
Punctate	*-tsi; -tse*	*-tsiko; -tseko*
Unmarked tense		
1. Continuous aspect		
reportive	*-ta; -tu; -ti*	*-tako; -tuko; -tiko*
conditional	*-fota*	*-fotako*
hypothetical	*-ŋalï; -nalï; -ñalï*	*-ŋalïko; -nalïko; -ñalïko*
potential	*-tani*	*-tanini*
2. Punctate aspect		
reportive	*-lï; -dyï*	*-lïko; -dyïko*
conditional	*-folï*	*-folïko*
hypothetical	*-ŋi*	*-ŋiko*
potential	*-luiŋo*	*-lukoiŋo*

relationship between the structuring of Kalapalo discourse by means of temporal reference and these grammatical categories; for time as process is the medium out of which the most fundamental aspects of Kalapalo ideas of action are created.

Tense and Mood

Tenses are grammatical forms that linguists usually understand as references to the relations between the time of an event described and the time of the utterance. But in Kalapalo, rather than simply expressing "distance" between one objectified event and another, tenses (which are marked in both verbal and nominative suffixes) lay emphasis upon the boundary or continuation, estrangement or development, of personal feelings and relationships. The remote past tense, for example, can refer to events that effect completion of a crucial life process, events that are irreversible and final. Ulutsi uses the remote past to speak about his previous storytelling in line 2 of his Kutsafugu story. Elsewhere, the tense helps to create a picture of action occurring just before a person's exit from puberty seclusion (for example, a young man having his hair painted or a woman having her bangs cut); action occurring before a person's death; or to convey the sense of finality of death. This remote past tense can also be used to express action that occurred in remote time, particularly to emphasize the temporal and ecological distinction between the present time (*ande*) and the distant past, especially the Dawn Time (*iŋila*), which is the time "of the Beginning" (*iŋilaŋo*); it would be a misnomer, though, to call this a "mythic tense."

The unmarked tense in the potential mood (*-tani; -tanini*) also has special functions. In referring to actions that will occur in the future, the tense complements the uses to which Kalapalo speakers put the remote past tense. The continuous potential form is used only in quoted speech of a powerful being or otherwise strongly dominant character who is about to cause a permanent change in another person. Hence the expression frequently heard in stories, a curse actually, *lafa itsani*, "As s(he) is now, so s(he) will remain." When one hears this statement in a story, one realizes that the character about whom it is made will shortly disappear from the action, usually by being killed but also, in a milder psychological setting (as is the case during conversational speech), by being made irrelevant to any future action in which the speaker and listener are to participate. The sense of such a statement is that the victim will be permanently fixed with the attribute that has caused the curse to be uttered. Declarations in the continuous potential mood thus have the character of what J. L. Austin calls "performatives" or John R. Searle "declaratives"[9] because something occurs in the near future as a consequence of their having been uttered. The character making the declaration is thereby symbolized as dominant, the most powerful being in the story. The continuous potential is never used by the narrator.

There seem to be similar restrictions upon how a speaker uses what I call the punctate potential mood. This mood occurs only when the speaker claims assurance that the action described will occur. Although narrators use it in storytelling, it is rare and seems to have a specifically clarifying function, serving to indicate an intended consequence in the future of a character's present action. (This usage contrasts with that in conversational speech, in which the punctate potential mood implies that the speaker can personally assure that an action so referenced will occur in the future.) On the other hand, when a character in a story is made to express the hypothetical mood, there is a clear sense of that character's relatively weak authoritative position vis-à-vis the rest, for this mood is used to wish and to make generic claims that are independent of personal experience and understanding. With the use of this mood, the narrator becomes a neutral commentator, an observer from contemporary time.

Quoted Speech

In Kalapalo stories, the use of a character's quoted speech, which may constitute as much as 80 percent or even more of a narrative, is the most important way to suggest mood and motive, in turn the most elaborate means of fleshing out individual characters and the most usual way of making etiological statements.[10] Efficient causes or reasons seem to be of particular interest to the Kalapalo, judging from the frequency of their appearance, but they are rarely described by means of designative statements that are part of a narrator's commentary. In addition to revealing features of a character's motive, quotation of course conveys considerable information about the relationships between specific characters by their use (or more frequently misuse) of the language of social—especially in-law—etiquette which should be pervasively filled with grammatical forms that mark that speech as emphatically truthful.

Ideas about a character's motive are expressed through that character's own statement of feelings concerning a situation or another character. These sentiments are normally expressed in clauses incorporating a modal verb suffix associated with intentionality (*-omi*). The motive of a character is thus linked to a statement about the action occurring, so as to connect the motive logically with the action in a causal way. What is especially interesting about these statements of motive in quoted speech is that such quotation is nearly the only context in which reference to the future (in the manner I have just described—that is, by means of the continuous potential mood) is made. Given that such reference sets up a character as dominant, not in the sense of most important to the story but as the most powerful, quoted speech can be considered an important means of constructing characterological hierarchies. In fact, such hierarchies occur by virtue of the entire patterning of sound symbolism in a story, a structuring that reflects the relationships that occur between entities and helps to develop a sense of setting. Sound symbols contribute substantially to that other component of narrative action, the *who*, *what*, and concrete *whereness* of events. They round out what is merely suggested by pronominal verb prefixes indicating person status of subjects and objects or names that tell us "what place." Sound symbolism thus develops in a consistent and precise way what Kalapalo grammatical categories leave vague.

At the beginning of this chapter I pointed out that in narrative discourse everything is significant and that a good performance is one in which nothing is said that is not meaningful to the story. Having described in a general way a variety of agents of narrative structuring that are possible in Kalapalo mythic discourse, I conclude with the idea that discourse structuring is what makes each statement in a story significant. Such structuring occurs by virtue of the creation of multiple cross-referenced meanings, and the process works because of the Kalapalo speakers' constant uses of a variety of forms that develop ideas of anticipation, connection, perpetuation, progression, and conclusion.

Chapter 3

Myth as an Explanatory Mode

Becoming aware of the explanatory messages in Kalapalo stories is yet another way of understanding and appreciating their significance as performed events that involve interpretive processes. Kalapalo stories are an important source of information concerning how these people make inferences and organize them into models of experience, how they use inference to construct an explanatory message, and how listeners signal their understanding and acceptance (or rejection) of clarifying statements.

Western explanatory speech events are usually associated with didactic argument in which the explainer communicates the necessity for legitimating or justifying assigned meanings in a new context of use, as well as for having used a particular explanatory principle in solving the problem. Didactic arguments are also frequently used to legitimate disputes and to form the proper contexts for debates. The vehicles for conveying these arguments are types of oral and written genre that are associated with and are considered especially appropriate for convincing others: philosophical dialogues, learned papers, formal lectures, written "Replies to . . . ," and the like. Many anthropologists, accustomed to our culturally created conditions for explanation, have had difficulty recognizing similar intentions and even forms of reasoning they can easily identify as logical when they are faced with exotic cultural forms. Mythology in particular is perceived as a mode of expressing the irrational, entertaining people while serving as an outlet for their improbable fantasies.

In Kalapalo narrative art, many of the tropes can best be understood as highly condensed explanatory constructions best suited to characterizing phenomena that are inherently difficult and complex, psychophysical states that are uncommon or are experienced by only a few persons (insanity, possession, trance, acute narcosis, unconsciousness, nightmares), or, on the other hand, that are forbidden explicit confession in ordinary life (hatred, fears of persons of another gender, dislike of one's own children). The content of these figures of speech, drawn from commonly shared experiences with the natural and social worlds, is readily understood by at least some members of an audience. The depth and subtlety of understanding, of course, will vary with the person listening, and personal qualities play a major role in determining how someone will interpret a myth (or whether it will be enjoyed or even understood). The point is that there are many possible ways of interpreting Kalapalo myths, and even if they have never heard a particular story before, people can immediately comprehend what is being said by reference to their own personal experience. Children begin their understanding of stories at the level of acquiring concrete knowledge: learning place names, species names and habits, the functions of objects and activities, and the kinship relations of the characters in the stories. All these facts are closely tied to a child's earliest experiences of the world and are the basis for subsequent understanding of allusions and metaphors. This heterogeneity of Kalapalo interpretive frameworks and of the themes in Kalapalo myths is clearly connected to the diversity of age, gender and social position of Kalapalo audiences.

But there are other important aspects of Kalapalo mythology bearing upon the problem of interpretation: the persistence with which certain motifs appear within the corpus and the tolerance for multiple variations—the "bricolage effect" in which distinctive logical solutions, as Lévi-Strauss would say, are presented. The same figures appear over and over again because the Kalapalo seem to imagine many plausible explanations for how they are to be experienced and understood. This does not suggest that the problems represented by such motifs are insoluble, but that they are complex and constrained by situated relations with other matters that are perhaps less fascinating or provocative.

Concepts of Time in Explanation

In the last chapter I described how images of time are used to segment narrative and to indicate shifts in character focus. Another temporal narrative image of considerable importance is the cumulative aspect of time. The Kalapalo believe that effects can be created by repeating the events, feelings, and acts that occur in the same "kind" of time. That time is cumulative and has cumulative effects is in turn rooted in the idea of time as recurrent. This idea is the basis for the explanatory proposition that an event can serve as causal precedent for similar future events, though Kalapalo mythic precedent does not fit Bronislaw Malinowski's idea that myth establishes a model or rule to be followed. Rather, a mythological occurrence "in the Beginning" is necessarily followed by persistent repetition and uninterrupted flow of action, an enduring unbrokenness of recurrence that is "endless," "everywhere," and "forever," perhaps even "eternal," ideas expressed by the word *titehemi*.[1] Past, present, and future are all one in the sense that what has once happened may continue to occur and has a chance of recurring in the future.

Time, then, is imagined as repetitive and successive as well as cumulative. The successiveness of times within time is conveyed in mythic discourse by means of temporal images referring to an individual's experience of it, as I described in Chapter 2; the cumulative aspect of time is indicated by using persistence of an act or feeling (the idea of *titehemi*) and the ways in which that idea of repetitive persistence is used as an explanatory proposition, which is that of precedence.[2] Hence to understand etiology and precedent we must understand how history and causality are conceived and how causal statements are made in keeping with indigenous standards for constructing explanations. As we shall see later in this chapter, in formulating their historical perspective Kalapalo easily incorporate both a linear and a durational sense of time into narrative discourse. The durational aspect of time links characters' activities or objects located originally in the past with current phenomena. In part, this is a manifestation of the concern of Kalapalo with incidents in narrative as precedent for much that occurs in contemporary life. What takes place now is not, however, perfectly identical with events or conditions described in myth but rather is seen in terms of "representations" (*ifo*) or "images" (*futofo*, "helps one to know"; "used for knowing") of them.

A good idea of how the notions of *tïtehemi* and *futofo* work together to explain contemporary life is found in the Kalapalo explanation for eclipses. The celestial sun and moon (considered "living things" by the Kalapalo) are described by them as *futofo* of the mythic characters Sun and Moon (also known as Taugi and Aulukuma, their adult names). These characters are often engaged mythologically in fatal combat with powerful beings, temporarily succumbing to their opponents but eventually vanquishing them. Solar and lunar eclipses (*Giti eta*: "Sun is being killed" and *Dune eta*: "Moon is being killed") are explained by the Kalapalo with reference to specific mythological events in which Sun and Moon fight with dangerous monsters. Because these events not only occurred "in the Beginning" (*iɲilaŋo*) but continue to recur in the *tïtehemi* sense, the eclipses people observe in the sky are part of the same phenomenal world, are identified with those events, and thus are explained by what is known of them through myth. The first point of inference is the recognition that the sun and the moon are *futofo*, iconic symbols of Sun and Moon described in myth. Thus an eclipse of the sun is a representation of any one of Sun's struggles (usually athletic) with a powerful being. Furthermore, because Sun and Moon are always ultimately resurrected, the Kalapalo know that an eclipse cannot be permanent. The fear they express of eclipses is not of the eclipse itself but of the unusually intense, violent power over life (or more appropriately, the power to kill magically) that is unleashed. Sun is using this power—the power of witchcraft—and it is therefore easily and intensely available to human beings. Hence during eclipses, witches are said to attempt to harm as many people as possible because they believe their power to be most efficacious at such times. The fear is that an epidemic will soon follow. But similarly, because Sun and Moon are using their physical powers to overcome the monsters with which they are struggling, this is also a time when wrestlers will try to enhance their own powers by making use of the medical practices associated with athletic competition. And finally, it is the time when the Dead, particularly the recently dead, are said to return to the living; for this reason gifts are put out for them by their relatives, and the interiors of Kalapalo houses suddenly are bright with strips of cloth, arrows, shell ornaments, and bead necklaces that have been placed just inside the entrances where the Dead are supposed to appear.

In this example, we see expressed in the idea of *futofo* the principle of homeomorphic identity, which underlies the indexical relation between mythic time ("in the Beginning") and the present. Such an idea is important not only within the context of mythological precedence but throughout Kalapalo culture, finding expression in ideas of medicinal efficacy, interpretation of dreaming symbolism, and the construction of metaphors.

History in Myth: A Kalapalo Experience of Europeans

An anthropological understanding of a people's history must be effected both with respect to their particular ways of remembering and understanding events and to how they communicate this understanding and memory within an oral narrative.[3] Thus if we are to know how people construct an awareness of historical processes, we must learn why certain events become memorable, how they are given explanatory meaning, and how they are integrated into older, long-accepted cosmologies and social models. We also need to investigate how new views of the world and of personal identity arise from a people's attempts both to shape and to express solutions to new situations, particularly in contexts of dramatic environmental change. As a system of meaning—a set of related, coherent principles—history has an explanatory or clarifying function which is inherent in its constant creative involvement with changing worlds of experience. Being a theory of the relations between events as well as a narrative description of those events, history is thus narration that contains an explanation or clarification of what occurred. In this connection, E. E. Evans-Pritchard reminds us in his essay "Anthropology and History" that "history is not a succession of events, it is the links between them."[4] And as Lévi-Strauss has pointed out,[5] different versions of a narrative reflect different explanatory motives of the tellers, hence different histories with different goals have to be considered acceptable alternates and not evaluated for their relative scientific accuracy.

Kalapalo narratives are the symbolic forms that must be taken into consideration if their historical sense is to be understood, and these stories can therefore be treated as primary sources of information concerning the explanatory principles that inform Kalapalo historical models, especially notions of causality. I have already written about how Kalapalo narratives contain within them clues concerning how events are linked together (and distinguished from others) as significant and temporally distinct segments of experience. Hence procedures for analyzing the historical in these narratives must take into consideration not only the symbolic significance of mythic events, activities, and characters and the semiotic relations between these elements but the entire discourse structure. In this chapter I will show how such a discourse-focused analysis can result in more precise understanding of how events are interpreted within a causal framework, in other words, the special significance given to events and their organization into a model. Using a story that has historical implications for ourselves, I will show how events are linked together within a Kalapalo narrative sequence, how temporally distinct events are isolated from one another, and the relationship between this segmentation of the narrative and certain functions of explanation. Narrative form and discourse structure code the narrated events and thus form an interpretive matrix.

For Native Americans, the experience of European contact and conquest was unusually dramatic and had far-reaching consequences that, if not immediately grasped, were implied by the perception of fundamentally different moral representations and judgments and the great miracle of metal tools. These two attributes were used to distinguish the Europeans as strangers with extraordinary power over both the natural environment and the peoples whom they encountered. The events of early European contact were everywhere preserved in oral tradition, but as Fred Eggan clearly demonstrated in the case of Hopi narratives, they were remembered in ways that differ strikingly from the accounts preserved in contemporary European documents.

The most lengthy and detailed description of relations between Kalapalo and Europeans is the story of Saganafa and his four sons. A particular example of this story that serves as the text for my analysis was told me by the *anetu* Muluku in February 1979. His story is remarkable for its vivid depiction of events that have no parallel description in archival documentation of European contact with the people of the Upper Xingu Basin, yet may have actually occurred in what is now Venezuela during the time of the Conquest.[6] The entire story is said by contemporary Kalapalo to have come from original narratives constructed by eyewitnesses: Saganafa, his grandfather, and others who participated in the events wherein the sons of Saganafa figure prominently. The narrative, like many others in Kalapalo mythology, is regarded by Muluku as being directly connected to, and a consequence of, past experiences of real, named individuals who participated in the events described.

In the analysis that follows the story, I make use of symbolic, structural, and discourse analysis procedures showing how necessary each is for an understanding of the narrative as a textual whole. This unity results from Muluku's use of many different verbal artifices, including metaphors, syntactic forms, discourse elements, and entire phrases (such as temporal reference and imprecations) that have special significance beyond their contributions to referential meaning. Both the communicative success of the story and the literary or artistic nature of the text are a consequence of the skill with which Muluku used these symbolic elements to formulate the narrative images.

Saganafa
Told by Muluku at Aifa, February 2, 1979

Some Christians stole Saganafa.
    He was secluded at that time,
        secluded.
        It was at Kwapïgï that that was happening,
          Kwapïgï.   5
      Saganafa was there,
        secluded.

1

a. Then on one occasion someone slandered him to his father.
  "Well, your son certainly did something,
      your son is staying near women," I'm told they said.   10
  "All right then," his father replied.
      His father was really disappointed with him.
      He approached him feeling that way.
  "Is it true then that you've just spoken with your sister?" he asked.
      "Someone was just telling me about you."   15
  The other was silent.
  His father was angry with his son,
      he was angry indeed.
          He was enraged.
  There was no reply.   20
  "Well, I'll really beat you hard!"   ·
  He removed the chord from his bow,
      the father did.
      Next he whipped him.
      Because he was not allowed to have sexual relations,   25
      Saganafa was whipped.
  When that was done his father scraped him all over.
  When he was finished his mother said,
      "That's enough, stop doing that to your son.
          Beat him only a little," his mother declared.
      "If you are disappointed with your son use your speech for   30
      now."
  Following that it was over.

2

a. Saganafa was secluded at that time.
  He remained silent, then he fled.
      "I'll go to Grandfather and his companion," he said,
          "Grandfather and his companion."   35
  At that time they had come,
      his grandparents had come to pull out salt plants at Kafindsu
      where they had a house.
b. Then when night fell,
      he collected his arrows, I'm told.
          It had become dark.   40
  "All right now."
      His father thought he was still there inside his seclusion
      chamber.
      Well, it was very windy by now.
c. *Very* late in the day he arrived.
      "Here is our grandchild," they said,   45
          as he arrived.

"Very well," they said.
"I've come here now to see you both, Grandfather," he said,
"To see you both."
"Very well." 50
Then he stayed there and they all slept.
And the next day.
d. After they had slept two days,
"Grandfather," he said,
"Let's go meet the fish migration, 55
let's meet the fish."
"Let's go as you suggest," he replied.
"Go ahead," she told him,
"With our grandchild," his wife said,
so they left, 60
they left *pupupupu*
paddling toward Kafindsu Meander.
Bah, a flood of migrating fish were approaching.
They went shooting at them all the while,
shooting all the while at *wagiti* 65
Saganafa went,
shooting all the while at the migrating fish.
Then it was over.

3
a. It was still very early, before dawn.
While they continued to do that others were coming toward them, 70
some Christians were coming toward them.
They saw something white on the sandbar, a lot of them,
some distance from where they were just then.
"Look at all the jabiru storks," he said to him,
to his grandson. 75
"Grandfather," Saganafa answered,
"At night I'm not well because of that very thing,
not well at all.
At night that's how I am."
"I see." 80
He continued to go, shooting *wagiti*.
Toward Tefupe.
While he was doing that the Christians had already come there.
"Hey, Grandfather. Some Christians are here!"
They held onto their canoe, the Christians did. 85
"Well, where are you two going?" the Christians asked.
"We've come here for fish."
"Well, come along with me."
"All right!" Saganafa answered.

"Well, come with me, come be my daughter's husband."   90
"I will! Grandfather, I really am going now, I'm going away."
        "Very well."
"I came here because of the pain of my father's speech,
Grandfather," he said.
"I arrived because he was never pleased with me.
            Now that is how I will leave.   95
            Tell the others. You will tell our descendants the story of my
            departure," Saganafa said.
                "Now that is how I will leave."
            How sad he was when he said that!
"All right now," *bok* he got into the canoe.
            Bok, payment was given by the Christian.   100
            Bok, a knife to his grandfather.
            "Here, take this."
            Again, *bok* an axe.
            "Here, take this."
            Again, *bok* a spade.   105
            "Here, take this."
            Again, a pair of scissors.
So, payment was given to him,
            payment for Saganafa was given by the Christian.
            "Take this, because now I'm taking this boy of yours with   110
            me for good.
                I'm taking your grandson away.
                I'm leaving right now."
b. "Grandfather, go away!
            I'm really leaving for good right now with our grandfathers.
            I didn't just come to you before for no reason, you know."   115
            "Very well," his grandfather replied,
                "Go then if you wish."
            "Grandfather, my necklace must be where I left it a long time ago, at
Ogi.
            I put it inside a tree there.
            I hid my necklace there.   120
            You must take it," I'm told he said.
Then they all left right away,
            they all left that place,
                they all went away.
c. When the sun was at its height his grandfather paddled home.   125
            He arrived.
            "Our grandchild no longer exists.
            A Christian has just taken him away."
            How sad they were!
            They left there *ti ti ti ti*.   130
d. Very late in the day they arrived at Kwapïgï.

"*Kaah*! *Kaah*!" shouting out the elderly man went on.

"Your son is really no longer alive.

Our grandchild is really no longer alive.

A Christian carried him off." 135

How sad he was!

The other had been so angry with his son,

with his son he had been angry.

"You never wanted to speak calmly to your son.

Here is your son's payment, here." 140

The axe.

"Here are your possessions, here,"

and the old man went away.

e. After that the others were all paddling home on Kafitsekugu, the
Culiseu River.

This was how the Christians used to go to their canoe landing. 145

"Let's go now, far away from here."

Well, they all went on the road after that.

Well, they slept, they slept, they slept.

f. For a *long* time they went on,

toward the place where the sky ended. 150

To where Kagifugukuegï the Monstrous Toad stayed.

"Quickly, hurry everyone!"

They all scraped some vines.

"Quickly, hurry everyone!"

Next they threw the balls of vine scraping in front of the creature 155

and it pounced on them.

That was how it was done.

The edge of the sky rose up,

and while it was like that

they went on. 160

"Quickly, hurry now, let's go,"

and they went on.

g. After a *very* long time

they arrived at their settlement.

He arrived with the Christians. 165

Saganafa was with the Christians,

he was.

It was over.

They had arrived.

"Well, it's over. Now you may become my daughter's husband." 170

He became so,

Saganafa became so.

"You may now become my daughter's husband as I told you before."

"Go ahead," so they were married.

Saganafa became his daughter's husband. 175

Then it was over.

4

a. She became pregnant,
         his wife became pregnant.
    When she was ready a boy was born.
    Again she was pregnant with a boy.   180
    Again she was pregnant with a boy.
    Again she was pregnant with a boy.
         There were four children of Saganafa.
    Kagayfuku (that's his name,)
         and Kagasafegï,   185
         and Paymïgasa,
             and then Paypegï.
             Four of them.
Teh that last one [*points to his fifth (pinkie) finger*] was the most
beautiful of all his sons.
         Beautiful.   190
             Just Paypegï.
                 He became the most beautiful of all his sons.
    That was over.
b. "You may go now to hunt deer."
    Saganafa went to do that,   195
         he always went to do that.
    Those who talked with one another were Saganafa and Paymigu,
         and I can't remember the name of the other now. . . .
    There were three of them,
         people like us who were Kalapalo,   200
             all of them always worked together when they went to their
             tasks.
    That's all.
c. Kagayfuku was this high at that time, I'm told.
    Another was still this way, smaller.
         Another was still this way, even smaller,   205
             like that.
    Then, he went to kill fish at an oxbow lake,
         Saganafa went there.
             He went fishing.
    By that time he had become a Christian.   210
    Then it was over.

5

a. He went to work,
         Saganafa went.
    One of our people was feeling lazy.
         "Go to work," the Christian said.   215
         "Very well," he told him,
             "But I won't just yet."

       "All right, go on."

       "I won't just yet," he replied.

b. Then it was over.   220

       "Go now!" the Christian told him.

       "You're really feeling lazy."

       "Yes, I'm feeling very lazy."

       "Then you will remain as you are," the other said.

       "Come along with me.   225

           Come along to be eaten by the Christians' Grandfather."

Next he tied him up,

       the Christian tied him up.

He was one of us.

       Saganafa had gone to hunt deer,   230

           he was fishing.

Then they went away.

       "Now, you'll remain as you are since you don't want to live any

       longer," as he took him away.

He took him far away,

       far away from there,   235

           the Christian did.

They came to the edge of some water,

       the edge of a lake.

In the middle of the lake was a house,

       the house of the Christians' ancestor.   240

Then "*Kaah!*" he called out to him,

       "*Kaah! Kaah!* Come get your food over here!"

Then he came,

       the Christians' ancestor came.

           He arrived.   245

       "Here," the other man said.

           "Here is your food."

       "Very well," he answered,

           "Very well."

Then the Christian took hold of the Kalapalo man.   250

       "Look," the Christian said,

           "Look.

       Because of your laziness you must be killed by this

       Christian.

           He's an evil Christian."

       "Very well."   255

c. Then he brought him to the other man,

           and that person took hold of him.

On the back of one knee the Christians' ancestor *tsïk!* cut him.

Blood came.

       On the other side *tsïk!*   260

       On the inside of one elbow, here on the inside of the other, *tsïk!*

One wrist *tsïk*!
and when he died the other took his body away.
He carried him away with his daughter.
With his daughter he carried him away.   265
He was the Christians' Grandfather.
He was a very old man.
"He was very old," Saganafa used to say I'm sure.
Saganafa used to teach us about him long ago.
As he carried him away,   270
his axe coagulated,
his knife coagulated.
"Now, let's go," the Christian said to another who was with him.
Then he arrived home.
Saganafa was fishing and hunting deer.   275
He had gone to hunt wild animals.
d. Then his friend told him what had happened.
"Say, where have you been?" his friend said.
"I was traveling around far from here."
"We must escape,   280
let's escape from here."
"Why should we do that?" Saganafa asked.
"Our brother is really no longer alive.
He is dead," the other told him.
"The Christian killed him."   285
"Where was he?"
"Far from here."
"Very well then," Saganafa answered.
"But if I were to do this I would truly miss our dear children," he
said.
"Only one of our children,   290
our son.
I would certainly miss him if I were to do this."
"No you wouldn't," the other replied.
"Let's flee.
Forget about our children.   295
You wouldn't miss them."
"Let's flee, certainly we'll flee as you suggest!
But I must take one of our sons with me.
Our son."
"All right."   300
"We won't do that yet.
We'll come and go carefully from time to time for a while."
"All right."
Next they left for the oxbow lake,
Saganafa and his companion left.   305

"Let's go to the oxbow lake," he said.
    "All right."
Then, another time,
    "Let's go to the oxbow lake."
    "All right." 310
        They went away.
    "How many days will you sleep there?"
    "Two."
    "All right," his wife replied.
Then they returned. 315
Once again, "We have to go to the oxbow lake again."
    "All right, let's go," he replied.
"Now let's go, let's run away!
    Because the Christians are sure to kill us over that matter of
    theirs.
Let's run away right now, 320
    let's go far away from here right now!"
"All right!" the other replied.
They left.
    "We two must go to the oxbow lake," Saganafa told his wife.
        "All right," she answered. 325
    "I must take this son of yours with me."
        Paypegï.
    "Come along, come along with me, my son."
    "Where?"
        "To the oxbow lake." 330
    "Now, you must not go there with him.
        I'm sure your father is running away," his wife told him.
    "All right."
"Father, let *me* go there with you," Kagayfuku said.
"You continue to stay here, 335
    I'll take you another time,
        another time.
Right now I want to take this boy here,
    your youngest brother."
    "All right." 340
"Now, none of you must go," his wife said,
    their mother said.
"Because your father is running away.
    Your father is going to a place that's far from here."
e. They began to come and while they were still far away, 345
    they slept.
The next day they were still far away and they slept,
    and on the following day
        the Christians went to search for them,

to search for Saganafa and his companion.   350
They came on the backs of horses,
    the Christians came.
A GREAT many of them were searching for them.
Then the others saw them as they were approaching
    "Oh, they're right here!   355
        I'm sure we'll die!"
    "We'll wait for them to come here to *us*," Saganafa answered.
    "Look, let's exterminate them *now*.
        They've been waiting to destroy you, and me too."
    "I think the Fierce People have been waiting to kill   360
    them all, so they won't do that, no."
They waited there for the others to come.
    But they didn't.
    They were afraid of the Fierce People,
        the Christians were afraid.
Following that the two men kept coming.   365
f. After a very long time had passed they arrived.
    They arrived here, at Kwapïgï,
        Saganafa arrived.
    He had become VERY old
        by the time he arrived.   370
All that time the ones he had left behind were looking for their father.
    Kagayfuku left as soon as he had grown into an adult person.
        He went all over to each of the settlements.
        He went here to get them.
Kagayfuku killed all of the people as he went.   375
    The Christians stole everyone.
        Leaders,
        men,
        women,
        children,   380
            everyone.
g. During one dry season of theirs they came,
        during the next dry season of theirs they came.
    The Christians continued *over and again* to come here to us, it is
    said.
Kagayfuku was the *worst*.   385
    He had become an adult person.
Kagayfuku was the leader of them all.
Kagayfuku, Kagasafegï, Paymïgasa, and Paypegï, look. [*holds up
four fingers*]
    He was their beautiful one,
        teh their beautiful one.   390
He then became a leader.
    Paypegï then became so,

          he became a leader,
          and they all left for a place far from here
              called Aŋafuku.   395
     "All right, now is finally the time.
          Let's go get *Kagasa*."
     (That's what Kagayfuku used to call us,
          Kagasa.)
     "All right, let's go get *Kagasa*."   400
     That was how Kagayfuku spoke.
h. Concerning something someone once did to them before.
     Once someone shot at Kagayfuku and his companions.
     This person was a member of Aŋambutï Community.
     That was the name of his settlement.   405
     They killed this Aŋambutï person, he was killed.
          He had come to fish, the Aŋambutï person came.
          While he was doing that the Christians killed him.
               They cut him with a knife,
                    Kagayfuku did, all of them.   410
          Teh! he was a magnificent person.
     So he died.
i. Then his father left, weeping for him.
     "Your younger brother is no longer alive, Children.
          No.   415
     The Christians killed him."
     "Very well," the others replied.
j. After the boy died, I'm told, his father arranged for someone else to
  avenge his son.
     The Aŋambutï person went to a Kwapïgï man,
          to Kwigalu.   420
     That's his name, Kwigalu.
     He was their exterminator of Christians.
     He was their clubber of Christians,
          he was their avenger.
               Teh, that boy had been beautifully pale.   425
               The one I spoke of earlier.
     So then the father gave this man a shell belt,
          a shell collar,
          a toucan feather ornament,
          eagle tail feathers,   430
               payment.
     "Very well," he replied,
          "You did cherish your son."
     "Look," the other told him,
          "Go ahead, do it once and for all.   435
     I've come to you because they wanted to murder our son."
     "Yes, you have," Kwigalu replied,

"Very well."
"Very well."
So he remained there.   440
It was over.
k. Once again they came for them.
"All right, let's go."
The others arrived.
It was just before the end of our rainy season when they   445
came,
the Christians came,
Kagayfuku and his companions came.
"All right everyone," he told them.
They arrived.
They went to a place far from here,   450
they came close to Aŋafuku.
Then they went to Kwapïgï,
and to Kalapalo,
the real Kalapalo,
that's its name.   455
Kwapïgï and Kalapalo were two settlements,
Kwapïgï here,
and Kalapalo here.
There was just one watering place, only one.
The others arrived there.   460
There they slept, they slept, they slept, they slept,
five days the Christians slept.
l. Then they went looking for their father.
looking for Saganafa.
He had fled to a distant place,   465
he was far away.
Kagayfuku and the others,
the Christian went looking for his father.
He wasn't there,
because he had fled from them.   470
Then it was over.

6
a. Kwigalu waited for them.
"You must kill their older brother, their Kagayfuku."
"All right," he answered,
"I'll certainly kill only one of them.   475
Paypegï, he's their beautiful one," I'm told he said.
"Very well."
b. Then he came to bathe,
Paypegï came right there.
Right there was the hidden one.   480

He shot him right here in the chest with an arrow,
        Kwigalu did.
           He shot Paypegï.
    "Ahkam!" he fell down.
        He didn't move.   485
"Go ahead," others said.
    Others went to inform the Christians.
    Some children went,
        those who were blood of the Kalapalo.
    "Your younger brother is no longer alive."   490
He came, Kagayfuku came.
    He was furious, furious.

c. Then he fired his gun
and the other ran away from where he was.
    The one who had killed Paypegï ran away.   495
He wasn't shot.
    He ran, he ran.
        He wasn't caught.

d. Enraged,
        so enraged was the Christian there at Kalapalo.   500
"So, now this is the last time we're going to do this,
    the last time.
'Now that it's our dry season, all right, let's finally go take away
Kagasa.'
    you won't say that any longer."
Then he beat his followers,   505
    Kagayfuku beat them.
They carried Paypegï away,
        they carried him away.
They left,
    the Christians then left.   510
So, they slept.
    The next day they slept,
        the next day they slept.
            Three.

e. He had died,   515
        Paypegï had died.
        They were so sad!
    They buried his possessions when he died.

f. It ended.
No longer did the Christians come.   520
    No longer.
They gave it up once and for all.
    They gave it up.
This was to be the last time.
No longer did the Christians come,   525

did Kagayfuku come.
no longer.
Those people were his children,
Saganafa's children.
That's all.   530

There are six thematically distinct parts to this story, corresponding to major divisions in the discourse structure. The first concerns Saganafa and his relationship to his father; the second focuses upon his separation from Kalapalo society; the third describes his capture by Europeans; and the fourth continues with his life among them. The fifth division, the most lengthy and complex, proposes a certain judgment about Indian-European relations. Finally, the sixth presents the culmination of all those preceding, what can be called the consequential effect. Each thematic division is located in a distinct setting, all six places or sites being linked together by the characters' experience of traveling, that common Kalapalo narrative device that serves to contrast—by means of spatial symbolism—qualitatively distinct forms of experience. Traveling, in other words, is a way of establishing boundaries, which seem to be treated less as visual entities than as spatial relations experienced through the sensitivity of human beings to time.

Correlations of temporal reference, thematic shifts, and focalization in the story of Saganafa are shown in Table 5.

Explicit Reference to Mood

Because mood and motive are so commonly emphasized by temporal reference, it is important to examine more closely how Muluku refers to a character's feelings. He makes eight statements regarding how a character feels toward others. In verses 1a and 3d, Saganafa's father is described as "angry" with his son; in verse 5b the Christians' Grandfather (or "Ancestor") is called "evil" because he is a cannibal; in verse 5c Saganafa declares he would miss Paypegï if he were to flee the Christians' settlement; in 5i the Aŋambutï father is said to have cherished (or "loved") his son, and Kwigalu later in the same verse is

Table 5.
Correlation of Temporal Reference, Thematic Shifts, and
Focalization in the Story of Saganafa

Stanza number	Line number	Temporal reference (introducing verses)	Thematic shifts	Focalization
2	38	"then night fell"	mood to motive	Saganafa
	44	"*very* late in the day"	motive to enactment	
	51	"they all slept"	concludes paragraph	
	53	"after they had slept two days"	keys new theme and focalized character	

Table 5 (cont.)

Stanza number	Line number	Temporal reference (introducing verses)	Thematic shifts	Focalization
3	69	"it was still very early, before dawn" (a liminal time)	new mood of Saganafa provoked by memory of a dream	Christians
	125	"when the sun was at its height"	marking of grandfather's mood	
	131	"very late in the day"	enactment of grandfather's motive	
	148	"they slept, they slept, they slept"	keys new theme and focalized character	
	163	"After a *very* long time"	last activity in stanza	
4	176–81	reference to pregnancies	marking of extended period of time; introduction of new characters	Paypegï
	203–5	reference to growth of children	as above; further description of new characters	
5			stanza shifts to climactic events of story all of which concern Indian-Christian relations	Christian; Christians' Ancestor
	345–48	"they slept. The next day . . . they slept, and on the following day"	keys new focalization; duration of motive	Christian
	366	"After a very long time"; reference to aging	resolution of old theme (Saganafa's life with Christians)	
	372	Reference to Kagayfuku's maturity	duration of motive	Paypegï
	382	"During one dry season of theirs"	marking of Kagayfuku	
	402	"Concerning something someone once did to them before"	reference to an indefinite past event (new theme)	Christian (Kagayfuku)
	445	"just before the end of our rainy season"	duration of motive	
	461–62	"they slept"	keys new focal character	
6	511–14	"The next day they slept"	keys new focal character	Kwigalu
	515	reference to Paypegï's death	end of Christians' motive	Christian

described as this boy's "avenger" (which later motivates him to kill Paypegï). Finally, in 6d, Kagayfuku is said to be "enraged" with his own followers for having let Paypegï die.[7]

In each of these verses the content focuses heavily upon some socially marked event, so that the action is halted temporarily by a description of the unusual relationship. Indeed, each of these references to mood appears at an especially critical moment in the story, when the feelings of the characters for one another have particular significance for the future course of events. The descriptions of mood in this story also seem to form two sets of contrastive agent-patient relations (with the Christians' feelings toward other human beings standing as unique). These relations are shown in Table 6.

Narrative Structure

The introductory section of this story does not receive a number because it is a capsule summary of the text that follows; as I noted earlier, the Kalapalo do not consider the story-line summary part of the narrative. The content of this introduction is important, however, because it orients the listener to the most significant elements of the text to follow. In the present case, the main event around which Saganafa's story pivots, his "theft" by the Christians (*kagayfa*), the particular stage of life during which this theft occurred (adolescence—the most important time of life—during which a person is held in puberty seclusion), and the setting (Kwapïgï, a community abandoned during this century) are called to the attention of the listener. In this introductory section, the Christians are focalized, indicating that they are the main concern of the story.

The first stanza of the narrative establishes Saganafa as a saddened victim of unjust parental abuse. The young adolescent, secluded so he can develop the highly prized virtues of physical strength, beauty, and moral goodness, should

Table 6.
Contrastive Relations of Mood in the Story of Saganafa

Agent–Patient	Verse number and reference*	Line number
Father–youngest son	3d. Father–Saganafa (*itsotu*, "angry")	lines 17–18
	5c. Saganafa–Paypegï (*waykeiŋatiga*, "I would begin to miss him")	line 288
	5i. Aŋambutï father–son (*funita*, "cherish" or "love")	line 433
Killer–victim	5b. Christians' ancestor–lazy Kalapalo man (*atïtifïŋï*, "evil")	line 254
	5i. Kwigalu–Paypegï (*imïtoŋope*, "the avenger"; lit., "resulting from the grave")	line 424
Leader–followers	6d. Kagayfuku–followers (*tsuekugu itsotu*, "enraged" or "furious")	lines 499–500

* References are to feelings of focalized agents toward other characters.

be the most beloved and cherished of all persons within the family. Rather than showing such *funita* for his son, Saganafa's father (perhaps unfairly, but more likely not) believes the malicious gossip of someone outside his household and angrily punishes his son. As a consequence, rebellion turns to grief, and Saganafa is motivated in the second stanza to separate himself forever from his father.

These events are formulaic. They constitute a conventional and frequently used narrative device for beginning a story about a young hero by moving him out of his community into the world of adventure. While this occurs, the adolescent is portrayed as contemptuous of convention, unwilling to remain in celibate seclusion, but more positively, as a person whose moral judgment and social curiosity is beginning to extend beyond his own family. He is most vulnerable to the social difficulties that so often prove tests of his composure and resilience (*ifutisu* is the word used by the Kalapalo to speak of this highly valued personal quality).

Events described in the third stanza are a consequence of the father's rage, the subsequent resolve of Saganafa, and his apparently successful life among the old people. He is now at his grandparent's camp, but the action shifts quickly to a fishing trip, when Saganafa begins to fish for the *wagiti* that are swimming downstream during their spawning migration. This event suggests that the time of year is late April or early May namely, the onset of the dry season, when the forests are beginning to be drained of floodwaters. As the canoe moves upstream, Saganafa's grandfather sees a group of large white figures on a distant sandbank, which he mistakes for a flock of jabiru storks. Saganafa corrects him, recognizing their appearance in dreaming he often experienced while still secluded in his father's house. Mention of dreaming tells us that what is to occur in the future has been fated to occur, because the Kalapalo think that dreaming makes the future happen. Saganafa's dreaming is represented as "unfortunate dreaming" (*siŋufesu*), thereby advising the listener that future events in the story will be characterized by Saganafa's misfortune. To be sure, the two Kalapalo men next meet the Europeans, who abruptly "steal" Saganafa; he willingly accompanies them as a fitting means of fulfilling his desire to separate himself from Kalapalo society. Stanza 3 is thus linked to stanza 2 by means of the initial motives of Saganafa and the dreaming, which occurred within the setting from which those motives arose. This suggests the inevitability of the occurrence, an inevitable conclusion that is a consequence of a specific psychological complex rather than abstract and indeterminate fate. When the grandfather returns to Kwapïgï and implicates the father's anger in Saganafa's capture (which is doubly stated by Muluku, in his own words and those of the grandfather) this relationship is made very clear.

The conclusion of this section describes the departure of Saganafa in the company of the Europeans, followed by a long journey to the Christians' settlement. The travelers first encounter Kagifugukuegï, the Monstrous Toad, a dangerous powerful being (*itseke*) who lives at the "edge of the sky." The sky is held down like a sprung curtain by the body of this monster, who has to be fed balls of vine scrapings before the travelers can pass. (In another version, they come across Kagiñekekuegï, the Tick Monster suspended in a web stretching across their trail.) The presence of such a monster as well as the fact that they have traveled beyond the edge of the sky seem to refer to Saganafa's entrance into an unknown and dangerous region occupied by powerful beings. Muluku's description of Saganafa's journey to the European settlement emphasizes the extraordinary endurance necessary to arrive successfully, and this conforms to other mythological accounts of trips to the places occupied by powerful beings. The developing image of Christians as humans whose attributes are those of powerful beings actually begins with Saganafa's dream and continues when he exhorts his grandfather in 3b: "Grandfather, go away! I am really leaving right now for good with our grandfathers." Here reference to human beings as "grandfathers" is an allusion to the extraordinary hyperanimate power of *itseke*, in this context the power of mysterious enticing spells that are deadly.

In the final segment of stanza 3, Saganafa is taken away in order to marry someone's daughter, an event that recalls 3a. Verse 4 continues this theme by describing the subsequent birth of four sons to Saganafa's wife. The last-born, Paypegï, is now focalized and given the special status associated with this birth-order position: he is the most beautiful of all the siblings. By contrast, the others, especially the firstborn Kagayfuku, are (by implication) boys who arouse aversion and even disgust. Later on, Kagayfuku fulfills this impression by showing himself to be the most repellent of the European raiders. The relative birth order of these two sons and their respective moral and physical attributes are crucial for the unfolding of later events because these attributes are not important in and of themselves but as indications of how others will perceive and act toward the sons and how they in turn will respond. Just as the adolescent Saganafa motivates certain acts in others, so these brothers are the source of crucial moods and motivations in others.

Verses 4b and 4c inform the listener of Saganafa's life among the Christians and the conditions of servitude under which the Kalapalo worked for them. Over a long period of time they ceased to be Kalapalo. We might think of this as the first strategy proposed for Kalapalo-Christian relations: to assimilate fully to the ways of enemies.

In stanza 5, this strategy is shown to be fruitless and dangerous, as the vicious power over human life that is characteristic of the Christians is first mentioned explicitly with the Christian's use of future reference in his imprecation (5b), "So you will remain then" (*lafa eytsani*); he means "As you lived lazily, so you will die a lazy person." This statement indicates to a Kalapalo listener the imminent death of the lazy man to whom it is addressed; such curses are another use of the future performative (by means of potential continuative verb categories) in narrative. Paragraph 5c continues this theme by describing the murder of the lazy man by the extraordinary figure of the cannibal executioner, the "Christians' Grandfather" or "Ancestor." The use of future performatives in the speech of the Christian who conducts his victim to this place of death is, as in the preceding paragraph, an example of how his power over human life is characterized by the narrator. This power, expressed initially as a mood, is developed into a particular motivation in these two paragraphs, concluding with the victim's horrible execution. For the Kalapalo cannibalism re-calls ferocity, violence, or wildness (*aŋiko*). And that in turn is a distinctive attribute of both Fierce People (*aŋikogo*) and powerful beings (*itseke*). Such unpredictable and intrinsic violence is another associative link between Christians and powerful beings.

The line in verse segment 5c concerning coagulation of an axe and a knife is Saganafa's original explanation of the origin of miraculous metal tools (such objects having no apparent source in the Kalapalo world). As with other objects whose creation is mysterious (such as paper and radios), the association of metal tools with Christians lends credence even today to their ability to use and control the hyperanimate, hyperillusory power of *itseke*, the power of creative transformation (*itseketu*). The dreadful manner in which Saganafa described the creation of metal tools is a forceful allusion to the most significant attributes of Christians, their *aŋiko* and their *itseketu*. Although Saganafa (and later the other Kalapalo) are not yet aware that this is the case, these two attributes later prevent them from ever fully assimilating themselves with Christians. (The same theme occurs in many other stories of relations between people and powerful beings.)

On numerous occasions people asked me to describe the manufacture of certain objects; paper, metal tools, wire, and machinery seemed to fascinate them most. After each of my fumbling explanations of our technology, someone would triumphantly say, "But you people are powerful beings!" Although the Kalapalo are intensely interested in our things and how they are made—clearly realizing that it is our power—they never let me forget how that very technology separated us unreconcilably. The unflattering moral connotations alluded to by the label *itseke* were the closest to condemnation of European culture I heard to my face.

Each of these characteristics is a complex mental process that accomplishes both feeling and motivated action. The construction in this section of the psychological attributes of Christians (in Kalapalo terms, the particular feelings and motivations that govern their behavior) serves to contrast them neatly with their victims and with Saganafa and his own people. Saganafa's sons exist in a structurally mediate position with respect to this opposition, having been born of a union between a Kalapalo father and a European mother. Though they intensely desire reunion with their father, they engage in slaving and murder while they attempt it. This is the dominant side of their nature: the maternal.

Returning to the narrative, 5d concludes with the decision of Saganafa and his friend to flee the Christians. Saganafa expresses his desire to leave with his youngest son, the most beautiful Paypegï (who is temporarily focalized). Paypegï and Kagayfuku are now contrasted through their father's respective attitudes toward them rather than (as elsewhere) through their own qualities. Kagayfuku will not be missed by his father; Paypegï will be. Saganafa's refusal to allow Kagayfuku to accompany him sets up his future relationship with his son—his refusal to reveal himself and reunite with him.

Segment 5e describes the return of the two Kalapalo men, pursued for a time by the Christians. In this paragraph, Muluku describes the presence of

Fierce People three days beyond the margins of European territory. As in stanza 3, where the figure of the Monstrous Toad appears, stanza 5 establishes a territorial boundary between the known and unknown, through personages whose relationship with human beings is so violent as to preclude effective penetration of their territory.

Segment 5f describes Saganafa's successful return to Kwapïgï, fulfillment of his goal of 5d, and action directed toward that goal described in 5e. (Again, Saganafa's future performative utterance in 5d sets up this action.) Saganafa's sons' continual search for their father and Kagayfuku's search in "all the settlements" are also attempts to realize a motive established in 5d (line 334): Kagayfuku's wish to be with his father. Segment 5g describes the conditions under which this search was effected: the killing and stealing of the people by all four brothers, led by the firstborn. Muluku again mentions Paypegï's beauty, this time as seen through the eyes of his older brothers. The shift in emphasis from Saganafa's attitude toward his youngest son to that of the older brothers is of great importance.

In 5h Kagayfuku is focalized, and the killing of the Aŋambutï boy (also a "beautiful person") motivates his father to seek revenge through the person of Kwigalu the executioner. Segment 5j describes the enactment of the Aŋambutï father's motive to take revenge through the contract he establishes with Kwigalu, who now becomes focalized. This paragraph is important because of the future performative of the father, who directs Kwigalu to enact revenge. This man's love for his son clearly contrasts with Saganafa's father's loveless attitude, while Saganafa is somewhat ambiguous in his attitude toward Paypegï (his love for his son does not prevent him from returning to the Kalapalo). This ambiguity of feeling toward the youngest son of mixed parentage compares with the ambiguity of feeling Saganafa receives from all his sons.

Paragraphs 5j and 5k create the conditions for the resolution or realization of this motive of revenge initiated by the future performative in the preceding paragraph. Here, the psychological context for the climactic events of the story is created through Muluku's emphasis on the repeated, even compulsive nature of the behavior of the Christians. The particular place where the revenge is to occur is also mentioned: a settlement that was occupied as recently as the turn of the century.

Stanza 6 realizes the Aŋambutï father's motive to have his son revenged. Because Paypegï is killed, Kagayfuku decides he will no longer return. This decision is linked with Muluku's earlier description of Paypegï (in 5) as the brothers' "beautiful one," an indication of their feelings of intense affection for him. Kwigalu also comments on these feelings in 6a.

Finally, the conclusion of this story (6b–6e) is an explanatory summing up of the reasons for the eventual failure of Christians to return once again to the Kalapalo. The attitude of his brothers toward Paypegï is the reason underlying the subsequent end of European depredations upon the Kalapalo. In other words, the explanation for why they never returned is a causal one, and their feelings or mood is the efficient cause used in this explanation.

Kalapalo History

The lineal sequence of events in this Kalapalo story is constructed by means of conventional narrative formulas that break up the flow of time into distinct and structurally significant elements. All these elements seem especially concerned with people's psychological qualities and with how they effect concretely motivated action. The links between one element or segment of the narrative and another is the motivational system; the backbone of this story seems to be constructed of motives, which serve as causal explanations of events. The narrative structure therefore tells us a good deal about how the Kalapalo understand and go about constructing history. They are particularly concerned with the reasons underlying events, reasons that are a matter of peoples' attitudes toward one another. In this story, these attitudes are implicated by the physical distinctiveness of the characters and by the underlying tendency to reinforce the contrasts among them, to assert the differences between Kalapalo and Kagayfa. By their violence and creativity, Europeans or Christians are associated with powerful beings, and this association results in the attribution of certain feelings or moods to them. Saganafa is a symbol of the good relations between Kalapalo and Christians, both from the perspective of the Kalapalo themselves (for whom he is a Kalapalo with knowledge of the ways of Christians) and of the Christians (for whom he is a nice young man, who works hard and can be trusted to marry one of their women).

Although a character's feelings are usually portrayed as inherent to the person, the relationships between that person and others are the contexts in which strong—and usually related—motivations arise. A character's action is thus the result of relationships with others, not a spontaneous outburst devoid of an underlying cause. Moods are therefore portrayed as causing motivation and motivation as causing actions and events, which as a consequence of their own logical relations (subsequent-prior) are thereby linked together into a narrative sequence.

At the beginning of the chapter, I defined "history" as a cultural form that combines narrative discourse with a theory of past events. My subsequent analysis demonstrated that the Kalapalo sense of history is based as much upon ideas about actors, their moods, motivations, and goals, as upon events. Moreover, actors are treated in terms of their relationships to one another, the feelings they provoke within each other and the motives arising from these feelings. It is this focus that gives Kalapalo historical narrative a distinctively different character from that of contemporary European scholarship, in which personal motive is subservient to generalized processes, forces, ideas, or interests that are held to exist in the abstract, independently of individuals. It is similar to the "Great Man" view of history, which stresses personal motivations as pivotal, but the Kalapalo emphasis upon interpersonal processes suggests that even this European view of history, like more modern ones, is concerned with different problems and manifests differing ideas of causality.

Myth and History

In anthropology, the distinction between myth and history emerges from an assessment of how accurately a narrative form reflects or describes reality. Myth, considered an essentially metaphorical form of narrative, is seen less as a representation of reality than as a commentary upon it (for Evans-Pritchard, probably influenced by Ernst Cassirer, this is a moral commentary). History, on the other hand, is conceived as a form that focuses upon the succession of events, resulting in a more or less accurate representation of those events. The less literally interpretable the content, the less historical a narrative is taken to be and the more distorted and inaccurate the representation of events that are the narrative content. The distinction between myth and history thus seems to parallel attempts to distinguish the communicative and formulative functions of language, trying to sort out imputedly rational elements from those that seem not to obey the laws of logic and are considered peculiar and fantastic.

From the perspective of Kalapalo culture, no easy contrast can be drawn between history and myth because all narratives are constructed by means of discourse elements and verbal images that are symbolic and that imply others within a general world view. The story of Saganafa is clearly concerned with describing the successiveness of certain events held to have occurred in particular times and places, but the selective nature of the description of these events (how they were remembered), the treatment of places and times when they occurred, and the properties of persons who participated in them suggest that they are themselves symbols. They are symbols that stand for the abstractly conceived contrast between Europeans and Kalapalo, as represented by these peoples' respective ways of feeling and behaving. Indeed, it would be difficult if not impossible to separate what is historical from what is mythological, even on the basis of some imputed truth value of the description (which for some would be measured by accuracy of correspondence with European accounts). The most difficult images for a non-Kalapalo (metal tools coagulated from human blood; a monstrous toad whose repulsively bloated body holds down the edge of the sky) are far more significant as allusions to certain ideas about Europeans and about the known environment than statements of literal belief. Rather than obscurantist, illuminating these ideas allusively makes them both plausible and comprehensible, even concretely meaningful, in a way abstractions might not be. In these allusive descriptions, tropes assist in comprehending what may be inherently difficult or complex notions rather than distorting or fantasizing them.

Chapter 4

Sound as Symbol: Orders of Animacy

Listening to a Kalapalo narrative, one is often struck by the richly textured sound of the performance and how readily one's ear responds to the tones and rhythms in what is being said. This response is a consequence of a speaker's frequent use of onomatopoeia, expletives, quoted speech, and song to create a text. Alternating these sounds with straightforward, narrated sentences creates abrupt changes in rhythm and pitch and a resulting sense of simultaneous presences that helps a listener to visualize the characters and events in the story by imposing a mythic and a musically poetic order on Kalapalo discourse.

There are several reasons for thinking that this alternation of sound is neither accidental nor done only for evocative purposes. First, there are clearly distinct varieties of sounds: monosyllabic unrepeated sounds, monosyllabic and polysyllabic repeated sounds (both fall into what are called *ideophones* by linguists), quoted speech, and music. Second, these sound classes occasionally appear in nonperformed speech, where evocative imagery is far less important. Third, different sounds are closely correlated with different entities. It would appear, then, that an underlying sound symbolism in Kalapalo texts implicates how entities are conceived and spoken about. Development of these meanings through sound symbols is one way the specific characterological configurations in a particular story are effected by a Kalapalo narrator.

I have already shown that one important reason for breaking lines as I have done—in keeping with a speaker's pauses—is to account for the role of the what-sayer. With the text broken this way, the minimal construction of a line can be seen to involve one of several possibilities: first, an ideophonic construction (especially onomatopoeia, recognized by its characteristic repeated monosyllabic or polysyllabic form); second, a human expletive or the call of an animal (usually monosyllabic or a repeated monosyllable); third, a quoted song or line of music; fourth, a portion of quoted speech or part of the actual narration. The occurrences in the fourth instance consist minimally of any form of noun (a lexeme, pronoun, or nominalized verb or adverb) and one or more particles that qualify through mode or focalization the noun's function in a preceding verb phrase. If the ideophonic forms of speech that I am considering substitute for noun phrases, which always include information about the noun's relation to a verb as subject or object, then music, quoted speech, expletives, calls, and onomatopoetic forms must not only evoke different entities but also symbolize them with reference to the particular relations of transitivity or intransitivity to which the entities in question must confrom.

Considered in this way, specific entities in Kalapalo myths can be grouped into five distinct categories, distinguishable according to the syntactic functions they perform, the suffixes attached to their names, and their representation by the sounds they emit. These syntactic functions, noun suffixes, and sound symbols together implicate distinct notions concerning the relative degree or level of animacy of the entity in question.

Table 7 includes a list of entity categories in Kalapalo discourse, the sound symbolism pertinent to each, and their various subject/object relations. In addition, I have indicated how sounds are to be interpreted and the noun suffixes associated with each category.

The Symbolism of Sound

Onomatopoetic forms constitute one important class of ideophones. Many are so standardized that they are used in almost all storytelling (for example, *titititi* to represent a barefooted person walking hurriedly along a dirt path), but it is a class that is constantly being added to and broadened in meaning as new phenomena are closely and precisely observed. An incident during one of my visits to the Kalapalo helped me understand how this can occur. One day, as I sat cleaning my glasses in Kambe's house, his granddaughter Kaitsa (then about fourteen) squeezed herself down next to me in the doorway. She was apparently watching carefully for the moment when I would start to put my glasses back on. Then, following my motions with great care, she smiled and suddenly said, "Nnnguuruk!" I realized she had exactly reproduced through sound the motion of my having moved the glasses onto my face followed by the act of settling them on my nose and ears. By her utterance, she had solved the problem of how those outlandish objects, through which only I could see anything, actually stayed on my face. For Kaitsa, understanding how my glasses worked was an aesthetically pleasant event.

In a similar manner, the variety of onomatopoeia in a story attests to the narrator's skill in making sense and then creating in the listener's mind a vivid image of the action that takes place. As the earlier examples (and those presented in Table 8) show, Kalapalo onomatopoeia does not involve representation of an entity by means of a verbalized symbol of a sound it emits. Rather, an onomatopoetic form refers metonymically to actions upon certain entities sometimes (but not always and only incidentally) accompanied by noise. Examples from the texts in Table 8 either substitute for, clarify, or expand the sense of a noun phrase. In all cases the forms refer to actions suffered by two categories of entities: (1) inanimate objects (such as smoke from a fire dispersed by the wind, a hammock cord snapping under the weight of an excessive number of people, or a pile of wood being thrown to the ground), including what are

Table 7.
Animacy Orders in Kalapalo

Degree or level of animacy	Category of entity	Syntactic functions	Sound symbol	Noun suffixes
1. hyperanimate; inventive, creative, unbounded, dangerous	*itseke*: "powerful beings"	sTV; oTV only when *s* is *itseke*; active verbs	*-aŋ-*: "music"; no sematic interpretation	*-kuegï; -tsuegï; -fuegï* (augmentatives)
2. beings capable of lying, fantasy, of social relationships	*kuge*: "human beings"	sTV; sIV; oTV only when *s* is human or *itseke*; *itseke* patient when passive verbs	*-ki-*: "speech"; nonliteral (iconic)	various; having to do with verbs of which they are agent-subjects
3. independent, animate beings; goal-oriented	*ago*: "living things"	sTV; sIV; oTV only when *s* is a higher-order entity; higher-order entities patients only with passives	*-tsu-*: "calls"; indexical	various; having to do with appearance, behavior
4. inalienable organs of the body; zones capable of independent motion and of feeling	no cover term?	sIV; oTV only when *s* is a higher-order entity	*-tsu-*: "calls"; indexical	inalienable possessive suffixes (*-gïpe*)
5. inanimate body parts; inanimate objects	*iŋko*: "things"	sIV; oTV when *s* is animate	*-tifi-*: "noises"; indexical	possessive suffixes (*-gï-*)

Key
s: subject
o: object
TV: transitive verb
IV: intransitive verb

thought of as passive or inanimate body parts (such as the feet, head, finger-nails, and trunk of the body); and (2) active or animate organs, which for the Kalapalo include the eyes, pulse (a concept that includes the heart as well as pulsing veins and arteries), the intestines, the inner abdomen (including womb and stomach), the anus, and the genitalia. All these are considered the zones of human feeling, the loci of emotions.

Table 8:
Examples of Ideophones in Kalapalo Texts

A. Onomatopoeia:

1. *puk*, ah tafaku, isiña
    "*puk*, well tafaku wood to her mother"
    puk / sound of wood being placed before recipient

2. *ti ti ti* ifaki ekugu
    "*ti ti ti* a long way"
    ti ti ti / sound of human feet walking on a path

3. *tsidik* ataŋembefa
    "*tsidik*, he climbed onto what he had been concerned with"
    tsidik / sound of man's body hitting tree as he climbed onto it

4. aimbegele *tsïgïtsïgïtsïgï* uletofona,
    dididididididididiiiii didik buuk!
    "Once again he did as before *tsïgïtsïgïtsïgï* to do that,
    dididididididididiiiii didik buuk!"
    tsïgïtsïgïtsïgï / man climbing tree, pushing feet against trunk
    dididididididididiiiii / man sliding down tree trunk
    didik / man's body bumping off tree trunk at bottom
    buuk / man's body (feet) hitting the ground

B. Expletives:

1. *achew achew*: sneezing
2. *oĩ oĩ oĩ oĩ*: crying adult
3. *wa wa wa*: crying infant
4. *hi hi hi*: giggling
5. *kïtah*: expression of frustration
6. *ah ha ha ha*: laughter
7. *akam*: cry of pain
8. *ah aaaa* (with sharply ascending pitch): death cry

C. Calls of living things:

1. *õ a õ, õ a õ*: call of the banded tinamous
2. *kwakwakwa*: call of the long-tailed potoo
3. *ŋa ŋa ŋa ŋa*: call of macaws
4. *siiiissss*: call of a snake

The sounds produced by inanimate body parts are represented by onomato-poetic forms and occur when they are used in action or are being acted upon by an animate being. The word used for these sounds is a nominalization of the verb stem *-tifi-*, which refers to the noisemaking caused by an agent but produced by an inanimate object. Hence at one end of the animacy continuum are inanimate objects or body parts that by implication are incapable of intentionality and goal-oriented thought; they are only acted upon. They are owned, or "possessible" but are not related to anything in an active sense—that is, in Kalapalo terms, by means of a communicative sound symbol. Onomatopoeia is a way of referring to some quality of their essence, what they do, or what happens to them when acted upon. This quality gives them a significance in discourse beyond their simple naming in a sentence. It is a way of making objects memorable even though they do not participate actively as agents in the story, and it helps us to envisage concrete aspects of action that is taking place, as well as the setting.

The next set of entities consists of animate or active organs of the body that are "inalienable" in that their loss is said to result in the death of the individual. Sounds these entities produce occur as a consequence of their motion. While animate organs of the body are thus capable of motion and feeling, they are not capable of motivated or goal-oriented action upon another entity. They do not think, in other words. Being animate, such organs are capable of emitting noises independently of their being acted upon. These sounds thus implicate the idea of independent feeling expressed through motion, which in turn is implied in the idea that animate body parts are the source of feeling in living things. Perhaps for this reason their sounds are called by the same term as that for the calls of living things: *itsu*.

Living things are *ago* and are frequently represented by their calls (*itsu*). As presented in narrative these calls occur only within the presence of a listener, usually a human being. They are meaningful only because someone is interpreting them as an indication of the presence of the being in question. A woman hearing the sound of the banded tinamous in the wilderness, "õ a õ, õ a õ," responds by remarking on its presence and attempting to make contact with it. Calls are thus not only indexically constructed (they are sound: sound correspondences), they are indexical symbols in that they indicate in the story the presence of the being emitting them; they are an assertion of identity.

Living things can serve as subjects of intransitive verbs and as both agents and patients of transitive verbs, but as agents they can only act upon entities of the same or a lower degree of animacy; they cannot be agents of activities in which human beings or powerful beings are suffering the action as patients. Living things are treated as independent animate beings capable not only of independent motion and of feelings (as subjects of intransitive verbs and because they emit calls) but also of goal-oriented action. Hence they are more animate than inalienable body parts, which are capable of motion and feeling but are not independent and therefore are incapable of goal-oriented action.

Human beings are classed with other life forms as *ago*, "living things," and as such are capable of producing *itsu* (which we can refer to as expletives, following the English speaker's practice of distinguishing human and animal sounds in a way the Kalapalo do not). These human utterances are, like animal *itsu*, constructed indexically (some examples are given in Table 8), and, again like animal *itsu*, human calls are also indexical symbols; they are associated in time and space with the feelings from which they arise. For this reason human beings can express truthful and empirically motivated feelings best through *itsu*.

Pain of varying degrees of intensity, deep sadness, shame, joy, sexual passion, frustration with oneself, indeed, the entire range of human emotion is expressed most succinctly (and by implication as truthful feeling) this way.

Human beings are distinguished from other *ago*, however, by their ability to speak, and it is through language that they are most commonly symbolized and distinguished from other categories of entities. In narratives, the quoted speech of human beings is the most important sound symbolism, sometimes consituting as much as 80 percent or even more of a text, and quoted speech in the form of conversations, short narratives, oratory, curses, or the various signaling outcries is the characteristic means of representing them as distinct characters in the stories. But language allows people to do something very different from animals. Human beings were created by a trickster, whose name "Taugi" means "speaks deceptively about himself," and whose epithet *tikambïŋï* means "without telling (or revealing) anything about himself." Hence human beings are in essence deceitful beings because of their ability to speak. Therefore, people are capable not only of truthfully expressing their feelings, but—and this is the unmarked understanding of human speech for the Kalapalo—of creating an illusory screen of words that conceals their true thoughts.

Among the Kalapalo, the truth value of speech is always marked in one or more ways. Most commonly used are particles that indicate the speaker's evidence for accepting or disagreeing with a statement. There are at least sixteen of these in Kalapalo, marked for tense, that express positive or negative confirmation, doubt, eyewitness certainty, supposition, hypothesizing, hearsay, and vagueness. Hearsay evidentials are commonly heard in mythological narratives, especially when speech is being quoted.

A second means of declaring the truth of one's own speech is to use the expression *augindaf ïŋï*, "it isn't a deception." Also, speech acts that are in general considered truthful and good by the Kalapalo (such as a leader's oratory or statements made by one affine to another) are flamboyantly marked by emphatic modal particles (*-ketsaŋe*; *-fetsaŋe*) that also seem to function as truth verifiers in contexts that demand unquestionable sincerity.

When these forms do not occur in speech, a person is assumed to be speaking illusorily, though such illusion may be the consequence of a person's indecision, confusion, or lack of knowledge. In any case, the Kalapalo receive verbal statements that are not marked as truthful in a psychological state of doubt, while the speaker (creating them with the intent to convince a listener) engages in assertion.

The verb for illusory speech is *augï-*, which can be applied both to a variety of different speech acts and to the use of special figurative language. Figurative language that is called illusory is typically integrated into speech acts that are considered truthful (such as the narratives I am considering), but the underlying intent of speech acts which Kalapalo label illusory varies considerably. For example, a distinctive way of speaking that is characteristic of new in-laws, who are the most intensely formalized relationship (*ifutisundako*) in Kalapalo life, is to "speak deceptively" to one another by labeling certain objects in distinctively "beautiful" tropic language, by verbally diminishing the worth of certain first gifts through labels that refer to badly made, disgusting, or worthless objects, and by referring to one another as if they were close kin rather than affines. Used in this way, *augï-* is extremely benign in intent; along with the actions it accompanies, it is a demonstration of the deepest respect and aquiescence to social form that is possible. In the speech of in-laws, illusory speech is immersed in speech acts that mask potentially threatening difficulties connected with affinity (see Chapter 6).

In contrast, there are entire speech acts labeled by *augï-* that are governed by the opposite of respectful feelings; here, Kalapalo speakers are not motivated by *ifutisu* but by such feelings as vague contentment and friendly warmth toward a person (*atutu* or "goodness") or any one of several ideas of feeling that in English are conflated by the word "anger." For example, *augï-* is used to refer to a joking discourse (*tegu-*) in which men tease each other about their love affairs, grossly exaggerating the victim's desire for an absurd partner. This way of speaking is characteristic of men who are friends (*ato*), one of the few enduring Kalapalo relationships based upon affection and personal choice. Malicious speech acts governed by violent anger (*itsotu*) and the desire to create anxiety in another, to confuse, delude, or perplex someone (*iŋgugi-*) are also called *augï-*, which in these cases can be translated as "lying."

From speech, then, depends creative power that extends human consciousness far beyond that of other living things. This power to create illusions has crucial implications for the relations humans construct with one another, for these relations are typically ambiguous, often masking true feelings and even true identities. So although humans are capable (like all living things) of goal-oriented action, what is important for their distinctiveness among *ago* is their capacities for deception in these relationships and for imaginatively creating their goals. Being relatively more animate in their ability to construct imaginative images of themselves and others, they are "acted upon" only when the agent is human or a powerful being.

The final category of entities in narrative discourse consists of powerful beings, *itseke*. Their distinctive character is plainly evident in the cast of mythical personages: Agouti, Taugi, Thunder, Jaguar, Kafunetiga, Nightjar, Tick Monster. It is also evident in their actions as characters: Agouti is a sneak and a spy, Taugi an effective trickster who can penetrate illusions, Thunder the most dangerous of powerful beings, Jaguar a violent bully who is easily deceived. These psychophysically distinct characters are unified by their experience in a space-time dimension that allows them to be in more than one place simultaneously, to be continuously doing now what they are described as doing then, to be ambiguous with respect to sex and age (or to lack these attributes), to change form from that of a natural species, celestial object, or material object to human shape, and even to be singular and plural at once. Powerful beings are different from concrete historical figures because they and their acts are "always" and everywhere; they are *titehemi*. This multiplicity of essence or "hyperanimacy" is coupled on the one hand with a multiplicity of feeling and consequent unpredictability and on the other with a monstrous intensity of some feeling or trait; hence powerful beings are dangerous beings. The hyperanimacy of powerful beings is suggested by the fact that they serve only as subjects or objects of active verbs and act as patients only when the agents are themselves defined as powerful beings. Their hyperanimacy and multiplicity of essence are perhaps what is deeply metaphorized by their association with musical invention. *Itseke* are powerful because of their *itseketu* or transformative power, their ability to create effects or achieve goals by means of *kefege* or "song spells." *Itseke* are thus the most creative and inventive of all beings, capable not only of thinking about things that do not exist (as do humans) but of causing these things to come into existence by means of their musical incantations. The Kalapalo story-tellers were sometimes careful to point out that, although they spoke of power-ful beings as if they performed actions as people would, in fact they understand these events to have actually been the performance of song spells. Song spells really effected (and still effect) what occurs in myth. Some people do indeed possess spells, but these are weakened replicas of the originals that were first invented and used by *itseke*, who are their true owners.

Powerful beings are thus capable of inventing musical forms, whereas hu-mans are capable only of copying those forms in their performances. Human beings can invent only through language, and their language should best be interpreted most broadly by understanding it as essentially figurative because of its main use in deception. Although humans are creative in contrast to other *ago*, they are limited in their creative capacities in a way powerful beings are not because music is amenable to far more complex and highly varied, even idiosyncratic, interpretation than is language, and it subsumes or encompasses speech. In the myths, although powerful beings communicate with people by speaking to them, they are preeminently and essentially musical.

Creative transformation, the quality of animacy that is associated with pow-erful beings, is marked by their pupilless eyes, from which dazzling beams of light radiate (these eyes are represented on masks by oval pieces of mother-of-pearl) and, in Taugi's case, by the brilliant feather headdress he wears on his visits to powerful beings (a sign to them that he intends to destroy them through his magical power). The sparks of light in the eyes of human beings are a sign of the paltry morsel of creativity that has been inherited from Taugi and his illusionary linguistic powers, but the decoration of dancers during ritual perfor-mances replicates the original model or image (*futofo*, "used for knowing" or "permitting understanding") that myth describes. It is then that Kalapalo men and women complement and thereby enhance their humanly verbal powers of illusion and creativity by means of the closest approximation of *itseke* action they are capable of engendering: musical performance.

What appears syntactically and also at the interface of Kalapalo syntax and semantics is a hierarchy of animacy, ranging from inanimate objects through animate body parts, living things, and human beings to the hyperanimacy of powerful beings. This hierarchy takes the form of successively encompassing subject/object relations and also of successively encompassing levels of sound productivity. Inanimate objects produce sound only when acted upon; animate body parts produce sound through their motion; living things are capable of calls; human beings of speech; powerful beings of music. In turn, the hierarchy of sound symbolism implies, along with the subject/object hierarchy, essential capacities of entities. Inanimate objects and body parts are possessible and are acted upon. Animate organs of the body can act independently but do not orient themselves toward goals. They exhibit alternate states of being (motion and therefore feeling, or states of rest and inaffectuality) and are associative or in-alienable rather than strictly possessible. Living things enact goals that are truthful, whereas human beings are capable of deceit, ambiguity, and fantasy; they are imaginative beings. Powerful beings are essentially musical and sub-stantially or naturally creative through this form of sound. Therefore, in J. L. Austin's sense they are performative beings, capable of reaching the limits of awareness of meaning by constructing action through a process that is simulta-neously mental and physical.

"When We Could Approach Powerful Beings"

The human beings who existed in the Dawn Time were different from those of the present because, as Ugaki suggested, they were capable of "approaching powerful beings." People were once able to engage powerful beings without danger of being killed merely by coming into their presence (in such instances, powerful beings are called *afitsatu*, or "dangerous transforming visions"). Dawn People often lived intimately with powerful beings and were themselves pow-erful by virtue of the song spells they controlled, which enabled them to survive such relations.

The word *itseke* can be used to designate a specific category of entity (or, as we saw in Chapter 3, underscore certain attributes associated with those entities), but its use more deeply implies a special mental experience that in-volves the weakening or loss of a form of material consciousness in which things are held to be concretely present in a place outside the mind, and a substitution of illusions. The Kalapalo say powerful beings appear to people during dreaming or as monstrous apparitions (*afitsatu*) when they take the form of a human being; the most monstrous and powerful of them all (the demonness Ñafïgï and Atugua the Whirlwind) are typified by their "poisonous pungency" (*piŋegï*), causing dizziness and general disorientation that ultimately leads to death.[1] Controlled disorientation, which is the shaman's ability to understand and interpret his tobacco-induced visions of powerful beings under conditions of severe narcosis, is the only salubrious means of dealing with them (if indeed it can even be called that).

The manner of describing these experiences of dreaming, of shamanism, and of contact with specific powerful beings suggests a contrast between the careful steadfast focus on material forms that is particularly characteristic of Kalapalo observation and another consciousness that is less focused and less material than it is illusional. Under these circumstances, what are first held to be doubtful apparitions—first appearing out of the corner of the eye and from a distance—assume a central and convincing place in rational discourse, serving both explanatory and rhetorical functions. Although these experiences have been called "altered states of consciousness," they are more exactly forms of self-enchantment, during which an illusionary state of consciousness is recognized as such and made valid through its meaningfulness. This meaning contrasts with that of material consciousness in the manner by which it is understood.

Powerful Beings in the Form of Human Beings

When the Kalapalo speak of a powerful being appearing to a person in human form, they are referring to active manifestations in human shape of the essential properties of entities. The word they use for this human form is *akūa*. The most common experiences of *akūa* occur during dreaming.[2] When a person becomes visually aware of the physical self engaged in activity, however, the term is applied to the manifestation of nonhuman entities in human form when they are involved in an active relation with a human person. Because the term *akūa* refers to the appearance of an entity in the shape of a human being, active manifestations in human shape of the essential properties of entities, I translate the Kalapalo concept "interactive self." I am especially concerned to emphasize by such a translation the two distinctive features of this concept. First is the idea that *akūa* are manifestations to a human person who is aware but not awake or materially conscious of both human and other animate beings, of manufactured objects, and of powerful beings. Second, the *akūa* is an interactive concept in that a person's awareness of it is always achieved in a communicative context (one that may be verbal [conversationally or through expletives], visual, musical, or any combination of the three) that constructs a relation of transitivity. In this connection, it is because such "selves" are making themselves visible to human consciousness that they take human shape.

The idea of *akūa* participates in the notion of an experience shared between a particular human being and some other entity, and such a shared experience can occur only when that entity takes (or is apprehended as taking) human form. Human form is necessary for communication to take place involving the mingling, with intense consequences, of the powers inherent in human language and in the spells of powerful beings. The *akūa* is not so much a "thing" as an interactive phenomenon, a special perceptual and conceptual experience for which "soul" seems a very crude, offhand gloss. The staleness of this translation is compounded when we remember that *akūa* are the human manifestations of material objects as well as living things and of powerful beings. "Self" seems more appropriate because in English it can be applied to many different entities, living and nonliving (we can say, for example, "itself" as well as "herself"). Furthermore, "self" is appropriate because the notion of *akūa* involves the entire entity, governing and thus pervading its physical wholeness. The *akūa* is, then, more than the immaterial "essence" of a thing. It is an interactive relation, and therefore the *akūa* can best be understood as an hypostatization of the principle of imaginative awareness of some being or essence, the interactive self of an entity as engaged with the mind of a human being. The idea of *akūa* suggests how the careful perception of the independent existence of things, each under-stood by the Kalapalo to be motivated by internally generated goals and feel-ings, can be concretely represented by a human figure that uses language when engaged with human beings, but by natural life forms or inanimate things that emit *itsu* when unconcerned with their relations with human beings.

Having now described some implications of the Kalapalo idea that a pow-erful being is an entity that can appear to a person in human form, I shall pursue this idea with respect to the main focus of this chapter, sound symbolism.

Identifying Characters by Sound Symbolism

In many stories, it does not always seem clear from the actions of characters whether they are material objects, living things, human beings, or powerful beings. Some stories concern human characters (Dawn People) whose eccen-tricities are symbolized by the species name that they bear (such as Tapir). Yet in others, humanlike characters are actually powerful beings (such as Storm, who can take the form of thunder and lightning but also that of mature men, their most common manifestation when they appear before human characters in myths). Finally, all the physically human characters called Dawn People or *aŋifolo* are also considered powerful beings. Although confusing at first, sorting out the existential nature of a character is not difficult if we remember that the words *itseke*, *ago*, and *kuge* ("human being") do not designate exclusive classes of entities but can be situationally distinct manifestations of the same being. These words imply categories of relationships. Although a character may man-ifest situationally varying properties of more than one entity category, by listen-ing to the sounds being emitted by the character one can easily understand whether the narrator is referring to the powerful manifestation of a character or to that same character taking the form of a particular natural species, an inani-mate object, or a human being.

I cannot emphasize too strongly that the labels for these categories may be applied to the same material form of entity, the selection of a label conforming to a situationally specific judgment made by the speaker concerning the degree of animacy the entity manifests in a particular context. To make such a judg-ment is to imply something about the relationship of the entity in question to human beings. For example, to call a particular species of fish a "powerful being" rather than a "living thing" is to deny its suitability as food. Or to call a child someone's "pet" implies that the "owner" has adopted it as if it were a wild fledgling accidentally discovered in the wild. Animacy is therefore not only an aspect of material being, it is inextricably connected to Kalapalo notions of the suitability of certain entities for mutually satisfying, social relationships. Animacy, in short, has moral implications, not in absolute terms but only with respect to a person's own situated experience of it. What happens to one Kala-palo when confronted by a powerful being will be different from another's ex-perience. In one case, *itseke* might kill a person; another time a man might be given some of their power by being taught song spells.

All the nonhuman characters in myths about Dawn People are considered powerful beings (because they are transformative entities), and they can take the shape of human beings and communicate with Dawn People through language. In the form of natural species, they emit calls, and the style of their actions as natural life forms is indicated by the speaker's use of the *-su* ("customary") mode. Finally, when they are manifesting their power by means of song spells, the sounds they emit are musical.

Alamigi

The story of Alamigi, a young woman who heckled the nightjars while they called outside her house at dusk, nicely illustrates the use of sound as symbolic of different entity relations and processes of communication. The narrator of this story was Agakuni, who told it to his large household with his brother-in-law playing the what-sayer's role. Agakuni was a terrific storyteller, taking on the various character's roles with a masterful sense of the comical spirit of the myth. This story seems especially concerned with playing with the ambiguities inherent in interpreting sounds in contexts where the margins between human beings, living things, and powerful beings disappear. The Nightjars, Banded Tinamous, and Tiger Heron appear as birds when the narrator represents them through their calls. They take human form when they speak but turn back into birds when they "fly away in the manner of" their species (a use of the "customary mode" I spoke of earlier). Finally, Nightjar is most surely represented as a powerful being when he performs his musical sleep spell in the unwitting presence of Alamigi's family.

Alamigi
Told by Agakuni at Aifa, February 14, 1979

Alamigi was a Dawn Person
　　　　of the Beginning.
　　　She was a human being.
　　　　a human being.
　　"Fokugeu', fokugeu',"
　　　　at dusk they called out.
　　"Maah! Go away, go away!" she told them.
　　　　This time it was the woman speaking, the woman.
　　"Maah! Go away stupid Fokugeu,' Kuaku.
　　Right now! Ugly Beak," as they went about.
　　　　"So get going, get going," she told them,
　　　　　　"Stupid Fokugeu', Kuaku.
　　　　You're forever eating biting ants, you're forever eating biting
　　　　ants.

Biting ants, our biters, you're forever eating biting ants."
Fokugeu' the Nightjars left.

The next day she heckled them,
 the next day she heckled them,
 the next day she heckled them,
  the next day she heckled them.
  She despised them,
   that woman did.
When all the people went to the manioc fields,
 then very early at dawn *tiki*,
  he entered the house.
  A woman with a newborn child was there by herself.
   Tiki, he entered the house.
"Oh!" she said,
 "Who could that be who just came in?" she said, "Who are
you?"
"It's me." Nightjar was a man.
  "It's me, me."
"I see." She stared at him.
"Who is this talking to me?" she asked herself.
"Who *are* you, who?"
"It's me, me.
 You've actually been calling me 'Kuaku.'"
So, "I see," she said, "I see."
"You've actually been calling me 'Kuaku.'"
  "I see."
"Whose hammock is this?"
 "Alamigi's," she answered.
"I see, and whose hammock is *this*?" "So-and-so."
 "Whose hammock is *this*?"
That side of the house was finished.
The other side as well.
"Whose hammock is *this*?" "So-and-so." "Whose hammock is this?"
"So-and-so."
"Listen carefully to what I say."
"What's that?"
"Who is the person who heckles the Nightjars? 'Ugly-beaked
Nightjar, you're forever eating weeds,' who says that to them?"
"She herself is who, Alamigi."
 "I see," he replied, "I see."
"Alamigi is the one who fights with them.
 When the Nightjars come here, 'Oh, get going!' Alamigi tells
 them. 'You're forever eating termites,' she tells them.
  She herself is the one."

"All right, I'll be going now," he said.

"Go then."

He went away. "Alamigi, Alamigi, Alamigi,"

a short distance,

and he forgot!

"What did you just tell me, what's her name?"

"Alamigi."

"Alamigi, Alamigi . . . ," he went on a little farther,

and he forgot again!

He came back there again.

"What did you just tell me?" he said.

"*Alamigi, Alamigi* is what I've been saying!"

"Yes, that's right."

Tututu

"Alamigialamigialamigialamigi. . . ."

Far away,

and he forgot again.

Tiki, he came back there again.

Tititi tiki.

"What did you just tell me?" he asked.

"*Alamigi*, I keep tell you.

ALAMIGI is her name, ALAMIGI!"

"Yes, that's right," he replied.

He left the way nightjars do and he went on to his own settlement.

There he remained.

At dusk,

"I know who our enemy is now, I have it, it's Alamigi," he said.

"We should go see her."

"Let's go."

At dusk, in the darkness they called,

so, "Kuakukuaku!"

They became still.

"Oh, go away, go away right now.

Oh you stinging anteaters, Ugly Beak!" she told them.

They listened to her.

"Let's wait, let's wait," he said.

Then while they stayed there

[breathily, as if blowing a spell]

"*Fu fu* go to sleep, *fu* go to sleep," so he told them that, Nightjar spoke.

He placed a spell on them.

He placed a spell on them.

"*Fu fu fu*," so that was what he declared.

Then they sle—ept

and they were dead.
They didn't really die,
   I mean they slept, just slept.
     They didn't wake up.
All her relatives, her people slept,
   because he had blown a spell over them.
     "Nightjar-our-sleep" is a sleep spell.
"Now let's go there."
   Tiki they came into the house, *tiki*.
     She was there.
"That's her!" "Come on!"
They untied her hammock *kidik*, *kidik*
   the other side *tidik tidik*.
The others were all asleep while they carried her away,
   but she didn't wake up,
     because they were placing a spell on her.
Tititititi a long way,
   into the middle of a lake,
   into the middle of one like this one here, a big one.
There they tied up her hammock,
   and the other side was tied up.
   She still slept,
    she slept,
     she slept.
      Then it ended.

When it was daylight the sun was here,
   perhaps a little lower,
tuh, he threw some water over her,
   Nightjar did.
   Buh he threw some over her.
"Na na na," he mocked her.
   She woke up.
"Hey! How did I ever get *here*?" she said.
   The Nightjars went away,
    they fluttered off in their usual way.
   "Too bad about you, you always want to heckle the Nightjars,"
   they told her.
While she slept,
   lying there in her hammock,
   "Oi oi oi," how she wept!
    They had brought her to a very deep place in the lake.
By dawn she stopped.
   "All right." She got down from her hammock *kukuku . . . tum*!
    into the water.
   It came up to her thighs,

it wasn't deep,
>no.

Far away in the wilderness, far away,
>"Ō a ō, ō a ō,"
>Akā the Banded Tinamous.
>>"Ō a ō, ō a ō," it declared.

"Well!" she said,
>"There must be someone over there,
>>someone.

>I'll go to them,
>>I'll go.

>I'll go to that place way over there."

She got down from her hammock *tï tï tï*
>into the water,
>>and she went on *tï tï tï*.
>>>The water became shallower.

Tik she came, she was on land.
>"That's all of *that*," she said.
>"I'm still all right," she said.

"Ō a ō," but it wasn't very far away in the wilderness.

"I'll go on now,"
>and she went on *ti ti ti tiki*,
>>Banded Tinamous was there lying down,
>>>just ahead of her.

>She had made a small fire.

"Well," she went, "I'll go on to her,"
>and she came toward her, as she lay in her
>hammock.

"My!" Banded Tinamous said to her,
>"What made you come here, who are you?"
>>"I'm me."

"I see, you must be Alamigi, Alamigi.
>Isn't it true the Nightjars brought you into the water?"

"Yes, that's right."
>The other knew all about her.
>"Yes, that's right, that's me."
>>"I see. You're the person who likes to heckle the
>>Nightjars.

Don't you heckle the Nightjars the way you like to.
Don't say 'Ugly Beak, you weed-eater,' don't say that.
>The Nightjars aren't nice at all, they aren't nice at all."

"Very well. Oi, oi, oi," she wept as she stood beside
Banded Tinamous, who continued to lie there.
>She had a tiny hammock.

Then the woman began to shiver *tï tï tï*,
>she was shivering.

"All right." She was damp all over.

"Granny," she said, "Grandmother," she said,

"Granny."

"What?"

"I want to lie down with you, to lie down with you."

"I can't do that, no.

Now see how tiny my hammock cords are."

Her hammock cords were really snakes.

On one side was *fü* the two-headed snake,

and on the other was *fïnafïtse* the little green snake.

Snakes were her hammock cords.

"If we were to lie down together

tik . . . bom!

we would both fall down."

"Never mind, I want to lie down with you."

"You'd better watch out for our hammock cords."

As the woman began to lie down,

tik bom!

the hammock collapsed.

Tik tsik Banded Tinamous rubbed out her fire

tik tik

Buuuh she flew away as the banded tinamous do,

she flew away.

Alamigi remained there.

"Why did I do such a thing?"

Poor thing, she was left by herself at the camp of

Banded Tinamous.

The fire hadn't gone out completely.

She was standing there.

Poor thing, she stayed there.

"It's still very far," she told herself.

Then "Ho ho ho,"

Ogoñi the Tiger Heron.

"Hey!" she said.

"There must be a person over there,

a person.

I'll go on."

She went farther on as she had done before

tsai tsai tsai through the dry leaves into the wilderness.

She was no longer in the water,

but in the forest.

Tsa tsa tsa.

"Ho ho ho,"

now the other called out from a tree,

it was a large one like an eagle.

Finally the woman reached it and from high in the tree it saw her.

It knew all about her.

"You must be Alamigi."

"Yes," she said, "I am she."

"The Nightjars stole you, didn't they."

"Yes, that's right."

The other knew all about what had happened to her.

"Don't heckle the Nightjars the way you've been doing," it said to her.

"Don't say 'Ugly Beak,' nor 'You eat stinging ants,' don't.

The Nightjars aren't nice at all."

"Very well.

Say," she continued, "You could guide me back, couldn't you?"

"Where is your settlement, your house?"

"It's far from here," she answered. "Far away."

"I see," Tiger Heron went.

"You could guide me back, couldn't you?"

"All right," it said.

"All right, but wait here for now."

"Very well."

Pupupu Tiger Heron flew away,

it flew *pupupu* far away,

and it stayed there.

"Ho ho ho," it called out.

Then *tse tse tse tse tse*

she went farther on,

she went farther on until she came to where it perched.

"You're here aren't you?"

"Here I am."

"All right, stay here for now."

Then *pupupu* once again it began to go on,

and it flew far away.

"Ho ho ho," it called out.

So she began to go on *tse tse tse tse tse*

she went farther on until she came to where it perched.

"Alamigi."

"What?"

"You're here, aren't you?"

"I'm here."

"Stay here for now."

It was the last time.

"Next you'll come very far."

"All right."

And so, *pupupu* it went very far away as it had before.

"Ho ho ho," very faintly.

She went on *tse tse tse*.

When the sun was here,
>   *Tse tse tse, tiki.*
>>   There was Tiger Heron.
"Alamigi," it said to her.
>   "What?"
"You're here, aren't you?"
>   "Indeed I am, I'm right here."
"All right.
>   Go now, go now.
You'll go just a short way *ti ti ti* to the trail.
Don't heckle the Nightjars, you will no longer heckle the Nightjars,
no.
>   The Nightjars aren't nice at all," it said to her.
"I'm going right now, I'll go now,"
>   and she went on again as before.
She was coming back,
>   Alamigi was coming back *ti ti* through the wilderness *tsa tsa*
>   *tsaaaah*
>   and she came to the trail.
"How far it was!" she said.
So she came back *tititi*
>   *tiki* she came into the house.
"It's Alamigi!" everyone said,
>   "Alamigi!"
>>   As she wept, "Oĩ oĩ oĩ."
"What could have happened to her?"
>   "Who knows."
"The Nightjars stole me, it was the Nightjars.
Don't you all heckle the Nightjars, don't.
>   The Nightjars aren't nice at all,
>>   they're not nice at all," she told them.
That's all.

The underlying theme in this story (represented in Table 9) is the communicational contrast between Alamigi and the Birds. This contrast is developed in various ways, most notably through the speech acts that constitute the major

Table 9.
Contrasts of Character in the Story of Alamigi

Alamigi	physically indexical	verbally illusory
Birds	physically illusory	verbally indexical

action of the story. Initially, the characters are delineated and contrasted by their seeming inability to interpret each other's utterances correctly. Alamigi heckles the nightjars because she misunderstands their calls to be deliberately annoying, whereas they merely indicate the presence of the birds outside her house. Later, she cannot understand that Banded Tinamous is telling her the truth when warning her about the hammock cords. Alamigi's problem is that she cannot see how speech can express directly or indicate literally a truthful matter. Being human, she too often interprets speech as illusory. Similarly, Nightjar can learn by indexical specification or enumeration, as when he visually associates the empty hammocks to which he points with their owner's names (listed by the woman left alone in the house). He has trouble remembering Alamigi's name, however, because he, being the producer of indexical calls, cannot easily envisage something that is not present before him; as a bird, he has trouble imagining. The questions asked by Alamigi and Nightjar also develop this opposition. Nightjar's questions to the mother of the newborn alone in the house are requests for information of an indexical nature: he requests indentification of a person. Alamigi's question addressed to Tiger Heron is very different, for this speech act represents her ability to formulate a future goal for herself. Nightjar's initial problem—an inability to imagine (or, stated more positively, that he persistently interprets speech by a thoroughly literal understanding of its use)—is the means by which he solves the problem of identifying his enemy. Alamigi's difficulty is with understanding speech as truthful, but this ultimately helps her to invent a way to reach home. This contrast between the essentially illusory interpretation and use of speech by Alamigi and the indexical understanding of the three Birds she encounters is paralleled by the opposition between the visual appearance of all these characters.

Nightjars (*Caprimulgidae*), tiger herons (*Tigrisona*), and banded tinamous (*Tinamidae*) are among the most physically deceptive birds in the Kalapalo environment; their spotted and streaked appearance easily camouflages them from the sight of predators. Furthermore, these birds are very common crepuscular species whose ventrilocal calls are heard at the most mysterious times of day (at dusk and before dawn). The complex physical deceptiveness of the bird characters from a human point of view (implied by their species names, which immediately call to mind their familiar characteristics and habits) contrasts with the straightforward physical indexicality of Alamigi (from the birds' point of view), for they always immediately recognize and name her on sight. When Nightjar appears as a man (in order to communicate directly with a human woman) he cannot be identified until he names himself, thereby giving his illusionary (that is, linguistic) identity. Finally, just as Nightjar achieves success by learning to think abstractly about or to remember Alamigi, there is a correspondence in the end when Alamigi ultimately understands the truth of the Birds' lesson: "The Nightjars aren't nice at all." We know she has learned her lesson, for upon returning home she pedantically repeats this formula to her friends.

Turtle Monster

Another story also plays with sound as symbol but in a quite different manner. The story of Turtle Monster, the enemy of the Birds, concerns how sound can serve as an identifier. When Turtle Monster is finally killed by a human being dressed as a powerful eagle, the flesh is consumed by the victorious (and verbal) mob, which thenceforth can only "call." These "calls," however, are like musical songs, since they are measured and repetitious.

Turtle Monster
Told by Muluku at Aifa, March 25, 1979

Listen. I'm telling you a story.
   Eugukafagu and Ugakifagu his father went to kill Turtle Monster.
      They went to Tolofïtï the birds' settlement to kill Turtle
      Monster.
     "All right, Older Brothers,
      think about how to do this for us," the Birds said.   5
   Their language before at the Beginning,
      the Birds' language was our language.
   They lived on the Other Side of the Sky.

The Birds dressed him in their skins,
      the Birds dressed Ugakifagu.   10
     He was their brother.
  All their skins,
     their feathers,
      and their claws were placed on him,
       so that he became just like a harpy eagle.   15
   Turtle Monster was a real monster,
    enormous.
  The Birds came to Ugakifagu,
     not knowing how to kill him themselves.
   "All right, go ahead.   20
   Try it right now."

So he left,
  and he came close to where the other was,
    at a very distant place.
   The other came,   25
    Turtle Monster came.
   He was very large,
    Turtle Monster was very large.
      Bah! Turtle Monster had a great many birds' tail

feathers strung behind him on a cord of burity,
          by means of which he had flipped over before.   30
He arrived that way,
          he came,
               at dawn he came.
     He began to sing,
          Turtle Monster sang: 35

[*Sings*]

          "Kusetaŋe the Big Turtle they are unlike us, the disguised ones.
     Tagu tagu tagu,"
          he went.
               Turtle Monster was speaking.
                    He was breaking his possessions as he came.   40

[*Sings*]

          "Is there anyone like me?
          They are unlike us, the disguised ones.
          Tagu, tagu."
     Ugakifagu waited for him there,
          perched on top of the house,   45
     When Kusetaŋe came outside very close to where he was,
          he came outside.
          "You must wait to club him," the Birds said,
               "You must wait."
     As Turtle Monster began to come outside just then,   50
          Ugakifagu came to kill him and he carried him into the sky,
               circling above the others.
                    "Hoh hoh!"
     Now, the Birds shouted, "Don't circle above the lake, not above
     the lake!"
He circled,   55
     he circled,
          he circled.
     "Not above the lake!"
          "Hoh hoh!" the Birds were cheering.
Turtle Monster flipped over and Ugakifagu's wing feathers folded up,   60
     so he died.
Then the monsters in the lake ate him,
     Ugakifagu's body was eaten,
          when he died.
The others left,   65
     the Birds left.
          "So he will remain,
               so he will remain."

Then Agipiso—Ugakifagu's brother—
          came to them.   70

Agipiso had gone to see his son,
>one who was still like this,
>>very small. [*holds up his hand to show height of a
>>small child*]
>Eugukafagu was here,
>>he was his son.   75
"Let's go there right now to see him.
>Let's go there to see our brother's offspring."
>Agipiso came there.
>>He himself was widowed from his wife,
>>>he was widowed.   80
He met him,
>he met his son.
"Why are you here this way?"
"Well, Son," he told him,
>>"I've come to present you with food," Agipiso said.   85
>>"I've come to present you with food."
"Very well."
"Father just died,
>he died.
>>It was Turtle Monster who flipped him over."   90
>>"Yes, he did," the other told him.
"You must come and put this red paint on," Agipiso said.
>"Here is some red paint."
>"All right," the other answered.
"Mother must smear it on you again and again."   95
>"All right," and he gave it to the boy.
>>"Mother, Father has just given this to me."
>>"All right."
Then he ate the fish.
>"You must take this, so you can be painted with it," Agipiso
>said.   100
>>"By Mother," he told him.
>>"Very well."

Then the next day and the next day his mother painted him.
When the red paint was all used up he had become fully grown.
>Eugukafagu had become an adult.   105
Then his father came to get him,
>Agipiso came.
"Well, my dear child," he said.
>"Avenge your father."
>>"All right."   110
"Go to your relatives."
Next he came to where *moh*, all the Birds were.
>"Go ahead, disguise yourself,"

so he disguised himself.
He put on wing feathers.   115
And all the parts of a bird,
he put on claws.
When he had finished,
"You must be sure to watch him carefully,
you won't try to kill him right away, no.   120
Beware of being like your father.
Tomorrow it will happen."
At dawn
as had happened before the great monster,
Kusetaŋe the Great.   125
That is his name, Kusetaŋe.
He sang once again,
Turtle Monster sang.
He was breaking his possessions as he sang.
"He's coming out right now!" the Birds said.   130
As he came out Eugukafagu was perched there on top of a dead
tree.
Then as Turtle Monster approached he came to him and once again as
before
bitsuk, he picked Turtle Monster up and carried him,
he carried him up into the sky.
"Huu huu!" the Birds cheered.   135
"Now he's done for!" they told one another.
"He's no longer as great as he was,
He's no longer as great as he was!" the Birds said.
Eugukafagu came toward the center of the sky.
"Hoh hoh!" the Birds were cheering,   140
the Birds.
Toward the center of the sky he touched the sky.
While he was above the plaza,
he broke Turtle Monster's body.
He broke his body, *tik*!   145
"Hoh hoh," the Birds cheered,
the Birds.
"Hoh hoh! Oh, now he'll really die!
Just as we thought he would, our son has avenged his father.
Yes, he has!"   150
"All right, come here!"

They came back,
and they arrived home.
"Go ahead, go now.
Some messengers must go," the Birds then said.   155

So the messengers left.
"Go ahead, go get the others."
"This person is a messenger and this person is a messenger."
"All right, go now."
It was tiny Piñu Hummingbird.   160
The messengers left.
When they still hadn't returned,
"All right let's go get it.
They probably won't come,
no."   165
"Very well," the others replied.
"All right now,"
pu pu pu they flew to the body,
the Birds did.
They all pecked at Turtle Monster's body,   170
all the Birds did.
That was what was to be used for their calls.
They were trying out what they were making,
the Birds were doing that.
Following that the Birds called.   175
All their calls.
The Birds' speech was like our own when they began to do that.
But that no longer continued.
As it is now the Birds call.
A long time ago we were like that,   180
it was still at the Beginning.
They were making it so.

"Say, Friend," someone said.
A Bird spoke.
"Listen to my musical instrument,"   185
Kutsu the Ornate Hawk-Eagle spoke.
"*Kwi, kwi*," he told him.
"All right.
Now you listen to my musical instrument."
Kuña the Smooth-Billed Ani spoke.   190
That person was his friend.
"*Kuju Kuju*," he told him,
"Say, Friend, I want that for myself."
"No, this is just my song."
"No, I want it for myself," Ornate Hawk-Eagle said,   195
"I want it for myself."
"All right."
Then Ornate Hawk-Eagle went, "*Kuju kuju*.
Say, this suits me."

"All right," the other said, "Keep it." 200
Smooth-Billed Ani:
"*Kwi kwi* this suits me.
When you're unlucky in hunting,
  you must sing my way.
Mortals will then say, 205
  'That person over there is unlucky.'"
    "All right," Ornate Hawk-Eagle answered.
Then again, Kusauka the Yellow-ridged Toucan.
"*Oha oha*," he went,
  Toucan went. 210
"Listen to my musical instrument, Friend."
  Then, "*Oha oha*," he went.
Akā the Banded Tinamous was his friend.
"Listen to my musical instrument, Friend."
  "I'll do just like you." 215
So, "*Kiokaka kiokaka*," he went.
"Now, since you don't play it well, I want it for myself."
"Beware lest mortals will say about you,
  'That person over there doesn't live in high places.'
    Go ahead, take it," 220
      and he gave it to Toucan.
Then again, Ka'akiso the Horned Screamer,
  with Tsitshaha the Giant Kiskadee,
Then again all the Birds did the same.
  Because of that all the birds' calls are as they are now. 225

Their messengers were arriving just then,
  the Hummingbirds were arriving.
    They arrived.
The others were still there pecking hard away.
  The Hummingbirds found only tiny bits of Turtle
  Monster's flesh. 230
Then Turkey Vulture arrived.
  "There isn't anything left at all."
    "There isn't any left."
"So, let it be."
  Since then turkey vulture doesn't speak, 235
    it doesn't even call.
      "Uh uh uh," is how it calls.

All the birds' calls came from Turtle Monster's flesh.
  They no longer spoke,
    they all sang. 240
      That's how they have all been since then, long ago.

Following that Eugukafagu became the Birds' leader,
     at the Other Side of the Sky.
         The Other Side.
He himself,   245
     Eugukafagu,
         whose father was Ugakifagu.
He who had died when Turtle Monster killed him,
     who had then been eaten by monsters.
         The other one was his son, Eugukafagu.   250
         He became the leader of the Birds.

Notes to Turtle Monster

29–30   An ornament of different kinds of birds' feathers with magical properties enabled the wearer to fly in any direction. This ornament also appears on the *atugua* (Whirlwind) costume.

36   The victims were not really powerful beings.

40   Breaking of one's possessions is usually done in mourning, hence a sign of Turtle Monster's wanton destructiveness.

92   *Bixa orellana*, known as *urucu* in Brazil.

157–59   The leaders are selecting and directing their messengers.

160   *Lophornis gouldii*. This marvelous creature is feathered as if it had been decorated with earrings and a white cotton sash, suggesting its role as a ceremonial messenger.

186   *Spizaetus ornatur*.

190   *Crotophaga ani*.

208   *Ramphastos culminatus*.

213   *Crypturellus undullatus*.

222   *Anhima cornuta*.

223   *Ptangus sulphuratus*.

231   *Cathartes aura*. This bird has a very faint call and is said to fly higher than any other bird. The messengers were late because Vulture lived so far away.

Loss of speech is associated with Turtle Monster's carrion because Turtle Monster embodies literalness. As his song asserts, he is "undisguised," as if the birds are actually lesser humans with the ability to appear as birds but without the true capacity of flight. But Turtle Monster flies with an object made from a great variety of bird feathers. This ornament allowed Kusetaŋe to fly in any imaginable manner, even to flip himself over in flight so as to rid himself of an enemy (lines 29–30).

In this story, the most salient feature of the birds—their speech—is lost when they eat the flesh of this literal monster, and they become birds that can only emit calls. But some of these calls are songs, and the voices of their owners are described as "musical instruments." Having been exchanged among friends, these songs carry specific residual meanings that refer to the original owners' manner of behaving because, being "bird songs," they are strictly indexical. Also, because they have musical qualities that other bird calls do not, these songs have performative functions; the particular calls—or songs—represented are unusual and rarely heard. When the species in question emit them, they are held to create certain events—usually unfortunate—in the future and therefore are interpreted by human beings in a manner that extends their literal meanings. There is no contradiction in thinking of these songs as both indexical and iconic at the same time, for it is in terms of the bird's own actions or behavior that they are interpreted literally, but in terms of what will happen in the future to a human being that they are interpreted iconically.

Chapter 5

The Government of Grief

The sound symbols Kalapalo use in their narrative art are also the substance of a series of events that give ritual meaning to a mourner's apprehension of grief. Sound in these activities serves as a code for interpreting states of mind, for conveying ideas about feeling, personal identity, and the emotions that accompany changes in one's personal relations. As cultural forms, the meanings in mourning rituals are shaped by the performance of sound. Expletives, speech, and song—and the very processes through which one kind of utterance is transformed into another—convey to the listeners distinct and concrete ideas about the participants' thoughts and feelings.

Burial and mourning among the Kalapalo are part of an extended series of events (taking a year or more to accomplish) that publicly shows survivors how they must reorganize their social obligations, and how mourners must reorient themselves while undergoing a psychodynamic process that involves changes in their feelings about the recently dead. Deliberate evocation of a remembered image of the deceased is engendered while the Kalapalo create a series of materially and temporally discrete dramatic settings, in which mourners are expected to mourn their dead in particular ways. Undergoing periodic but always necessarily different experiences of remembering the recently dead seems to help the mourners to transform their spontaneous outbursts of grief and the sensation of numbing shock into a gradual awareness that the finality of death is reconcilable with remembering, making it possible for them to return fully into the society of the living while actively preserving that memory. There is also what might be called a Kalapalo mythology of death; images from these stories are from time to time called to mind or even replicated in ritual performances that serve as step-by-step models for subsequent ritual action.

This ritual process coalesces the culturally meaningful, the network of social obligations that envelops people living in a particular place, and the psychodynamic, which is the evolution of feelings of grief. The performance of sound symbols in these rituals molds all three experienced meanings into a symbolically expressed unity by requiring mourners to express specific ideas of feeling concerning their grief and memory. And these symbols are instrumental in orienting survivors toward the specific social meanings given to the contexts in which the sounds of their feelings demand to be heard.

Kalapalo attitudes toward death and the Dead form the substance of the story of Ugafïtaŋa, a man whose pact with his beloved friend accorded him the great privilege of visiting the Dead, perforce with unfortunate consequences that he could not have predicted. In this story (told to me by the old leader Kambe), we learn about life after death: the astonishing rituals in which the Dead and the Birds club each other in a replication of the act of revenge by mourning survivors among the living. But most poignant are Kambe's descriptions of the causes of death and evocations of the anger, depression, and fear that are felt by survivors in their grief over the loss of a cherished relative or friend.

Ugafïtaŋa, The Man Who Visited the Dead
Told by Kambe at Aifa, February 21, 1979

They went to get wood,
        they used to both go there.
    Almost always these friends would go there together.
        They were inseparable.
    They would also go together to bathe,   5
        and they would go together to the plaza.
"Friend," one said to the other.
    "If I happen to die,
        if I happen to see a monstrous apparition, Friend," he
        told the other man,
            "In death I will surely return to get you,   10
               in death."
"Very well, I will return to you the same way in death.
    I will return to get you,
        to get you."
"Very well, I too will return to get you."   15
    "Very well."
So he remained there.
    Soon after he became feverish because he had been bewitched.
Then after he slept,
    he had slept three nights,   20
        he died, that having been done to him.
        His friend wept over him.
Then he was buried.
    He was taken from his house to the plaza.
        Then the other went into his house and remained there.   25
Then his friend spoke to him in a dream.
"Friend, when the moon is fully eclipsed I will come to get you,
    I will get you so we can kill Birds together,
        we can kill Birds.
            We'll do that to the sky-dwellers."   30
            "All right."

Then he remained there in his house.
    He never walked around outside,
        never.
        Everyone was released from mourning,   35
        they were all bathed,
        but he still didn't walk around,
           not yet.
    Then finally once again he walked outside,
        he began to go get firewood just as they had always done.   40

The new moon had already risen after the sky had opened,
    and finally it was eclipsed,
        the moon was killed,
          killed.
        "Kuu kuu kuu," they all called out as it was killed.   45
        "I'll see if my friend has come to get me,
          I'll see.
            He should be where we used to go together."
    Then he went to get wood.
        He went to get wood at dusk.   50
          On that occasion he went to get wood.
    There he began to weep.
        The splinters of his firewood reminded him of his friend.
    Then he split his wood *tsiuk tsiuk tsiuk* and tied it up.
        Just as he was about to come back,   55
          his friend came,
            the dead man came to get him.
    The dead man threw a piece of wood at him *tuk!*
        and as he glanced behind him,
          there he was.   60
    "Friend, I have really come to get you,
          I have really come to get you."
          "Yes, you have."
    "Now I have come to get you so we can slaughter the Birds."
    "All right, let's go as you say."   65
    "I'm coming back with you."
        The dead man came back with his friend.

It was dusk,
        the sun was here.
  Pom, he threw down the wood.   70
    He arrived.
        They were both there.
    "Friend, we must steal some *tuafi* now."
        They rolled up a lot of *tuafi*,
          they rolled up *tuafi*.   75

They took them along to the sky to hold their
feathers,
to hold their Bird feathers.
"How's this, Friend?"
The man had just a few.
"Yes, that's all right but take a few more."   80
The other took some old manioc processing mats as well,
the kind we use for squeezing manioc.
Finally he came back to the dead man.
"That's fine. Let's go."
"Let's go, Friend."   85
"Tomorrow the guests will be leaving.
Tomorrow the Dead will be going as guests,
tomorrow."
"All right."
They walked away *ti ti ti ti*.   90

The sun was here,
at dusk.
They were coming to the Other Side of the Sky,
no living people were doing that,
only the Dead were going as guests.   95
The Dead were going to kill the Birds.
"Let's go, Friend."
They had already left and were going on,
following the Dead.
They came to a creek,   100
a shallow one,
where the others were.
Tuk tuk tuk,
they began to cut clubs,
they began to cut *ugifaŋagï* wood.   105
These were for their clubbing of the Birds *tuk*,
for their clubbing.
"From here we'll be leaving, Friend,
we'll be going on."
"All right."   110
They went on right then from where they had stopped,
from where they had stopped.
They went on.
"Let's go, let's go!"
"All right."   115
[*The story was interrupted for an hour.*]

(I'll go back a little.)
The Dead had already cut their clubs.

"Let's cut our clubs."
    "All right."
Tik, they cut some.   120
    His friend cut some,
        the dead man cut some.
            Long ones, look.
Long ones were being cut,
        the person cut them,   125
        still from that same place.
            Long ones.
                The dead man had also cut some long ones.
"Let's go, Friend," and they went on.
    They went following the others.   130

At sunset they came to a place just outside the settlement,
        outside the Birds' settlement.
The Birds were all cheering,
        the Birds were like this,
            human.   135
They were disguised as Birds,
    all kinds of Birds,
        all kinds.
Buh! *ah haa*! so many guests arrived,
    so many Dead arrived!   140
        Everyone had gone on together.
"Um um um," the Dead smelled him.
    They smelled his odor.
    They wanted to paint him with red paint.
"Friend, I want to paint you right away with red paint.   145
    That way you will smell like a dead person."
        "All right."
            "Um um um, we're doing this to you because you
            smell like one of the living," the Dead said.
Over to one side were the guests' campgrounds,
    there were two of them.   150
For they themselves and for others whose leader was Itsaŋitsegï.
    The mother of Taugi and Aulukuma was leading those other
    people.
        The two co-wives were their leaders,
        the seated ones.
            yes.   155
Ugakifagu was the Birds' leader,
    Ugakifagu.
    He eats us,
        he's a very tall person.
            His name is Ugakifagu.   160

"Come on now," the Dead said.
They stayed there and soon they all fell asleep.
   they all slept.
"Friend," the dead man said.
   "Stay here and we'll sleep together.   165
      Let's lie down together."
         "All right."
            The other had left without his hammock,
               without his hammock.
                  "All right."   170
"You mustn't be afraid of me."
   "All right," as they fell asleep.
Heat from a *kune* was warming the place,
      heat from a *kune*.
         teh it comforted the Dead.   175
            They were all asleep,
               warmed by the heat from the *kune*.
"Friend," the man said,
   "I feel cold.
      Let's build up the fire."   180
"We can't," he said.
   "This isn't fire.
      that's still a person."
"That can't be so."
The other came to look at it.   185
He touched it slightly and it stood up.
   It turned into a person.
      He was the *kune*.
         It was nice and warm, *teh*.
So then they fell asleep right away.   190
   The man slept on one side of the hammock *bok*,
      opposite his dead friend.
         His friend was on the other side *bok*,
            opposite him.
The friend woke up,   195
   the living person woke up when he felt a snake there,
      a snake was in the hammock.
Boh! "Friend! A snake!"
The other woke up.
   "Friend, that's me, that's me," the dead man told him.   200
When the sun was rising,
   "Come on," they said.
The messengers came to get them.
   The messengers had come.
"Have our children begin to come forward now, have our children
come forward."   205

"Very well. Come along Children," Itsaŋitsegï said.
　　Itsaŋitsegï was the leader of the Dead.
　　　　Segufenu was her co-wife.
　　She had a single breast,
　　　　only one.　　　　　　　　　　　　　　　　　　　　　210
　　Taugi made it that way so we would recognize her.
　　　　Tsiuk! he had cut it off.
　　　　　　Teh, she was beautiful.
　　　　　　　　She was Segufenu,
　　　　　　　　　　she was Isaŋitsegï's companion.　　　215
　　　　　　　　She is not the same as Tanumakalu,
　　　　　　　　　　but still another person.
There she was.
　　　　"Go ahead," she said.　　　　　　　　　　　　　220
　　They danced up to the Birds,
　　　　　　all of them came together just then.
　　　　　　　　When they came together,
　　　　　　　　　　the Birds appeared as people.
"All right come on everyone,"　　　　　　　　　　　　225
　　the Birds kept coming as people,
　　　　they came from where they had stood,
　　　　　　then as they danced away they became birds again.
　　"Children, they are different from us,
　　　　those who do that are different from us.　　　　230
　　　　　　All right, go on, Children."
The Dead went first.
　　The first ones to have died, the most ancient ones were the
　　killers.
　　They had their clubs with them.
　　　　their clubs.　　　　　　　　　　　　　　　　　235
　　Their clubs *bah haa!* there were so many!
　　　　The Birds had them, too.
　　　　　　Tspiñokuegï the Sparrows, the red ones.
　　　　　　　　Many Kïŋua Oropendolas, many Kuña Anis,
　　　　　　　　　　all kinds of Birds.　　　　　　　　240
　　　　　　　　　　　　"Kaa, kaa kaa kaa kaa kaa kaaa!" they
　　　　　　　　　　　　went,
　　　　　　　　　　　　　　the Dead said.
Finally they went on in a line.
　　Tok tok! They finished approaching and began killing each other
　　tok!
　　To one side seated on his leader's stool was Ugakifagu.　　245
　　　　The Birds' leader was seated on his leader's stool.
　　The dead people were brought and placed before him.
　　　　He blew over them in order to revive them with his spell,
　　　　　　and they returned.

Once again as before the Birds were clubbing them.   250
    They kept returning.
Itsaŋitsegï sat nearby so that she too could use spells.
    When they went to her she simply wiped off their blood and
    they went on.
When they were finished,
    the mature ones were next.   255
"We must go now, Friend."
    "All right."
They all came in a line again,
    this time the Dead who were mature people.
"Kaa kaa kaa kaa kaa kaa," they all went,   260
    the Dead said.
        They shouted their war cry,
            for dueling with the Birds.
They approached the others still doing that.
    Tok tok tok tok they kept clubbing them, *bam!*   265
        Many of them died but even though they were clubbed
        they came alive again.
        Tok tok tok tok.

When the sun was here at its height,
    the friend was killed by a Bird.
        The friend was killed,   270
        the dead man was killed.
            The one who was dead was killed by a Bird who
            carried him in his claws to Ugakifagu.
Then the dead man returned because of what had just been done to
him.
    "Come on, Friend,"
        he himself was the only one left,   275
            the person still hadn't done it.
    His name is Ugafïtaŋa,
        Ugafïtaŋa.
    Tok tok tok tok!
        A Bird died and never got up,   280
            because it was a man who had clubbed him.
            Others as well were scattered all over.
Over to the side were some Kuaku, Amazon parrots who had
been pets of human beings.
    They had become dead beings.
They looked at him.   285
When they looked at him,
    they saw him,
        they saw he was a human being.
"He's alive,

that man who's killing us."   290
    "All right," the Birds answered.
        Buuh! They suddenly flew off.
The dead man came to his friend.
    There was blood on his forehead where a Bird had clubbed him.
        Wiping the blood from his face,   295
            the dead man came back.
The Dead wanted the feathers,
    the tail feathers of the Birds whom Ugafïtaŋa had clubbed.
        They had died once and for all.
Ugafïtaŋa pulled out the tail feathers and filled up one *tuafi*,   300
    and filled up another *tuafi* after that.
        Another *tuafi* was filled up,
            another *tuafi* was filled up.
                Bah ha haa! so many!
His friend also had some.   305
    Every one of the Dead had some,
        they all had some.
When they were done they put their *tuafi* away inside a house,
    the guests put them away.
        Then they all remained there.   310

Then when the sun was here,
    "Friend," the dead man said,
        "Let's go walk over to the other houses,
            let's go walk over now to the other houses."
                "All right."   315
They left.
    "'Fiŋgegi' you have to say."
        He had one silo of manioc starch
            and three baskets of dried balls of manioc mash.
The man looked about him.   320
        Their visit ended.
            "Let's go," the dead man said.
They left and went to another house. *Tikii*.
        Into Tō the Ema's house.
    "Look that's Ema, Friend."   325
        Tikii. "Continue to stay here."
        "Very well."
            He had only one silo of manioc starch,
             one that was very narrow.
They came out again and went to another house.   330
    Tikii into Kofoŋo the Duck's house,
        Duck,
            the one that rises up in the sky.
    "That's the real Duck, Friend," the dead man told him.

"I see." 335

"Look."

"Continue to stay here."

"Very well."

He looked about him.

Duck had a large silo of manioc starch, 340

and also some baskets of dried manioc mash.

"Let's go now," the dead man said.

Tikii they came to another house.

"Look, Friend," he said,

"This is really Ndïtï the Motmot." 345

"I see."

"Stay here."

"Very well."

He had a manioc silo like this one here. [*Indicates one
of average size in his own house.*]

"Let's go, Friend." 350

Tikii, they came into another house.

Ogomïgï,

a Bird.

He eats us.

Ogomïgï. 355

Tikii.

"Stay here."

"Look, Friend, that's the real Ogomïgï.

He eats us,

he eats us." 360

There were human skulls there,

mm mm mm, a great line of them hanging from the rafters!

There were many eyes.

Small locusts called *fakuasa* were there,

they were his crickets. 365

"Those are his crickets, his crickets."

Those insects eat the chords holding the skulls.

Taku, giruk! one of them fell.

Aiugugo bugs had eaten through the chord.

"Let's go, Friend." 370

To Tute's house,

Tute the Hawk.

He had a large manioc silo.

To one side was his drinking water,

roiling *hum, hum*. 375

His drinking water was in a large gourd vessel over to

one side of the house.

Because Tute is the period of water.

This was what was happening.

Their visit ended.

To Embisa's house. 380

"Stay here."

"Very well."

Teh, his eyes were red as could be!

His eyes were red as could be.

"Let's go to another house." 385

Tikii.

Ogo the Storage Platform.

He was always well fed.

One manioc starch silo of his,

another manioc starch silo of his. 390

His dried manioc roots as well,

bah ha

he was the one who had so much of everything!

His dried manioc roots, what are called *ñaŋo*,

ñaŋo. 395

And his manioc starch was also

abundant.

"Look, Friend," the dead man said,

"I used to call him Storage Platform. 400

He's very well fed,

well fed."

The sun was here,

it was late afternoon.

They had gone around the entire house circle.

"Let's go."

The sun was here, 405

the sun was beginning to set.

They came back,

the Dead returned.

They came back with those two in the rear.

"Look, Friend, look now." 410

Then they all arrived at their own settlement,

at Añafïtï, the Place of Many Dead.

They arrived.

"Come on, Friend," he told him,

"I'll escort you home." 415

"All right," the man replied.

They both came back.

At the very end of the day they arrived once again at the man's own settlement,

here, at the person's place,

at Ugafïtaŋa's settlement.   420
"Go, Friend," the dead man said,
    "Go.
Leave, Friend, and be sure not to look at me."
    "All right," Ugafïtaŋa said.
As he began to return he glanced behind him.   425
    The other was betailed,
        he was going away as a maned wolf,
            he had become a furred animal.
    "Waaa, beware of looking at me.
        I just told you not to look at me!   430
    You will only sleep a few more days!"
        The dead man counted on his hand.
    "Friend, I just told you not to look at me!
        I just told you not to look at me!"
The other came back,   435
    he returned,
        and he fell asleep.

The next day everyone talked about it.
    "Ugafïtaŋa is here once more from having killed Birds.
    Ugafïtaŋa has just arrived home again," the people said.   440
He gave his neighbors the tail feathers which he brought,
    the Birds' feathers.
        There were so many tail feathers.
Ugafïtaŋa took some out *buk*
    but he kept five *tuafi* for himself.   445
He carried the others outside to his leader,
    to his people.
He went outside and he gave them,
    they were given by him to that other person who was the
    one who gave them out.
        Everyone got some.   450
There were still some others who had gone to an oxbow lake,
    some friends were still away at an oxbow lake.
    "I'll set some aside for them,"
    and he put two aside.
There were still three *tuafi*,   455
    he still kept his treasures.
        Teh they were the most beautiful of all!
He still had them,
    long feathers,
Birds' feathers,   460
    tail feathers.
"I'm going to the manioc fields."
    He went away.

There were no people in the house.
Then the others arrived.   465
 Their wives told them what had happened.
  "Your share of feathers is right here."
   "All right."
 There still were some more,
  teh, the most beautiful of all.   470
There were no people in Ugafïtaŋa's house,
 by the time those two came from the oxbow lake,
  the two friends.
 No one,
  because he had gone to the manioc fields,   475
   Ugafïtaŋa had gone to the manioc fields.
 Those two approached and *tikii* they came inside,
  the two friends together.
   "Let's look at our brother's things!"
Then they took down the *tuafi*,   480
 two of them,
  and opened them up.
   Mbisuk bok bok.
    Teh his own things were beautiful,
     the most beautiful of all!   485
"Why didn't our brother bring these out,
 Why didn't he bring these out?" they said to each other.
"That's just how he is.
 Our brother must remain as he is now.
  He will die as he is now.   490
  Let him be this way.
   He will take these with him to cover his face,"
  they said to each other.
Then Ugafïtaŋa arrived.
 By then it was dark.
The friends had gone away to kill him,   495
 to kill him.
He was to sleep—look—
 he would sleep,
  his friend had counted the number of days he was to
  sleep,
   the maned wolf had done that,   500
    his friend did that as he went away.
     "Waaa, there are still these many days,"
      he had said.
After the man slept these many days they began to shoot him,
 on this fifth day.   505
  At night while he was asleep they shot him.
  They both shot him.

Suddenly at dawn "Eh he he!" he was crying out with pain,
    having been shot in the way I described.
So, when the sun was here he died,   510
    that was still happening to him.
      He wasn't cured.
        The others wept.
After that he was buried,
    he went into the ground.   515
The others placed the coverings over his face,
    his feathers,
    the Birds' tail feathers,
      buk buk buk that way.
His shroud was placed over him as they carried him into the
ground.   520
    He had died once and for all.
    He had met his friend,
      yes.

Notes to Ugafïtaŋa

41   "After the sky had opened" means that the rainy season had ended.
73   *Tuafi* are mats made from burity palm leaf ribs, in which feathers are stored.
103   Witches are clubbed to death by avenging survivors.
151–52   Itsaŋitsegï, the "first mother," bore the twin tricksters Taugi and Aulukuma, who created human beings.
156   For Ugakifagu, see Muluku's Turtle Monster story in Chapter 4.
173–75   A *kune* is an instrument of revenge made from the ever-boiling body parts (skin from palms, finger joints, or little toes) of a person whose death is attributed to witch-craft. The heat from the *kune* is thought to result in the witch's death from internal combustion. Here, Kambe suggests that the Dead were both warmed and mentally comforted by one while it was destroying the witch.
208   Segufenu was a sister of Itsaŋitsegï.
311   After a ceremony, guests "walk around" the circle of houses hoping to receive presents. In this stanza, Ugafïtaŋa and his dead friend visit the powerful beings whose images (*futofo*) are the constellations that serve calendrical functions for the Kalapalo. The amount of rain associated with each constellation is suggested by the amount of manioc stored in each of the houses.
317   The dead man begins to tell his friend how to address his hosts by name.
352   Ogomïgï: According to Ulutsi, when the crickets eat through one of the skull cords, it crashes toward earth, where it is seen as a shooting star. For the Kalapalo, this means a leader will shortly die.

As I saw on all-too-many an occasion, after a Kalapalo dies, or even during the final moments of life, relatives gathered around the sick person's hammock succumb to their feelings of despair and anger by crying out their grief to the victim. When the curers declare a person dead, a great commotion arises. Those looking on rush shrieking to embrace the corpse, crying out that death has occurred, wailing to the dead person by means of the kinship terms they used so soon before in addressing their relative in life. Hearing these sounds of grief, nearly everyone else in the community runs to the house, joining in the outcries in sympathy with the survivors, moved by the loss of a member of the settlement community. Many of these people run over to the deceased's closest relatives and sit in turn with them in a close embrace, continuing their wailing. A man occasionally runs to his house for a rifle, firing it at the sky, women smash the household's smaller cooking pots, and the smallest children of the deceased (who are sometimes forgotten in the turmoil) scream and prance back and forth in confusion and fear. The Kalapalo call this time of succumbing fully to grief *ifetunaluko* ("they cry out noisily"). These noisy *itsu* are the first sounds of mourning that are heard. From now on, the dead person's house is no longer used.

After approximately two hours, a burial will be organized by the hereditary leaders. Nonrelatives decorate the corpse, painting it and covering it with ornaments as if it were to participate in a dance. Others prepare the grave in the center of the plaza; when this work is completed, the corpse is carried out, wrapped in the same hammock in which death occurred and lain in the hole. The survivors who are close kin (parents, children, and spouses) are helped down to embrace the corpse for the last time; often they have to be torn away from the body before it can be covered with dirt. Once the grave is filled in, most of the onlookers return home, leaving the closest kin to weep over the site.

At this point, and for the next day or so, the survivors begin to transform their noisy weeping into musical lamentation, singing out in standard rhythms their kinship relationship to the deceased. Now, the kinship term is grammaticalized, modified by the suffix -*nika*, which has an evidential function meaning "it's true, isn't it?"; also, in calling the deceased by a sibling term, the survivors de-emphasize their often antagonistic and competitive relations and emphasize a unity among all relatives on the model of the natal family: mother, father, children, brother, sister. A lament for a deceased wife, for example, consists of the repeated line, *wiŋandsunika* ("Isn't it true, my sister?").

At this time, still longing intensely for the dead person, the Kalapalo mourners frequently modify their singing to call out (more rhythmically than in speech) to the dead, as in *Yatsi umukugunika, wigakafo eteta fetsaŋe!* ("Alas my poor child, how true. You have to go on ahead of me, don't you?"). Turning outcries of grief directed to the deceased into *ifatafisunda* ("mourning through song") is a gradual process, and at this early stage grief and shock may prevent the mourner from fully controlling it.

Toward dusk, food is placed over the grave for the trickster Taugi, called on this occasion the "dead person's parent" because he is the creator of human beings. This invisible visitor comes to weep for people who have died, and he is expected to partake of the food that is left for him. After he eats some of this food the remains are distributed among the assembled gravediggers. The possessions of the deceased are unpacked over the grave by the mourners, then destroyed and burned. In this way the dead owner can travel with the *akūa* of these objects. Next, waving fragrant *kejite* leaves, the gravediggers urge Taugi to leave the world of the living.

By nightfall the weeping relatives have returned to their houses. Sometimes the house of death is abandoned and the survivors taken into households of relatives in the community.

On the following day, the debris left on the grave is removed by a woman who is a hereditary leader (*anetu*) after which the gravediggers distribute food that has been contributed by relatives of the deceased. These events mark the end of the burial phase of the mortuary process and the beginning of the important mourning seclusion phase. This is the occasion for cutting the hair of close survivors of the deceased. A man's hair is cut quite close to the scalp; a woman's long tresses are cut above her shoulders. The haircutter—often a brother or sister of the dead person—receives a gift from a close relative of the person whose hair is cut, and the survivor then enters strict seclusion, lasting as long as a year. Several days after a widow enters seclusion, her dead husband's lovers are publicly marked as possible bearers of his children by having their hair cut, the amount of hair removed being a sign of how close their relationship was to the deceased.

Mourning seclusion is but one of several types of seclusion practiced by the Kalapalo, during which an individual lives in a compartment built within the large, open communal family house. The others are connected with physical maturation, preparation for the role of shaman, childbirth, and when a *kune* charm is made in order to execute a witch. During puberty seclusion the goal of this extended withdrawal from social life is to transform the scrawny body of a child into the seductive corpulence of a young adult and to change the impetuous, selfish feelings of children into the purposeful, considerate, and modest motivations of responsible adult Kalapalo. The external appearance of the body is a sign to them of the inner feelings and thus the moral worth of the individual, and to effect these conjoint ends, they maintain a stringent set of body techniques that emphasize learning how to control the physical urges of the self. When an apprentice shaman is in seclusion, he withdraws from contact with women (whose bodily substances repel the powerful beings with whom he establishes contact) and learns to smoke tobacco and to call his spiritual helpers, in short, prepares himself for the role of curer and diviner. Both puberty and shamanistic seclusion are ascetic experiences during which one learns to control bodily processes and to develop certain qualities of thought. A woman's seclusion occurs for as long as three months after the birth of her child, during which time she eats no fish and strengthens her body and that of her child with medicinal plants.

In mourning seclusion one also attempts to create certain feelings or moods, in this case learning to accept the occurrences of remembering the deceased. Indeed, what we call reclusivity is for the Kalapalo a matter of constructing powers of presence; the more deliberately isolated the self, the greater the need for withdrawal from society and the deeper the mystery and hence the fascination on the part of the rest of the community. Like the field cleared around a hermitage, the wall of the Kalapalo seclusion chamber is both a boundary and a barrier. We are aware that the doings inside are not of our world, and the person within is trying to keep at bounds sinister powers through the discipline of isolation.

In contrast to puberty and shamanistic seclusion, however, the mourner does not attempt to control inner feelings and bodily processes (these being different aspects of the same thing for the Kalapalo) but rather is expected to give in to grief and perforce to assist the journey of the deceased to a final celestial home. Following hard upon burial and the sending off of the deceased to Añafïtï, the dead's sky settlement, the survivors are made to realize the finality of death in a most vivid manner, the experience of traveling suggesting to a Kalapalo the contrast between their earthly existence among the living and their deceased's ultimate existence as a powerful being in a domain known to most only through mythology and the reports of shamans who have traveled there.

The requirements of mourning seclusion are to mourn through song virtually throughout the day, while reclining in a hammock within a small, close chamber, withdrawn from the pleasures and diverting occupations of normal life. The mourner, weeping alone in the seclusion chamber, perhaps surrounded by small children, must remain covered with the substances of mourning—tears, mucous, paint from the victim's body, and soil from the grave.[1] The hair is allowed to grow but remains unkempt. All this creates a special experience for a mourner that involves forced concentration on grief and memory as the progressively stultifying atmosphere of the seclusion chambers causes those feelings to begin to dissipate and the mourner to feel, at the end, a little bored. (There are some songs about people who made plans at this time to remarry.)

Like other seclusion practices of the Kalapalo, mourning seclusion thus involves attempting to create certain feelings or moods, in this case learning to accept times of remembering the deceased. Mourning seclusion forces the survivor to remember the deceased constantly, to think about the circumstances of the beloved's death, and indeed of death itself. Consequently, mourners are expected to dream about the dead person toward the end of this process, considered a positive sign that the deceased has successfully completed the trip to the sky settlement.

Secluded mourning continues for ten days. While the close relatives are in seclusion, the others in the settlement must refrain from decorating themselves and making loud sounds, especially collective musical performance. During this time, relatives from other settlements often arrive to mourn over the grave, and their mourning songs are joined by those of the local relatives. These visitors also cut the hair of the deceased's spouse and express anger at the local community for having allowed witches to go undetected.

During these ten days after a person's death, the dead person's *akūa* is said to be drawn to the living by the noisy outcries and weeping of the survivors, these sounds indicating the miserable hope of the living that the dead person will reappear. At this early stage of grief, the survivors are not fully reconciled to the dreadful finality of death and still think of the one who has gone before them (as they sometimes call the deceased) as temporarily absent. The dead person, in turn, wanders around the outskirts of the settlement, not yet fully convinced that there is a more suitable place to live among the other Dead in their settlement located across the sky in the direction of the rising sun. It is during this transitional period that the interactive self (*akūa*) of the deceased most clearly displays its character as a powerful being. It manifests power of transformation, occasionally taking on visible human form, but it may change unpredictably into an animal, most often an *isogoko* (maned wolf), a creature similar to a coyote that roams around human settlements and whose nocturnal cries are thought to inform people of death in distant places. Experiencing such visions can be dangerous, even fatal, for one usually cannot bear to see a powerful being and continue to live. People are afraid of the dead at this time and also during lunar eclipses, when the Dead are said to return temporarily to the living so as to acquire weapons with which they fight their bird counterparts in the sky. When not fighting the Birds, the Dead manifest yet another quality of powerful beings: they spend their time performing music. Feeding from a never-empty manioc silo, the Dead engage in none of the activities necessary among the living for sustaining and perpetuating life; rather, these functions are conducted through their musical powers. The living think of the dead as undergoing a passage from the physical condition of immobile and consciousnessless death through a transitory phase of wandering when they are dangerous to the living, and finally entering an existence that is fully independent of the living. Then they appear as active and violent participants in ritual battles with their former pets and are called by a special name: Aña, the Dead.

After ten days, a washing and painting ritual (*koŋitsofo*) is held. All the relatives who have been in seclusion participate in this ritual held in the plaza while a surviving spouse undergoes the ritual inside the house. By now the dead person is thought to be fully beyond the range of the living, being held in a kind of puberty seclusion in the settlement of the Dead, once again growing fat and strong.

If the deceased was a member of the hereditary class of leaders the rituals that follow are more complicated than for ordinary people. These ceremonies occur in approximately half of the cases of death in accordance with the relative proportion of leaders to nonleaders in the settlement. But because leaders do not necessarily marry only other leaders, the experiences of mourning that occur at this stage are shared by leaders and nonleaders alike.

The mourning relatives are led outside to the plaza and seated before a line of specialists who are to sing a song (in a local Arawak dialect) variously known as "Bat's Song" (because it was first sung by that personage), "Vulture's Song" (because Vulture was the leader of the settlement in which Bat sang the song), or "The Genitals of Ukwaka Cut Out Long Ago," referring to the events of a story in which Bat is the most important character and sings the song. Here is the story as it was told me by the storyteller Kudyu, a superb joker who clearly relished the trickster role of Bat.

Atsidyi the Bat or Ukwaka's Cut-Out Labia
Told by Kudyu at Aifa, July 7, 1979

Continuing with someone else.

He was going to deceive her.
   As a deception he went on in his usual way shouting,

"They're all there, they're all there!"
That's what he did as he arrived home with his fish catch.   5
   Watsaja had killed some fish.
"You have returned," that was what I'm told was said to him.
   His wife spoke,
      Ñuku spoke.
         "You have returned again."   10
"Yes," he said, "I have returned."
   "Very well," she said.
      His wife saw his fish catch,
         his fish catch.
Then at dusk, when the sun was here,   15
   they went to get firewood.
He had lied to his wife,
   he had lied to his wife in order to do something else.
      He wanted to cut out his mother-in-law's labia,
         Ukwaka's labia.   20
Moh, her labia were like this,
   the things he wanted to cut out were unusually large!
      It's said that because he wanted to have red paint, Bat
      wanted to cut out that part of her.
"Ñuku," he went.
"Yes?" his wife said.   25
"I've been thinking about asking you.
   Has our parent already decided not to go?" he said to her.
"What's that?"
"Today the Gikigifïtï Community have gone to pull out salt
plants.
   I can tell by their footprints how they are going," he said,   30
      Watsaja told her.
         "I see," she said.
         "Listen, Mother," Ñuku said to her mother.
   "Listen, Mother.
      Your grandchildren's father is going to where the   35
      Gikigifïtï Community are pulling out salt plants."
"That sounds nice," the other woman answered.
   "That sounds nice."
"'Has our parent already decided not to go?' he asked me.
   'By doing that you and I will have flavoring for *fesoko* fish,
fesoko.'"
      "Yes, that's true."   40
"'I'll put them on the drying rack for our parent,' that was what
he said."
   He was lying.
      He wanted to cut out her labia!
Now this is what happened.
They prepared some food to take along.   45

"Does he want to go?" Ukwaka said.
"I'm not sure why my young relatives' father wants to take
me.
I'm not sure why my young relatives' father wants to
take me so far from here.
Very well," she said.
"Let's go now, Their Grandmother. 50
Permit me to take you."
"Yes, it will be all right.
We're just going to get our *fesoko* flavoring.
Let's go get our *fesoko* flavoring."
Manioc bread was made, 55
manioc bread was made.

Then at the beginning of the day they left.
"Let's both go, Their Grandmother," he said.
"Let's go as you say."
They untied their hammocks, 60
their hammocks were untied.
Then they went on to that place,
where the footprints were.
These footprints were *his*.
Bat's footprints. 65
Bat had made the footprints.
In order to deceive his mother-in-law,
in order to deceive his mother-in-law.
This is what she said:
"Yes, this seems to have really happened," as they went farther
on, 70
to the salt plants.
There weren't any salt plants.
"Where could they have all gone, Their Grandmother?
Let's sleep right here where we can eat some fishy ones,
some fishy ones."
"All right," she said to him. 75
"He's always the same," she said.
"He's begun to lie to me as usual!"
Tuk he killed some fish,
Watsaja killed some fish.
He killed some fish. 80
When he had finished they ate them.
They ate them.

It became dusk for them.
Then when it had become dusk for them, almost nighttime,
"Kwakwakwa," someone went that way for the first time. 85

Ajafi the potoo called.
"Listen to that, Their Grandmother," he said.
    "Listen to what that one over there said, listen to that," he
said.
"Well, what did it say? What?"
"'Lie down together, lie down together with your affine.'"   90
    That's just what he told her!
        That's just what he told her!
"How can I do that?" I'm told she said.
    "Oh, how can I do that?
        You can't lie down with someone in your own family.   95
      Oh, no!"
            "I'm just saying what that one did," he went,
            Bat said in his usual way.
Now this is what happened next.
    From far away *oɲogu* the tiger heron "Oh oh oh oh."   100
"We must listen to that, Their Grandmother.
    We two won't sleep well at all tonight."
"What did that one tell us?"
"'Quickly, lie down with your mother-in-law,' it told us."
"Oh, how can I do such a thing?   105
    How can I do that?
      How can I do such a thing?"
        "I'm just saying what that one did," he said to her.
Afterward—now it was night—
"Waaa," *isogoko* the maned wolf spoke.   110
"We must listen to that, Their Grandmother!
    That one doesn't leave any of our remains!"
"What did it just tell us?"
    She was beginning to be afraid of the maned wolf's call.
      "What did that one just tell us?"   115
"'Hurry up, lie down with your affine!
    I'll eat up your relative until there won't be anything left' it
just said to me."
"How can I do it?"
    I'm told she said, Ukwaka said.
      She was his mother-in-law,   120
        she of the lengthy labia.
        Ukwaka's her name.

Now this is what happened.
    Very early in the morning all the birds called.
      They all repeated what had been said earlier, when it was night.   125
        How the birds all called!
          The singing ones whom he had sent there.
"Listen, Their Grandmother.

'He never leaves any of their remains.
   Hurry up, lie down with your affine,' they're saying to
   you."
"How can I do such a thing?" I'm told she went,
   "How can I do such a thing? How?"
      She kept repeating that over and over to him.
         Ukwaka spoke to him,
            Ukwaka spoke.

He was lying to her.
   He was deceiving her.
      He wanted to cut out her labia with a very large oyster shell.
         A large oyster shell.
            Teh he a very beautiful thing!
For a long time it was used for doing things like that.
   Tsiuk! it was used when we had to cut something.
With it fish were cut open,
   food was cut open.
Arrow cane was scraped,
   with *aue*.
It was this long.
   Ke he he! it was very sharp!
That's how it was, but no longer.
Now there are knives.
   A very long time ago Dawn People had *aue*, so they could
   do such things.
      That's its very name.
         Aue.

As the day was almost about to begin,
   and the night was almost over it happened again.
      Ikege the jaguar called.
She was beginning to believe him.
   When she heard it she was about to lie down with him.
   When she heard it she was about to lie down with him,
      when the jaguar began to call.
"Say, that wasn't very far from here!" Bat said.
"What did it just do?" she asked.
"'I'm coming right now to eat you.
   Even though you want to lie down with your affine you will
   both die,' it told me."
"How can I do such a thing?" was what she said.
   "All right, for now."
Now she wanted to lie down with him.
Now she was terrified,
Now Ukwaka was terrified.
"How can I do such a thing?

130

135

140

145

150

155

160

165

170

All right."
"Come here to me.
It may just be a lie, Their Grandmother, it may just be a lie.
That one doesn't leave anything of us, that one doesn't
leave anything of us."
"No it doesn't," she said. 175
Pok. She lay down with him.
She lay down with him!
They were lying opposite each other.
"I will do it this way," was what she said.
"Please tell me what is being said." 180
Again, "*Hïm, hïm, hïm,*" that was done very near where they
were.
"Listen: 'I'll probably crunch all your bones when I eat you.'"
That was how he spoke to her.
It was right near them!
For the last time, from far away. 185
"Go to sleep, you must go to sleep.
I'll stay awake, I won't sleep."
"All right, all right."
She fell asleep right away,
she slept. 190
After she had begun to sleep soundly, he got up very slowly,
he got up.
He wanted that other thing,
he wanted to cut it out,
to cut out her labia while she remained lying down. 195
Then while she was that way he opened her legs, *giuk!*
Boh! oh ah! her vulva was huge!
That was what her labia were like.
He wanted them.
He grabbed hold of her vulva and with the large oyster shell 200
he cut them off.
He cut off Ukwaka's labia.
With one large stroke, *giuk!*
She died when he did that to her.
She died once and for all.
Then *uubok!* he put them down. 205
Next *tsikiti*, he carried them and held them above the water.
Tofïkï, the blood was dripping down,
the blood was dripping down.
Bok. A *wagiti* fish touched it with its tail.
Since then it's on the *wagiti*. 210
That's its body paint,
its body paint.
Its body paint,

on *wagiti*.
A *ketïti* fish touched it.   215
A *dyofi* fish touched it.
An *afi* fish touched it.
All the fish that were there.
That's how it came to be on the fish, *tsik tsik*.
It happened that way.   220
Ukwaka's labia.
That's her labia.
Then he brought her back to her own hammock.
Now it was early morning.
He aimed his arrow at an *ulugi* fish.   225
He killed it.
Then he put it inside her throat.
This was what he said:
"Now I'll carry this stuff to the other side."
Popopo.   230
He took it to the Place of Many Birds, to Tolofïtï.
His mother-in-law's body was still back there.

So listen.
Then he went,
taking it with him.   235
This is red paint,
this is red paint,
this is the red paint that he wanted.
"I've got it!" he said.
"Here, I've made it."   240
He made red paint from it.
It had become red paint.
That other thing was red paint.

Then after a short time he came back.
"Let's go," he said.   245
He put her on his back.
"Kaa kaa!" he cried out.
He was mourning.
Watsaja was mourning his aunt although he had just
done that to her.
[*Sings*]
"Ahwawagani inukaagamani nakinu, nakinu, nakinu, nakiu.   250
Nakiyusini nakiyu nakiyu nakiyuu nakiyu nakiyusini."
That was how he said it.
He entered the path from the oxbow lake.
He did that mourning with the Agafïtï song, Agafïtï.
"It was the painted one my aunt ate," he said.   255
Agafïtï.

Agafïtï use the word "painted one" for speaking about
    that fish.
So, he was on the trail from the oxbow lake.
    Mourning in the Agafïtï way,
        Agafïtï.   260
He was lying all along.
    He himself was the killer all along,
        he himself was the killer.
            He had cut out her vulva.
"The jaguar ate her bones, it was the jaguar."   265
    He was lying when he said that.
        That was how he mourned.
            He cried that way for his aunt,
                he cried that way for his aunt.
"Auntie ate the painted one," he told the others: 270

[*Sings*]

    "Nakigukini, nakigu nakigu nakiguu nakigu nakigutsini nakiguu.
    Awawagani inukalamani, nakigu nakigu nakiguu nakigu
    Nakigutsini nakisu nakisu nakiguu nakigu nakigu,"
        That was what he told them as he continued to mourn.
His cousin Tuga the Crested Caracara was listening.   275
    "Here he comes crying for my aunt."
        Crested Caracara spoke about his cousin.
"What did he do to my aunt, he who has done such things
before, the benosed one, the rotten-smelling one?" was what he
said.
The other came home.
He came back mourning for her this way: 280
    "Kaa no more, no more!" he kept on saying.
"Oh! What did he do to my aunt, he who has done such things
before?"
        That's what he said,
            what Crested Caracara said about him,
                what his cousin said.   285
"What did he do to my aunt, worthless one?
    Apparently that person we all dislike has done something to
    my aunt, that worthless one," Crested Caracara said.
        He was angry with his cousin.
"Our parent is no longer alive.
    Our parent hungered for the fishy ones."   290
        That was what Bat said.
            "It must have been the spines," he said.
He arrived home.
    "Ñuku, our parent is no longer alive.
        She was craving *fesoko*, our parent was."   295
        That was what he said.

He was lying to her, as usual.
Then it continued even further this way.
Her daughter looked inside her mouth.
The *ulugi* fish he had put in her throat was still there. 300
"Yes, it does seem to have happened that way."
She embraced her mother.
She held the dead woman close to her.
Bat buried her after that, worthless one, he buried her.

Then it continued further this way. 305
They slept, they slept, they slept.
After three days had been slept,
he came to his own people's place,
to the Place of Many Birds on the Other Side of the
Sky.
Bat went there. 310
"Ñuku, tomorrow I'll go see my own relatives.
I'll go see them."
"All right," she said, "Go then."
Then at the beginning of the next day,
at dawn *pupupu* he went on as bats do, 315
the way a bird does *pupupu*.
He soon arrived.
They were preparing to paint their heads with red paint.
He had really lied to them.
"Here he comes!" 320
He arrived.
"That's enough, that's enough."
So finally he put it on Kwakaga the Chicken,
and on Ugufu the Turkey Vulture.
They were still like our people then, but it's no longer
so. 325
The day after he kept doing it, and again on the following day, he put
it on them.
This is what he said:
"All right everyone, come here to me."
To Chicken.
Then Chicken was wattled. 330
It was that very thing.
Her labia,
Ukwaka's labia.
"All right now, come to me.
I want it on you, my little one," was what he said, the uncle 335
said.
"For me, Uncle," Agati the Spix's Guan.
"I didn't speak to you.

I just spoke to your younger brother, to your younger
brother.
      But come here anyway so I can decorate you."
With his hand he put on a very small piece.   340
      Since then Spix's Guan has a small dangling piece.
      He put on a very small piece with his hand.
"All right, I want to put it on you."
Bah ah, he put a BIG piece on the head of Chicken.
      A very big piece indeed.   345
            How it dangled back and forth when he did that!
            Since then her labia is this thing that's on the
            chickens.
"All right, come here to me to be decorated.
      Come to me," was what he said to Ugufu the King Vulture.
"For me, Uncle," the whiteheaded one who was another kind of
guan,   350
      the other one.
            This was Tuala the Whiteheaded Guan who was saying
            that.
                  "For me, Uncle," he said.
"No, I wasn't speaking to you.
      I just spoke to your younger brother.   355
            All right, come here to me so I can decorate you."
                A ve-ery little piece again, yes.
                      Whiteheaded Guan became wattled.
Then he placed a lot on King Vulture.
      It was really torn by then.   360
This was her labia,
Ukwaka's labia.
Our women have small ones but hers was enormous.
      That was just what it was like.
            This was her own, not like what's on other women.   365
            Her own.

He arrived at his own settlement,
      Bat arrived.
He had gone first to his own people,
      to see them.   370
            He was deceiving them, as usual.
            He was deceiving them.
"You have just come back again," his wife said.
      "Yes, I have come back."
"It's true our parent is no longer alive," she said.   375
      She spoke that way to the same person who had killed her
      mother.
"Our parent is really no longer alive.

The day before yesterday our parent really died."
"We must go there, we are going.
　　While we leave our parent here, they will bathe us there." 　　380
"All right, as you say.
　　We must go as you say, let's go."
"We must go there to have that done to us.
　　So we can be bathed there for our parent.
　　　　She herself who is dead, 　　385
　　　　　　our parent shall be left here."
That was what he said.
　　That was what he kept saying.
　　　　Bat kept saying that.
　　　　　　Bat spoke. 　　390

Then at dawn the following day he put a crab—the pubic-ornamented
one—on his eyes.
　　　　This one eats tears.
　　Now, they became very red indeed when he did that!
　　　　The pubic-ornamented one kept doing that to him.
When it was daytime, 　　395
　　"Look at me now, look! I can't go."
　　　　"All right," she said.
　　"You yourself must go.
　　　　You must go with our relatives."
　　　　　　"All right," she said. 　　400
　　　　　　　　"With our relatives."
　　　　That was what he said.
　　　　　　He was lying as usual!
　　"Quickly now, pour some water into a pot."
　　　　She filled it up. 　　405
　　"Pay careful attention to my friend's face.
　　　　He is just exactly like me!
　　　　　　Exactly like me!"
　　　　　　　　That was what he said.
　　　　　　　　　　He was lying. 　　410
　　"He himself has been told about it, and has told me he will go.
　　　　He will go."
　　　　　　"All right," she said.
　　"When he brings you fish . . . (this is what he said to her) . . .
when my friend brings you fish, when he speaks to you, you will
say, 'Your friend hasn't come at all. Your friend isn't well, his
eyes are sore.'
　　　　You will tell him that. 　　415
Look well at the father of our children.
　　He is exactly like me.
　　　　My bent nose, my head, my rotten smell, my smooth

wings, my extended shoulder bone,
　　　that's how he'll be!
'Now, why doesn't he come, the father of our children?'　420
　　You'll tell him why, you'll tell him why.'"
　　　That is what he said to his wife.
Then when it was morning,
　　"Go now.
　　　I can't walk very well, I can't walk very well, I can't　425
　　walk very well."
　　　The others left.
When they had gone onto the path and were far away,
　　　he also went up through here [*points toward the roof*],
　　　he went through a hole in the roofing thatch.
　　　　Pupupu he went away.　430
His wife saw him as he went away, high up in the sky.
　His wife saw him.
As soon as he arrived he painted himself with red paint.
　He painted himself all over.
　　　As soon as he arrived he painted his hair.　435
Now, listen well!
　　Now, listen!
　　　That person was Watsaja.
When he arrived his wife was still approaching on the path.
　He kept painting himself.　440
　　He painted his legs,
　　　he painted his back.
　　　　All over.
Then when the sun was here,
　late in the day his wife came.　445
　　The others arrived.

The next day they got ready to bathe her,
　　they got ready to bathe Ñuku.
　　　The Birds were all lined up.
He himself who had done all this was the song leader,　450
　he himself!
When the sun was here,
　cold manioc soup was brought out,
　　fish were brought out.
　　　Pok.　455
When this had been done, the songmaster came out.
　Bat came out.
　　His wife didn't recognize him,
　　　she didn't.
"Friend," she said,　460
　"Your friend hasn't come at all.

Your friend is suffering from sore eyes," his wife said.
When his wife looked at him,
   "Yes, it's just as he said.
      This person is really just like him."   465
It was he himself of course.
   It was really he,
      it was he.
         This is a story about him: "Ukwaka's cut-out
         labia."
When the sun came here next,   470
   he began to sing,
      he himself began.
He had a black bow,
   a black bow which he grasped.
This is what he said: 475
   "Her labia were cut out," he sang.
In his song he named her.
I am a knower, I have it now.
      Fatty taught it to me.
         Because he did that I have it now.   480
Should a leader die,
   I sing it here.
Since that time on the occasion of a leader it is done so that red
paint can be passed over all of us here.
   It's King Vulture's song.
      It's King Vulture's song: "Ukwaka's cut-out labia."   485
This is what he said:
   "Someone put an *ulugi* fish in her throat."
This is the song.
   This is how it goes:
      "Ulugi, ulugiigeki saa, getsiiyuu."   490
         That was how he went,
            what Bat said.
While his wife sat right there he was singing about his own
mother-in-law.
   He sang about her, he sang, he sang, and when he came to
   this verse, look,
      he mentioned her name.   495
         He named Ukwaka,
            he named his mother-in-law!
            Really!
            He always deceived a great deal and he
            was deceiving then.
               That is what he said.   500
When he did that her daughter spoke,
   Ñuku spoke.

"Hey!" she said to herself.
 "Why has he named Mother?
  Mother has been named by her grandchildren's   505
  father," she said.
When that happened, when that happened,
 right then he took up some dirt and with great sadness he
 himself spoke about what had happened,
  Her heartless husband kept doing that.
   Really!   510
Then, this is what he said.
 He sang this way.
  Listen, I'll sing it next.
  Afterward her daughter was going to know about him.
   Ukwaka's daughter,
    Ñuku.   515
I'll sing it, listen:
  "Kukakaaa kumakumaawi
  kuwatiii kaga atuasu
  iikisuuu uwefenee atuaasuu
  ikefeneehi nifanukaa nawamii   520
  wajiiii, yaawanii, jukawigii jukawagii tawakuu tawakuu,"
   he told them.
Listen.
Then because he did that her daughter knew.
 "Why did he just mention Mother that way?"   525
  That is what she said.
 "He himself must really be the one, he himself!"
  It was over.
Then this is what happened next.
 His wife covered herself with water,   530
  Ñuku covered herself with it.
   Next she was painted with genipapa.

Then after that was done the next day when it was still dark,
 at the very beginning of the day Bat returned.
  He arrived at the house ahead of his wife.   535
 He went to the water's edge and washed himself.
  removing his red paint.
 He cleansed his heartless self of the paint on his head.
  He became unpainted like this, look.
 But here behind his ear some red paint was still left.   540
  Bat was going to do something,
   he wanted to be beaten by his wife.
 Here behind his ear was some red paint.
  A little bit of it.
   The rest had been removed.   545

Listen.
This is what has been told.
When he arrived right away he bathed himself with water.
He put just a little bit in his eyes,
only a small piece of crab.   550
Ouch!
Then when the sun was here,
it was dusk,
the other arrived.
"You have just come again," he said to his wife.   555
"Yes. Are you all right?" his wife said.
"Yes, it's dead. Look if you want."
"Yes, it is. It's dead."
"Was our children's parent there?"
"Yes."   560
"You see, that was my friend.
He is *just* exactly like me!
I really miss him."
That was what he said!
"All right," she said.   565

Then the next day at dawn when the sun was here, this is what he said.
He made an opening in the thatch, down over here, *pëpëpë*.
"Look for my lice, my lice.
My lice are almost eating me up."
"All right," she answered.   570
Then his wife began to look for his lice.
"Right here," he said.
His wife was occupied with his lice.
Finally she did that in this place,
she picked his lice behind his ear *pëpëpëpëpë* . . . it almost   575
. . . some red paint was there!
"Hey!" she said.
She released Watsaja.
His wife grabbed him by his hair.
"Watsaja! Where is this red paint of yours from?"
Puk! she dropped him to his feet!   580
He was really ashamed.
There was a stick nearby that she was going to use to beat him.
"From where?"
His wife grabbed it.
"Where is it?"   585
"Here! The truth is it was you who did that before to our
parent, you killed her for us!
It was you who did it!"
"It wasn't me who killed your parent!"   590

"Then you placed that thing on the others.
  Afterward.
Now I see you in another way. I know all about you.
  You.
The truth is it was you who killed Mother before, it was you.
The truth is it was you who wanted to sing about what you did
before, a piece of her. Why did you mention Mother in your
song, as if you were her grandchildren's father?
  Her name.
   Because you *did* do it.   595
Why did you mention Mother before in your song, as if you
were her grandchildren's father?
Then you mentioned her name.
All the time you were singing about Mother's murderer you were
really the person who had done that!
  Go away! Go away!"
She began to beat him.   600
  She grabbed the stick, *tuk*!
   Bat ran outside when she did that.
    She almost beat him to death.
He ran away.
  He went to that same place as before,   605
   to his own settlement.
Listen! Then *tikii* someone else came to her.
  "There's no doubt he killed our parent," Tete the Bat Falcon
said.
   "There's no doubt he killed our parent before, your husband
  did it, your husband.
    Then he left ahead of you, ahead of you.   610
     I know he was the one who was singing there
     before."
Because he told her that Bat's wife cried,
  his wife cried.
"It was he himself who was singing, he himself, that same one
was her killer."
   "Yes, he was."   615
"Now you must become my wife, my wife."
  "All right, that will be fine with me."
"He will remain as he is. You have become my wife.
  "All right."
   Then she became his wife.   620

At night he returned.
   Bat returned once again.
"Ñuku, open the door for me!"
  She didn't answer.

The next night he came back.   625
        "Ñuku, open the door for me!"
        "Why do you keep coming back here again?" she said.
        "I miss you very much," he said.
                "You don't feel that way at all," she said.
                He went away.   630
Once again, at night he came back.
                He brought her some wild *kofi* fruit.
        "This isn't food, it's just fruit from the forest," so he went away
        again.
Then she said to Bat Falcon,
        "Go ahead, kill him if you wish."   635
                "All right, I *would* like to eat him."
The next night as Bat was arriving,
                Bat Falcon watched him from inside the house.
        Suddenly he flew out and killed him.
        Then he carried Bat up to the roof where he ate him.   640

Listen.
        That's certainly all there is.

Notes to Atsidyi

29   Gikigifïtï is an ancestral community of Carib-speakers from whom descended the
Jagamï people.
34, 47–48, 50   Conversations in this and the following stanza include the markedly
polite speech of affines, which reinforces by contrast the murderous deception of Bat. Typical
affinal words for relatives in this story ("your grandchildren's father"; "my young relatives'
father"; "Their Grandmother") make reference to the offspring of a marital union. Also characteristic of affinal speech is the expression "the fishy ones" for "fish" (see line 290, for
example).
35   Salt plants are water hyacinths from which an edible salt is made by leaching the
ashes of burned stems and leaves.
38   *Fesoko*, *Hoplias matabaricus*, is a common fish about eight to nine inches long,
usually caught in traps.
41   Before being burned, the water hyacinths are dried on racks, a frequent sight as
one travels through the swamps of the region.
86   *Nyetibius griscus*, the common potoo, is a nocturnal bird with a distinctive, haunt-
ing cry. It is related to the nightjars.
100   *Tigrisoma lineatum*.
110   *Chrysocyon* sp. is the nocturnal canid scavenger associated with death and witchcraft.
209   *Bryconinea* sp. (Portuguese, "matrinchão").
215   *Anostomidae* sp. (Portuguese, "piau"; "piaba").
216   *Boulengerella cuvieri* (Portuguese, "picuda aracu").
217   *Hydrolycus* (Portuguese, "cachorra"; "pirandira").
225   A small fish of the *Cichlidae* family.
250   This song is in the Arawakan dialect of the Yawalipiti people, whom the Kalapalo
call Agafïtï, after a former settlement of theirs.
275   *Caracara plancus*.
323   *Cathartes aura*.

336   *Penelope jacquacu.*
349   *Sarcoramphus para.*
352   *Penelope* sp.
391   "Pubic-ornamented one" refers to the triangular shape on its carapace.
593   Bat gives himself away by mentioning his mother-in-law's name, which violates affinal name-avoidance rules.
608   *Falco ombigularis.*

Just as Kudyu describes in his story, the song performance is followed by washing the mourners. Each person is assigned a washer, whose task is to throw water over the mourner and see that the body is completely cleansed of the substances of mourning. Afterward, the male mourners are painted with red paint by their washers, whom they pay with arrows, eagle feathers, or cotton thread. Then all the other men are washed by the male mourners, and these men enter the ceremonial house to paint one another. While they do this, two of the principal mourners walk from house to house to wash all those who have not participated in the activities in the plaza but who "cried during the time of burial."

A widow or widower is similarly washed and painted inside the house but almost immediately removes the paint with which he or she has been decorated, thereby letting the in-laws know that it will be some time before he or she will be willing to return to a normal life. "He wants to keep crying," or "She still remembers her dead husband," it is said. But even such a persistent griever and all the other people who wept for the deceased must be publicly washed in order to release them from the ritual state of mourning that prevents furthering the life of the settlement. Washing and painting thus symbolize the return of the mourning kinsmen (but not a spouse) to a certain condition of social life in which they actively sponsor collective economic and musical activities that characterize Kalapalo public ritual.

What must we make of the association of this washing and painting ritual, an act that releases mourners from their seclusion from social life, and of that curious story about Bat? Specifically, what occurs during the singing of Bat's song over those mourners? First, it is important to remember that this event occurs when mourners appear in public for the first time. The mourners are said to be as yet "bashful," "unwilling to show themselves" (*ifutisundako*). They "long for the dead person" (*apïŋifïgï ifunita ifekene*), and they are "melancholy" (*otonunaluko*), emotional conditions that are incompatible with public roles. After the ritual, they are no longer "bashful"; they "walk around" and are sponsors (*oto*), spending all their time working for the memorial ritual. The washing not only prepares them for the social role as organizers of a memorial ritual (turning their passive secluded state into active relations with the rest of the community) but helps them to reconcile that public, active role with their continual memory of the dead and sadness over the death of a beloved person. This transition seems to be effected by having them think about something else: a mythological character who is dreadful and funny at the same time, who reminds the survivors of the absurdity of death, thereby helping them to think of death in a far more objective manner than they have been. For the myth evokes the death of an absurd Dawn Person ("she of the lengthy labia") at the hands of a clever but even more ridiculous trickster, who in the end receives his comeuppance at the hands of an avenging relative of his wife. Performing the song thus evokes a certain kind of story and certain characters, all of which suggest to the participants that their memory of the dead, while in seclusion and still strongly evoking grief, can eventually become controlled and compatible with normal social life. The song ritual thus helps keep people from falling into perpetual melancholy by providing a model of feeling action—involving re-marriage and revenge on the part of a mourner—thereby assisting in their return to the world of the living.

The fulfillment of important, complicated obligations begins almost imme-diately for these people, starting when the newly cleansed and painted mourners wash the other members of their community. But even more important now is the start of their active involvement in collective preparations for a memorial ceremony, the Egitsu, that will be attended by several hundred visitors from other communities. These preparations require the participation of all the people in the settlement and must be carefully planned and coordinated. These events involve principally economic and scheduling tasks, and have clear instrumental goals which together constitute a community project. To effect these goals, the special hereditary ritual officers called *anetaū* manage, organize, and plan the ritual events. The relatives of the dead are considered the sponsors (*oto*) of the memorial process, and they are responsible for providing food and other pay-ment in return for the performance of the ritual and assistance in preparing for the visitors. The sponsors serve as nodes in a complex redistribution network and are thus actively involved in the work. As the level of these activities inten-sifies throughout the dry season, the period of such preparations, the work of the sponsors becomes more and more public and increasingly significant to the success of the whole.

Returning to the mortuary ritual process, following the washing ritual, the men, now fully decorated, begin to perform a dance called *auūgufi*, accompa-nied by two singers playing rattles. Both the singing and the dance suggest snakelike motions, and indeed it is said that the *auūgufi* was taught to human beings by some Snake People. The story of the origin of *auūgufi* associates the musical performances directly with mourning and with memorial, but rather than following death, they occur mythologically when the man who has learned them decides to leave ("once and for all") to live with his Snake Wife. The *auūgufi* is thus an evocation of the finality of death and of the complete separa-tion between the living and the dead.

The *auūgufi* performance has the most complex texture of all Kalapalo mu-sic, for it consists of up to four integrated parts, each of which has its own distinctive rhythm. Three of these parts are always present: voice (the leading or dominant part, which is sung by a pair of male specialists, one of whom initiates a stanza organized into four-beat measures, which is then repeated by the other—usually less skilled—man); rattles played by each man that support his dance by introducing a three-beat counterrhythm; and bodily motion, as the singers sway in imitation of the movement of a snake. The fourth part allows for collective participation by all the men who are not sponsors or singers, dancing in a line before the memorial posts and the singers. (The best way of describing the motions of this line dance is to say it evokes the struggles of fingers inserted into a Chinese finger puzzle, or—a more South American image—that of the stretching motions of the basket-press, the *tipiti*, used by some [not the Kalapalo] for squeezing manioc.) Each part in its own way contributes to a distinctive impression of snakes.

Kumagisa
Told by Kambe at Aifa, July 5, 1982

Fagagi ekugu, "Many Sariema," was a settlement of our ancestors, Fagagi ekugu.

    Kumagisa
who had been married to his wife,
    he had married her, he cut her bangs, he cut his wife's bangs,
        when she was a maiden.   5
    (You've seen it yourself, someone cutting the bangs of one of
        my people.)
Then she was brought to him after that,
    she was brought to him.
She kept rejecting him,
    his wife kept rejecting him.   10
She kept rejecting him.
No, she never went with him, never.
When she went with him at all, she hid herself.
    She would go, she would hide herself.
    She kept rejecting him.   15
So that he would divorce her, his beautiful wife,
    so that he would divorce her.
Then, I'm told,
    she went to the water's edge, she, his wife would go,
    her husband . . . she, his wife would walk some distance from
        him.   20
        She was rejecting him.
        Yes, she was certainly rejecting him.
    As I've said, they were there.

After a while,
    after they had been there together a short while, it ended.   25
    While she slept beneath him,
        his wife rejected him.
"I'll go get some firewood," he said.
    It was late in the day, the sun was over here.
        Kumagisa spoke.   30

"I'll go get some firewood," that was to his mother.
"Go if you wish," his mother said.
Well, he came close to a visitor's path.
They began to talk among themselves.
They began to sing.   35
Snakes were doing that, Kakakugu were doing that.
Snakes, Kakakugu.
Snakes, Kakakugu this size.
They began to sing.
They themselves.   40
They were performing *auūgufi*,
how they all performed!
They are the protectors of the *aŋukwagi*, the *aŋukwagi* palm.
The ones that stand on mounds.
So there beneath the ground was their house.   45
Their settlement was underground.
"Koh hoh hoh huehhh," they began to sing.
"Ah! Who are they?" he said.
He went toward them to see,
to see the *undufe*.   50
Outside, they all began to perform.
Teh, a beautiful daughter was doing that.
A daughter.
A Snake Daughter was doing that.
The daughter of Kakakugu was doing that.   55
Teh! She was a beautiful maiden.
"Well! Kumagisa.
Are you here for some reason?"
"No," he answered,
"I've come to collect some firewood."   60
"You have a wife, don't you?
You have a wife, don't you?"
"Yes, I'm that person."
"Why didn't she come with you?
Why not?"   65
"She always does this to me," he answered.
"She has no interest in me,
she has no interest in me."
"I'll never lose interest in you at all,"
the Snake Daughter said.   70
And so she became his true wife.
He wanted her to be his wife.
The Snake became his wife.
The Kakakugu Woman became his wife.
Then, listen: 75

It was there, long ago, that he heard it.
"Listen Kumagisa. Listen, that's the *undufe* being performed,
  the *auūgufi* is being performed.
He listened carefully to it.
He was still inside her house,   80
  he had gone inside her house.
She had brought him there, *teh* his magnificent wife did that.
She had become his wife once and for all.
  She had become his wife, yes.
She had become his wife,   85
  and so he listened to the *undufe*.
    He must have begun to listen carefully to it after all that
    happened to him.
  He was listening, Kumagisa was listening to it.
    He was listening to it.
They were singing, they were singing.   90
  They were singing after that, in the plaza.
"Listen, Kumagisa," she said,
  "That's the *auūgufi*,
    the *auūgufi*."
"I'll go now," he said,   95
    "I'll go now."
  "All right, go then," she said.
The tree split open and he came home.
    He had been listening to the song.
  "Tomorrow I'll come to you, tomorrow."   100
Now he was very glad because of all that had happened to him.
Teh he, after all that he had acquired a very beautiful wife.
His wife who had lost interest in him still slept beneath him.
And so he arrived home, *bum*.
  By then it was dusk.   105
  He had become very happy.
"You have arrived, haven't you?" his mother said.
  He came to his wife.
    The one who slept beneath him.
His wife still remained with him.   110
She didn't greet him.
    Yet the powerful being had greeted him.
"You must leave now," he said,
  "You must leave.
  Go to your mother,"   115
  he said to this other woman.
  He had just married someone else.
He had just married her when all that had happened to him
before.

He had just married her.
    Teh she was beautiful, the daughter he had just   120
      married.
"You must leave."
But she wanted to stay there with him just as she was.
    She wanted to stay there with him just as she was.
Then, she stayed there.
    She still slept there with him.   125
    They fell asleep.
The next day again,
    he went, he didn't take her along.
    The sun was over here.
But once again it began to happen as before.   130
    He began to hear it,
      he began to hear the song.
        He began to hear it,
    I think it was his wife who told him about it long ago.
    "Very well," he said.   135
      I think it was she.
He stayed there while his wife did that,
    after he arrived in order to learn about it.
      At dusk.
    What they had been doing stopped then, the *auūgufi* stopped.   140
    His other wife was still with him,
      still beneath him.
The next day he went again.
    And once again—look—
he went over and over to be with her.   145
    He went to hear the song.
    Over and over again.
When at last he had gone through the entire song in his mind,
    the entire song was completed,
"Mother," he said.   150
"I haven't been well,
    I haven't been well."
"What is wrong?"
"I'm actually married to someone else,
    I'm married."   155
"You are? Where did that happen?"
    "At her own settlement.
    I was married at the Kakakugu's.
    That's who my wife is.
    A Kakakugu."   160
"Is that so?"
    "Yes."
    "When I kept going away it was to listen to a song,

to listen to a song."
"It was well that you did that," his mother agreed with what he told   165
her.
"I will have to sleep there later Mother,
        I will sleep there tomorrow."
        "As for you, go away."
    So he sent his wife away.
            "You must go."   170
    It was the other one, his other wife who was accepting him.
        She was accepting him.
Then I'm told he stayed there.

He finished sleeping there.
    The next day the song began   175
            It began.
As he came back to his wife, near where he walked he heard it.
            Near where he walked.
They all came outside the house and went beside him.
        He stood right next to the singer.   180
    He was listening to the song,
        standing there he was able to hear it clearly,
            he was listening to the song.
It was over.
    I'm told the day began.   185
    So the day began.
    Before dawn he had been listening to that thing.
        he had been listening to it.
It was over.
    "I must be going now,   190
        I'm going now that it's over."
    So he went away,
        he went away after all that had happened to him.
            He left right away.

But the next day he continued to go there.   195
Then he kept going there the following day again,
        he kept going and going to listen to the song.
It was over—look—it was over.
    He listened well to the song when he did that.
    And so every part of it was clear in his mind.   200
Since he was doing that her bangs were cut because he wanted her.
            That was over.
He was listening to that other thing,
        so he listened to it after that.
    He must have heard it perfectly after that.   205
So then while he was there,

"Mother," I'm told he said.
"Tomorrow I must bring your daughter-in-law here,
   tomorrow.
Think of it, I am bringing your daughter-in-law here."   210
"Very well," she answered.
  His wife will be going to his mother, he will bring her,
    he will bring his wife there.
  "Very well," she said. "Bring your sister here if you wish.
    Bring her here."   215
He went to get her,
  he went then after he said that.
So he went,
  he had already sent the other one away because someone else
  had chosen him.
Teh. That woman was just right for him.   220
  He had sent the other one away to her parents.
    He no longer wanted her.
Then, he went after that.
  Soon after he was there after he did all that.
  He did all that at dusk, and he came to her.   225
Tiki, her husband came inside.
  Think of it, his wife came there.
    The Kakakugu came there.
  His older siblings, his older siblings who were women,
    she came with him to his siblings.   230
   His siblings were three women.
   There was only one man, he himself.
   He was the single one of all of them.
Tiki so anyway he came inside.
  The sun was here, it was dusk.   235
  The others sat here, in the doorway.
  They had just been preparing the hot manioc soup, his sisters were.
  His mother was lying in her hammock over to the side of the house.
  His mother's hammock was hung by itself, hung by itself.
Tiki, "I'm right here, Mother,   240
   I can just see your daughter-in-law,
    Now I can see your daughter-in-law," he said to his mother.
Then *chuu!* the Snake came toward them after that.
  "Oh!" his sisters screamed when she did that,
   she frightened his sisters,   245
    they were frightened of her.
  She came toward them after that and she came inside.
  Her husband walked close to her, ahead of her.
When his sisters saw her following him,
   "Umah, umah," they were very frightened.   250
  So he went to lie down in his mother's hammock,

so he went to lie down in his mother's hammock,
>while she curled up beneath her husband, coiled up.
"Mother," he went, "Your daughter-in-law is right here.
>>Your daughter-in-law is right here. 255
>>Your daughter-in-law is right here," he went.
>"Very well," she answered.
"Dear child," she went,
>"You are indeed here with your relative."
"Shuuuuuuu," the other went. 260
>"Shiiiiiiii," was how she answered her.
>That was how she greeted her,
>>she greeted her mother-in-law.
"You should speak to your sister-in-law,"
>>their mother said, 265
>>>to her children, to the women.
"You are indeed here with your relative."
>>The other was curled up beneath her husband.
Teh! but how beautifully painted she looked that way.
>>They saw how well the Kakakugu design was conceived. 270
>>She had used the *tiŋufifitse* design, the *egitsu* design.
"You are indeed here with your relative."
>>"Shiiiiiiii," she greeted her, she greeted one of her sisters-in-
law.
>>She greeted her. 275
>>"Shiiiiiiii."
>"Very well," the woman answered, "Stay here."
Once again a sister-in-law came to her.
>Again she did the same thing after that.
>>"Shiiiiiiii," she greeted her.
When that was over, "Let's go," he said. 280
>"I'll take you back,"
>>her husband then said.
>>So they both came back after all that.
Her husband got up from where he had been lying down, from where
he had been on the side of the house.
She came, she came next to him, "Shiiiiiiii." 285
>*Mbisuk*! But now she was transformed again.
>>They both approached after all that.
And they both went to the entrance path toward her house,
>>on the entrance path. 290
"Mother, look," he said
>to his mother.
"Look at your daughter-in-law."
"I was wrong to think of her that way.
>>I thought I would be afraid of her when she came here," his
mother told him.

        "Because she's a snake."   295
And so that ended that.

Then he slept, he slept, he slept, and so then
    they kept talking to each other after that.
    They kept talking together, they kept singing after all that had
    happened to them.
    They kept singing after that had happened to them, they kept singing.   300
    They kept singing after all that because that was how they were.
    The dawn performance by the Kakakugu.
        This was the origin of the dawn performance.
[*Sings*]
        "utalikugu tëikege ugimina
        Oh ha ha je."   305
        "Put my feather armbands around my head
        Oh ha ha je."
            That was what they were doing after that.
            That was what they did when daylight appeared.
            That was the Kakakugu dawn performance.   310
            That was their dawn performance.
[*Sings*]
        "Wah hi je he,"
            that was what they were doing after that.
      "Listen, listen," she then said to him.
        "That's the very thing we perform at dawn,   315
           the dawn performance."
        "I see," he answered her.
He was listening to what was being done, he was listening perfectly
to what was being done.

Once again they came again to his mother,
        once again they came, you see,   320
            and again they came once more.
        This time however she came as a person,
            as a person this time.
      "Mother," he said,
        "I must bring your daughter-in-law again.   325
           I will bring her again," he went,
           "I will bring your daughter-in-law."
      "Very well," she went.
This time it was dusk when he went to do that,
        this time it was dusk when he went to do that.   330
        It was dusk, the sun had already set.
They came back
      He came *tiki*, she came behind him *tiki* her husband came inside.
      Think of what I've just said, it was dusk when he did that, the sun

was very low on the horizon, outside all was silent.
Tiki,   335
   "Now we're both here, we're here."
Her sisters-in-law were seated near the doorway.
   They were fixing hot manioc soup near the doorway.
The others came up to them from their side trail.
      Came up to them.   340
No one else knew about them, not at all.
   None of the people in the other houses knew about them.
      His mother was the only one who knew about his wife.
      And his sisters also knew about her.
Then he approached them,   345
   "Here we are."
   They had come up to them from a side trail that had taken them
   around the settlement.
Tiki, he came behind her, they came there.
      Teh! How beautiful she was as she came!
   "Here is your younger brother's wife, your sister-in-law!   350
   Here comes your sister-in-law, but now she's a human being!"
   they told one another.
   Teh, her painted thighs were beautiful, *teh he*, they were more
   beautiful than ever!
   Her forehead was painted as she came, her feet were painted as
   she came.
"You are here with your relative," they said.
   "I'm certainly here," she answered.   355
   She spoke to them like a person.
   This time she spoke to them like a person.
   After she came to them.
So they stayed there.
   "You must take some of our hot manioc soup to your sister-in-law.   360
      Our hot manioc soup.
      To your sister-in-law."
   "Very well," the others said.
They dragged some over to him,
   and then they packed it up for her husband.   365
   It was ready.
Then they put it before him.
   "Let's go," he said.
   He had brought her there so the others could see her, so they
   could see her.
   So her mother-in-law could know what she was like.   370
He kept coming to her,
   "Let's go," he said.
   "We'll sleep at your place."
      The sun was here, it was late in the day.

Teh! she was the beautiful Kakakugu. 375
She was a small-breasted woman.
The design she had painted on herself was that of a powerful
being.

He stayed there for a short time.
        He stayed there for a short time.
When he was ready they came back again, 380
        once again they came back,
        but this time they came back for the last time.
He was bringing her back for the last time.
        He brought her back once and for all this time.
"*Teh heh*, what's-his-name's wife is beautiful!" The others were 385
telling each other about her.
They had seen her after he came back with her.
He had brought her around to all the others.
        Teh his wife was still beautiful.
        That was how she was when he brought her around to the others.
She was certainly very different from all the rest of us. 390
        They had come to his settlement.

And so one of his dry seasons passed, and his dry season passed.
        Then while it was raining,
"Mother," he said.
"I must go. 395
        I will go.
            I will go.
I must go to show you what will happen.
She and I will live over there.
        That place over there. 400
            By the entrance path.
Make a belt for me right now Mother," he went,
        "A belt for me."
        One made of cotton.
            Cotton. 405
"I will have to hold a ritual," he went,
        "I will hold a ritual,
            I will hold a ritual."
"All right," she said.
His mother spun a belt for him, 410
        she spun some cotton,
            which she rolled into a very large ball.
Then, he wanted to teach the others.
        They will be singing about him.
            They will do just as he was about to. 415
But they were going to alternate with him.

They were going to alternate singing the song.
They began to listen to him,
    they were going to dance with him.
He was ready.   420
    They were listening to him.
    Because of what he was doing his mother was making his belt.
    She spun a huge amount of cotton!
Then the others cut down a tree, his followers cut a tree down.
        His followers cut down—um—they cut down his image.   425
        A *wegufi* tree was what they did that to,
            they all cut it down.
    She was still showing them how to do it.
        She still looked like a human being.
He was going to go away once and for all.   430
    To his wife.
    Underwater, underground.
    He was living elsewhere, he was living elsewhere.
    He was about to create the original event.
        He was about to create our first performance.   435
And so it happened.
They all went to the oxbow lake.
    For the memorial post work they all painted themselves,
        after they had all returned from that place.
They set up the memorial post.   440
Then at dusk they carried the post into its hole.
    They had made a place for it,
        and so they set up his image.
    They set up this thing of his that they remembered him by, made
    of *wegufi*.
And they went to cry for him,   445
    his mother went to mourn him,
    she was brought outside after all that happened.
When that was done the others began to shake their rattles,
        the *auūgufi*.
    Wearing macaw headdresses.   450
    Wearing earrings of macaw tail feathers.
        Yes.
When that was done he blew a spell over it.
    "You must seclude yourself, Mother, but not just yet."
He started the *auūgufi* song.   455
His mother had built his fire,
    she had built his fire.
"Make our fire," he said,
    and so his mother stayed there weeping,
        seated beside his memorial post,   460
        while he sang,

until he was finished.
When it was morning, he sang the dawn song,
      he sang the dawn song when that happened.
    And he stopped.   465
Then when it was truly day,
    the sun had risen,
    "Mother," he said,
    "Bury my fire,
      my fire."   470
    "Very well."
So she buried his fire in the ground.
    She buried his memorial post fire.
    And so, she buried his fire.
She buried his fire, and it was done.   475
    His mother had buried his fire.
He had really sung his song well.
    While everything else was being done he was singing.

And so he finished.
    "Mother, I'm going right now," he said.   480
      "I'm going right now.
        I'm going."
And so he went after that.
      He went.
He went on the entrance path.   485
    He wanted to go and he went once and for all,
      and so he went once and for all.
He never came back to his mother, no.
      Not at all.
That was why all that was done, that was why.   490
So that he could go away forever.

Then his mother distributed his belt to the others.
    She did that with the cotton.
His mother distributed his forehead wrappings to the people in the
other houses.
    She distributed his forehead wrappings to the speech   495
    masters.
    All of it.
    She gave it all away.
    What he himself had owned.
    That was his belt.
He went away while she did that,   500
    he had gone away once and for all.
    To his wife.
    He was Kumagisa.

His name.

His wife, the one who had discarded him was left behind.   505
    because he wanted to marry someone else.
    His other wife had been rejecting him.
"I want this one for myself," the Snake Daughter chose him for
herself.
    His other wife rejected him.

That's all.   510

Notes to Kumagisa

37   *Kakakugu* is an unidentified nonpoisonous snake.
43   *Aŋukwagi* is a low palm on the cerrado that bears clusters of almond-flavored fruit
prized by the Kalapalo.
77   *Undufe* is the Kalapalo term for any collective musical ritual.

When the Kalapalo perform *auügufi* and play the flutes they call *ataŋa*, they mark the beginning of their ritual season. The *ataŋa* performance marks the entire period as part of an *egitsu*, while the *auügufi*, performed repeatedly over the many weeks of ceremonial preparations, is held in the area of the graves of the dead and focuses attention on this central, communal, and sacred space. Shortly after the first performance of *auügufi*, an enclosure of logs called *tafite* is built on the grave of the person who is being memorialized. The *auügufi* performances in effect bracket the period of time during which work on this structure takes place. Pairs of male flute players and their female partners dance around and around the settlement, moving from one house to the next as many as eleven or twelve times before relinquishing their turn to another set of performers; they repeat this ritual over many months until the final, climactic day when—taking turns—the invited guests do the same in the hosts' settlement.

The climax of a Kalapalo memorial ritual process comes when memorial posts are set up in the plaza to represent each of the dead who are being honored. These posts are decorated with symbols of their gender identity, after which the sponsors are again formally painted by ritual officers. Then the posts are decorated with cotton belts. At the moment these belts are placed upon the upright logs, all the relatives of the deceased suddenly rush from their houses to weep, for it is now that the Dead return, this time (it is thought) as onlookers at their own memorial. Once again, mourning through song occurs because of a deliberate evocation of the memory of the dead (as it did during mourning seclusion), and it still means that the dead are being remembered, but mourning through song has now become more controlled than when the survivors lay in seclusion: it is now periodic, occurring at prescribed moments. Kalapalo also perform mourning songs more purposefully than before, doing so in some fashion of unison and as part of the role of ritual sponsor. At night when the sponsors—illuminated by fires—sit next to their relative's effigies watching the visitors dance into the plaza, this scripted mourning occurs once again; now even further separated from thoughts of death, it is emblematic of their roles as sponsors.

Conclusion

I have described a ritual process that takes mourners from an experience of spontaneous grief and anger into a seclusion chamber in which memory of the deceased is never allowed to diminish and during which time the mourner is encouraged to succumb to all the forces of both grief and memory—to focused, planned, goal-oriented participation in complex, collective work. Memory of the dead is again deliberately and finally evoked during a public mourning event that demonstrates how successful the cultural forms have been in the government of personal grief.

Throughout this process, sound plays a crucial expressive role. Initially, grief is expressed through *itsu*—human noise or expletives—not through music, for at the moment of death despair takes precedence over imagination and utterances are fully indexical of feelings. As memory begins to form out of grief, illusionary thought returns, now orally expressed through spontaneous mourning songs in which desperate outcries directed toward the dead in an attempt to bring them back to the living are transformed into rhythmic, melodic evocations of them. Song thus alludes to memory; in seclusion, this memory is spontaneous and unpredictable. Eventually, however, memory is engendered through activity shaped by ritual symbols· and almost fully controlled. Ultimately, singing becomes stereotyped and thus emblematic of a particular social position or role, now associated with a memory that is reconciled with a return to the community.

The mythological imagery and organization of mourning rituals seems to have a useful influence on the consciousness of the participants, affecting their attitudes toward the deceased while helping in this process of controlling the consequences of a persistence of memory by giving meaning to death and the experience of remembering. Kalapalo myths refer, of course, to the first instances of various parts of this ritual process, yet they seem to serve less as justifications of particular practices than as poignant, evocative models of feeling. As such, they effect particular ways of thinking about death and the dead; in contexts that demand immediate, performed responses to the symbolic structuring of the stage and to the formulaic roles of onlookers, these myths seem to have major importance for assisting the continuity forward of ritual action. For those performed responses contribute to the progression toward and ultimate completion of the ritual goal by engendering the appropriate responses of nonmourners in a process that is as much artistic and improvised as it is traditionally scripted and formulaic.

1. Standing before the *kuakutu*, the song masters Muluku, Kudyu, Kākaku, and Kambe sing "Bat's Song" over four mourners. The mourners and two young spectators sit on the *tafite*, an enclosure built around the grave of an *anetu*.

2. *Koŋitsofo*: the washing of mourners by *anetaŭ*.

3. An *auŭgufi* at Aifa, 1967.

4. An *egitsu* at Aifa, 1979: As cotton belts are tied around the memorial posts, relatives crouch beside to wail to their dead.

5. Juĩ, newly married, enjoys a piece of fish in his father-in-law's house. The young couple's hammocks are intertwined, the hearth has been freshly swept, and the floor has been moistened with water. At his feet is a pan of hot manioc soup prepared by his mother-in-law.

6. Kākaku prepares his youngest daughter, Kumafu, for a wrestling match by scraping her body with a blood letting tool.

7. At the end of the rainy season, streams draining off the grasslands are fished with these *utu* traps. The clothes help protect against biting gnats that proliferate at this time of year.

8. *Ataŋa* players Agakuni and Kafusala during an *egitsu* season at Aifa, 1967.

9. Kwambï singers carrying wealth (cloth, land snail shells) in a ridiculously flamboyant gesture of display.

10. Kwambï masks escorted
by the water beings called
Pidyë.

11. Yamurikumalu *ataŋagï*
Kefesugu and Kaigu
"preparing" the *egitsu* July
1980.

12. *Oh-ho-me* singers. The *taiyope* song leader Ugaki dances at the center of the line. The two decorated women are song leaders who are also *anetaū* and wrestling adepts. The third, younger woman (also *anetu*) has been made to dance with them so she can learn the music and acquire the poise her mother feels she lacks.

13. Tsëfi brings some piqui fruit to the plaza, where the *taiyope* Ugaki and Moge stand accepting the day's harvest, October 1979.

14. Cutting open a morning's piqui harvest for the sponsor's wife, who will boil it and store it for redistribution.

15. The *taiyope* Agikuagï distributes the sponsor's piqui soup, to women seated before the *kuakutu*.

16. As two pair of young women practice wrestling, Kafuga challenges an opponent.

17. The *taiyope* Ondo distributes boiled fish on pieces of manioc bread, brought to the plaza by the Yamurikumalu sponsor.

18. One afternoon during the Yamurikumalu season, these young women and girls ran singing towards some men in the plaza: "His red penis goes in and out, in and out, in and out."

Chapter 6

Fantasies of Erotic Aggression

One of the most notable aspects of Kalapalo mythology is the elaborate psychodynamic treatment of social life that makes explicit the conflicts and ambivalences inherent in social relations. Anxiety about certain aspects of the self and the roles one must play that are generated by Kalapalo social praxis are played upon in disturbing images of concealed feelings and fantasies. As we have already seen, Kalapalo myths contain a good deal of quoted speech that would ordinarily be private, inaccessible to a casual eavesdropper and concealed if possible. Such is the speech of lovers, children's conversations, those of husbands and wives beyond earshot of their parents, of elders criticizing their juniors, and of people planning to kill someone. Second, characters are often identified primarily by their kinship and affinal classifications. Through their adherence to or violation of significant codes for conduct, they are used as symbols of personalities and varieties of moral-ethical judgment. Finally, verbal fantasies about human existence and its absurdities are created through the telling of ridiculous stories about "disgusting Dawn People" who foolishly pervert a "good" human feeling. Collectively, the various characters and their doings portray the Kalapalo understanding of their developmental processes from early puberty through sexual maturity. They focus upon changes in a person's ideas of self and attitudes toward others during this time of life, as the changes undergone by the human body are conditioned and enhanced by elaborate and constant work that involves a complex system of body techniques behind which are both medical and social intentions.

The difficulty of reconciling inner feelings with standards of demeanor prescribed for persons engaged in one or another class of relationship (particularly people who are related by marriage) is a standard refrain in Kalapalo myths, many of which describe people manifesting respectable social personae while concealing distinctly impolite or hostile feelings toward those around them. Social life in these stories is a masking process behind which antisocial and even violent attitudes are concealed.

The Last-Born or Youngest Sibling

Adolescents like Saganafa often represent strategic thoughts and actions that conflict with the values and norms of ordinary social life. These characters are models of the suitability and even necessity of strategic thinking and ethical choices that seemingly violate social norms, decisions that expand the universe of *ifutisu* so as to extend ethical judgment beyond what is normally accepted or anticipated in the domain of kinship. Rather than expressing purely negative antisocial feelings, these acts often express universalized values, feelings of moral community and equality of self and others that contrast with the restrictive ethics, hierarchic order, and nonspontaneous nature of family life.[1] Although strategic thinking conflicts with ideas about how ordinary life should be conducted, it can be presented positively as a means of asserting the solidarity of people who are not relatives, similar to a "strength in numbers" principle, for example, with reference to the conflict of the Birds against Turtle Monster or (in the myth of Monstrous Women considered in Chapter 7) the women of Aŋambïtï Community in opposition to all their men. Of course, on some occasions such attempts at expansion of the moral community fail, causing new and irreconcilable conflicts within the family (as in the story of Saganafa). Last, an undifferentiated group organized and led by elders (but gloriously represented by an adolescent who is the personification of *ifutisu*) can accomplish what individuals or small groups of kin cannot. This is appealing to Kalapalo in ways I will more concretely demonstrate in my discussion of collective ritual in Chapter 7.

The character most clearly associated with this expansion of moral community is the last-born or youngest of a set of brothers or sisters. The last-born sibling in Kalapalo mythology is distinctive because the character is always portrayed as an adolescent who dramatically breaks away from family life by violating the exclusivity of familial morality and who either establishes important relations with strangers or deliberately performs a suicidal act. We saw how this happened to Saganafa; another story in which this theme figures prominently follows. Chronologically, the events precede the story of Bat, as the names of some of the characters suggest.

Akwakaŋa
Told by Kambe at Aifa, February 18, 1979

I

A person went to his settlement,
        to his mother's settlement.
    He went there from Ñatasa,
       this person went from that settlement,
         from Akwakaŋa's settlement.   5
            A person of the Dawn Time was doing so,

a long time ago.
Akwakaŋa was a powerful being,
    he was Kwatïŋï's grandson.
        Kwatïŋï was his grandfather.   10
    Teh he was beautiful,
        beautiful.
Ukwaka at that time was his aunt,
        Ukwaka.
Her daughter at that time was Ñuku,   15
    her daughter,
        a woman.
            Her bangs had already been cut.
Her younger sister was a secluded maiden,
    her younger sister.   20
The visitor arrived there.
    "Kaw kaah!"
    He slept two days.

Ukwaka wanted to invite her nephew.
    The mother's name is Ukwaka.   25
    Ñuku is her daughter,
        Ñuku is her name.
            Her bangs were already cut.
Then she told her husband Kaŋaŋatï,
    "Our nephew is invited so he can be together with our daughter.   30
    I have invited our nephew to be her husband."
    "Very well, later I will escort her to his own house."
    "You must be sure and go to him," she said to the man.
        "Yes."
    "Implore your brother to come here.   35
        Urge him to come," his aunt said.
        "Urge him to come,"
        and so he left.
When the sun was here he arrived at his settlement,
    at Ñatasa.   40
    "What's-his-name has just arrived."
        I have no idea of his name,
            so I'll continue to say "the person."

Then when it became dark,
    at dusk,   45
        he came to where the other was.
There he was,
        seated inside his seclusion chamber.
    "Akwakaŋa," he said to him.
    "What? What makes you come here?" he asked.   50

"Your aunt has just invited you, your aunt wants to invite you."
"What did she do that for?"
"She wants you to go to her daughter.
 She wants you to be her daughter's husband."
"I certainly will go if she wishes. I will go," he told him.   55
His grandfather Kwatïŋï asked,
 "What did your older brother just say? What?" he asked him.
"It seems to be our deception, what he just told me.
 Aunt has just asked me to visit her.
  So that I can become her daughter's husband,"   60
 Akwakaŋa said.
"In that case you must go immediately to your aunt.
 Go to your sister, go to your sister," he told him,
  his grandfather replied,
   Kwatïŋï said.
   He slept two days while food was being   65
   made.
"Go now," he told him,
 his grandfather said.
Next he covered him with sores,
 running with pus.
  He became disgustingly ugly.   70
Inside he was still *teh* beautiful!
 Here, here, here was pus,
  disgusting, disgusting.
   He put on his necklace and arm wrappings.
When the sun was here,   75
 "Kaw koh!" he arrived.
 "Akwakaŋa, Akwakaŋa," they said.
His aunt led him inside.
 "My young relative," she told him,
  "You are certainly here."   80
 "Yes," he replied,
  "I am certainly here."
"We were the very ones who invited you here, who invited you."
 "Very well."
He strung his hammock above that of her daughter.   85
 Her daughter was seated in the doorway.
  She glanced at him from where she was sitting and saw the
  running pus.
"He really is disgusting," her daughter said.
  "My mother sent for someone like this because he was
  ugly."
Pus covered his ENTIRE body.   90
 Inside, he hadn't changed, *teh* he was beautiful!
She went to lie down.

"Make something to drink for your younger brother," her mother
said.
    He was seated nearby.
"That's even more disgusting!"   95
    Her younger sister was in puberty seclusion, a maiden.
"You should go now to the water with your younger brother."
"How can I go with that disgusting person, pus-covered as he
is?"
    So he went by himself.
Atsidyi the Bat . . . look, he misled her,   100
    at the water's edge he misled her.
        Ta ta ta he tapped her on her back.
"Disgusting, disgusting," he said to her.
    "Don't touch me with your sores," he misled her.
    "He's disgusting," he repeated.   105
        "Don't touch his sores, go away now."
She never greeted him.
    He went alone to get firewood.
        She did nothing.
Only his aunt made his food.   110
    His wife never touched him.
"You're disgusting," she said,
    as she kept pushing him away from her.
In the water was piqui pulp,
    which was to be used for his ear-piercing.   115
        Because they were going to pierce his ears.
He slept, he slept, he slept,
    he slept five days.

She hadn't spoken to him.
    She would visit Bat's house,   120
    "Let's go to the water," she would say,
        and he would go there with her.
            She would go there with the same person.
            She would go there with Bat.
            Bat was really ugly.   125
He himself used to wrestle,
    Watsadya used to wrestle.
        His name is Watsadya.
"Look, my younger brother is going to wrestle someone."
    She took her seat and put it by the doorway in order to   130
    watch him wrestle,
        to watch Watsadya wrestle.
Her husband was right there,
        nearby.
    His uncle wrestled with Watsadya.

Then he slept,   135
    but nothing changed.

That was how he was when a storm began to rain,
    his grandfather was coming to him,
        to scrape him.
He appeared there at the water's edge.   140
    "I am going right now to the water," Akwakaŋa said.
        He went away,
            and his grandfather scraped him there.
Then he removed the covering *kïkïkïïïsok*!
    Mbok, he put it down.   145
    Teh! Akwakaŋa's body was still as it had been made,
        beautiful.
            His grandfather was the one who had disguised him.
            He had made him ugly.
                The other was still unpierced   150
                    Akwakaŋa hadn't yet been pierced.
Tsiu tsiu tsiu his grandfather scraped him.
    Every part of him, all over.
"Mother," she said.
    Her daughter,   155
        the secluded girl, spoke.
    She already walked to get water.
        She had already been presented.
"Mother," she said, "I'll go for water."
"Go ahead if you wish."   160
Then she picked up her water gourd,
    the *tafa* was what she carried—this kind of thing, our
    container—
        and *pu pu pu* she left.
As she ran there his grandfather was scraping him under his arms.
    "Who is that?" she asked him.   165
        "Is that Akwakaŋa?"
    "Look, my grandchild.
        Look at your younger brother, look.
    While he has always been like this,
        your older sister has rejected your younger brother.   170
            He has been like this all the time."
              Teh, he was beautiful!
                Tsiu tsiu tsiu.
She washed herself and then she returned,
    the maiden returned.   175
Then it was over.
    His scraping was finished.
    "Go now," his grandfather said,

"Go now."
"Tomorrow I am leaving, Grandfather," he answered.   180
"Tomorrow I will leave.
She doesn't speak with me," he said about Ñuku,
his wife.
Then he came back,
while his grandfather went away to his own settlement.   185
His grandfather disguised him, *kïdukï*.
How disgusting and ugly he became!
The mother was making cold manioc drinks from piqui pulp.
She removed the water gourd from her daughter's head.
"Mother," she said,   190
"I am going to bring down Akwakaŋa's serving bowl, his
tuku."
Teh! she was so pale!
"That's what's-his-name's container.
Unfortunately you're never supposed to prepare his manioc
drink.
Unfortunately you're never supposed to prepare his manioc
drink,"   195
her older sister said.
"I intend to do so," she said,
"I do intend to prepare his food."
They had seen each other at the water's edge.
Teh! They had seen each other's beauty.   200
Her older sister was repelled by him,
but she had never really seen him!
Then he returned.
Tikii, he came inside.
Disgusting running sores covered his body while still inside,   205
teh he, he was very beautiful!
He sat down.
"Akwakaŋa," she told him,
"Over there is some drink I've just mixed for you," the
younger sister said,
the maiden said.   210
"Very well."
He drank it.
He consumed it,
he consumed what she had prepared for him,
the piqui drink she had prepared for him.   215

When night fell,
"Mother," she said,
"Let's go out to the latrine area."
"All right," her mother said.

The sun was here.   220
   The rain had ended.
   "Mother," she said,
      "Your nephew seems to be pale, pale.
        Teh, he is beautiful!
   You've made your daughter marry such a person.   225
   I think he's been really deceiving my older sister.
      I think your nephew is probably very beautiful,
        beautiful."
When night fell he arose.
   "I'm leaving to cut some wood."   230
     Tafaku wood cut in long lengths.
   "Aunt," he said,
      "Tomorrow I will certainly leave," he told her,
        "I will leave.
   Your daughter has rejected me,   235
      your daughter."
   "Very well," she answered,
      "I agree, you must leave if you wish," his aunt said.
   "I certainly think your sister has deceived us again.
      She has always criticized those who would lie down with   240
     her."
        Then his aunt prepared food for him when night fell.

At the beginning of the day,
   at dawn he packed his things and went away,
      he went away.
        "I am going right now," he said.   245
His wife was still at the water as usual.
   She was at the water as usual,
     she had gone to the water.
   She was there with Watsadya her lover,
     with the ugly one.   250
        Akwakaŋa left while she was still there.
Then his wife returned,
     abandoned by him.
   Undik she came inside.
      He had started to leave while she was at the other place.   255
   "Your younger brother has left you once and for all," the mother
   said to her daughter,
     Ukwaka said.
   "Let him go if he wants,
     even now he's as disgusting to me as ever," she replied.
Then, "Mother," the younger sister said,   260
     the maiden said.
        "I will go with Akwakaŋa."

"Go if you wish, go with your younger brother if you wish."
She untied her hammock,
    she rolled up her seat and her mats,   265
        pï pï pï she walked quickly away.
        She went away,
            following him in order to become his wife,
            the younger sister was now his wife.
At a place very far from there   270
    she asked her younger brother to cut her bangs,
        to cut her bangs.
"How disgusting for her to have gone away with him," she said,
        the older sister said.
        "She has gone with the pus-filled one, gone with such a one   275
as he,"
At the water's edge he removed his covering, *kuuu tsok*!
    He threw his covering away,
        he threw it away.
He was a powerful being,
    a powerful being.   280
Bok!
    The name is *fugikï*, "running sores."
"You must stay here," he said.
    He left it behind on a tree stump.
        Teh! when he did that the color of his body lightened.   285
Then they went on.
"Akwakaŋa," she said,
    "Here I am with you."
"All right, come along if you wish."
    They went away after that.   290
Teh both wife and husband were beautiful!
    His covering was left on a tree stump,
        his sores were left behind,
            but his body was unchanged.
He was still unpierced.   295
Because someone else had to do it his people went to the ear-piercer.
When he came to his grandfather he was told about it.

When the sun was here he arrived.
"Koh, koh," when he was seen that was shouted out.
    Standing in the plaza,   300
        his followers said, "Akwakaŋa has just arrived!"
    "Leader, leader. Look, his wife is with him!"
As they came to a bend in the road,
        the others would see his wife walking behind him.
        "Yes, he does seem to have a wife."   305
He had already cut her bangs,

and on the road she had painted herself.
Teh he he she was magnificent!
They came into the plaza,
and they entered the house. 310
The sun was here.
She was seated there,
his wife was there.
She was another wife,
not Ñuku. 315
She was her younger sister.
Then Watsadya stayed with Ñuku.
Watsadya became her husband.
He was Ñuku's husband.

At dusk it finally happened. 320
The Bird's followers,
Kakasatsuegï the Fishing Buzzard,
and all the Birds,
Akaga the Jabiru Stork was there,
all the Birds were in the plaza dancing the
surrounding dance. 325
They were beginning to perform their ritual.
Akwakaŋa was beautifully made!
The Birds performed.
They were the ear-piercers.
When they stopped, 330
he went to the water with his wife.
"That's enough, that's enough," their leader said.
"When my dry season comes, the organizers will request the
performance.
I want to go to the oxbow lake.
I want the bark net to be set there, 335
so fishing can be done that way.
So that the others can perform the ritual."
Next they prepared manioc bread.
Manioc bread was prepared right away after he said that.
Their food, after he said that. 340
The women made manioc bread because the men were
leaving for the oxbow lake.
They all left for the oxbow lake.
With the bark net that was being done.
They were going to poison the lake.
They began to kill the fish. 345
So many were to be used for his ear-piercing!
(Be sure to watch carefully when it happens here.)

They arrived,
    they came from the oxbow lake.
        Their carrying baskets were filled with fish when they   350
        came.
    That person's house,
        and that person's house was filled with fish.
After a while they put the fish on grills,
    the fish were put there.
        This was their food distribution.   355
Another house was filled with what was to be eaten right away.
        And the fish in another house was for when they sang,
            set aside for their performance.
Late in the day they all came together,
    completing the circle.   360
    Their food distribution was fish,
        beautiful.
The next day they prepared the messenger's food.
    The messenger left to go to that same place,
        to his father's town.   365
When the sun was here,
    "Kaaoh, kaaoh, here comes the messenger!" they said.
    Boh, the followers cheered their messenger.
    They had left for a distant place, another settlement,
        a place just like this.   370
Someone led the visitors by their wrists to the plaza,
    and seated them.
        There were three to whom that was done.
The leader greeted them,
    and his father-in-law came outside.   375
        Kaŋaŋatï came outside to greet the messenger.
Following that he did the same to the one seated next to him.
    And continued once again.
Then they were ready.
    Three of them had come.   380
        Their messenger had come.
        "Tomorrow you must surely go, tomorrow."
        "Very well, we will escort our children."

The following day,
    "Children, Children, Children," he said.   385
    He asked that food be prepared.
        He asked that their food be prepared.
            To be eaten on the road.
    He asked that their drink be prepared.

He had asked for it. 390
They made some manioc bread.
All the manioc drink was put outside.
They were to take with them what they had just
prepared.
"All right, now."
They all began to leave. 395
They had just cut up their cotton.
Watsadya had just cut up his belt.
The ugly one had just cut up his belt.
Ñuku his wife had just cut up his belt,
his cotton. 400
So they all left.
Boh, she went as a guest with her mother and her father.
Everyone left.
"Tatata" went his bell,
Watsadya's bell. 405

Very late in the day when the sun was here,
they came close to the settlement.
When the sun was here the others sang,
the hosts sang.
The guests were standing still 410
they were standing still.
they were the ones who were standing still.
"Hooh!" the hosts shouted.
Those on the other side,
the guests shouted as well, "Hooh!" 415
They too shouted again.
Akwakaŋa's father's followers were approached by their messengers.
Fish were brought to them.
In his silly wife's carrying basket was her belt,
Ñuku's belt, 420
in her carrying basket,
heartless one.
In her own,
in Ñuku's carrying basket.
The messengers approached to get their cotton. 425
They were arriving.
The singing stopped,
They were finished.
Manioc bread has been prepared by their daughter.
"You must go to your parents, to your parents with what 430
you have prepared.
Get it ready."
This time she prepared food for her parents.

"All right."
She prepared manioc bread,
  she did that to wrap fish in,   435
   and she came to them.
They tied up their hammocks,
  the guests began to tie up their hammocks.
 Their followers, *boh* were cheering as they came.
  The followers arrived.   440
   Their newly ripened ones began to arrive.
"Let's go," Akwakaŋa told her,
 "Let's go to our parents.
  We'll take them manioc bread."
She also had cold manioc drink.   445
  Manioc bread was on his wife's head,
   wrapped up in her mat.
 Going that way, his arms were wrapped with cotton,
  he wore his cotton belt,
   his head was painted.   450
    Teh he was so beautiful!
Close to the path her father had tied his hammock.
 He was seated on his leader's stool.
As Akwakaŋa approached them Ñuku glanced at him.
  His mother-in-law glanced at him.   455
 As they approached them his wife was painted.
  When his wife did that,
   teh she was beautiful!
She held some fish in her arms.
  "Here comes your younger sister!" the mother said to Ñuku, 460
   to her older daughter.
She glanced at her younger brother as she continued to lie in her
hammock,
  while he approached.
   Teh ah hah!
    He was so beautiful now!   465
     Earlier she had found him disgusting.
      "How disgusting." She had been misled
      by the other man.
"Mother, he must be Akwakaŋa,
 all the while my younger brother has been this way."
"He was always like this before you rejected your younger 470
brother.
 He was always like this before."
"Mother, that's certainly he!"
 She sat up just as her younger sister arrived ahead of
 Akwakaŋa.
Her younger sister stood before them.

"Mother," she told her, 475
    it was his wife who spoke.
"Here indeed is manioc bread and fish which I have brought
you."
"Bring it to us then," her mother replied.
As they talked with each other he stood close by.
"Aunt," he said, 480
    "Indeed it is you."
"Indeed it is I and no one else who is here.
    We have come together with your uncle," she said about
    their father.
"Uncle," he said.
    "Indeed it is you." 485
"Indeed it is I and no one else who is here.
    Humbly I have escorted your brothers, my young relative."
    They talked with each other.
Nearby Ñuku sat up.
"Akwakaŋa, let's speak to each other now." 490
    He said nothing.
"Akwakaŋa, let's speak to each other."
    Akwakaŋa continued to talk with someone else.
    Her mother poked her.
"Let's go," he said to his wife. 495
"Mother, I want to leave with Akwakaŋa."
"When he was just exactly like this you rejected your younger
brother."
"Mother, I want to leave with Akwakaŋa."
    He was going to be the only one she desired.
The others left once more. 500
    The younger sister went with him,
        she went with him,
            he and his wife.
                After that.
"Mother, that's really Akwakaŋa, isn't it?" she said. 505
"You can't stay with Akwakaŋa.
    Because when he was just exactly like this before you
    rejected your younger brother."
    She was angry with her daughter.
        The others arrived having left Ñuku behind.
"*Ta ta ta*" her husband approached her. 510
    In order to participate in the ear-piercing he came to get his
    cotton belts.
"Ñuku, Ñuku, where are my cotton belts?"
"Waa! Those aren't your cotton belts, they belong to my younger
brother,
    they're Akwakaŋa's belts."

"Are they really no longer mine? 515
   Tiji tiji tiji," he giggled,
The others were dancing for the last time,
   since the next day they were to be pierced.
And so then they got ready for the wrestling to begin.
   They were all painted in order to wrestle. 520
    They were all painted.

When the sun was here the messengers went to escort them.
   To escort them so the guests could come.
They approached after that.
   From all sides people converged. 525
    Bah ha ah! So many different communities were in the
    plaza!
     Gathered together in a crowd.
The ones to be seated came, over here, over here, over here, like
that.
Some were already seated while the messengers came with those
to be seated,
   and they were seated. 530
It was done.
   Look, the sponsor of the gathering,
    he himself was his grandfather and Dogfish was his father.
     He was Dogfish's son,
      Akwakaŋa was Dogfish's son. 535
     He was his son.
      Together with the other,
       Dogfish was the leader,
       their leader.
His grandfather announced the wrestling champions. 540
   He himself was such a one,
    Akwakaŋa was the first to wrestle,
    and the next one,
     and the next one,
      and the next one. 545
     There were five counted.
Then the guests came to them.
   Tutututu, but they could do nothing.
    His grandfather had put a rock inside his palm,
    causing him to be heavy. 550
     Fuh! as he blew on it it entered Akwakaŋa's palm
     where he had put it.
They came together and they wrestled one another.
When they were done they began to play the *ataŋa* flutes.
   First those of one settlement went around,
    and then those of another settlement went around. 555

When that was done the messengers brought the guests inside.
They were housed,
in order for them to sleep.
In order for the guests to sleep,
they were housed.   560
When the sun was here,
"Mother," she said.
"I will tie my hammock beneath Akwakaŋa."
"No, don't tie your hammock with his!" her mother said angrily.
Her mother was angry.   565
His wife had lowered her hammock considerably,
the younger sister was very low.
"Mother, I will tie my hammock . . ."
Tuk! her mother hit her.
"He was always like this before when you rejected your   570
younger brother.
He was always like this before."
Tok! Her daughter wept.
"Mother, I will tie my hammock beneath Akwakaŋa."
She wanted to tie her hammock below his in order to be his
wife.
He didn't want her.   575
"Akwakaŋa, let's talk together now."
But nothing happened.
He didn't want to talk with her because she had
divorced him after what she had done to him,
she had divorced him.
Then they all slept, after that happened.   580

The next day it was finally done.
Look, their ears were rubbed with *tupagafotugu*,
their ears were rubbed with it.
Then at dusk they did that again,
on the front of where they were to be pierced.   585
All the Birds did that.
While they were singing his wife sat by herself nearby.
She didn't go to sing.
They were singing and rubbing the boys' ears so that
the blood would recede.
At dawn they came to the plaza.   590
His wife had made *sagaga*, the foamy manioc drink.
She had made their drink.
Sagaga was done for that because it was weightless.
Inside a large gourd bowl.
It was taken out to the plaza so that those who were to be 595
pierced could drink it,

and they drank it all.
When the sun was here they were taken to the plaza singing *egi*
together,
   with the howler monkey's song.
  Close to,
    in front of the house,   600
     inside the house.
  Then on the Birds,
    on Kakasa the Yellow-billed Tern.
  Next Akaga the Jabiru Stork,
  Kaka the Laughing Hawk,   605
  Ugisa the Great Egret (he was very young)
    and Tegutegu the Southern Lapwing.
  They were all painted with charcoal,
    it was put on the Birds,
     on all the Birds,   610
      on Southern Lapwing,
       on all the Birds.
        They were taken back to the plaza.
When the sun was here,
  they were turned around in the plaza.   615
    They were held seated on the laps of others.
  Close by were the people who were going to pierce them.
    They clutched the ear-piercing sticks which they had made
    from the wood of cotton plants.
"Tuk tuk tukjuhfo!"
    And finally,   620
     tuk! on one side
      and again *tuk*!
       The plugs were snapped off, *ndak*!
  Then they cured them with spells.
  When that was done, "Kaaw!"   625
    the ones who had been held were carried to the house.
  They were brought on one person's back like this,
    on someone else's back,
     and on someone else's back.
      They lay down without moving.   630
  They couldn't drink at all.
    No.
  They didn't eat any fish.
The others went away,
  the guests went away.   635
    Her father went away.
"Mother, I will stay here, Mother I will stay here, Mother I will
stay here."
  But no.

Her mother took hold of her by her hair,
      while she wept.   640
Because she wanted to become his wife,
      the rejected one's wife.
            She wanted to become Akwakaŋa's wife.
Her younger sister had become his wife,
      her younger sister.   645
She finally left weeping,
      because she wanted to be his wife.
            They went away,
                  Ñuku and her husband.

Their ear plugs fell off after a while   650
      They cut off a piece of the Amazon parrot's wing feather quill,
            it was cut off.
After a while they cleansed their stomachs with medicine.
      Their stomach-cleansing medicines were brought,
            the kind called *ketïti utuŋu* "piau's gas." 655
They slept, they slept, they slept.
      They hadn't yet drunk anything.

On the sixth day they cleansed their stomachs,
      in order to do something else,
            in order to drink some cold manioc.   660
                  So that afterward they could eat.
Late in the afternoon when the sun was here they were lined up
before the doorway.
      "U u u u."
            They vomited.
Their charcoal designs were still on their bodies.   665
      They washed themselves in order to remove their charcoal
      designs.
Those who wanted to eat right away couldn't wash off their
charcoal design.
      Laughing Hawk,
Yellow-billed Tern,
Jabiru Stork,   670
Southern Lapwing,
      that was what happened to them.
Only Great Egret hadn't eaten anything,
      so he remained white after he washed.
            Think about it carefully for now.   675
                  You will see it later on.
Then they came outside and were seated.
      Tih! We become so thin because we don't drink anything while
      we are doing that.

Although manioc bread is made,
    we don't yet eat any starchy food.   680
      We don't.
      We continue to sleep.

The next day "Kakagah koh" others began coming to see.
    Some manioc bread was eaten.
    Cold manioc drink was made,   685
      inside a pot this large,
        in that house, that house, that house,
          by the parents of the pierced ones.
            Their fathers and their mothers.
When it was finished they brought it from this house,   690
    from this house,
      it was carried to them,
        to their pierced ones.
          Bok, it was set down,
            and they went away.   695

      II
Then, look, he played his flute,
      Akwakaŋa played his corn flute:
[*Sings*]
    "Sun's wife, Sun's wife.
    The wife of the one who is jealous of us."
"I'm listening to all of you."   700
    He was their uncle,
      Sun was,
        Sun.
        He was their uncle.
          Akwakaŋa and his companion's uncle.   705
Next the other answered him.
[*Sings*]
    "The large gourd bowl, the large gourd bowl
    Akwakaŋa is the lover of his uncle's wife,"
      he said.
    "Well!" Akwakaŋa said.   710
      He had made love to the other's wife,
        so Taugi replied that way.

Not long after Sun made a dangerous being.
      a dangerous being.
While they were still all lying stiffly in their hammocks,   715
    it came toward them,
      Alagaga the Hyacinth Macaw.
"*Turuh! Turuh!*"

It was Hyacinth Macaw,
      large like a blue and yellow macaw,   720
         the dark one.
"Go away," Akwakaŋa told it.
    They were still lying stiffly in their hammocks.
      Those on the opposite side of the house were the Bird's
    followers.
"Here's something,"   725
      some corn was thrown at it.
      It smelled it.
Then, wanting it badly,
      Hyacinth Macaw chewed it all up.
When it was finished,   730
      Akwakaŋa grabbed it, *bok!*
         and put it away.
When the sun was here,
      "*Turuh! Turuh!*"
      It became his pet,   735
         it became Akwakaŋa's pet.
"Well, I didn't say I wanted to send you to him to do that,"
      his uncle said,
         Sun said.
"I sent you to chew them all up."   740
      Because the other had wrongly made love to his wife
Then Jogojogo Parrotlet came toward him.
    "*Tatatata*" that's how it calls.
    It entered, *tikii.*
    "Akwakaŋa," it asked him,   745
      "Are the misbehaving ones here?"
      These were his followers.
"Over here," he said.
    He threw wild *kutëgë* fruit to it.
      Kuh, kuh, kuh, it chewed it up.   750
Next he grabbed it, *bok!*
    It became his pet, *ti, ti, ti, ti.*
Again Kafugu the Howler Monkey came toward him.
    It entered.
"Akwakaŋa, are the misbehaving ones here?"   755
"Over here," he said.
    He threw wild *tapago* fruit to it.
And, again *bok!* it became his pet,
    Akwakaŋa's pet.
"Well, I didn't send you to do that!"   760
Then from a pubic ornament his wife had rolled up,
    Sun made Ekekuegï the Snake Monster.
      He painted it.

It was *very* long.
"Go now," he said. 765
  Mohoh! It was huge!
Its teeth were like dogfish teeth,
  its teeth.
Tuh tuh tuh tuh it slithered up to the door and pushed it open.
"Akwakaŋa, are the misbehaving ones here?" 770
  The other was thinking hard.
He didn't send his followers,
  send his followers.
    He cherished his followers.
He did that with his old ugly ones. 775
  He did that with his ugly people.
"Here, take this one," he said.
  He held one out by the wrist,
    close to the Snake.
It bit into her and ate the person up after it did that. 780
  It went away having done that,
    it went away.
And once again,
  "Akwakaŋa, are the misbehaving ones here?"
    One of his old ugly ones again, *buk*! 785
    Once again it bit into someone and *kuk*! *kuk*!
    once again it ate someone.
    Once again it went away.

The next day, once again it came at dawn,
  dududu, 790
    once again it approached him.
"Akwakaŋa, are the misbehaving ones here?"
  It wanted one of his followers.
Kok! one of his old ugly ones.
  It bit into that person after she was given to him. 795
    Buk! it ate her up.

Then night fell.
Again the next afternoon,
  it approached them again.
It had by that time—look— 800
  it had eaten three people.
This time when it came it poked its head inside,
  Snake Monster did.
"Akwakaŋa, are the misbehaving ones here?"
  "Here's one!" he said. 805
    Kok, again.
Then it swallowed her, *kwik* and went away as it had before.

Then there were some arrows there like this kind.
 The next day Taugi was planning to close up the house with a
rock.
  Bok! the house was completely sealed up with rock.   810
   They weren't able to go outside so the Snake Monster
   would be able to eat all of them.
When that was done Hyacinth Macaw flew to the top of the house.
 Tik tik tik it nibbled at the stone,
  tik tik tik.
 With Parrotlet,   815
  with its relative.
   Chew chew chew.
 Its teeth were an axe,
  its teeth were strong and hard.
   Together they were chewing on the rock.   820

At dusk they were still doing that and by nightfall they had made a small
hole.
 "Akwakaŋa. Go ahead, try this out."
  "All right."
 Tiki tiki, he was caught around the shoulders.
  Only his head and neck emerged.   825
 "Do it a little more," Akwakaŋa said.
  "All right."
 Tik tik, it was enlarged on one side,
  Then the other side was made.
   Chew chew chew it became this large.   830
   Tik tik tik on top of the house.
    Tik tik tik.
 Many people inside were going to climb up to it.
  Because his followers left through it,
   they went away.   835
"All right now," he said.
 Tik! He shot an arrow onto the sky,
  onto the sky.
 He shot his arrows one after another.
  Onto that place the arrows went.   840
 Tuu . . . tsik! like this,
  tuu . . . tsik, tuu . . . tsik.
   They were shot one after another,
    one after another.
    Tik! *tik*! *tik*! *tik*!   845
    Doing that they were used up, all their
    arrows were used up.
"All right, come on."

Cotton thread from one side of their knee wrappings was
unwound,
    also that from the other side,
        and it was all tied to an arrow.   850
Tititi, pupupupu it was pulled up to the top of the house.
    It was that long.
Bok! Then he thew it wa-ay up to the sky.
"All right now," Akwakaŋa said.
Their sister,   855
    Akwakaŋa's sister was Nzueŋi the Cicada.
She was the sister of those same people,
    they were her brothers.
She was lifted up,
    having been put inside a small basket.   860
Titi when she was only a short way up,
    "Umah umah umah umah!"
        That was the woman doing that,
        the woman.
            She was doing that,   865
            being very frightened.
"No, she's too frightened."
    The others were leaving.
"You must continue to remain here,"
    Into the earth she went,   870
        underground.
She dug into the earth beneath the main house post.
    They buried her,
        her brother did,
            with her griddle placed on top of the hole,   875
            a cover placed on top of the hole.
            Her griddle.
Her large mussel shell was nearby,
    a kind of long mussel shell,
        that same one.   880
"You must cut it up with this."
    "All right."
They left right away,
    Hyacinth Macaw with them,
    Parrotlet with them,   885
    Howler Monkey with them.
"*Kaw, kaw kaw,*" the Howler Monkey sang out.
    Taugi heard it.
"Go then, go with the mortals, become their food.
    So he will remain, as their food," he said,   890
        Taugi told him.

They were going at last,
finally they all went away on that thing.
It became a plant,
a very useless kind of plant that grows near the FUNAI   895
Post.
Kalapalo say, "Akwakaŋa's ladder."
They were all on it as they went away,
all of them,
his wife with him.
They became powerful beings,   900
their bodies eventually became stars.
The pierced ones became stars.
Their ear-piercing companions were Birds down here.
They all went away.

At dusk after that happened   905
The Snake Monster came as before,
again,
Early in the morning it came as before,
again.
Tuhtuhtuhtuh,   910
it approached them as it had before.
Only their ear plugs were left there.
Then *bok*, it came inside.
Then *tuhtuhtuhtuhtuh* it came further inside,
the Snake came inside.   915
It entered the house,
it was looking around.
"Akwakaŋa," it asked,
"Are the misbehaving ones here?"
No answer.   920
"Akwakaŋa."
"*Tsiu*! *Tsiu*! *Tsiu*!" their ear-plugs whistled.
"*Tsiu*!"
"Akwakaŋa, are the misbehaving ones here?"
But nothing happened.   925
"*Tsiu*! *Tsiu*! *Tsiu*!" they replied.
Akwakaŋa was by now very high above that
place.
It waited but there were no longer any of them left.
They had all gone away,
every one of them,   930
except their sister who was underground,
with her griddle covering her.
A griddle,

like this thing used for making manioc
bread.
Next the Snake came straight toward her as she stayed hidden.   935
Well, it had come inside the house again.
It came further inside again to search for them.
It searched for them after that.
It kept lifting up its head.
No one was there.   940
Well, the others were very high above that place.
It lifted up its face.
There was the chewed-out place,
their exit.
"Where were they able to go?   945
Where were they able to go?"
It crawled up onto the main house post,
the one in the middle.
On this its tail ascended.
Pupupupu.   950
As it approached
she removed her hat.
Tsiuk!
Dzududududududu duluk!
She cut off part of it.   955
Then once again it began to crawl up on its foreparts,
having had part of its tail cut off.
Tsiuk!
Bom!
Once again,   960
onto the house post.
Then *tsiuk*!
Uububububu bum!
And once again up on the house post.
The next piece began to ascend again to eat them,   965
to go toward the sky.
When the next piece tried to ascend,
it was cut,
tsiuk!
Uuu buk!   970
She closed her hat while it searched about,
it searched about further.
Nothing,
Once again it went. . . .
tsiuk! *bom*! it fell down again.   975
And once again it searched about.
She was underground so it didn't see her.

Much shorter than before,
    it went on.
    Tsiuk! *bom*!   980
    That time the head *tsiuk*! *bom*!
    There was nothing left
        So it died.
She picked it up,
    bububububu and whirled it about her head.   985
      "Oh, go far from here 'Rests on Mortal's bread'!"
      Tum! she threw its head into the water.
It became *ugake* the electric eel.
You've already seen it.
    Our people eat it.   990
      It became the electric eel
      that's what the head is.

Notes to Akwakaŋa

3   Ñatasa or Iñatasa is the name of Kwatïŋï's settlement where Akwakaŋa, the son of a daughter of Kwatïŋï, lived. The Kalapalo identify this place as located near the original Xingu Carib territory, in the southern region of the Upper Xingu Basin between the Culuene and Culiseu River headwaters.

30–32   The mother suggests that Akwakaŋa come live with her family so he can marry their daughter, after which the father will escort her back to her husband's settlement, where she will live permanently.

58   By saying "seems to be our deception," Akwakaŋa lets us know he realizes there may be something wrong with the daughter, since she is being offered as an adult. In the case of a maiden in seclusion, a boy's relatives would have first proposed the marriage take place. The stories "Kusimefu" and "The Tree Termites' Nest" in this chapter begin with descriptions of these acts of betrothal. Indeed, Ñuku turns out to have rejected all her parents' earlier choices, preferring her lover Bat.

134   Ñuku's father's wrestling with Bat is a sign that he did not consider the love affair between his daughter and this man worthy of public recognition. Had that been his inclination he would have initiated some form of affinal avoidance with Watsadya.

396   New cotton belts are made for dancing and wrestling during this ritual. They are "cut up" from very long strands of cotton that have been spun by a man's wife over several months' time for this purpose.

406ff.   This stanza describes the behavior of guests and hosts during the initial greeting stage of these rituals.

425   The "messengers approached to get their cotton" means that gifts of cotton were given by the guests in exchange for their having been invited and fed by these *anetaü* messengers.

486–87   These lines represent extremely formal speech between men who are acting in their ritual *anetaü* roles.

582   *Tupagafotugu* is the dried fruit of a cerrado tree of the same name that is scraped and mixed with water; the infusion is repeatedly rubbed over the initiates' ears to prevent excessive bleeding during the piercing. For a description of the ritual, see Basso, 1973: 65–70.

591   *Sagaga* is a very light and foamy manioc drink drunk cold by the boys, before the onset of their fasting. It is also served in other circumstances to any person who must fast.

697   A "corn flute" is a small oval-shaped gourd flute.

707 "The large gourd bowl" refers to liquid food Taugi's wife frequently gave Akwakaŋa in such a serving dish.

715 Boys must lie stiffly in their hammocks directly after their ear-piercing. The difficulty of maintaining this posture in their hammocks (they are used to sprawling and swinging about) diverts their attention from the pain of their ear lobes.

901 After climbing up to the sky, Akwakaŋa became the stars we call Archerner and Ankaa in the constellation Phoenix.

Kalapalo Adolescence

For the Kalapalo, adolescence is the time for developing moral and physical attributes of self that will remain throughout much of a person's life. As the point of departure for adulthood, Kalapalo adolescence must be carefully worked on, so as to initiate the correct processes leading toward a healthily beautiful, socially complete, and therefore fully satisfying adult life. This is why a Kalapalo in puberty seclusion follows elaborate, precisely directed rules for behavior—a rigidly circumscribed and formalized experience for the Kalapalo.

At puberty, when boys are said to begin to feel sexual interest and to wish to separate themselves from younger relatives, or upon a girl's first menstruation, a seclusion chamber is built within the parents' house by walling off a section of the living space. Living within this chamber for a period of time that varies from one year (for daughters who are not *anetaū*, or "leaders") to as many as six or seven (for boys who are attempting to become wrestling experts or bowmasters and who are also *anetaū*), the young person undertakes arduous ascetic practices that are designed to add flesh to the body—both height and plumpness (gross body mass) as well as luxuriant hair being considered especially beautiful. These practices obviously contrast with the more familiar European and Eastern forms of asceticism, which seek to diminish awareness of the corporeal self, but the goals of engendering control of immoral feelings are similar. The Kalapalo customs are designed to inculcate in a young person the desirable physical and mental characteristics that will be distinctive during adulthood.

Men and women agree that the practices of puberty seclusion are painful or at best uncomfortable. Medicinal practices include taking stomach-cleansing medicines that must be forced up (*tuwaki-*), a dangerous practice when the medicines contain a concentration of plant poisons,[2] and young people must frequently submit to bloodletting (*fifi-*), which involves being scraped over most of the body with an implement set with dogfish teeth. Virgin youths who dream of the powerful beings controlling wrestling magic (*īoto*, "masters of perspiration") can acquire special strength and skill that enables them to achieve the status of *kindoto* ("wrestling masters") but only after a lengthy period of regulated diet, the use of special (and sometimes very dangerous) plants for *tuwaki-*, and the strict avoidance of contact with procreatively active women. The virgin youth cannot eat hot food, turtles, grilled flesh, fats, or sweets; he must eat only cooled boiled fish. His manioc bread must be made by a young girl or a woman past menopause, and he must have no contact (even through speech) with a sexually active woman. Of course, he must remain celibate throughout this period. While the youth remains secluded he uses *tuwakitofo* (infusions "used for watering") made from the milky residue of roots from the *afusagī* plant (*Clitoria* sp., the bush pea), the sap from *ijalitefugu*, "tapir's stomach," or the plant called *ketïti utuŋu*, "piau's gas." All these plants have milky sap, which is supposed not only to strengthen the boy but to make him virile by causing the production of considerable seminal substance. (Some of these plants are also used to enhance a woman's milk-producing ability.)

After he has finished using this substance, the youth is visited by the *ïoto*, who instructs him about the rules of seclusion. Then the boy ties a single cotton string on each arm (to delineate the site of his future muscles) and paints himself with piqui oil (*ñukau*) from the edge of his eye to his ear (a line of intelligence; the "hard-eye" and "careful listener" are descriptions of intelligent persons), a spot on each hand and on his arms (again, sites of future strength). He uses a small gourd of the men's wrestling paint (*itali*, a tree resin women must never touch), which the *ïoto* prevents from ever being depleted. The use of these essentially colorless, transparent substances effects the acquisition of muscular strength and wrestling acumen that builds upon visual and aural skills while preserving the highly admired pale and unpainted skin tone of the secluded adolescent. After several years, the youth who has followed these medical practices turns into a champion wrestler whose strength is never depleted. When the *kindoto* dances during the great ceremonies attended by visitors from other communities, he is privileged to wear a belt of jaguar fur, the claws of the giant armadillo, and a decoration made from the skin of the anaconda to which is tied the stretched hide of a squirrel, all these animals being considered *kindoto* because of their unusual muscular strength. (The inclusion of the squirrel was explained to me by the fact that this animal has unusually muscular arms.)

In the past, boys also attempted to acquire the special powers of the *tafaku oto*, the "bowmasters." They experienced an initial period of dreaming that was interpreted to mean that such powers would be acquired in the future course of seclusion. Like the boys who became wrestling masters, these youths were expected to rub certain plant substances into their body scrapings, eat special foods, and refrain from contact with women. Other customs were supposed to ensure that a man's eyes never failed him and that he remained invisible to an enemy. Today, during the few years before he enters seclusion, a young boy's arms are scraped and rubbed with the plant called "dogfish's air bladder" (*afi atandaŋagë*), but in the last twenty years or so no men have trained to be *tafaku oto*.

The *masope* or maiden in puberty seclusion also attempts to cultivate physical qualities that will turn her into a beautiful, corpulent woman, a hard worker, and a capable mother. Initially, her seclusion practices are related to her menstruating for the first time. Just as adult menstruating women do, she must refrain from eating fish, but this prohibition extends throughout the first month of seclusion. She must fast severely during this first menstruation, and is allowed to drink only cold manioc soup for the first three days. After her first menstruation ends, she "cleanses her insides" with a *tuwakitofo* while her father hunts monkey for her to eat during the remainder of the month. The first month of seclusion is also a considerable change from unsecluded childhood for the *masope* because she must not touch anything lest she become a thief in adult life. She must remain celibate until she is "presented," when she is allowed to dance with wrestling champions during the great ceremonies. Although she may return to seclusion after such an event (daughters of leaders are usually secluded for three years), like the maiden who married Akwakaŋa she can draw water and bathe alone. She now begins to receive lovers and may by this time be engaged.

In other ways the puberty seclusion practices of both young men and women constrain activity and result in considerable sensory deprivation for extended periods. These practices include seclusion in a dim, restricted space within the house, maintaining a strict and spartan diet, whispering or avoiding speech entirely with people to whom one is not closely related, avoiding persons of the opposite sex, and reclining in one's hammock only late at night after the other household members have retired. All these austerities require the youth to learn to control hunger, thirst, sleep, sexual desire, the wish for visual and verbal communication, and even the expression of musicality, particularly during the early phases of seclusion, when it is important to begin absolutely correctly so as to proceed to the desired end. Young people who correctly engage in these practices are said to become especially knowledgeable about their bodies because they pay close attention to their organs of feeling—the animate organs of the body I discussed in Chapter 4—and to emerge a physically and morally beautiful person.

These young people are believed to be morally beautiful because they have been able to control polluting substances and potentially destructive feelings toward others. They are motivated by their *funita* for parents or other older kin who instruct them, and those who violate the stringent taboos or refuse to continue to seclude themselves and undergo the unpleasant body techniques after the first enthusiastic year or so (these are invariably young boys) suffer the serious disappointment of their elders. The older people sometimes deliberately neglect these young rebels for a time, refusing to feed them and insulting them in public if they fail to wrestle successfully. (One mother ridiculed her son by suggesting to an old widow that she marry the boy, who refused to enter seclusion long after the proper age. On a later occasion, after he lost too often in a competition at Waura, she tried to embarrass him by making obscene gestures that told of his love affair with a mature woman.)

Through the symbolic strategy of asceticism (of which puberty seclusion is the most elaborate but also including menstrual taboos, a range of dietary prohibitions, and requirements of temporary but lengthy celibacy for widows and widowers and for men in training for the role of shaman), the potential dangers of the Kalapalo body are held in check. Benefits accrue not only to the self but to those most likely to be harmed—one's family and community—hence the morality of asceticism. The individual turns the self into a physically pleasing object, neutralizing the evil forces within, thereby becoming a cherished and respected person and in rituals the active symbol of a community's moral worth. Kalapalo asceticism is thus one specific expression of the more general Native American principle with which Lévi-Strauss concludes the third volume of his mythological excursion (1978); "good manners" are the means of controlling dangers from within of protecting others from oneself.

The Kalapalo adolescent can thus serve as a particularly apt image of moral as well as physical beauty. A euphemism for a woman's lover or husband is to call him her "younger brother" or her "younger relative," the normal terminology when her parent speaks about the husband to her daughter. He is her "beautiful one" in both a moral and a physical sense. Yet in the myths these are the very people who most often provoke jealousy and anger in others and who in response withdraw from society or in various ways are especially responsive to the suggestions of powerful beings, thereby providing a test for themselves as well as certain members of their families. The repulsive disguise of parasites and running sores with which Kwatïŋï hides the beautiful Akwakaŋa is one example of such a test. It is a test of his tact for Akwakaŋa and a device for confirming Ñuku's nastiness, and it ultimately results in punishment that makes Ñuku regret her pitiless arrogance. As a motif, the disguise of running sores opens the way for Ñuku to come to understand her own faults, making her recognize that she has deserved what she got: Watsadya the Bat who (in another story) turns out to be a murderous nuisance.

Myths about adolescents clearly show the relationship of the "beauty" of a properly secluded person with a special moral authority that emerges from that person's behavior, for one who completes a rite of passage is allowed to make judgments and is held responsible for them, being expected to face the world as an adult, not an uncontrolled child. The varieties of physical work to which the body can be subjected during puberty seclusion result in differences in feeling and especially in moral action after young people—now about to face the world as adults—leave their seclusion chambers. Later, the social settings in which they find themselves, in particular the restraints and demands imposed upon them within the domain of sexual activity, provide the contexts for the emergence of these passively contained feelings. The most important context in this regard is of course marriage, with its imposition of stringent affinal avoidance, a careful—even stilted—and highly marked set of speech forms, and the injunctions to reproduce and to obey menstrual and postpartum taboos. In the domain of affinal relations, the Kalapalo impose what are undoubtedly the harshest moral rules, thereby creating a situation that conflicts markedly with the relative freedom—of speech, personal choice in the selection of associates, and lack of clear-cut obligations—of a child's early family life.[3] Affinal experience thus creates the prime conditions for emergence of aggressive feelings, which if not contained develop into explicitly violent resolutions. Kalapalo myths such as the following one about Agakuni, the man who married a jaguar's daughter, express fantasy—and anxiety—about how these motives might be realized and the inner struggles that people undergo in order to control them.

Agakuni
Told by Ugaki at Aifa, February 2, 1979

This is about their pet,
        the pet belonging to someone's children.
The sister was in puberty seclusion and her younger brother was also
secluded.
        They were there together.
    Being that way they often made love.   5
        They were there together in the younger brother's seclusion
        chamber.
He made love to his sister,
        Agakuni did.
                He made love to his sister.
Their pet bird was perched on their seclusion wall.   10
        Takugugu the puffbird.
    "Takugugu, takugugu, takugugu, takugugu."
        It kept doing that.
    It was calling out, "Takugugu, takugugu, takugugu, takugugu."
        It hadn't yet told anyone.   15

Once again, the next day,
    the next day,
        the next day,
as they continued that way over and again,
    it was his sister whom he desired,   20
        it was his sister.
The two lay down together in the hammock,
    he and his sister.
        They were *real* brother and sister.
Probably while he was making love to her their pet was watching   25
them.
    Their pet was a puffbird.
    It was watching them.
And once again the next day,
    he made love to his sister.
And once again the other watched them doing that.   30
    They were making love once again.

Because they kept on that way
    she became pregnant.
Their mother came to see her.
    She entered the seclusion chamber, *tikii*.   35
    "I want you to bathe yourself now," she said to her,
        to her daughter.

To the side was the younger brother's window and his sister's
window.
"You must bathe yourself now," she said to her daughter,
    to her child.   40
"All right," she answered.
Her mother saw that she was very thin.
    Teh, she had become very pale because of what had happened.
    She had become skinny because of what had happened,
        because she held something inside her.   45
            Her mother saw her.
"Why is she this way,
    Why has she become so thin?" she said to herself.
She noticed her breasts were dark,
    her breasts.   50
        The mother observed all this.
            She went outside right away.
After she went outside,
    their pet told her, "Takugugu takugugu takugugu takugugu,"
        it said to her.   55
"Takugugu takugugu takugugu takugugu,
    it was Agakuni who made love to his sister,
        made love to his sister," it told her.
"Oh! What is Takugugu saying now?
    It's always saying stupid things."   60
And once again, "Takugugu takugugu takugugu,
    it was Agakuni who just made love to his sister."
    Because we were able to approach powerful beings.
That was how they were,
    those of the Beginning.   65
        They were Dawn People.
We were coevals of powerful beings,
    so we were able to approach them.
And once again, "Takugugu takugugu takugugu," it said in its usual
way.
    There was no one else around.   70
"Agakuni makes love to his sister,
    Agakuni makes love to his sister," it kept saying to her,
        it kept saying to their mother.
Their parent said,
    "What did that one just say?   75
        What strange thing did that one say to me?
        Well, I just saw our daughter."
She thought about what she had seen.
    Having something seated in her womb because of what she had
been doing,
        she was beaten by her mother.   80

Next their father came to whip his son with his bow string.
He was furious with his son,
>he was angry with his son because he had made love to his
>sister.

Then he remained there,
>their son remained there.   85
He had become sad,
>their son had become sad.
His mother had not beaten him at all,
>she had only beaten her daughter.
Only his father had beaten his son.   90

Then when the sun was here he collected his arrows.
"Little sister," he said to his sister.
>"I must leave," he said to her.
>>"I'll go some place far from here," he said to her.
>>>"I'll go some place far from here," he said to her.   95
"Very well," she said to him.
"You must not tell Mother,
>don't tell her," he said.
"Very well," she answered.
Then he shoved his arrows outside,   100
>he shoved his bow outside.
Then when that was done,
>he plunged through it,
>>he plunged through the house wall.
He went away after that.   105
>He went away to a place far from there
>>because his father had whipped him in the way I
>>described.
>>>With his bow chord.
And so he went away after that.

The sun moved, moved, moved . . .   110
>until at dusk their mother parted the thatch to speak with his sister.
>"Where is Older Brother?" she asked her.
>>"Where has Older Brother gone?" she said to her.
>"I don't know, he went away.
>>'I must go far, far away. I'm going now,' Older Brother
>>said."   115
>>>It was late in the day when her mother appeared.
>"It's too bad that man of yours had to beat your son," said her
>daughter about her husband.
>>"It's too bad that man of yours beat your son," she told her.
She became angry with her,

and then she began to cry. 120
      Their mother was crying because she missed her son greatly.
Teh! He was so beautiful, Agakuni's fingernails. . . .
    Plants never were able to wound him.
Teh, he was beautiful! He had gone to the forest.

Just as the sun was setting, 125
    at the very end of the day he came upon a tree,
      as he walked in the forest.
    It was very large,
      a huge one that had fallen down.
He looked at it, he examined it carefully. 130
    "I'll sleep here," he said.
    "Because my father beat me that way,
      let all the wild things bite into me."
He placed his arrows inside the log.
    Then he looked inside. 135
      Lying on his back he crawled in,
        ti ti ti ti that was how he started to go inside the tree.
He went far inside,
      entering a tunnel which led to a side branch.
He went into a huge tunnel, 140
    he went farther into the tree.
There he remained,
    sadly musing,
      when just then what must have been the tree's occupant
      came,
        a snake came. 145
But it didn't come in the shape of a snake,
    it looked like a wild thing,
      a powerful being.
While he was sleeping,
    tu tu tu tu it came toward him! 150
"Well," he said to himself, "let this monster eat me.
    My father always used to torture me,
      so I will remain as I am," he said.

Then just in front of the entrance to its house,
      right in the entrance of the snake monster's house, 155
        tsuk it left its arrow outside.
        Tsuk it put down its arrow.
This was its weapon.
    Its weapon.
It came toward him after that. Crawling alongside Agakuni's neck, 160
    it came toward him.
      Dodododododododododododododododododo ahh!

He didn't move!
Then it went on top of him.
  Mbisuk, the last of it passed over him!   165
He went to his feet as it slithered past.
 Yes! He started to leave!
  He went very slowly,
   shifting himself along on his haunches
   tsuhguh, tsuhguh, tsuhguh, tsuhguh   170
    and he went outside.
He picked up the arrows.
 Tsuk the other arrow came together with his own so he picked it
up.
He went some distance farther and slept.
 "My arrows are still intact."   175
  The other arrow was still there.
   "The monster's arrow has allowed me to carry it away."
   He carried the monster's arrow away since it was
   friendly towards him.

Just at dawn the next day as darkness ended
  and the sun was rising, he said, "I'll go far away." 180
 To Adafa Dove settlement.
  Dove.
Tikii, he came very close to that settlement.
  The Birds still appeared as people.
 "I'll go there," he said.   185
  Tikii there was a woman there,
   a Dove Woman,
    a woman.
As she came outside she said,
  "I think there is someone outside,   190
   I think someone is right there outside the house."
 "*Tsiu, tsiu, tsiu*," he whistled to her.
  "Come here," he told her.
Then she approached him,
  she herself, Dove Woman.   195
 "Why are you here?" she said.
 "For no special reason," he said.
 "Are you really Agakuni,
  the one who made love to his sister,
   whose father beat him?   200
    Hi hi hi," she laughed.
 "Yes," he said, "I am he."
 "Why are you here then?"
 "I've come to be with you," he told her,
  "To be with you."

     "Very well, come on, come on," so they went on.   205
He became Dove Woman's husband,
        Agakuni became so.
He slept, he slept.
     "I'm going far away," he left her behind.   210
        "I'm going," he went far away.

He went towards a Jaguar's settlement after that,
        he went close to a Jaguar's settlement.
Tikii, as he entered the visitor's trail
     the daughter was walking towards him,   215
        Jaguar's Daughter.
She saw him.
     "Come here," she said.
He went to the Jaguar.
     "Who are you?" she said.   220
        "Are you really Agakuni?" she said.
     "You must be the one who made love to his sister,
        who was beaten by his father."
     "Yes," he said.
     "I see," she answered.   225
        "I have come to you, to you," he said.
     "Have you? I should tell you that Father has eaten all my
friends.
        He never allowed them to remain here,
           but Mother is not that way."
     "I see," he replied.   230
     "Now look, Father ate my friends.
        These are their bones."
           Bah! All those bones of her husbands!
             It was her father the Jaguar who had eaten them.
When he had finished doing that,   235
        someone else would come to be their daughter's husband.
"Woman's Ugliness,
        come here to me,
           I want to examine you for flaws."
             That's what he would say to the man,   240
               to his daughter's husband.
"Very well."
        Then that person would come to him.
           Outside they were still there,
             their bones,   245
               outside.
     "Very well," Agakuni said.
     "Let's go now, come on."
They went farther on after that.

"Mother," she said,   250
    "Mother, your son-in-law is here."
"Who is my son-in-law?" the other asked.
"Agakuni."
"All right, I will conceal him from your fiercely protective
father.
        Unfortunately your father always eats your friends,   255
            your father.
                Bring him inside here," she told her.
"All right," her daughter answered.
"Go get your younger brother if you wish.
        Have your younger brother come to me if you wish," she
        told her.   260
She left to get him.
    "Come on, now," she said to him,
        "Come on."
"All right."
        He came inside, *tikii*.   265
His father-in-law was far away.
    His father-in-law was someone who traveled around all over.
    The Jaguar was someone who traveled around that way.

The sun was here
    when he approached.   270
        "Quickly, come here to me," she told her daughter,
            the wife said.
            The Jaguar's wife spoke.
"Quickly, come here to me," she told her.
        "Your younger brother will eat toasted corn."   275
            "All right."
She filled a gourd with toasted corn for her daughter.
    "Here," she said,
        "You must be sure to make your younger brother eat all of
        it.
        Be certain, because your father will surely want to eat   280
        your younger brother."
        "All right," her daughter said.
Finally the Jaguar arrived.
    He arrived with his game,
        a few deer and a peccary.
"I am certainly here, Children," he said to them,   285
    to his children.
This was what his children were like:
    there was a woman, a man, a man, a man, a man—five of
    them.
        His male children had been full grown for some time.

Then while he sat there, 290
 his wife came to tell him about Agakuni,
  his wife did.
  "Old Man," she said.
  "What?"
  "Our daughter is in trouble, 295
   in trouble.
   Our son-in-law is here to be with our daughter."
  "I see," he said.
He rose after she said that.
  "Woman's Ugliness, I want to see you. 300
   Come over here so I can examine you for flaws,
    I want to look right now for flaws," he told him.
  "Very well," Agakuni said.
  "Go right now to Father so that he can look at you."
  "All right," he answered. 305
Agakuni rose
 and came to where the other was seated by the front door.
 The Jaguar examined him very carefully.
  He turned him around on each side.
  He looked at his feet, 310
   he looked at his nails,
    this way, he looked at his hands, between
    each finger,
     he was searching for wounds made from
     sticks.
      There were *none*.
  "Well, Woman's Ugliness is really acceptable, 315
   he is flawless.
  Yes, he is acceptable."
"Come here now," he told him.
 He wanted her younger brother to eat toasted quartz pebbles.
 He always gave them toasted quartz pebbles to eat. 320
  He wanted him to do so,
   her younger brother,
   her husband.
  He wanted him, her younger brother,
   to eat it. 325
Corn had been placed there next to some cold manioc drink.
 Corn had been placed there.
  Real corn that his wife had toasted.
 "You must be sure to eat this," she told him.
  "All right," he said. 330
Puk, the daughter came and picked up the other dish.
 The daughter ate that,
  she ate the toasted quartz pebbles.

Her husband didn't touch it,
  he was able to eat the real corn,   335
   "Kurn, kurn, kurn."
This was very old, hard corn that she had toasted.
"Well, Woman's Ugliness is really acceptable!
  He is really acceptable,
   the flawless one.   340
    The flawless one has eaten."
His daughter ate the toasted quartz pebbles
   while Agakuni ate the corn until it was all finished.
  "Father, there's nothing left at all."
  "Very well," he said,   345
   "I want the flawless one to join my children."
Then after that he married their daughter and became her husband.
  He was the Jaguar's Daughter's husband.
   Agakuni remained there, for a *very* long time.

Then she became pregnant,   350
  it was a boy.
   "Old Man," they said to him, the brothers said,
    "Let's go hunting,
     let's go hunting."
  "I agree, we should certainly go."   355
   For their game.
  "I agree, we should certainly go right now."
  "All right now, as you've said, let's go hunting," they said.
   "For deer,
    and tapir,   360
     and capivara.
      We should go for them," they told him.
       "We should be hunting those," they told
       him.
  "Very well, I agree, we should certainly go right away."

At dawn the next day,   365
  "Let's go gaming now Old Man."
To kill deer and capivara as they always did,
  they all went to the *akuloki* trees.
  "Stay here," they told him.
   "Stay here.   370
    They really came after this fruit here!"
  "All right," Agakuni answered.
Bok! One brother-in-law seated himself on the branch of a tree.
  Another of his relatives, of his brothers-in-law, was over there
   and their youngest brother was wa – ay over on the other 375
   side.

Soon after it approached them,
> a tapir approached.
>> The gluttonous one.

Agakuni was going to kill it with that thing belonging to
someone else,
> I mean with the Snake's arrow.   380

Now as it came toward him,
> *ntsako*! he shot it,
>> and it died.

He killed it with the snake's arrow.
> *Ntsako! Ubom!*   385

Once again something came,
> just a deer.
>> *Ubom!*

A capivara.
> *Ubom!*   390

By the time it was over it had become light.
> Those he had killed lay on the ground,
>> he had killed the beautiful ones.
>>> A deer had been killed but it was called "the beautiful
>>> one."

"*Tsiu, tsiu*, Brothers-in law," he whistled to them.   395
> They were all finished.
>> "*Tsiuu, tsiuu, tsiuu,*"

He called them to come to him.
"Brothers-in-law, come here!"

His brothers-in-law had only killed one.   400
> When the game approached they would growl,
>> and the others would run away because they were
>> frightened,
>>> so they only killed one.

Those of their brother-in-law were lying where they had fallen.
> He began to pile them together,   405
>> he did that to the tapir, the peccary, the deer, the capivara.

"Well, Brothers-in-law,
> how were you able to kill all these?"

"How were *you* able to kill these Old Man?
> Although this happened to them,   410
>> it wasn't our arrows which made them die."

"Very well," he answered, "You've observed correctly that I was
the one who killed them.
> But I cannot tell you how I did that."
>> He didn't tell them about the Snake's arrow.

The others then sucked the heads of the tapirs and drank.   415
> Here, they sucked on the heads.
>> They sucked, how disgusting, don't you agree?

"Let's roast some of the meat now,
          let's begin roasting it."
               "All right."   420
"I must not eat this, no," Agakuni told them.
     "All right," they answered,
     "Go over there to collect your own food if you wish.
          There are fish there.
                    Go over there to collect your own food."   425
                    "All right," he answered.
His brothers-in-law left,
     and they came to a camping place where they prepared a fire.
     They prepared a fire over which to place the deer,
          a small morsel of it.   430
               In order to eat their beautiful ones.
While his brothers-in-law were eating
     he brought something back,
          wagiti,
               and more *wagiti*.   435
                    There were four of them.
     He brought this to them,
          to his brothers-in-law.
     "Go ahead, eat it," they said.
     "All right," he said,   440
          so they all ate.
After they scorched the hair from their deer,
     they ate it.
          "*Tchew tchew tchew.*"
Then they divided some up between them,   445
     and they wrapped up the leftovers.
          They had become full.
"Let's go now," they said.
     "We'll return some other time to carry the rest of the food away,
     to carry away the tapir."
          The tapir would be carried away after that.   450
Finally the brothers-in-law were returning home.
     The youngest brother put some on his back.
     Next, *buk tuk* the oldest brother put some on his back.
When they were ready,
     "Let's go."   455

When the sun was setting
     one brother-in-law who was there sang,
          "Mmmmmm."
     "Well! Listen, Old Man!" she told him.
          "Listen.   460
               That must have been our children who just did that."

They understood that the others had successfully acquired game.
They understood them.
Then the others approached carrying the game on their shoulders.
When they were close by they called out once again, 465
"Mmmmmm."
"Well, our children are certainly successful, Old Man!" she said.
"Quickly, build a fire,
for our children really seem to have had success this
time."
They came while that was being done. 470
On their backs were tapir,
on the backs of his brothers-in-law and on Agakuni's back.
Tapir, peccary, capivara,
so they approached.
"Our children are just beginning to arrive," she said. 475
They arrived.
"Well, quickly, go get some mats!"
"We were certainly successful," they told them.
They put down what they had been carrying, the tapir was put down.
Bok! bok! Oh, a great pile of meat! 480
Then their father stood up.
"Old Man," she said, "Look at all this game your own children
have brought!"
"All right," he answered.
The father rose,
the Jaguar rose. 485
So, he came to suck on a joint of meat,
to suck on a piece of it.
Tsuu.
As he was accustomed to do,
he sucked on this side, 490
here on the top of its head,
tsuu.
And once again after that.
They spoke to their father.
"Go ahead, you must go prepare a grill," they told him. 495
"Grill this,
just a morsel of it,
so we can eat it
Your daughter's husband has used someone else's
possession to kill these beings.
That was what happened. 500
This same one would have been missed by his own arrows.
I tell you that he, your daughter's husband, did it that way.
That was how my relative killed all my game.
The *tañe*, what's-it's-name to whom that was done,
the tapir. 505

This is our relative's game,
> the game your daughter's husband killed.
We weren't the ones who killed them before.
> Only one person was the killer of them all."
> > "I see," he said,   510
"We don't know how he killed them," they told him.
> "I see," he said.
"He didn't eat any of this, none of it," they said.
"I never eat this," he told her.
> "All right," she went,   515
> > "All right," his wife said,
> > "All right."
"I must not eat it," he told her.
> "All right," she answered
> > "All right," she kept agreeing with him.   520
> > > "All right."
"Your daughter's husband must not eat it," they told him.
> "No," they told him.
"He must be allowed to eat fish, however."
"All right, that will be done," he said.   525
"So you must go shoot his food,
> because only that kind of thing is his food."
> > "All right," he answered.

Then about that time his wife gave birth.
> It emerged, a boy.   530
Once again it happened to her.
> A boy.
So there were two children.
> Two children of Agakuni.

Then he went to get firewood,   535
> to get firewood.
"I'm going to get firewood," he told his wife.
> "All right," she answered.
While he was there doing that a jaguar tried to eat him.
> another kind,   540
> > from another settlement's community.
This one was not at all like his own relative.
> It was another kind of jaguar who apparently tried to eat
> him there,
> > and so Agakuni killed it.
It died when he did that with his arrow as he had done before.   545
> With the other's,
> > the Snake's arrow.
It died after he did that.
> It died there.

Then he arrived home.   550
    "Who from here was traveling about?" he asked his wife.
    "No one," she told him.
        "I see," he answered.
    "Ask our parent, 'Who has been traveling about?'"
    "Father, who has been traveling about?"   555
    "No one," her father told her.
        "I see," she answered.
Next he removed his arrow from inside the place where he kept it,
    inside his wrist wrapping,
        and *tsik* stuck it between the house rafters.   560
Then at night it left,
        the arrow left for its owner.
    It went back to the Snake.
        It fled.
    It was ashamed.   565
        It was ashamed of having killed the jaguar,
            it felt ashamed.
    And so, it went away after it had done that.

When he awoke it had vanished.
    Agakuni got up to look for it,   570
        to look for the arrow.
        It wasn't there.
    It had gone away as I described,
        it had gone away.
"I must go now," he said,   575
    "I'm going away."
His discomfort,
    his discomfort grew because he was without his weapon.
        That was what the arrow had been.
    "I must leave now," he told her.   580
    "I'm going now."
    "Don't go," his wife cried as he went away after that.
    Agakuni went away.
He went back to his mother after that.
    He went away leaving his children behind.   585
    They were like this,
        still very small.
            Two of them.
    The younger brother was very small,
        and the older brother had just begun to walk when he left.   590

In his own settlement he remarried,
    he remarried a real woman this time.

With his own kind of woman he remarried.
Then he went with her to the manioc fields.
    Agakuni went there with his wife.   595
"Go to Daddy," his wife said.
    The Jaguar's Daughter spoke.
        They were this high by then,
            somewhat taller.
"Go to Daddy, to your father,   600
    make your father look at you."
"All right," they said.
    They went to their father.
Then while he was there,
    they saw him!   605
They came toward him,
    to their father.
They weren't at all afraid of him.
    They came up to their father to see him.
"Here we are," they said to him,   610
    "Mother sent us, Mother."
        "I see," he said.
Then when they were there another time
    his sons came toward him again.
He was far away in the manioc fields   615
    with his wife and her sister,
        two of them.
            They had gone on ahead.
The others came toward him as they had done before.
    Their mother went with them.   620
        Their mother came toward him.
Their father was in the manioc field planting their crops,
    with his wife.
        They were planting their crops.
"Go quickly to him," she said.   625
    "Go to Daddy," she said.
        "All right."
The others were coming near,
    tik tik, breaking off manioc stalks.
        They saw them.   630
"Hey! There are some jaguars!" his wife's sister said.
    "Jaguars! Jaguar children!"
"Well!" their father said, "These must be your brother's children,
    your brother's children.
        They've come to me."   635
            They came up to her.
She, the aunt, stroked them.

                They didn't run away from her.
            "Be sure you don't hurt them.
                Those little ones are your brother's children," he said,   640
                    their father said to her.
                    "Those people.
                        Indeed they are the ones," he went,
                            their father said.
        They didn't run away,   645
            they remained there while
                he squatted beside them.
        They were all seated together while his wife watched.
            She appeared there in the form of a human woman.
        Then she came to him.   650
            She was angry with him,
                with their father.
        "You seem to have married someone else."
        "Yes," he said to her.
        "Well, you will sleep these many days," she said to him.   655
            He will sleep five days.
        "So I will remain," he said.
        Then he became sick,
            and after five days he died.

    That's all.   660

Notes to Agakuni

   394   That is, the animals were spoken of as if they were fish.
   421   Agakuni only ate fish, asserting himself thereby as a peaceful human being. Presently, the Kalapalo do not eat what they call *ŋene* (land animals that are furred), this dietary
taboo being part of the general moral code called *ifutisu* (see Basso, 1973: Chapter 2).
   505   *Tañe*, Portuguese *trairão* (Hoplias lacerdae): a large, primitive Characin common
in the quieter waters of the Upper Xingu Basin.
   513ff.   See note for line 394.

Demonic Transformations

One of the most dramatic social configurations in Kalapalo mythology is the
crisis that arises when an individual (usually male but in one instance an entire
community of women) seeks to separate himself fully and finally from his relatives, humiliating or even trying to kill them in a particularly obnoxious manner
as he does so. In especially striking imagery, apparently ordinary human beings
transform themselves into dangerous monsters by means of extraordinary self-
induced torture or, less violently, by the application of poisonous substances to
their bodies. Their pain leads to acquisition of power dangerous both to themselves and to others; this is transformative power over life (*itseketu*), a power
that is clearly linked in the stories to sexual feeling. The theme of demonic

transformation appears prominently in the four Kalapalo stories reproduced in this chapter (and a fifth, that of Monstrous Women, that I consider in Chapter 7) that develop bizarre and fantastic images of sexuality and violence. To explain what they mean, I turn to the ways Kalapalo social life might have contributed to certain characteristically Kalapalo experiences of and attitudes toward sexuality and aggression and the relationship of the images of these debauched mythic specters to those experiences and attitudes.

Fitsifitsi
Told by Muluku at Aifa, July 6, 1979

"Let's go look for land snails,
   land snails.
  Let's go look for land snails."
  "All right," someone said.
Then they went to gather land snails.   5
   They went on to that place.
  They looked around,
   gathering land snails.
    There were so many!
  He found one,   10
   he found another.
    He found some land snails.
Then he shaved off the flesh of his leg with a shell,
   ti di di, ti di di, ti di di.
  He was working on his leg bone *ti di di.*   15
"Let's go," his friend said,
   "Let's go now."
  "Very well," the other said,
   "I'll be here just a while longer, I'll be here just a while
   longer."
Ti di di.   20
"Come on! I'm going right now."
  "I'll be here just a while longer, I'll be here just a while longer!"
  But *ti di di* he was working on his leg bone.
   He was trying to get it very sharp.
  It became a stabbing spear,   25
   a stabbing spear.
"Say, there's something wrong with him!" the other said.
  He ran away,
   the other one ran away.
    He was his friend.   30
  "There's something really wrong with my friend."
  He ran away,
   and he arrived home.

Tsik, tsik the other was coming back.
  Tsik.   35
At dusk and then at night,
 tsik, tsik, tsik, he was coming back.
  The door was tied shut.
   Tsik, tsik.
  "Hey, I want you to open the door for me!   40
   Friend, I want you to open the door for me, I want you to
   open the door for me!"
  Nothing happened.
   They were sleeping,
    so he went away among the trees.

The next day he came again.   45
 "I want you to open the door for me!
  I want you to open the door for me.
   I want you to open the door for me!"
  Nothing happened.
   The door was never opened.   50
 "This is how I will always try to stab you all.
  Like this."
   Tsidik! he stabbed the door.
He went away having done that.
  The monster went away,   55
   he had become a monster.
  What had been a Dawn Person went away,
   he had become Fitsifitsi.

Aulati
Told by Muluku at Aifa, July 6, 1979

"Let's go chop down the *aga* nest,
   aga.
    I've found an *aga* nest."
  "Very well."
   "It will happen at dusk."   5
Then as it was becoming dark,
  "Come along, you two," he said.
   "Let's go, Brother-in-law," he said, and to his sister.
    Three of them,
     two men and a woman,   10
      his sister.
  So then they went away to where the tree was,
   to the tree.
   "This is it!" he said.

His sister had a large pot.   15
    "Go ahead," he said. "Put it right here."
She put it beneath the tree.
He went up the tree *pu pu pu* on the tree.
    "All right now," *tuk tuk tuk*.
He was chopping it out.   20
    When he did that honey poured right out.
        "This one really did that nicely!" he told them.
            "There's plenty here."
                Tik tik tik, into the large pot below.
They came,   25
    the bees came to chew up his hair.
    They were biting him.
As they did that the honey kept pouring out.
    Tik tik. *Ku ku ku* they were eating his eyes,
        and his hair *ku ku ku ku*,   30
            while his blood dripped down.
    As it did so,
        a great deal of honey was pouring out.
            There was so much honey that kept on pouring out,
                so much of it!   35
The other sat there,
        his sister and his brother-in-law.
They dipped their fingers into it and as they kept on doing that
they tasted his blood.
        "Why is there *blood* in this?"
        His blood kept dripping down.   40
    "Hey! He just did a terrible thing.
        All this time we were made to taste blood, blood," his
    brother-in-law said to his wife.
    "There must be something wrong with your younger brother.
        He's not right.
        Let's leave him here."   45
The brother-in-law removed his ear plugs from his ears.
    Bok he put them down beside the big pot,
        and they fled,
            they ran away from there.
Tik, tik, tik.   50
    As he kept doing that honey continued to pour out.
    "Here it all comes!" he said.
        "Brother-in-law!" he said.
        "*Tsiu!*" the ear plugs whistled.
    "Here it all comes, Brother-in-law!"   55
        There was no reply, just "*Tsiu! Tsiu!*"
    "They've left me here."
    He came down.

By then he had no more flesh on his head,
    nor any lips,   60
        everything was gone.
            He was all bloody.
The others had run away,
    and when they arrived at their house,
        bok they tied up the door.   65
            Bok! the Dawn People tied it up.
Then the other one came there.
    "Open up for me, Brother-in-law, open up for me.
        I've returned to you."
            There was no answer from the inside of the house,   70
        nothing.
            He had to sleep outside.

The next day he went behind the house,
    behind the house.
His brother-in-law didn't go to bathe,   75
    he didn't go to the water's edge,
        he didn't go to urinate.
            He kept inside the house.
He didn't bathe,
    he didn't travel about,   80
        no.
            Then he slept for a few days.

At dusk the other appeared once again.
    And the next day the other appeared once again.
        The next day,   85
            the next day.
            At dusk,
                at night.

After he stayed there a very long time the man went to the water,
        to the water.   90
The other grabbed him,
        his brother-in-law did.
    "Here is my brother-in-law!" he said.
        Pik he jumped on his back and stuck fast!
They started to come back together,   95
    and they slept together.
He was always on his back.
    He had become a monster.
When the other drank,
        "It will be for me, Brother-in-law."   100
When there was hot manioc soup,

"I want to drink this, Brother-in-law," he said.
Fish,
and all of his food.
His brother-in-law became very thin,   105
his brother-in-law was starving.
Really!
He was starving,
his brother-in-law was starving.
Really,   110
the Dawn Person was starving.
His brother-in-law had become very thin.
"Brother-in-law," the man told him,
"Let's go fishing, fishing."
"Let's go."   115
They went on.
They kept going,
while the man shot fish, *tsik*.
Ku ku ku, the one on his back ate them.
Tak, ku ku ku.   120
He ate the fish raw.
The other couldn't even roast them.
When they came back,
the man had no fish catch.

And again, on another occasion,   125
"Brother-in-law, let's go throw the *kundu* traps, *kundu*."
"All right," he answered,
They left,
they left and they went on to the place.
Tok tok,   130
in the water,
in the water *tok tok*.
Even when he caught a fish,
ku ku ku the other ate it.
The sun was here,   135
here at dusk like that.
"Brother-in-law, I'm really feeling very cold,
I'm feeling cold all over.
You should wait here, here.
I'm really feeling cold all over my body."   140
"All right."
So the man lifted him off,
and he went on *tsogo, tsogo* through the water.
Then as he came toward the head of the stream,
he ran away.   145
"Brother-in-law, you're leaving me behind here, you're

leaving me behind!"
The man then went on,
    and he arrived without his food,
      he had almost starved.
    "All right," the other one said. 150
      He sat there where he'd been left behind.
A tapir came by.
  "Here is my brother-in-law!
    Here is my brother-in-law!"
      He grabbed it. 155
  "Here is my brother-in-law!
    You carry me."
Buh! They ran away and when it tried to eat some wild fruit,
  "Give it to me, Brother-in-law,
    give-it-to-me-give-it-to-me-give-it-to-me." 160
  It was starving,
    the tapir was starving.
      It was just bones.
Then it died so he remained there.
  "Wherever is my brother-in-law now? Where? 165
  Wherever is my brother-in-law?"

Following that Ñafïgï came by.
  "Here is my brother-in-law!"
Then he grabbed her.
  "Here is my brother-in-law. 170
    You carry me."
  "Now you come along with *me*.
    I'm not your brother-in-law, I'm not your brother-in-law.
      Come on, come with me as my husband."
She took him away then, Ñafïgï took him away. 175
  She took him away to her house.

Listen.

Kusimefu
Told by Kudyu at Aifa, July 21, 1980

Listen.
  He was a Dawn Person named Kusimefu.
    He was a Lahatua man,
      a Lahatua ancestor.
        He was Kusimefu. 5
          He was a Dawn Person whose name was
          Kusimefu.

He went to get firewood in order to get a wife.
   She was still immature.
  He went to get firewood,
     for one who was yet a virgin child.   10
   Such was his wife.
    She was a Dawn Person.
"Very well," she told him,
   her mother agreed,
     the mother of the woman.   15
  "Very well," she said to him.
   "Very well."
    The man continued to stay there.
Following that the other made manioc bread for him.
  That was his wife who made manioc bread,   20
   and she took it to him,
    to Kusimefu.
Following that he appeared where she was.
  Finally she had become a maiden.
   She had matured.   25
  When that happened to her
   she had already grown tall.
    She had matured.
"It has just happened.
  Your sister has matured."   30
   That was what was said to him.
    Her mother spoke.
     "Very well."

Then Kusimefu went to collect materials for her seclusion chamber,
    to collect materials for her seclusion chamber. 35
     Small saplings.
Next he built it.
   That is what Kusimefu did.
  He enclosed his wife,
   he enclosed his wife.   40
    It was ready.
"It has just been finished," he said.
   "Very well."
  His wife went inside.
  There the maiden remained.   45
   Moh! Her calves were huge!

Not long after that happened her bangs were cut,
   her bangs were cut.
  Not long after that,
    not much longer after that her bangs were cut. 50

With a piranha jaw.
And with what's-its-name, with *ogopa*, a bamboo knife.
That's its name.
It's very sharp,
with it Dawn People shaved their necks.   55
Our hair was cut *tsiu, tsiu*.
It was held somewhat like this,
kiu kiuk kiuk kiuk,
It always did things badly.
This was the Dawn People's scissors,   60
the Dawn People's scissors.
They slept,
they slept,
they made love.
They were constantly making love!   65
Continuing always to be that way for a short
while they kept on sleeping still.

After a few more days were counted and they had slept a long time they
went to throw *taka* traps,
to throw *taka*.
To kill fish.   70
Taka.
The mother spoke,
the old woman spoke.
"Daughter," she said.
(The sun was here, low in the sky.   75
It was almost dusk.)
"Daughter," she said.
"Tomorrow ask your younger brother . . .
ask that he take us to throw *taka*," she said.
The mother spoke,   80
the old woman spoke.
"All right," her daughter said to her.
Then *tikii*, he came inside with his firewood, *tikii*.
After a while she went to lie down with her husband, *oummbok*!
"Listen carefully now to what I say," she said.   85
"Listen carefully now to what I say," she said.
"What's that?" he said.
"Mother just said something, Mother just spoke."
"What did she say?"
"'Tomorrow he will take us both to throw *taka*,   90
to throw *taka*.
He will take us both.'"
"All right," he said,
"All right."

Then their food was prepared,   95
    and manioc bread was made,
        for eating fish.
            He was lying.
                He was going to become a *tugufi* catfish.

Listen carefully while I tell you about it.   100
    At dusk it became dark.
    At the very beginning of the next day,
        "Let's all go now," he said.
    He picked up his arrows.
    Their food had been wrapped up,   105
        and they went away,
            they went away.
    The old woman was with them.
        The mother,
            the wife's mother, that is.   110
Then it continued this way,
    they kept on going farther.
        They were doing so on the trail, *titititititi*.
        They went on.
            The poor old woman as well.   115
Then when they were very far away,
    they were at Fish's Charcoal,
        Tugufi's Charcoal.
            This is "Fish's Charcoal."
                He painted himself with it.   120
"This is such beautiful charcoal," he said to his wife.
    "Paint it on me," he said.
        "All right," she said.
        "Right now, right now."
His wife went away.   125
    "Mother," she said.
        "I'll stop here for a while,
            Kusimefu wants to be painted with charcoal."
"Very well, do as you wish, go ahead."
Then she painted him.   130
        He also painted himself.
He himself *tïk* put it on himself.
    On one side.
His wife put it on his other side.
    On the other side.   135
        Tak, tak, with this kind of spotted design, look.
        With this kind of design, *tak, tak, tak*.
        This was to be his design,
            this was to be his design.

Tak, *tak*, she put it on him.   140
    teh he, it was so beautiful!
"Let's go now."
    "Let's go."
Ti ti, they went on after that was done,
    they went on.   145
When they had gone farther and were much farther away,
    he himself was first,
        the husband was first.
Then behind him was his wife.
The old woman was the last,   150
    the old woman.
Then when he had gone on ahead of her somewhat,
    not far from the fish traps,
        she began to pee,
            his wife was peeing.   155
While his wife was peeing the other one went on ahead of her.
    The old woman came up behind him,
    his mother-in-law came.
When they had both gone on still farther,
    he looked at his penis,   160
        he examined his penis carefully,
        Kusimefu did.
"Ouch!" he said.
    He paused.
        "Ouch!"   165
While they stood there together,
    his wife approaching from behind,
        giii he rubbed it.
        He rubbed it hard.
"Yesterday when we went to collect firewood you sharpened my   170
penis," he said,
    while he rubbed himself *biii*,
        he did that to his mother-in-law!
        His wife was still approaching him from behind
        when he did that.
"Oh, it's really me!
    It's me!"   175
        There he was having done that,
        truly ashamed,
        ashamed.
Bïtïïï he ran off,
    while the other one stood where she was.   180
Tum! he went into the water.
He went away as a *tugufi* catfish having done that.
    He deceived them.

He went away as a *tugufi*.
     Tum! into the water.   185
"Come here quickly!" his mother-in-law said to his wife,
   "Come here quickly!
  Why didn't you tell him you had to pee?
  I was far away when you peed."
"Why should I have done so?" her daughter asked.   190
   "Why should I have done so?"
"Your younger brother did a shameful thing which shocked me,
   your younger brother."
"What was it that he said?" she asked.
"'Well, it seems that when we went to collect firewood you must   195
have touched this thing here.'
   When he was there, it's true, you did sharpen your younger
   brother's penis,
     you sharpened your younger brother's penis."
"Ah ha ha!" her daughter laughed,
   "Where did this happen?"
"Close to where the *taka* were thrown,   200
  the *taka* were thrown."
    "I see."
"Why didn't you let him know you were peeing?" she went,
   the old woman said,
     her mother said.   205

Mbiii, his arrows were scattered all over.
   He had thrown away his arrows.
  "Your younger brother's arrows have just been left here."
  "We'll wait here, then."
   Buk, they sat down.   210
They waited, they waited, they waited . . .
   until the sun came here.
  "What a long time!
  Where could he be?"
   He had already turned into a fish.   215
  "What could he have done?"
"Go look right away!" she went,
  the mother said,
   the mother said.
    "All right," her daughter answered.   220
Tsogo tsogo, she walked into the water and crossed to the other side.
  "KUSIMEFU!"
  Nothing.
  "KUSIMEFU!"
  Nothing.   225
  "KUSIMEFU, COME ALONG NOW!

Mother is hungry for fish.
  You were foolish to do that to her,
    you were foolish.
KUSIMEFU!   230
  KUSIMEFU!"
    Nothing!
"I will look some more."
  Tsogo tsogo his wife went on.
  Tsogo tsogo tsogo,   235
    well, fish had become caught in the traps.
      They hadn't been removed.
        In each one of them they had been caught.
  "Where IS he?" she said.
    "Mother!" she said.   240
      "Mother! where IS he?
        Where?"
"I don't know, I know nothing about where your younger brother
went."
"Mother, come here so we can look for him together."
Then they went looking for him,   245
  into a shallow pool where the water was not very deep,
    going farther toward where it became somewhat deeper
      there he was . . .
        floating.
His arms had become pectoral fins,   250
  pectoral fins.
His legs were the tail.
His penis was this part.
His little feet . . . his tail spines . . . *tugufi*'s feet had been his
own feet.
  So black!   255
Listen now!
  So black!
    With tiny spots spaced widely apart.
He had been a Dawn Person.
  He became something which remains in Lahatua Lake,   260
    he became so.
      Kusimefu is his name,
        Kusimefu.

"Mother, here he is!"
  "Come on!"   265
    They surrounded him.
  This part of him still was a human foot,
    still human.

All the rest here and here was fish
    fish,
        fish.   270
Just this little bit was still human,
    still human.
They tried to grab him.
    Nduk! he threw his wife off,   275
        his wife was thrown off.
He went away having done that,
    he went away.
They returned mourning for him after he had done that,
        they mourned for him.   280
"Why are they doing this for him?"
"Alas, there we began to mourn him!"
"What happened to him?"
"We saw it. Your brother is no longer our deceiver.
    He's now transformed into a fish,   285
        he's now transformed."
"Where did that happen?"
"Close by," she said.
    "Yes, he's just become a *tugufi*.
        When we touched him he pushed us away.   290
        He threw us both off from him.
            He was pushing us around."
                "Huu," everyone kept crying as she
                spoke.

Listen.
    He was a Dawn Person,   295
        a Dawn Person.

The Tree Termites' Nest
Told by Kudyu at Aifa, July 21, 1980

Listen,
    there was even someone else,
    who was another Dawn Person.
    An ancestor of ours, someone like we people here.
This time he was a Kalapalo,   5
    a Kalapalo ancestor.
Just as we do he also
    kept collecting firewood,
        he was collecting firewood.
In order to have his wife,   10

        his wife.
We collect firewood,
      we people here collect firewood.
We people here collect firewood
      for someone such as that person.
Such as her,
      for one of our nearly ripened ones,
In order for her to be someone's wife.

So, *tafaku* wood is what he collected,
      tafaku wood is what he collected
        for payment.
      Puk,
        why, *tafaku*
          to her mother.
Next her parent went outside to get it,
        to get it.
      "Well, since this is what he has just begun to do our relative will
      tie his hammock up, our children will eventually tie their
      hammocks up together," she said,
        she said.
      The old woman spoke after he did that,
        the old woman was the person who spoke after he did
      that.
She was talking about what he had done,
      she was talking about it.
"Very well," her father said.
For some time the woman's parent gave out the firewood.
      She gave out what the other kept bringing her
        among her brothers and sisters.
      She brought it *bok*.
      To this person,
        to that person.
So, she shared it among her brothers and sisters,
      they were going to be his parents-in-law,
        they were to be his parents-in-law.
So that was indeed how they were,
That was indeed how they were.
And *we* are.

She finally matured, you see,
        she finally matured.
      It was over.
"It's time for her bangs to be cut."
      That's what they did in connection with that, so someone came

15

20

25

30

35

40

45

50

to escort her to him.
That's what was done in connection with that.
"It's time for her bangs to be cut."
So our escort, her escort went,
    our woman went,
    a woman went.   55
When that was done she was brought outside.
Next payment for her was brought out.
    Shell belts were brought out.
    To her mother,
    To her parents,   60
        to her parents.
    Payment to her parents.
    Shell collars to the men,
        shell belts to the women.
    To others shell belts,   65
    Toucan feather headdresses,
    Oropendola feather headdresses.
    That was how it was in the past,
    That was how it was in the past.
    That was what he did,   70
    That was what he did.
    The woman was someone he paid for,
        someone he paid for.
However, had it been an ordinary woman he wanted to arrange this
for,
        there would have been no payment.   75
        None.
    Except for someone like this woman here,
        a widow, a widow someone wants to arrange this for,
        someone else's wife who becomes our wife,
    we pay for her.   80
    Yes, we pay her older brothers,
        her brothers.
    That's what must be done.
"Very well," they say to him,
        "Very well," they say to him.   85

Then she stayed there
    maturing,
    maturing.
Again he brought her outside.
So that he could seclude her,   90
        so that he could seclude her.
    That was done.

Then after a lo – ong time her bangs were cut for her.
Then after he did that they slept, they slept
                    five days.   95

"Let's go get some wood now."
            "As you say, let's go."
His wife painted herself.
            Elaborately,
                    his wife painted herself.   100
Ti ti ti a long way.
            "Let's look for our firewood around here."
            "No, let's go farther on over that way."
He was really lying.
He wanted to devour her.   105
            he wanted to devour her.
                    Her husband.
            He wanted to devour his wife.
                    Yes.
Ti ti ti "Around here."   110
            "Let's go farther on," he said.
            A long way.
Carefully he went looking for a *kwō* tree,
            looking carefully.
            One like this, this size.   115
Teh, he was looking for one that was perfectly straight.
            He wanted to find one like that.
            He wanted to find one like that.
There it was,
There it was.   120
            One like that was there.
"Wait right here,
            wait right here.
            I'm going now for our firewood,
                    I'm going now for our firewood.   125
            Go *way* over there.
                    Go *way* over there.
                    Be sure not to come toward me.
            Only when you hear me *tuk tuk* cut into it, will
            you come."
He really lied.   130
He was feeling estranged from his wife.
He wanted to devour her.
            "All right," she said.
His wife remained over to the side where he had told her to stay.
            "I'll stay here," she said.   135
So she cleared the brush around her,

      she cleared the brush around her,
         for what was going to fall.
Tsidik,
      her husband was on it,   140
         he was on it.
Tsïgïtsïgï, he climbed up to the highest fork in the tree,
         to a fork in the branches,
             gïrïk,
      he sat down on top of it.   145
However, he was going to slide down the tree because he wanted the
tree to cut open his stomach.
The tree really chewed up his stomach.
The tree,
         the tree.
Dizdizdizdizdiz tsidide dïïk!   150
Once again he did as before *tsïgïtsïgïtsïgï* to do that
         dididididididiiiii, didik buuk!
And once again he did as before.
Once again.
Look: Because he was doing that the tree rubbed it all off, it rubbed off   155
his stomach.
      His guts were exposed by the tree when he did that,
         his guts were exposed.
Kïtsikïtsikïtsïgïï
      but when once again he did as before,
         his eyes were rolling from pain when he did that.   160
      But this time he became a monster when he did that.
         Mbiih.
      When that happened to him these parts, the contents of his
      stomach were all exposed.
Think of it!
So much blood was there!   165
         on the tree.
      Blood, from his having done that.
      Mah haah! So much blood was flowing.
"It's been a long time, I wonder what he's doing?" she asked herself,
         his wife said.   170
      "It's been a long time, I wonder what he's doing?"
Meanwhile because he had done that horrible thing to himself,
      "Um!" I'm told he kept saying,
      "Um!" he had come down to the ground.
      "Um!" he was really grunting hard,   175
         he was grunting.
      "Um!" I'm told he kept saying.
Tsidik, pïtsïpïtsïpïtsï that was what kept happening after that to his
stomach parts.

These parts were all falling out.
He was a real monster now,   180
    he had just been transformed.
Having done that, you see, his teeth had grown out,
    his teeth had grown out.
They came from here because he kept wanting them to,
    so he could use them on her.   185
He wanted to devour his wife's body,
    his wife's body.
Listen to that!
    Listen.
He was a Dawn Person.   190
    A Dawn Person.
    A long time ago he chased one of us.
    Yes.
"Um!" he kept saying.
    "What could that be over there?" she kept asking herself.   195
She approached very carefully!
    Very carefully, very carefully she approached, very. . . .
Searching, searching, while searching.
Pïtsï pïtsï pïtsï
    so he kept coming toward one of us.   200
"Um!"
"What could that be?
I don't think this is safe at all for me," she told herself.
    "For me.
What could have happened here?" she said. "What could have   205
happened here?
I'll look some more, I'll see.
    I'll see."
So meanwhile he kept going on insanely toward the fallen tree,
    now, toward the fallen tree.
"Oh!"   210
    Now she was really frightened by what was happening.
"What could have happened here?
What happened?"
But meanwhile her husband still kept on going farther.
    "What could this be?" his wife said,   215
    his wife said.
        "What could this be . . . ?" "Um!"
He ran right toward her,
    he ran right toward her.
He was going right toward his wife,   220
    in order to devour her.
"*Kïtah!*"
    Well, but she saw him, just as he was coming at her,

she saw him.
And she dashed away!   225
She ran off.
He was running right at his wife!
Tututututu when they had gone on like that for a long way,
well, he left his wife,
he left his wife.   230
He returned after he did that to her,
he returned.
He returned to that thing he had been concerned with, you see,
and then he became stuck on the tree!
Tsïgïtsïgïtsïgï pïtsïpïtsï all the wa-ay up to the   235
highest fork *mbiih.*
BUT THIS TIME HE DIED ONCE AND FOR ALL, her
husband
died.
Mbiih, he died.
On the tree.   240

Kutufu the tree termites' nest,
that was he himself.
That was a human being.
Its red thing,
its red thing is his very intestines.   245
His intestines, the contents of his stomach,
his intestines.
His stomach parts, his intestines,
they're right on the tree,
like that.   250
That thing itself,
that's his very intestines,
that's the remains of a human being.
That was how that dreadful monstrous vision came into being.
Termite House came into being, a monstrous vision.   255
When we are about to die we see him, *teh he*, wearing
his beautiful necklace and his earrings.
Another time when we see it, it has become a termites' nest,
it has become earth.
That's what happens,   260
That's a human body,
a human body.

So she came back,
his wife came back,
mourning him,   265
mourning him.

"Whatever happened to him? Whatever happened to him?" they asked
her.
    "Well, he's no longer our deceiver,
       he's transformed himself.
          I'll never know why he transformed himself.   270
    Go see for yourselves,
       go see for yourselves," she told them,
          she told them.
    She told her brothers,
       her older brothers.   275
"Go see for yourselves," she told them.
    So they went on after she said that,
    Ti ti ti ti.
    "We were right here," his wife said.
When they had gone farther on,   280
    "We must remain perfectly quiet as we go,
       perfectly quiet,
      He is our devourer,
       he is our devourer."
    So she said that to them,   285
       his wife spoke.
Then they went
      toward his remains.
      Toward what was left of him.
    "Look, Older Brothers.   290
      Look.
    This is the place where I stayed before.
    Here is where he left me.
    Indeed it was he,
      he himself."   295
They went on very carefully looking for him.
    "Watch out for him! Watch for him!"
As they continued farther on they suddenly saw it *uumbuk.*
    So, there was the termites' house, there it was attached to the
    tree.
    Holding on fast like this, embracing the tree,   300
    He had become a termites' house.
    His intestines extended out as its cord,
      that was his intestines.
    That was just the way it was,
      that way.   305
He died doing that, he died doing that.

It's finished, look.
    It's finished.
      That's certainly all there is.

Although each of these stories is constructed around a focal character whose name is sometimes used as a title, it is crucial to understand the dramatic confrontation of the entire group of relatives, as is true for all Kalapalo stories. The reactions of these relatives and the responses of the focal character to their reactions are important, for what is fundamental in their drama is not simply one character's behavior and feelings but the dynamic relationships that unfold in the narrative. The focal character's temperament needs to be seen as a construct of his relationship with the others, rather than as an independent and inherent mode of relating toward them, uninfluenced by his social environment. Nonetheless, through the character's active relations with others we are able to understand a sadistic person who manifests compulsive violence motivated by the desire to achieve pleasure.

Each of the four myths opens in a household where the protagonists' relationships are characterized by their manner of addressing one another and, in some of the stories, by a somewhat stereotyped description of activities normally associated with persons classified in the relationship category in question. These activities and the conversations of the characters thereby engaged are a prefatory comment by the narrator that describes the character's life and comportment as normal and customary. The listeners are persuaded that the people in the story are conforming to etiquette appropriate to their relationship and by implication that they feel the appropriate *ifutisu* for one another. In the stories that begin by examining a relationship between spouses (Kusimefu, Kutufu, Monstrous Women), emphasis is placed on the feelings of *funita* and *ifutisu* between husband and wife, their sexual attraction for each other, and their mutual willingness to constitute a productive unit, all in keeping with their marital status.

In the story of Aulati, for example, a young man living with his sister and brother-in-law suggests that they all collect honey from a bees' nest he has discovered. In the stories "Termites' Nest" and "Kusimefu," each man is described in a lengthy introduction as having been recently married, living within his wife's household, and following the severe avoidance practices newlyweds follow in their association with parents-in-law. In "Termites' Nest" the man suggests to his wife that they look for firewood, while in "Kusimefu" the mother-in-law suggests to her daughter that they all go fishing; each is an activity typical for these relatives, particularly during the early period of a marriage. Finally, in the story of Fitsifitsi two close friends decide to collect land snails. Although the characters are not husband and wife, their relationship is also close and affectionate.

In the initial situation, then, relatives are about to engage in a familiar and respectable activity, during which the chief protagonist, either by suggesting or agreeing to participate, shows himself to be generous and helpful toward the others. The domestic household—the principal place in which these sentiments are expected to be generated and perpetuated—is the setting.

After this prelude, the action shifts to a site away from the settlement, where the characters begin their collective activity. This new site is often familiar to people listening to the story; it is frequently named and associated with a useful resource, and this identification reinforces the sense that the activity being performed is a normal one associated with social tradition. The new dramatic arena is still within the territory of human activity (not the domain of powerful beings). When the relatives arrive at this new site, the focal character speaks to them, indicating what he wishes to do and speaking as if everything continues to be normal. At this point, however, the narrator interrupts to comment upon the character's real motive for drawing the others to that place: he wishes to transform himself. The narrator's comment on the character's deceitfulness and his statement of motive serve to heighten the narrative tension and create among the listeners a deeper interest in what will happen next. This heightening of tension makes the listeners acutely aware of the entire social context that has just been described. Immediately the listeners become conscious of the dark side of social relations: the possibility that behind polite language and outward conformity lie unspoken resentment, a contempt for ties that are ostensibly enduring and impulses that are murderous.

Suddenly the focal character's demeanor changes. He begins to transform himself into a monster. In the stories of "Termites' Nest," "Aulati," and "Fitsi-fitsi," whose motive is to kill their relatives, this change is accomplished through bizarre self-inflicted torture: one man scrapes away the flesh of his own leg, another allows his face to be disfigured by biting insects, and a third rubs off the flesh of his stomach as he repeatedly slides down a tall, rough tree trunk. The resulting intense pain causes these insane characters' "eyes to roll" and their teeth to grow into grotesque fangs. They become monsters: devourers, stupefiers.

In the story of Kusimefu, the man plans to rid himself of his female relatives by turning himself into a fish; he paints himself in the spotted design of the large *tugufi* catfish, using a substance "belonging to" that fish.[4] Kusimefu's manner of separating himself from his mother-in-law is (from the perspective of linguistic etiquette) no less violent than that of the murderous characters in some other stories. Kusimefu speaks salaciously to his mother-in-law, with whom he is expected to observe a modest silence. His words are "painful," not only to his mother-in-law but to Kusimefu himself. Shocked and intensely shamed by his realization of this "mistake," Kusimefu plunges into the water. His transformation is achieved by the acute shame he has created in himself.

In all these examples, after the transformation process is described, the monstrous appearance of those with evil intent—their huge teeth, wildly unfocused eyes, loss of facial features, a leg turned into a stabbing instrument—signifies the true motives behind their transformation and specifically how they attempt to kill their victims: devouring, starving, piercing. These motives represent distorted or fearfully extreme physical processes (eating, fasting, sexuality) that are regarded in their restrained expression as the foundations of life.

Although the focal character in each of these stories is the agent of his own transformation, his relatives actually separate themselves from him. When the monster is discovered they flee from him rather than trying to overcome or kill him.

When the final break occurs, it is accompanied by a statement about the change uttered by the untransformed relatives: the person is described as being "no longer normal" or "good" (*atutu*, a word whose sense is also that of physical beauty; as we shall see later, this is a relevant connection). In response, the monster may temporarily attempt to restore his tie with his horrified kin, now with the overt goal of killing or harming them. These events occur once more in or close to the settlement, the return to this site underscoring the contrast between the present feelings of the relatives and those portrayed in the opening lines of the story.

Eventually the transformed monsters depart to live independently of their relatives; they have become true monsters moving within a third setting, that of the wilderness. This setting stands in marked contrast both to the scene of the transformation (a known region of exploited territory) and to the earlier domestic setting, and each of these three locales situates a stereotyped image of family life. As long as they remain within the settlement, people behave normally and appropriately in the myths, motivated by respect and affection. In a known environment away from the settlement (including to some extent the manioc fields and bathing place), relaxed behavior that reveals a person's true feelings is appropriate because the full range of a person's relationship network does not exist outside the settlement, and people can and do seek relief from society there. Thus Kusimefu, thinking he is speaking to his wife, addresses his mother-in-law in a manner that is obscenely inappropriate within the domestic sphere his mother-in-law represents. Finally, in the wilderness there is an ever-present danger of encountering powerful beings, monstrous in appearance and dangerously wild in their behavior. A focal character's demeanor in the wilderness is also bizarre, associated with psychic violence that is the opposite of *ifutisu* and *funita*.

Kalapalo narrators condemn the murderous feelings of these characters and what they do to themselves by selective application of the "customary" modal particle *-su* when speaking of the character's actions. In Chapter 4 I described one use of this mode. When the action so marked is performed by a living being (*ago*) that is not human, the *-su* mode simply signifies that the character in question has now taken on a natural life form, whereas previously it manifested itself as a human being. When the actor is a human being, however, the *-su* mode qualifies an act as compulsive, self-gratifying, and performed without consideration for others. In these instances, while uttering the relevant sentence in which *-su* appears, the Kalapalo adopt a distinctive whining tone of voice that means they are speaking critically. In the myths presented in this chapter, the *-su* mode occurs in commentary spoken by a relative concerning the "repeatedly foolish" behavior of the focal character.

The compulsiveness of the focal characters is also sometimes suggested during the transformation sequence, in which a marked change appears in the attitude of the narrator toward what is surely one of the critical events in the story. Despite the grotesque and often horrible nature of these events, the story begins to take on the quality of caricature, and rather than openly expressing horror, the Kalapalo seem to treat it as humorous. This attitude is conveyed by playing off the character's grotesque behavior with both the pleasure that he derives from it and the compulsiveness with which he accomplishes it. Devices for portraying such exaggerated imagery include emphasis on the compulsive repetition of behavior through description in the -*su* and -*gele* ("continuative") modes and use of onomatopoetic substitutes for descriptive phrases, substitutes that emphasize the effects of the character's action upon certain objects being acted upon. Kudyu, a master of Kalapalo onomatopoeia, used this device to great effect in his story about the man who turns into an arboreal termites' nest.

Demonic Transformation and Asceticism

I noted earlier that all the transformations motivated by murderous intent are accomplished by self-mutilation. Removal of flesh recalls by extreme contrast the ascetic customs of Kalapalo puberty seclusion which are designed to add flesh to the body. Recall the purpose of seclusion practices: to create a morally motivated adult who will personify the values of *ifutisu*. The contrast between puberty seclusion practices and the monstrous transformation in these myths links physical monstrosity with the ordinarily repressed feelings of pleasurable aggression, that are the diametric opposite of the cooperative feelings engendered by seclusion practices. Physical appearance in each case is thus associated with a person's inner character, as embodied in feelings, motivation, and ethical judgments. On the one hand is beauty (accomplished by developing the body's flesh), which accompanies ascetic self-control on both the physical and social levels. On the other hand is a horrible appearance that is accomplished by the removal or maltreatment of the flesh, accompanying undisciplined, conscienceless aggression toward others.

The models of *ifutisu* and *funita* are constantly kept in mind by the Kalapalo when they judge one another. In addition, there are other constant reminders of the inherent dangers within the human person in the form of polluting substances and violent feelings that result in fear and sometimes even hatred of those around one. Yet the unmistakable combination of aggressive and affectionate feelings, of self-mutilation and pleasure in these stories suggest a complexity underlying the immediate and obvious fact that bad feelings threaten social life. First, these myths suggest that ferocity, the manifest feelings of *it-seke*, is always present in people, hidden behind the social persona adopted during one's life. This ferocity is different from the various manifestations of anger that Kalapalo distinguish because it is hidden and ever-present, whereas the other feelings are all around but only in the form of relatively brief outbursts. Although people are often short-tempered, disappointed, and even enraged, these forms of anger are often justifiable or at least explicable, whereas wildness is an inherent condition of humanity that is always to be suspected to be lying close to the calm surface of even the most suave individual. Culture is portrayed in these myths in Freudian fashion as providing the means of repressing feelings of aggression against loved ones. When some people move away from the arena of normal life into a setting that is suitable for the relaxation of normal social etiquette, a change comes over them. They seem to lose what moral conscience they formerly had. They become (or, rather, reveal themselves to be) wild, turning into deadly monsters whose power is specifically transformative. This power is closely associated with hyperanimate creativity, another one of whose manifestations is sexuality. For this reason, metaphors of sexuality contribute strongly to the language of demonic transformation.[5]

Metaphors of Sexuality

In each of the five stories I have been considering, the activities about to be engaged in, the means of effecting the transformation, and the mode of the attempted attack on or humiliation of the relatives all have sexual implications. The content of these events makes reference to the genitalia, sexual intercourse, aspects of procreation, and childbirth. Before describing these symbols, I would like to review briefly what is said by the Kalapalo about the origins of human sexuality and discuss contemporary Kalapalo attitudes about it, for such attitudes help explain the salience of the mythic imagery.

In a long story Kambe called "Kwatïŋï," his description of the first women (the Made Ones) develops Kalapalo ideas about both the inherently "natural" reproductive powers of women and the pleasing sensual aspects of their sexuality. Sexual relations are portrayed as motivated by generous reciprocity on the part of women toward men. Women please men sexually, the Kalapalo say, hence women should not refuse themselves nor show excessive jealousy when their husbands and lovers approach others. But in a story Muluku told about Taugi we learn that had it not been for that trickster, who removed dangerous creatures from the vagina of his cousin Ñafïgï, sexual intercourse would be the death of men. Furthermore, in this story Taugi invents menstruation by placing a tiny gnawing piranha in his cousin's breast, so that women will have an excuse acceptable to men for avoiding sexual relations. As a consequence, menstrual blood (a disgusting and polluting substance for men) is the most significantly important fact of female sexuality that for the Kalapalo distinguishes the roles of men and women. For only men can become shamans (it is said) because powerful beings detest the smell of women, particularly their menstrual blood. Shamans in training (that is, in seclusion and attempting to make contact with powerful beings), young men in puberty seclusion, and boys during the ear-piercing ritual must all avoid contact with sexually active women. Men do not watch women give birth and are disgusted by bloody hammocks and afterbirths. Finally, there are strong injunctions against women preparing food when they are menstruating; men are so afraid of becoming "weak" (that is, prevented from wrestling well) by food contaminated by menstrual blood that when a woman begins her period, she tells the members of her household so that all the food prepared by women can be discarded.

Although men are repelled by these aspects of women's sexuality—but also strongly attracted to women—Kalapalo women often find men excessively aggressive in their sexual feelings. Though sexually active, Kalapalo women dislike men who are too persistent, who exhaust them by repeated demands, who penetrate too deeply, and whose penises are "too large, like the penis of the tapir." Furthermore, women say that seminal substance from too many men will make them sick because it will not congeal into a fetus. Unmarried Kalapalo women and those with several young children are reluctant to become pregnant and undergo painful abortions if they do. Kalapalo women blame the sexual aggressiveness of men for unwanted pregnancies, though women are expected to remain sexually inactive while their children are nursing for the sake of their infants' health. Clearly, there is a deep ambiguity about sexuality among the Kalapalo that combines attitudes of intense curiosity and active desire with an abhorrence for the undesirable consequences of sexual intercourse and contact with what are conceived to be repellent sexual substances.

In the myth of Aulati, the most prominent symbol in the early part of the story is the *aga* nest, its structure suggesting a pregnant womb. The species of bee called *aga* by the Kalapalo is *Trigona spinipes*, whose nests are built in the open, supported by tree branches.[6] The large, oval nest consists of a thick outer protective layer of earthen material surrounding the round inner region of the brood comb and storage "pots" or caches of honey and pollen. *Aga* (like other native South American bees) are stingless, but they are known for their ferocious bite. Because it is considered excessively sweet, their honey is tabooed to all but the aged, those beyond childbearing age. This species, whose nest resembles a procreative organ—the womb—is thus treated culturally as antithetical to procreation and to the continuance of life. When Aulati hacks this metaphorical womb to pieces a flood of liquid results that becomes mixed with his blood, suggesting a weird form of birth in which Aulati, bloodied and faceless, appears as a horrible antimother. That his face may suggest to Kalapalo men (who rarely observe childbirth and who are repelled by the idea of coming into contact with the polluting substances of that biological event) the appearance of female genitals postpartum is not unlikely because a woman's mouth and vagina are frequently equated metaphorically. (In a traditional song, a woman sings to her lover about a rival, "Walk quickly by us, even though Other Parrot's wide mouth is opened.") Aulati's subsequent attempt to starve his brother-in-law by clinging to his back and devouring everything the man tries to eat suggests the antithesis of the Kalapalo idealization of the conjugal relationship, the loving sharing of nurturing food and mutually pleasing sexual relations.[7]

In the story of Kusimefu, fishing with traps also alludes to the sexual, especially procreative, activity between spouses; the *taka* traps are womb images because the word for this organ can be used for the compartment in which the fish are held in the trap. After shaming himself by speaking of erotic matters to his mother-in-law, Kusimefu leaps into the water, becoming a catfish. Here the connection is less clear than in other sexual metaphors I have discussed so far, but the transformation of Kusimefu into a *tugufi* catfish—a particularly "fishy" fish to the Kalapalo—suggests again to them what is considered a disgusting aspect of sexual intercourse: the secreted genital fluids that are considered mutually polluting.

Both vaginal fluids and semen (as well as breast milk, blood, and the fruit of the genipapa tree) are classed together by the smell-taste category *ūegï*, and this term is also applied to fish.[8] Kusimefu's desire to transform himself into a species of fish that is considered particularly "fishy" suggests his refusal to continue sexual relations with his new wife. For the Kalapalo say that to eat *tugufi* is to cause pain, so that if someone is already in pain she should avoid eating it. Pregnant women do not eat this fish so as to avoid excessive pain in childbirth, and women with small children who are still nursing reject it so their children will not experience pain from having consumed the substance of the fish in their milk. The *tugufi* image, just like the *aga* bees' nest in "Aulati," thus suggests in a negative way activities associated with pregnancy, birth, and nursing. A man turned into a *tugufi* becomes a creature antagonistic toward women and their offspring. For these reasons, and because Kusimefu also flees from his mother-in-law, the action of the story suggests that he is motivated by reluctance to continue the social consequences of sexual relations, namely, procreation and the creation of a more extensive network of kin through his children.

In the story of Fitsifitsi, the friends collect land snails, a mollusc whose shells are commonly used as metaphors for womens' breasts and whose fleshy parts the Kalapalo explicitly liken to female genitalia. But Fitsifitsi is less interested in collecting this female object than in sharpening his leg into a stabbing instrument, interpretable as symbolic masturbation not so much because of the phallic image of the object but because the word "sharpen" is a metaphor frequently used in reference to a woman's mechanically causing an erection (such as is mentioned in the story of Kusimefu). Unable to stab his friend, Fitsifitsi is reduced forever to senseless and ungratified use of his member, the perpetual digging of ditches in the wilderness, possibly an allusion to something futile the Kalapalo see in the activity of masturbation.

In the story of the man turned into a termites' nest, we again return to the image of a man in a tree, this time a tree repeatedly described as "straight," a "good one" suitable for cutting into the carefully split lengths of firewood that a young man is supposed to present to his in-laws. Reference to such a tree is reminiscent of the common expression *i tsotunda*, "the tree is enraged," a metaphor for an erection. The Kalapalo male sexual feeling is likened to rage because it is most clearly manifested in a process of muscular stiffening caused by the outward compression of inner feelings of tension (said to arise in the hollow of the abdomen). Not only this image of the tree as phalluslike in its growth but the entire situation of wood-cutting is a direct reference to the sexual feelings of husband and wife because this is one of the few activities spouses engage in together that affords sufficient privacy for them to have sexual relations unencumbered by thoughts of prying eyes. In the story the man's wife paints herself elaborately, a Kalapalo woman's message that she wishes to make love to her husband.

In this same myth, the husband transforms himself by scraping and cutting open his abdomen so that his intestines spill out. This act might symbolize anxiety fantasy about frightening and disgusting aspects of pregnancy and childbirth. Again, as in the story of Aulati, the man attempts to kill his victim by an act alluding to the female role in sexual intercourse: devouring. In each case, the manner of eating is extreme or excessive, further suggesting a male fantasy of the destructive voracity of female sexual feeling. But it would be an over-simplification to say that these characters are specifically female, for the context of their voracity suggests the aggressive violence associated with male sexuality. These monsters therefore can best be understood as personifying the sexual attributes that are most feared by the Kalapalo.

One last story ties all the themes of this chapter together. The myth of Sakatsuegï concerns an unfortunate youth who becomes the victim of the relentless desire of some monstrously male women and the literally devouring sexuality of the vampirish Ñafïgï from whom he barely escapes from a horrible wasting death.[9] The story is also interesting because it stresses Kalapalo ideas about the pleasurable and positive aspects of human sexual activity. Despite its horror, the myth is—at least during Sakatsuegï's sexual tribulations—a funny story, which, by proposing a ludicrous erotic situation in which women behave like men and men like women, develops a remarkably close image of the playful sexual deceit that is a constant feature of Kalapalo life. The conclusion stresses the importance of the reproductive function, the means by which the beloved dead are replaced by their cherished descendants. For, rather than being horrible monsters, the offspring of the unions Sakatsuegï is forced to endure are benevolent, sympathetic figures, the objects of their grandfather's deep affection and (ultimately, but not described in this version) the beautifully decorated powerful beings who give game to unlucky hunters when they are encountered in the deep forests.

Sakatsuegï
Told by Kambe and Sung by Kofoño at Aifa, July 30, 1980

Listen.
    In that very same place was even someone else about whom I will
    now speak,
        another husband of hers, Ulejalu's husband.
            Sakatsuegï.
    You probably don't know about him yet.   5
        He was her husband.
    They were all at that place I spoke of earlier,
        while they did all that I described before.
    Her younger sister is still there even now.
    "You go on, I'm afraid of going underground."   10
        She had many followers,
            the same number as well,
                they were of the same number as those of the other
                sister.
        They were also frightened of going underground.
    "Umambe! I'm frightened!"   15
    "All right, you must continue to remain here. Here.

You will not show yourselves to mortals, don't.
That is something to be used for the mortal's dying." 20
"All right."
"You will hide yourselves well,
you will hide yourselves."
(All right, Kofoño.
Listen, Kofoño will sing.)
[*Kambe's wife Kofoño picks up the story here, since women's music needs
to be quoted.*]
They are still there.
One who sees her will die quickly. 25
She is heard, *teh* beautifully singing Yamurikumalu,
singing.
Her followers as well:
[*Sings*]
"ulegi jawagi kafatafigi, nukutege ifigi jahaa
ulewi jawagi kafatafigi, nukutege ifigi ja'aha 30
jahahujaha, jahahujahaa
jahaha ahuu

jokofigigijakaenegigijoko, negigijaka, negi
ijakafigigijaka finefigijoko, negigijaka, negii
ewenikuni afutakanini 35
jahahu jaha, jahahu jahaa
jahaha ahuu

kwakutigikuwajijahaa
kwakutigikuwaji jahaa
ulewi jawagi kafatafigi, nukutegeiwigi ja'ahaa 40
jahahu jahaa, jahahu jahaa
jahaha ahuu"
It began when she painted with *itali*.
When the Other Kagutu is performed here she listens.

[*Kambe resumes the narrative.*]
Now I am speaking to you about them. 45
The transformed ones, they were the transformed ones.
Some people went there.
Their father had been invited to visit.
"Children," he said,
"Let's travel now." 50
(Look you've probably seen our poor people going to
another settlement to trade.)
"Let's go now," he said.
They all went there to Aŋambïtï.
"Buh, hiih, hooh!" cheering they went on.

After they went on,   55
    "It's me, it's me, it's me," he went,
        their father said.
        "It's me, it's me, it's me."
The other leader came out to the plaza.
    "We have all humbly arrived here at your residence.   60
    I've brought them,
        I've brought our children.
    There are none among them who can seize you,
        I have not brought them,"
            that was what he said.   65
Then the other leader made a speech,
    and next the other leader discussed it with the residents.
Next they all wrestled,
    they all wrestled.
Then they presented objects, *pok pok*.   70
    You've seen them present objects *pok pok*.
        I mean at another settlement.
Then they were brought inside,
        to the ceremonial house,
            to the ceremonial house.   75
                They were brought inside the ceremonial house
                where they slept.

At dusk the older brothers remained there.
    Look [*holds up three fingers*], there were three of them,
        his older brothers.
    Their last born was this one [*points to his fourth finger*],   80
        there were four in number.
    This one, look, Sakatsuegï.
He was only a youth.
    The others were already married
        they, his older brothers.   85
    He was unmarried.
    Teh he was beautiful!
They were all there in the ceremonial house.
    They had yet to sleep another night.
    They were still untroubled.   90

Then next day they dance *undufe*.
    The *kagutu* flutes were played.
That day, when it became dark,
        it was their second night.
            They were sleeping two nights.   95

They went alligatoring to other houses,
        alligatoring.
    Just as those who are unmarried do here now.
        Tapualu and her companions stay unmarried,
        and Kamafu and her companions have remained   100
        husbandless,
            they are husbandless.
Then his older brothers went alligatoring,
        they were alligatoring.
    Then they went to those in a nearby house,
        they went to them.   105
    To one who was a secluded maiden,
        to one whose knees were bound.
    While they were staying inside the ceremonial house,
        they were staying there.
"I'll go," he said.   110
    He wanted to be like his older brothers.
        "I'll go alligatoring," he said.
    Then he went,
        Sakatsuegï went.
Tiki he entered a house,   115
        Ulejalu's house was where he entered.
    She was by then an old woman,
        an old woman.
    Teh, but think of it, she was beautiful!
    Teh he, she still remained youthful,   120
        she looked like a young woman.
As he went on,
    "Why have you come to me?" she asked.
    "I've just come to you," Sakatsuegï said.
        "Here I am to you,   125
        I am to you."
She bound her knees just like a maiden would do although she
was an old woman.
    She bound her knees,
        she was well-formed.
            Well-formed,   130
               Ulejalu the well-formed.
"Who are you then?" she asked.
"It's just me, me," he answered.
"What is your name then?" she asked.
"Sakatsuegï.   135
    I keep desiring you.
        I am desiring you right now."
"Come on then," she said.

She quickly wrapped her knees with her cotton *pu pu pu*,
she drew him to her by his wrist and *pok*, they lay down
together in her hammock.   140
She kept him as her husband forever,
she kept him there.
She kept him as her husband.
His older brothers had left by then,
they had left.   145
They were finished.
They had been to maidens.

At night their father remained awake.
"Where is he?" their father wondered.
He questioned his sons,   150
"Where is your younger brother?"
"I don't know, he went alligatoring somewhere."
His father went looking for him.
He saw them there doing as before,
he was still doing as before with Ulejalu.   155
She had made him her husband forever.

The next day they all went away his relatives went away,
his older brothers went away.
He himself still remained there doing as before.
Ulejalu had never returned him.   160
He had become her husband.
That is how he was with her,
how he was with her.
The others still were as they had been,
they had not yet been transformed.   165
He was always lying down with her!
Throughout the day.
He was very excited.
She was so beautiful Sakatsuegï kept desiring her,
he kept desiring her.   170

When night came he kept making love to her
over and again throughout the night.
He really made love to her!
She enjoyed his lovemaking.
Yes.   175
Then, her younger sisters were playing the *kagutu*.
Outside were the *kagutu*.
"Where is our older sister?
Come out here, come out here to the *kagutu*,
come out here.   180

Our older sisters,
  whom our spouses find so well-formed,
    our spouses find so well-formed."
Their spouses had been making love to her.
  Having done that she would go outside quickly. 185
Then she would return again,
  she would return again.
She went to check on her husband,
  because others would come to him to make love,
    her younger sisters would go alligatoring to him. 190
He stayed alone in the house,
  eating manioc bread,
    eating manioc bread,
      eating manioc bread.
Her younger sisters criticized her, 195
  criticized her,
    her younger sisters did.
"Let's go look for a meal for our younger brother,
  a meal for our younger brother."
While he was alone they wanted to make love to him, 200
  her younger sisters did.
They wanted to make love,
  they wanted to make love to her husband.
"Very well." Ulejalu had just heard them,
  "Tomorrow I plan to go far away to fish." 205
    "All right," her husband said.
"You yourself must remain here."
  "All right," he answered.

At the beginning of the next day
  when the chickens crowed she left. 210
Her husband remained behind.
The woman was the one who did as I described.
She went to kill giant *agouti*,
  giant *agouti*.
    Furred animals. 215
      That's Monstrous Women's food.
        She was going to kill some very large ones.
After she left her younger sisters came to him from where the *kagutu*
were being played.
  to lie down with her husband,
    to make love to him. 220
      They were going alligatoring.
One of them came,
  bok she lay down with him,
    she lay down with him when she came.

They gave beads to their lover, 225
    kaŋatsegë grass seed necklaces.
        That was the kind of gift they had for their lover.
He hid them *tu tu tu* Sakatsuegï hid them.
    He rolled the necklaces up into a ball,
        and put them here by the wall of the house. 230
Ulejalu returned,
    She returned from having gone hunting.
On her back she brought the game,
    their food,
        her husband's food. 235
        She brought the game.
"Here I am," she said.
    Bum! she dumped them off her back.
    "Sakatsuegï," she said,
        "You are certainly still here." 240
    "I am certainly still here, still here."
She had killed giant *agouti*.
    Giant *agouti* were their food.
So her husband ate.
    Right away she swept the floor, 245
    she swept the floor *pisu pisu pisu*,
        she swept the entire floor carefully.
        Beneath all the walls.
He had put his things in the ground.
    That was why she cleaned up. 250
Together they ate after she did that.
    She gave some to her younger sisters.
        Some of the meat was brought outside.
    It was a large one,
        that giant *agouti*. 255
    The others then ate it in the plaza.

After they slept three more times,
    she went once again as before.
    She went once again as before,
        gaming. 260
    And once again she arrived home.
Her husband had been given more beads by her younger sisters.
    Her younger sisters had gone alligatoring.
They came to him from where the *kagutu* were being played,
    into the house *tiki*, 265
        and they made love to him.
They gave their lovers' beads to him,
    they gave beads to Sakatsuegï.
He put them in the ground.

He did that so she wouldn't see them. 270
        So that his wife Ulejalu wouldn't see them.
Pisu pisu pisu she swept beneath the wall,
    she went looking for her husband's lovers' gifts.
Then *pok* they lay down together.
    Because they continued to lie down together 275
        she became pregnant,
            she became pregnant.

One more time then it was the height of the dry season just as it is now,
    she went away again.
        And once again she went to kill his food. 280
        And once again she brought it back.
    Again her younger sisters came alligatoring,
        they made love to her husband.

Finally it was ready,
        her stomach was ready. 285
            She had become very pregnant.
She still went hunting as before,
        with her very pregnant stomach.
        She was pregnant because of what he had done.
        It was her lovemaking. 290
They had made love through the night,
        They continued to lie down together.
    She always desired him,
        always desired him.
            She had made him very thin. 295
He was skinny because she had been doing that,
        skinny.
    It was his semen that had made him that way.
    It was his lovemaking that had made him that way.
    He was still unpierced, 300
        still unpierced.
        He still wasn't pierced,
            not yet.
So he stayed there while she went fishing.
    She went for the last time. 305
        It was the last time.
    She will find his lovers' gifts.
        His lovers' gifts will be found by her.

When the sun was here
    she returned. 310
        She had killed a giant *agouti*,
            she had killed some game.

Once again she brought out her husband's food to her younger
sisters.
Her younger sisters had been making love to him.
They were making love to her husband coming from where the   315
kagutu were being played.
One of them went into his house,
and they made love.
Then another went,
and she made love to him,
she made love to him.   320
Beads—his lover's gifts—*bah hah* there were so many of them!
He hid the ball of necklaces carelessly,
carelessly he had hidden it.
Ulejalu arrived home,
"You are certainly still here, Sakatsuegï."   325
"I'm certainly still here."
They ate as they had always done before, close to one another as
always.
Afterward she began to sweep up, she swept *pisuk pisuk* beneath the
housewall while her husband remained seated over on the side of the
house.
Pisuk pisuk pisuk pisuk.
As she came to the wall there *pisuk* in the ground was that thing—it   330
was this big—
he had rolled up.
When she saw it she picked it up,
and she became as angry as she ever could be,
she was angry.
"Sakatsuegï?" she said.   335
"What?"
"From whom did this come?
Surely these are the lover's gifts that the mothers of your
nonexistent children have been giving you!"
"That's not so," he said. "They aren't."
"But from whom else could this have come?"   340
The strings of beads had been rolled into a ball.
She was very jealous indeed.
"I'll shoot you, I'll shoot you!
I'll shoot you."
She would have shot him then and there,   345
she would have shot him.
But as she ran to get her arrows, her younger sisters grabbed her bow,
her younger sisters did.
They grabbed it, *bouk* while he ran off,
"Go away!"   350
"Go away Sakatsuegï!" they said.

"Our older sister is furious with you."
　　"Yes," he went.
Tututu, so he was running away, he was running away.
　　She was Ulejalu.　　　　　　　　　　　　　　　　　　355
　　　　So, he was running away.
And he came back, while he was fleeing her.
　　And her stomach was like this, while he came back.
Tututu he came close to someone's entrance path.
　　He came once again, this time on Ñafïgï's entrance path,　360
　　　　it was Ñafïgï's entrance path.
　　He had been coming close to Ñafïgï's entrance path without
　　seeing where he fled.
　　But as he fled he had been coming closer and closer, and he went
　　onto Ñafïgï's entrance path,
　　　　he went onto Ñafïgï's entrance path.
　　Back at the other place her younger sisters were scolding
　　Ulejalu,　　　　　　　　　　　　　　　　　　　　365
　　　　they were scolding her.
As he approached her
　　　　Ñafïgï came toward him.
　　She came right up to him as he ran from the other one,
　　　　as he ran.　　　　　　　　　　　　　　　　　370
　　He was fleeing the other one, he was fleeing her.
"Are you going somewhere?" she asked him.
　　　　"Are you going somewhere?"
"No," he went,
　　　　"I'm fleeing someone," he replied.　　　　　375
"Who are you?"
"Sakatsuegï," he answered.
"Come along as my husband," she went.
She grabbed him *bah*!
Ñafïgï held him tightly as she took him away.　　　380
He was still as before,
　　very small,
　　　　skinny.
The other one had an embryo in her stomach,
　　she was pregnant, Ulejalu was.　　　　　　　385
　　　　His former wife who had wanted to shoot him with
　　　　her arrow.
She took him away,
　　Ñafïgï took him away.
Again he was a husband.　　　　　　　　　　390
　　He still hadn't been pierced as yet.
She took him away to her settlement, to her house.
　　　　Pok.
　　　　　　(It's awful, isn't it?)

Again as before she was making love,   395
    throughout the night as before she made love to him.
        She was constantly making love.
            Ñafïgï was constantly making love as had happened to
            him before.
    Continuing at the beginning of the day when they went to the
    water,
        again when they returned they lay down together again as   400
        before,
            she was constantly making love.

He had slept two days.
    "Sakatsuegï," she said,
        "I'll hunt for your food," she said,
            "Your food."   405
                "Very well, go if you wish."
    Tsïkitsïki,
        she painted his feet with red paint.
            She painted his feet so that he would remain lying
            down.
    She tied him down so that he couldn't walk around,   410
        so that no one else there could make love to him.
            She was like that.
    Then she came to him, *bok*,
        straightening his legs and tying him down that way so that
        he couldn't touch the ground.
    Having done that she left for the forest.   415
        She went to shoot monkeys,
            to shoot his food.
Here in her house was someone who stayed behind,
    Akugefe stayed behind in the house.
        A woman.   420
    "Sakatsuegï," she said,
        as she untied him *pupupu*.
    Pok, she lay down with him.
        Really!
    She desired him,   425
        she desired him.
    Her vulva doesn't poison us.
        That other one's vulva does poison us,
            Ñafïgï's vulva does that.
    "Listen now Sakatsuegï," she said.   430
        "You'll find that my vulva is nice," she told him,
            Akugefe said to him.
    Then she made love to him.
    Next she painted his feet,

just as they had been before,   435
        because the red paint kept rubbing off while she made
        love to him.
                It had rubbed off while they were lying down
                together.

When the sun was here Ñafïgï returned, *tuu tsi*,
        while she played her flute.
The others could hear her when she did that.   440
        She had monkeys,
                she had killed toucans,
                        she had killed caciques.
Uubom! she threw them down inside the doorway.
        "Sakatsuegï," she said,   445
                "You are certainly still here."
                "I am certainly still here."
While he lay stiffly in the hammock,
        she untied him *pupupu*.
                As if he had always been like that since she had left 450
                him.
And then she was making love to him.
        Really!
        She untied him,
                she untied him,
                        so he could singe the hair off the monkeys.   455
And so once again as before they both ate as before,
        they ate.
And again when they had both finished eating they lay down together,
        they lay down together.
        They lay down together and made love.   460
        They lay down together,
                they lay down together.
        Together they made love throughout the night,
                she herself did that,
                        Ñafïgï did that.   465
        At night they went to the water and there they lay down together
        again,
                she wanted to lie down again.
        Really!

For a long time they remained that way.
        Again she went to the forest.   470
                When he was left behind Akugefe unbound him *pupu*
                in order to make love to him again.
        And once again she did that.
                "Listen, my vulva is nice, Sakatsuegï," she said,

"My vulva is always nice." 475
   She desired him.
Then she painted his feet,
   the same as before.
Pu pu she tied him down again.
   She tied him down after she made love to him. 480
Finally Ñafïgï was returning once again,
   she returned to them.
Then she came to him,
   she arrived once again.
Monkeys had been killed, 485
   they had been killed.
"Sakatsuegï, you are certainly still here."
"I am certainly still here,"
   her husband was lying motionless in his hammock as
   before.
"Singe these," she said. 490
The one who stayed behind was spinning cotton *duuu*.
   She never traveled about.
She always stayed alone watching the house,
      so she could make love to him.
And again Ñafïgï went, 495
   she went to the forest.
He had become skinny because her vulva's poisonous odor was
killing him.
   He had become even skinnier.
Having made love all the time as had Ulejalu the angry one,
   she had become pregnant. 500
Ñafïgï was pregnant from having done what Ulejalu had done.
   Her stomach had grown large.

Listen now. Ñafïgï went away while her husband remained behind.
   Her husband had become thin.
      Her vulva's poisonous odor was killing him. 505
When he was alone Akugefe took him,
   when he was alone he was taken by her.
"Sakatsuegï. Come see Ñafïgï's husbands' remains.
   They were killed by her lovemaking.
   She killed her husbands until they died. 510
Then she carried them *pom* and threw them outside behind the
house.
   Her vulva's poisonous odor killed them."
Their bones lay scattered about behind the house,
   her husbands' bones.
      Her vulva's poisonous odor was their killer. 515

Then Akugefe brought him to where they could see the bleached
remains.
      "Look at that, that is what you will become,
          that is what you will become."
      "I see," he replied.
      "You must go away!" she told him,   520
          "You must go away!"
      "All right," he answered,
          "All right," he said after she told him that.
               Akugefe was telling him to leave.
      "This is what you will become.   525
Even though you're still barely alive she wants your bones to
remain here.
      Tomorrow, 'You,' she'll say,
          'Sakatsuegï, tomorrow I must go to the forest!'
          'I'll go with you,' you must speak that way,
          'I'll go with you,' you will say to her."   530
               "All right," he answered.

The following day,
      "I must go now."
      "I'll go with you," he told her,
          "I'll go with you."   535
      "No, you can't go, you can't go," that's what she said to him.
      "I'll follow you."
          She left after he said that.
When Akugefe had retied him,
          she followed Ñafïgï.   540
She went with her to the forest entrance.
She plucked some *agafagu* leaves
          and she sat down on them, *pok*.
               There she stayed.
Later she moved farther over,   545
      to another place.
Tiny sweat bees were there,
      tiny sweat bees.
          With *afejo* bees,
               she sat on the honey of *afejo*.   550
Then she left,
          she went back to see him.
      "Sakatsuegï," she said, "You're still here."
      "I'm still here."
      "All right, come here," she said,   555
          and she shot him away with her bow,
               Akugefe shot him away.

Farther on *ndik* he landed outside his father's house,
  his father's house.
    Tiki.   560
He was very small,
  he had become emaciated.
Ñafïgï still had something in her stomach after what she had
done.
Her stomach had grown somewhat larger
  while the woman from the other place was almost ready,   565
    Ulejalu was almost ready by then.
Then Ñafïgï returned to him,
  she returned *tiki*,
"Was someone resting here?"
  The *afejo* honey was left after Akugefe had moved over to   570
  the side.
No one was there either,
  where Akugefe had moved farther over to the side.
"Where is he?" Ñafïgï said.
  She hurried back after that.
Akugefe had just begun to spin cotton,   575
  she usually did that,
    she who had sent him away.
Taa, taa, Ñafïgï was playing her flute.
Wind arose and then she killed monkeys in the forest, she killed
furred animals.
She killed cacique birds,   580
  she killed toucans.
"Sakatsuegï," she said.
  He wasn't there.
"Your younger brother followed you," Akugefe told her.
  "He did go,   585
    he did follow you,
      he followed you.
I think you told him he could.
'I'll go with you,'
  I think he told you that," she told her.   590
Ñafïgï went back,
  It's said she was still dripping with sweat when she went
  back.
She went to look for him at that same place,
  she went to the place where Akugefe had been.
From there she probably began to track the footprints, but she saw   595
nothing.
  Looking for him she went inside trees,
    inside big trees.
She went into the ground,

but no, she saw nothing.
Once again she came back.   600
    "Have you found him?" Akugefe asked.
    "I haven't."
        She was angry with Akugefe, she was angry with her.
    "I think you told him he could,
        I think you told him he could."   605
    She herself was the one who had just been deceiving Ñafïgï.
        She had thrown him away.
    "Yes," she told her.
Ñafïgï continued to look for him as before,
        but she didn't find him!   610
    Her monkeys were still unsinged.
        He had gone far away!
She went to all the other powerful beings' places,
    to their settlements.
    She kept looking for him as before,   615
        but she didn't find him.
    By then he was with his father,
        by then he was with his father.
    He had become terribly thin!
        It was her poisonous odor that had been killing him.   620
    So his father kept him inside the house,
        inside the house his father kept him.
        Inside the house,
           secluded.

I just remembered to tell you about this, listen.   625
    "She will certainly go,
        she will be looking for you.
    She will go as a man,
        She will go as a man.
           She will arrive at his own cousins' house.   630
    She will go there appearing as a person,
        appearing as a person.
Then she will come to you.
    'Who is that?' when she asks your father he will refer to you by
    someone else's name."
        "All right."   635
    "'Is it true he is Ñafïgï's former husband,
        is he Ñafïgï's former husband?'
    'Sakatsuegï's former younger brother' your father will say.
    'He is Fikigiwa, the former younger brother of the one poisoned
    by Ñafïgï's vulva,' he will tell her,
        your father will say."   640
        "All right."

"'He is just the image of his older brother,
he is just the image of him.
How I miss him,
how I long for him! 645
'His older brother was fat just as he is,' he will tell her,
your father will say.
All the other households will avoid naming you.
They will not tell about you.
they will not tell about you." 650
"All right," he said.
"Your father himself will not tell,
he will not tell.
He himself will warn those in the plaza—the men—not
to name you.
She will go to the followers as a maiden, 655
she will go as a young man,
she will go as a woman,
she will go as an old man.
That is how she herself will go.
She herself." 660
When others finally were to tell her
Ñafïgï was going to kill him.
She will bring their son there.

They went back.
Akugefe made love to him again and then she was going to shoot him 665
away on her bow.
"Stay here,"
pok she lay down with him once more and made love to
him.
"Ataah, ataah! How nice!"
That was what she kept saying to herself.
She really desired his penis. 670
"Stay here,"
she put him on her bow and shot him away.
Tiki, "There is my son!"
How thin he had become from Ñafïgï's poisonous vulva,
from making love to her. 675
She was going to have their son.

He remained secluded
cleansing his stomach all the while with plant medicines.
He did so with *tïkïgï*, the vine that twines around manioc.
Fikigiwa rubbed himself behind his joints to purify himself of 680
Ñafïgï's touch.

Secluded *teh* he was becoming beautifully fat once more.
Then he was really fat!

Then she gave birth,
 his wife gave birth,
  that was happening to Monstrous Woman   685
  She gave birth to a boy.
She accepted him,
 she picked him up.
  He was cradled when she did that to him.
Ñafïgï's swollen stomach was almost ready,   690
 while their husband Fikigiwa was in seclusion.
  Fikigiwa was.
His father had renamed him,
 he had renamed him.
  Sakatsuegï was still his real name.   695
  He had given his son the name of someone else.

For the planned ear-piercing,
 some others gave him piqui soup.
  Piqui was given to his father for the ear-piercing.
  Sakatsuegï was the father of an infant when he was pierced.   700
  Teh, he had fattened up beautifully!

He stayed there,
 and after one dry season of his passed the rains came once again.
  the rains came again,
   it was the rainy season.   705
  The piqui pulp was packed in soaking baskets during the rainy
  season for the ear-piercing,
   for the ear-piercing.
Then it came to her,
 when the waters had flooded Ñafïgï was giving birth,
  she was giving birth.   710
A boy was born once again,
 a boy.
As had been done to the other one,
 she accepted him.
The woman's accepted-one was walking,   715
 he was walking.
Ñafïgï had also given birth,
 also to a son.
Her son was still seated,
 he had not yet gone,   720
  gone to the other settlement, gone to his father's
  settlement.

"Koh koh!" when the sun was here,
  "Koh koh!" someone was arriving.
   "That must be her, Children," he went,
    his father said.   725
     "That must be her.
When you go about be sure never to speak of him,
   be sure not to speak of him," he said.
    "All right," the others answered.
He went around to all the households repeatedly warning the people.   730
   Around to all the households he went.
   He warned them,
    he warned them.
   When he was in the plaza,
    he spoke to the men.   735
   While they were all asleep she traveled as a man,
    she was traveling as a man.

The next day before dawn she went visiting,
     still as a man.
       She came there to visit his father.   740
  She looked like someone else,
    she went with the appearance of a person from another
    settlement.
Tiki she came inside with some people from other houses who were
escorting her.
   "Stay here," while Sakatsuegï said that he sat with his head
bowed.
   When she came inside he sat that way while they talked with 745
each other.
   "That is she," he informed his father.
    "She must have transformed herself to look like a person."
"Whose seclusion chamber is that?" she asked.
   "That's Fikigiwa's seclusion chamber.
    He's the younger brother of Ñafïgï's former husband   750
    Sakatsuegï,
     he's Sakatsuegï's former younger brother."
   "Where was he?" She kept changing the subject.
    "Where was Sakatsuegï?"
"Ñafïgï's poisonous vulva killed him.
First he was Monstrous Woman's husband.   755
   Monstrous Woman almost killed him.
   Then as he fled from her,
    Ñafïgï came to meet him,
     she came to meet him," his father told her.
      "She was the one," he said.   760
   "She was, was she?" she answered,

"I will go see him."
She came toward him to see.
"Here comes your older brother to see you," his father said.
    As she went, she looked like someone from another 765
    settlement.
Dïïï, "Stay here," he said.
She glanced at him.
    She recognized him, *teh* he was beautiful and plump.
    "He's the same one his father was talking about!" she said to
    herself.
    "Stay here, I'm going," she told him. 770
      "Go, then."
    "That's Sakatsuegï himself!" she said.
She went on to another house.
    She went to the water's edge with someone.
    "Whose seclusion chamber is that next door?" she asked the one 775
    with whom she walked.
      "Whose seclusion chamber is that next door?"
    "That's Fikigiwa's seclusion chamber,
      his seclusion chamber.
    A long time ago his older brother was Ñafïgï's husband.
      Sakatsuegï." 780
    "What became of him?" she asked the person who said that,
      as they went on.
    "I don't know.
      He was Monstrous Woman's husband.
    When she tried to kill him he fled," he said. 785
      "Ñafïgï captured him when she met him, she captured
      him.
    Ñafïgï is sexually insatiable, so she captured him."
      (But she would probably say the same about me!)
Finally, she went back to her own settlement.
    "You must be very careful not to tell her about your younger 790
brother, Children," her father told the women and also the men.

She remained, she remained, she remained and after she had slept a long
time there she came to him once again,
    She came to him once again.
    As a woman,
      a woman.
    She came as a woman, *teh teh he*, 795
      a real beauty!
        She came as a younger woman whose bangs had just
        been cut.
    "Kaw kaw what's-her-name!" they all said.
      When she arrived she looked like another person,

she arrived at that person's cousins' house.   800
Next she came,
    and again as before when she came she was taken visiting.
    She kept asking the women as they went,
        "Whose seclusion chamber is that?" she asked.
    "That's Fikigiwa's seclusion chamber,   805
        Sakatsuegï's former younger brother's seclusion chamber."
    "What happened to him before, what?"
        "It was the poisonous odor of Ñafïgï's vulva that killed his
        older brother.
    His younger brother is the true image of him,
        he looks just as he once did.   810
    How sad I am for his poor brother!
        'Sakatsuegï was once this way' that's what we poor people
        tell each other."
        "Do you?" she went.
She slept once,
    and she went away having done that.   815
        She went away once again.

Another time she came to him,
    she came for the last time she came as she had done before.
        Again she came as someone else.
After she had slept five days,   820
    once more she appeared at another house as a woman again.
        Teh, a lovely young girl.
    "That's probably she.
        Be sure not to tell about your younger brother,
            don't tell, Children," his father told them.   825
    "None of you will tell about your younger brother, no,
        you will not tell about your younger brother."
        "All right," they answered.
    He kept speaking that way to them,
        he told them all.   830
Then once again she went visiting,
    a woman was escorting her to each of the households to take
    away their possessions.
        She arrived to take them away,
            she arrived.
    "Who is he over there?" she said.   835
    "This is Fikigiwa's seclusion chamber,
        Fikigiwa's seclusion chamber.
            He is Sakatsuegï's former younger brother."
    "What happened to his older brother in the past? What? What
    happened to him?"
    "He fled from being Monstrous Woman's husband.   840

Monstrous Woman tried to shoot him.
Then as he continued to flee from her he came onto Ñafïgï's
entrance path,
    Ñafïgï's entrance path.
Ñafïgï met him.
    Again he was captured as her husband.   845
It was her vulva's poisonous odor that killed him then,
    her vulva's poisonous odor killed him.
How sad I am for him.
    I yearn for his poor older brother,
        his poor older brother,   850
            his older brother," she told her.
"Yes, you do," she answered.
Then, she continued to visit with her.
    "Whose seclusion chamber is that?"
She went away again as before,   855
    she stayed away for a month.

Then she came as a man, a person,
    she came as a beautiful youth.
        Once again she came as a youth.
            Before she had come as an old man,   860
                the first time I mean.
Once again she arrived as someone else,
    once again inside another house.
She went to that person's brothers,
    to his cousins *tiki*,   865
        she came inside the house.
Then she kept questioning them again.
Again she came to him.
    "Your older brother is right here to see you," his father said.
    "My younger relative, continue to stay here," his father said.   870
    "I'll go now to him."
        Once again she went to see him.
          "Go if you wish," the father replied.
    "Your older brother is right here," he told his son,
        "Your older brother is right here."   875
Tiki she came inside,
    into his seclusion chamber.
"Continue to stay here," he said to her with his eyes averted,
    because he didn't look at her,
        he didn't look at her.   880
("This is he doing this, he *is* Sakatsuegï.")
    She recognized him again.
She came back,
    she came back and again went away.

Once again she came to him carrying her son. 885
    this time they were piercing him.
        They surrounded him as she came carrying her son,
           They were piercing him.
She came to where the women were seated,
        she came as an unmarried woman. 890
        "Let's sit over there so we can watch the dancing in the plaza,
           in order to watch the dancing in the plaza."
           "All right," her young son answered.
She came outside the house carrying her seat of split palm wood.
    The others were encircling him. 895
        He wore a cacique feather headdress.
        He wore eagle feathers.
    (Look, you once saw our people wearing cacique feather
headdresses.
        Paže and his companions were wearing them before.)
"Who is he?" she said, 900
    "Who is he?"
"He's Fikigiwa, Fikigiwa.
    Sakatsuegï's former younger brother."
"What happened to him before? What?"
"He fled from being Monstrous Woman's husband. 905
When Monstrous Woman tried to shoot him,
    he fled onto Ñafïgï's entrance path.
Ñafïgï was nearby,
    and she couldn't resist making love to him,
        she couldn't resist making love to him." 910
"Yes, she's bad."
And once again, "Who is he?"
    and once again she questioned someone.
        She changed her appearance to look like someone else.
"Listen to me, I'll tell you about him." 915
    When the other woman whispered she held her ear close.
"I'll tell you about him,
    That's Sakatsuegï doing that!
    Sakatsuegï!
He returned from being Ñafïgï's husband, 920
    from being Ñafïgï's husband.
It was Akugefe who threw him away from there.
    Akugefe did that!"
"All right, go to Father!" she said to her son,
    "I wasn't the only one who made you." 925
He was this tall,
    already a walker,
        he was like Fetso.
She stood him up.

He went to where they were dancing and took his father's hand. 930
"Oh no! Who is this child of ours who just tried to hold my son's
hand?"
      his father said.
         He pushed him so that he fell to the ground and hurt his
         poor mouth.
The other one rose,
      the other one rose, 935
         his mother was furious with him.
Her pubic ornament crackled!
She picked up her son,
      and she ripped off a fingernail *bistsuki*!
Duu! she threw it. 940
    Tsiuk! *umbom*! it slashed his throat.
He died when she threw it at him.
      He died, as she went away laughing.
         "Ah ha ha ha," she was laughing about having killed him as
         she went away.
      "I already warned you!" his father was angry with the teller. 945
He was buried after that happened,
    they made a tunnel grave in order to have a leader's memorial.
Their grandfather remained there,
    everyone remained there weeping.

After four dry seasons of his passed, 950
    their grandfather went to get wood.
         The others had grown up by then.
      "My son once walked around right here, here my son would go."
They started to travel to their grandfather.
      "Go to your grandfather, 955
         go get your older brother,
            go get your older brother," his mother went,
               Ñafïgï said.
                  "All right."
He went to get his older brother, 960
      to the Monstrous Woman.
    The other son of Sakatsuegï was there,
      he had grown tall.
    "You," Ñafïgï's son said,
      "Come with me to our grandfather, 965
         to our grandfather."
    "All right, let's go now as you say."
They both came.
    He was collecting his firewood,
      far away in the old fields. 970
    They began to come toward him.

One of them threw a piece of stick at him.
    He hit their grandfather with the stick.
        Tooh . . . taki.
He hit him with a small piece like this.   975
That other one did something like toss dirt at him,
    getting him to turn his head toward them.
        Tunn, tak!
"Look over here at me."
    They were smiling.   980
"Grandfather," he said.
    "We're right here,
        you're with your grandsons!"
"Who are they, my grandsons?"
"We're the ones.   985
    He is one of your grandsons, Monstrous Woman's son,
        and I am Ñafïgï's son."
"I see!" their grandfather said.
    "Now my dear little grandsons are all here!" he embraced
them.
He smiled,   990
    he came away from his unceasing anger, he smiled.
He took them back with him.
"Here are my sons,"
    he had three other sons, men.
This one here [*points to his fourth finger*] was he,   995
    their last born,
        Sakatsuegï.
[*Enumerates on his hand*]
    Again an older brother,
    Again an older brother,
        again an older brother.   1000
        This one here was he,
            he was their last born.
"All right now," *buk* with palm thatch as was done before he secluded
them.
    He did that in order to pierce them.
    Piqui was given him.   1005
Then they remained there during the dry season,
    and when it ended they went as guests to the performance.
        The messengers went to invite them.
He was crying while he watched them being pierced.
    You've seen it yourself!   1010

Notes to Sakatsuegï

1ff.   This story followed another about Monstrous Women that I discuss in Chapter 7.
The introduction here begins with a description of the other story.

63   The phrase "without those who seize" is a polite deception about the wrestling prowess of his followers.

550   *Afejo* bees are a sweat bee that apparently collects human sweat and manufactures honey (?) on the spot, leaving a sign of human occupancy when the person moves away.

744   Sitting with head bowed is a polite greeting gesture made to a visitor who is walking around the house circle.

788   Kambe jokes about himself.

928   Fetso is his young grandson, then about two years of age.

947   A tunnel grave refers to the manner of burying dead leaders.

Ñafïgï (an *ifaü* or "cousin" of the trickster Taugi) is a demoness, the very image of utter destruction and of a wasting death. Even Taugi cannot fully subdue her, and he sometimes uses her to terrify his own enemies. Essentially female, Ñafïgï is able to change her sex and age, and she has the uncanny ability to appear in the form of any human person she chooses. Like Taugi she is a trickster, but her deceptions are invariably thoroughly destructive.

That such forces of destructive transformation are closely associated with human sexuality is no accident, for as we have seen in this chapter, the Kalapalo understand lust—of all feelings—to have inherently destructive consequences in its own right. Ñafïgï embodies the qualities of sexual feeling the Kalapalo most fear: that of men, which takes the form of violent passion that can easily turn to rape, and the insatiable devouring female sexuality that seduces young men like Sakatsuegï, jeopardizing their ability to survive by sapping the strength necessary for their growing to full adulthood.

Eroticized Aggression

The contrast between the insatiable voracity of female sexuality and the violent aggressiveness of male sexuality will be discussed further in Chapter 7 when I consider the relation between music and gender identity. Here, I have been concerned to show how metaphors of genitalia and reproductive functions are exaggerated and associated with hidden feelings of aggression, fear, and repulsion. Regarding gender identity, these feelings are mutually complementary: men fear and are repelled by certain female sexual things, and women fear and are repelled by men's sexual persistence. Because these eroticized feelings of aggression are expressed so markedly in the mythological context and in the related rituals of Kagutu and Yamurikumalu that will be closely examined in Chapter 7, we must consider them reflections of fantasy that achieve socially appropriate meanings through such performances. When these emotions erupt outside the context of ritual events, they are regarded as peculiar and dangerous, even though important cultural practices—menstrual and postpartum taboos, the avoidance of birthing by men, celibacy expected during puberty seclusion, shamanistic tutoring, widow seclusion, and beliefs linking a woman's sexual promiscuity to illness contracted by her children or herself—must reinforce those feelings throughout a person's life.

Although the symbols under consideration have specific semantic significance that gives insight into a Kalapalo perspective on aggression and sexuality, they also refer to the more abstract and more personal complexity and contradiction of feeling accompanying human relationships. Male and female, aggression and affection, feelings of erotic passion and of physical repulsion appear throughout Kalapalo culture in oppositional patterns, yet in these myths and the rituals I will describe in Chapter 7, they are merged within symbolic forms that seem internally self-contradictory and therefore semantically paradoxical. In all these myths and rituals the barriers between men and women that are erected by the manner in which Kalapalo construct their domestic lives and that tend to be insisted upon in the domestic sphere are reduced to arbitrary figures both textually and in the performance, where sexual identity is dissolved in a merging of listener and speaker, male and female, within a common performative experience. In Kalapalo fantasy, the openly expressed feelings of men and women toward their own sexuality and their hidden fears about the very persons of the opposite sex to whom they are drawn by passion are all blended into complex mythological images that create a sense of the ambiguity of gender classification and the artifice in the cultural construction of sexuality.

The reaction of listeners to these stories suggests further that these myths may reproduce hidden feelings. Although the feelings of the characters may be found in real individuals, Kalapalo find such mythic figures bizarre and even ridiculous, laughing rather than shuddering when the transformation is described. This attitude is clear from the expletives listeners use to commenting upon a speaker's discourse during the narrative and from the occasional interjected commentary of the speaker, who breaks the performance to laugh and express a personal judgment or, as Kambe did, to associate himself with a most dreadful character ("Sakatsuegï," l. 788). The Kalapalo apparently need to create a comfortable distance from these mythological characters, which is enhanced by portraying them as grotesquely exaggerated caricatures. However familiar the emotions may be to a listener, a strong sense of condemnation accompanies the mythic characters throughout their peregrinations, further creating distance between the complex idea of the character and the participants in the narrative event.[10] These mythic symbols thus have a deeply ambiguous quality, being fascinating and abhorrent at the same time, suggesting that they depend upon essentially privately held experiences of social processes for their deepest significance.

The end of the story of Kutufu, rather than giving an account of the origin of arboreal termites' nests, indicates that a *kutufu* nest sometimes appears as a human being—a dangerous vision (*afïtsatu*) that kills anyone who has the misfortune to see it. People are said to die by means of petrification at the sight of such "monstrous visions," a powerful being suddenly seen in human form, an idea that may have come from observations of animals in extreme fear. If this story is indeed concerned with male fears and fantasies about pregnancy and birth, the sudden vision of a termite nest turned human might be a metaphor for the sudden conscious realization of such fears, which would indeed prevent a person from continuing to live in society. The temptation to give up culture, to give in freely to the urges of the body (especially, in all these stories, to give in to an aggression that is linked to bodily processes), involves pleasure but also horrible suffering. The result is demonic self-transformation, a fascinating but dangerous undertaking. A monster in the form of a natural object that suddenly appears human is a truly petrifying phenomenon. Through it people come face to face with both their own—and their companions'—most hidden realities of feelings; their fear of these feelings thus prevents them from ever returning to the soothing comfort of culturally motivated life.

The themes in these stories are highly pertinent to an argument made by Melford Spiro several years ago (1979), who demonstrated convincingly that themes of aggression and sexuality are consistently "interpreted out of existence" by anthropologists practicing structuralist analyses of myth and ritual. Although Spiro used as his chief example the Bororo myth that served Lévi-Strauss as his key text in *The Raw and the Cooked*, his argument that aggression and sexuality are important concerns in both myth and ordinary social life was broadly framed and reconstructed within a Freudian model of the relation between culture and aggression, especially the argument in *Civilization and Its Discontents*. Spiro contrasted Freud's idea that aggression persists in a state of culture, albeit inhibited by the superego, with Lévi-Strauss's interpretation of the key text (in which conscienceless aggression among members of a family occurs) as representing the transition from nature to culture. Spiro noted, "Since absence of anxiety and guilt implies an absence of cultural norms prohibiting aggressive behavior, in Freud's view this myth could not possibly represent a transition from nature to culture."[11] Because he focused on the problem of whether there is an underlying interpretative opposition between nature and culture in the myth, Spiro's criticism did not include an examination of how Bororo social life might have contributed to specifically Bororo attitudes toward aggression and sexuality, as well as to the meaning of mythological symbolism of those themes in relation to such experiences and attitudes. The Kalapalo stories I have discussed in this chapter metaphorize the complex ideas of compulsive aggression, sexuality, and moral conscience and suggest ways of conceiving their relationship. Rather than being vague abstractions, each of these is understood by the Kalapalo as a motivational process, characterized by feelings, resolutions, goals, and specific enactments.

Chapter 7

Saturated with Music, Submerged in Sense

Although Dawn People and powerful beings are distinguished by their use of speaking and musicality, these symbolic channels in Kalapalo narrative art are also complementary communicative codes that establish a world to which both types of entities belong and in which they reciprocally attend to each other. This world is reproduced during ritual performances, in which Kalapalo collectively adopt the powerful mode of communication through which they engender the experience of a unity of cosmic forces, developed through the unity of sound formed by creative motion. In rituals, too, they most vividly realize their powers of presence. For by collectively performing music, they not only model themselves upon their images of powerful beings, but they feel the worth of those models by experiencing the transformative powers inherent in human musicality. Unlike trance states or those of alternative, illusionary states of consciousness, these transcendant powers unite within a heightened state of sensual consciousness bodily feelings of great intensity, transforming for a time the meanings given to the personal self and to the collectivity as well as the environmental setting.

Many Kalapalo rituals are associated with a mythological idea of the origin of some musical phenomenon (a song or a musical instrument) which is an integral part of that ritual. Rarely, though, is a ritual in its entirety as it might be observed today described in myth, and certainly never in connection with an instrumental goal. (Sometimes we learn the appropriate context for some rituals: the story of Kaŋasiŋi describes the first memorial ritual held by Taugi after his mother's death, while elsewhere we hear about Kumagisa, the man who learned the *Aũugufi* from Snake People, of Jagifunu, who learned the Fishes' *undufe* from the Fish People, or of the origins of the women's *Yamurikumalu*.) The most obvious way, then, that Kalapalo myth and ritual are connected is that myths describe something which we can observe in the present as the most fundamental aspect of ritual performance, namely music, and it informs us as well of some aspects of the context of music's origins.

Aside from the songs used in connection with shamanistic curing, the most important ritual use of music occurs in public, collective events which take place for weeks and sometimes months at a time during the six-month dry season (roughly between May and September). During that season, and especially

at the period of its onset, the Kalapalo are intensely occupied with these complex collective efforts that involve both a musical, performed component and
one that is economic and not performed. The Kalapalo at this time of year are
constantly involved in musical performances that are associated with the most
basic and unquestioned or sacred values and cosmological principles, and which
thus seem to be among the most fundamental religious events in their lives.

These public, collective Kalapalo rituals are—at first sight—rather different from what we have been told about certain African and Oriental events from
consideration of which anthropologists in recent years developed some of the
most influential and fruitful theories of religious action and ritual symbol. I am
thinking especially of Victor Turner's models of the ritual symbol, of liminality
and communitas,[1] of Geertz's ideas concerning the ritual event as a symbolic
text[2] and of Fernandez's notion of ritual meaning as metaphoric predication on
inchoate pronouns.[3] Despite their differences, all these scholars seem to work
with a set of unstated assumptions about the content of ritual action: that it is
built up from concrete symbols that carry discursive referential and exegetical
meaning; that this meaning tends to be metaphorical in a double sense—formally expressing relations of similarity to their referents and sharing meaningful
correspondence with other domains of a culture; and that the understanding of
ritual meaning must take into account the intent of participants, the goal of ritual
action. The anthropological study of ritual thus has a number of correspondences with linguistics (if it has not purposefully drawn from that field). For
anthropologists have analyzed ritual as if it were a language that can and should
be "translated" or "interpreted," even when (as Victor Turner has taken care to
emphasize) ritual symbols also "say the unsayable."

What must we make, then, of rituals that use few and at best stereotypic
symbolic objects and little or no speech? How might those extremely productive
anthropological theories of religion and ritual cited above apply to activities in
which the acts of musical composition and musical performance, while communicating and expressing deeply felt religious ideas, are even more important
as systems for constructing religious experiences, serving as symbols because
of inferences concerning what those experiences mean? Indeed, the phenomenon of musical ritual forces us to ask several fundamental questions. First, if
we cannot understand musical ritual chiefly from meanings given to the musical
content, must we consider it in the main a nondiscursive physical and emotional
experience? Second, what are the connections and differences at the formal and
logical levels on the one hand and of performance and experience on the other
between linguistic modes of constructing meaning and musical modes? The
answers to these questions will have implications for contemporary theories of
religion and for our anthropological understanding of musicality, which is (as
Zuckerkandl reminds us) as crucial to our understanding of ourselves as spiritual beings as is language. In this chapter, I address these issues by examining
several Kalapalo performances, showing what is distintive in general about Kalapalo musical rituals and how different musical performances create a variety
of transmundane experiences for them.

Talking about Music

For the Kalapalo, music is, like speech, a process of living, but, because it encompasses all other types of utterances, especially speech (thereby yielding song), it is the clearest manifestation of the highest degree or level of animacy: that of powerful beings. The transitive verb stem *aŋ-* is used in reference to collective instrumental or song performances during which people "dance," or more correctly, make rhythmic motions with their feet (*tetsuiti*, "shuffling"). By "collective" I refer (as do the Kalapalo) to performances of the same music by members of a community; from one instance of performance to another the relations between participants and observers change, resulting in virtually full group participation. "Collective," in other words, does not imply that everyone is participating at once but that all eventually do participate and also actively observe at some time during the ritual process.

In contrast to the performance of music, which is a collective process, a noun (*igi-*) is used in reference to a musical piece—a song or a line of instrumental music—and the verbalization of this noun (*igiñu-*) refers to an act of singing; playing on an instrument is *on-*. These acts may or may not be performed; the terms do not imply collective participation as does *aŋ-*. "Collective musical performance" thus is constructed from "musical pieces"; the latter may be played or sung independently of performance and are frequently quoted in nonritual contexts (such as storytelling) so that listeners may learn them. Finally, the word *itolotepe* ("birding") refers to the performance of songs that have concrete referential meaning and that, unlike music that occurs during *aŋ-*, have been "pieced together" by human beings (*fes-*; the same verb means "articulate a skeleton" and "sew together pieces of a garment").

By naming an aspect of life, the verb *aŋ-* implies animacy of a supreme degree, the hyperanimacy of powerful beings that involves dangerous creativity and lack of personal restraint, especially that control of aggressive urges with which the Kalapalo seem so occupied. The hyperanimacy of powerful beings, the source of music, is life in its most complete, unrestrained, and infinitely varied expression, the creative source but also one of dangerous transformative power, of violence, witchcraft, and destruction. Human beings can use music to charm and soothe powerful beings by engaging them in a performance that temporarily controls their ferocity, enticing them into forgetting for the moment their antipathy toward the performer. It is important, Kalapalo say, to be able to perform music when in the presence of powerful beings, for music disarms dangerous monsters so as to make them forget themselves. This is also an important theme in many stories about personages who outwit the most dangerous monsters. Music "soothes a savage breast" in ways that language cannot.

Similarly, the *kefege* or song spells that contemporary Kalapalo shamans own and the songs they use in curing rituals are forms of music that they receive from powerful beings so that the latter can be called to help cure seriously ill people. In addition, the music associated with particular powerful beings that is performed during collective ritual performances can be used in serious cases to attract those *itseke* to the settlement so that they may be persuaded to help a victim whose *akūa* has been temporarily lost.

In these several contexts of people's relations with powerful beings, then, music (or more exactly, musical performance) is identified by the Kalapalo as having controlling force over aggressive, transformative, and wandering power; it is also a manifestation of that power. The ability of music to control and channel aggression, to limit hyperanimacy in ways that are helpful to people, has further consequences for understanding its importance within ritual contexts. This is because in such contexts of use, political life—the relations of control that some people effect over others—achieves its most concrete and elaborate expression.

Musical Rituals

Musical performance as such does not have fixed or assigned meanings, but in ritual contexts music is always an important symbol. Musical performance is associated with the imagined characteristics of certain primordial inventors or composers, namely, the transformative and dangerous hyperanimate power of specific powerful beings (though not, it seems, specific kinds of transformative power). This meaning is further extended in the experience of "affecting presence" generated by music; music's power over a listener (and even more so, over the performer) is defined as the power embodied in the mythological creator. This meaning, however, refers to the phenomenon "musical performance," not to the particular characteristics of particular pieces. And in the case of performance of songs with words, *itolotepe* (see Appendix 3), the meaning of the songs is derived explicitly from the verbal component and not the musical one.

The association made between music and hyperanimacy appears at a number of levels of meaning and experience within the ritual performative frame, for it is expressed not only in the general ideas concerning sound symbolism that I discussed in Chapters 4 and 5, but in the contexts of costuming, the aesthetic of musical performance, and the complex semantic connections the Kalapalo make between musicality and sexuality.

Costuming

When masks are used in ritual performances to represent specific powerful beings, the features of the masks complement the musical effect. Kalapalo masks are generally crudely modeled objects made from gourds, slabs of wood, or pieces of old hammocks upon which are painted vivid, glistening, but very simple designs. All the features of masks are exaggerated because powerful beings are supposed to be intensely alive. The eyes of the masks are made from pieces of mother-of-pearl, representing the gleams of light that are the sign of hyperanimacy. If there are ears, they protrude considerably from the head, and the noses are long and unbridged. A pair of long red cotton strings representing the tongue and breath—from which music is produced—hang from the gaping mouths of masks representing beings who are closely associated with musical performances. The masks' mouths are surrounded with the long, spiky teeth of the dogfish or pieces of a large piranha's mandible from which protrude sharp, triangular slashing instruments. In contrast with the vivid, shining features of the mask, the rest of a performer's costume is made from dried burity palm materials, which have turned a greyish tan color. Feathers are not worn with masks except on the Whirlwind mask, to the rear of which is tied a long ornament of black and white feathers that represents the ability of this being to fly in any possible direction (Turtle Monster wore a similar ornament and had the same extraordinary powers of flight). Having been prepared over a number of days or even weeks, the dancers emerge from the ceremonial house in the center of the plaza into an environment that is dull in color. The grass-thatched houses of the circular settlement are uniformly grey in appearance, while the plaza, cleared of grass and packed hard by constant comings and goings, soccer games, and dances, has acquired the characteristically reddish yellow color of the local lateritic soil. Surrounding the forest are a variety of greenish bushes and low trees, whose colors also tend toward the greyish hues.

The effect of a mask emerging from the ceremonial house is therefore startling. The masks have bright black, white, and red designs that contrast with the rest of the costume, which blends in with the environmental background. And like the tails of sting rays, of certain large and dangerous lizards, and of hawks and eagles, this sharp contrast between dark and light on an otherwise dull background is a sign of potential for violence that galvanizes the attention of the observer and says, "dangerous powers: beware."

If performers are not wearing masks, they decorate themselves with brilliant body paint and feather ornaments. The colors available to the Kalapalo for decoration and use as symbols are red, black, white, yellow, and blue. Normally used in combination, these colors have symbolic values that should be understood both for the individual meanings assigned each color and their combined significance in particular contexts of use.

Singly, black is used when men communicate directly with powerful beings. Sleep, the night, states of narcosis, unconsciousness and death—the loss of externally visible light—are conditions for what I called "illusionary consciousness," what the Kalapalo understand to be situations of contact with powerful beings. In place of visible light is given sight of the world of creative, inventive, hyperanimate power, which shamans try to understand by inducing such states of consciousness. Hence powerful beings are associated with darkness and with the color black, because of their presence in a world that is different from the one accessible to ordinary sight, and which is far from the world of externally visible light that is provided by the sun and by fire. (Powerful beings are internally lit, and their eyes betray this inner illumination.) In the domain of powerful beings, fear is the prime emotion of the human traveler, and great caution must attend each visit. The shaman and wrestler darken their bodies and faces with pot black, leaving the area around their eyes unpainted, as a way of making themselves less visibly human and appearing more like a powerful being.

Black paint in the form of genipapa juice is used to paint the main participants (sponsors) in ceremonies that commemorate dead *anetaü*. Here, the design is associated literally with the original snake owners of the ritual, but the color of the paint makes reference to the connection between the ritual activities and death.[4]

But although painting one's body black is a way of creating a ritual identity between oneself and powerful beings that involves effacement of one's human qualities, *itseke* are strongly attracted by the "beautiful" color red. Red cloth, red feathers, and fragrant red paint in the form of *miŋi* or *ondo*[5] are dazzling enticements to powerful beings, a visual metaphor for the fearful attraction of power. Although hiding themselves with black paint, the shamans tie onto their heads red cloth or red feather ornaments to attract the powers they desire to communicate with. Red is the color that commands attention, that symbolizes heightened states of material consciousness: alertness, intelligence, vivacity, active engagement with the world.

Their bodies fragrant and gleaming with this red and black paint (sometimes set off with white so as to emphasize the designs), men decorate themselves during ritual with the feathers of toucans and macaws. Over their biceps they tie yellow and red breast feathers of the blue and yellow and red macaws. On their heads, over a plaited crownlike hat, they tie ornaments made from the "toucan's pubic hair" (soft yellow and red feathers that grow under the tails of these birds) and from the tail and wing feathers of macaws. Their ears are adorned with brilliant toucan feather earrings. Finally, both men and women try to supplement their traditional ornaments with blue and green beads: women wear long, very thick necklaces of glass seed beads which men sometimes make into patterned belts; men like to bind their knees with cotton thread, and though any color is acceptable, green and blue are preferred to red and yellow because of the contrast with the colors of ritual featherwork. The effect of this costuming is a vivid polychromaticism associated with the Dawn People. But feather ornaments are most closely connected with Taugi the trickster, who wore them as a sign to his hosts that he had come in anger, hoping to destroy them through his deceptive powers. Hence with their polychromatic costuming the Kalapalo have invented another reminder of the source of their own distinctive creative powers.[6]

Egitsu and Undufe Rituals

The Kalapalo classify their public rituals into two general categories. The word *egitsu*, meaning "visited" or "attended upon," refers to events that culminate in a climactic performance in which formally invited communities within the Upper Xingu social realm participate. Included in this category are the Egitsu proper, a ritual that commemorates dead *anetaü* or "leaders"; the Ipoñe or boys' ear-piercing ritual (an event that is a classic rite of passage); the women's Yamurikumalu and men's Kagutu rituals; the Katugakugu ("mangabeira sap object"), a rubber ball game ritual; Takwaga, in which flutes of the same name are played; and Ifagaka, the spear-throwing ceremony. All of these rituals involve repeated performances of music in the host community over a considerable period of time before the climactic performance that includes the visitors. In addition, because *egitsu* rituals involve athletic competition between guests and hosts, for several months before the appearance of the guests, the hosts practice their skills (as the guests are doing in their own settlements).[7]

The rituals called *undufe* are performances that include only the members of a particular settlement.[8] Among these are the Kaŋa undufegï, "Fishes' Undufe"; Eke undufegï, "Snakes' Undufe"; Fugey Oto, or "Arrow Master" ritual; Agë, the manioc ritual; Afugagï; and several in which masks associated with the *itseke* "owners" of the music are manufactured and used: Kafugukuegï (howler monkey ritual), Afasa (the forest cannibal monster), Žakwikatu, Kwambï, and Pidyë (powerful beings who were placed in the water by Taugi), and the Whirlwind undufe, Atugua.

The Structure and Experience of a Musical Performance

The climactic performance of a Kalapalo ritual always follows a series of preliminary events that sometimes occur over an entire year. For this reason, we have to be concerned with a long series of repetitive incidents and a process that extends over a long period of time rather than with single events. People often learn music and dances during these preliminary performances, so they are used by the performers to practice their skills and to try out the effect of their costumes, but these are not events designed solely for practice. Especially significant is the constant redefinition of space in the community as ritual space and of certain times of year as ritual time, or more precisely, as liminal space and time, "time out of time" and space that is literally siteless. These attributes result from the way musical performances are structured.

Most Kalapalo music is measured in that it is accompanied by rattles and dances in which the body is used as an instrument for measuring time, for establishing a common pace. A beat group is the dominating feature of a piece of music, repeated small groups of beats constituting the structure of the piece. Musical pieces are almost invariably structured in rhythmic and text patterns of four or eight: first, a softly sung or played tone center is rapidly repeated four times within a rhythmic beat that is measured by a performer's step or by a flute being raised and lowered (the tone center occurs within a four- or eight-beat measure); second, an initial part or "portion" (*akwalu*) of the piece proper in which the first melodic line is structured in four- or eight-beat measures that vary in rhythm; third, a second "portion" with a second melodic line (similarly structured as to meter but also rhymically varied); fourth, a third portion (less common); and fifth, the tone center repeated to mark the end of a section before a new verse or repetition of the whole. In full performance each of the constituent portions is repeated. When a single person or a group is performing, the repetition of each piece occurs either two or four times in each house or in the plaza, but some performances feature pairs of singers, in which case each singer takes a portion in turn, singing it twice before a new song is started. Pairs of singers or players are usually mismatched, in that an older or more knowledgeable person who teaches is coupled with a younger or less experienced one or one who is learning. Finally, when men and women sing in unison (during the *ipoñe* or ear-piercing songs and the Agë, a manioc-planting ritual) each gender-based group deliberately sings a whole pitch apart from the other, so that a sense of two distinct but united voices is evident.

The nature of Kalapalo musical motion seems designed to emphasize the hypnotic rhythm of the music. This rhythmic experience involves a structure of continuously repetitive motion: repetition of the steps of the performers, repetition of the tones, repetition of the performance by each participant in a single event, repetition of the entire event from day to day, repetition of the ritual through time, from the original performance that a Dawn Person saw (described in a myth, perhaps) until the present event. But this repetition is patterned; it is not simply the occurrence of precisely homogeneous forms over and over. For the aesthetic of ritual repetition incorporates the use of structured variation, which is as much a matter of individual differences among the performers as it is a consequence of the melodic, rhythmic, and textual changes in the music.

The continuously repetitive movements of groups of Kalapalo dancing in unison seem to bring out what Zuckerkandl calls the "ceaseless repeated beating of the metric wave."[9] A tune cannot be easily sung without the movement of the body, especially the legs (in nonperformative contexts, a person might swing in his or her hammock or merely tap a hand on a nearby house post to represent this bodily motion), nor is the song complete without the rhythmic accompaniment of the dancers' feet. The movements of Kalapalo dance also help to mark changes in the direction of the melody. As I discussed above, Kalapalo musical pieces typically consist of a pair of melodic lines of complex rhythm that are repeatedly exchanged, and with each change the dancers reverse their movements; sometimes this exchange is between a pair of singers. Dance motions also emphasize changes from one of these repeated pairs to the start of a new verse, a return to the beginning of the old melody, or the start of an entirely new melody and set of rhythms. Finally, Kalapalo dance brings out the spatial side of the musical symbol by uniting discrete places, dissolving the differences between autonomous houses, and uniting the residents into an undifferentiated whole. From a musical point of view, space is used as an important compositional resource, as important as are the tones themselves, for Kalapalo melodies are constructed from at most four tones (entire vocal pieces have no more than six tones and many flute pieces have but three), and those of a single ritual convey a somewhat stereotyped impression as a consequence, an impression that is compounded by the incessant repetition of the performance. Hence the salience of rhythm and space as devices for structuring a ritual event would seem especially important for developing the aesthetic of patterned repetition.[10]

Although everyone strives for correct performance, it is recognized that each person has a slightly different interpretation, an impression formed by the performer's physical appearance, the care taken in selecting the elements for a costume (and how well these conform to the generalized ideal to which everyone subscribes), and of course a person's musical abilities, the care with which an *itseke* is represented, and how the performer's own character influences what is actually done. Some people are said to know much more about a particular powerful being and thus represent that being more clearly than do others. (I have heard, for example, some people speak admiringly of how well their Arawak neighbors the Waura represent the difficult *auūgufi* polyrhythmic motions—body, voice, and rattles—of the Snake People.)

The patterning that involves this subtle variation in each act of repetition also occurs in collective performances, in which people group themselves into lines. When such a line of dancers moves from one place to another, it is led by the "beautiful ones" of the community, the young secluded boys or girls who are also *anetaū* (in the case of the *egitsu* rituals, which are always sponsored by *anetaū*), or, during an *undufe*, by the most experienced song leaders. In the middle of the line dance the "ordinary" (*talokito*) people, and at the very end, perfunctorily decorated and barely able to keep up with their elders, are the young children. When a line of performers remains relatively stationary, they face in a single direction with the song leaders in the center, flanked by the less experienced singers and finally the youngest of the group. As with the patterned repetition that occurs as dancers move from one house to another, uniting different houses into a spatial whole, this linear formation emphasizes personal differences among the participants while paradoxically uniting all those individuals into a collective whole. This unity creates a tension within patterned repetition that involves simultaneous collective homogeneity and individual difference.

The musical performances of both *egitsu* and *undufe* rituals typically involve a simple, recurrent patterning in which virtually everyone of the appropriate sex and age participates, either at once or sequentially. The first performance, marking the opening of ritual time, occurs in the central plaza (*fugombo*), the central communal space beneath which are the graves and in which is located the ceremonial house (*kuakutu*), where costumes are made and stored during the ritual period. The dancers move from this area to the house of the sponsor, performing either inside by encircling a central storage platform or dancing in a line facing the front entrance (there may also be a performance outside in front of the house), then emerge and continue the same performance in every other house in the village circle. The events end with a final performance in the plaza. Normally this first enactment occurs during a liminal time of day: at the very beginning of dawn (*mitote*) or at the end of the day just before sunset (*kohotsi*). I stress this timing because during such times of day people normally are at their most idle, reflecting upon their dreams of the previous night, seeking out their lovers, or sitting in the plaza or before the entrances to their houses gossiping about what has happened during the day. All these activities emphasize personal relationships, introspection, and thinking about the effectiveness of one's relationships with others, in marked contrast with those occurring during the ritual events. The timing of Kalapalo ritual performances thus seems to restrict people in their thoughts about matters that are potentially destructive of group harmony.

Just as the communally performed *aŋ*- establishes in a performative manner the time of year as that of ritual, so the interior movement of the event unites the two halves of each house (separated by the storage platform), and the house-to-house movement links each autonomous social space into a ritual whole that is communal and egalitarian. Similarly, because the performance is communal, people from different households and of different families are expected to work collectively for the ritual. In other ways there is a purposive homogenization of the factional divisions resulting from kinship and marriage ties. Men who are brothers do not dance next to each other, nor do they play flutes together, and women must not dance with their husbands but with men from other households. Furthermore, as the movement of the performers within the space of the settlement creates a spatial unity, so the dance and music together unify the bodies of the participants physically, thereby creating or at least enhancing an experience of unity of persons, of space, and of time that differs from that of nonritual life.

As the series of preparations continues (they may be year-long in the case of the *egitsu* or only a few weeks long in the case of the *undufe*), each performance intensifies—indeed, visually compresses or condenses—these temporal, spatial, and social images by means of the spatial movements and ritual components that occur. As the date of the climactic event draws nearer and the level of economic activity accompanying it increases, along with greater public work by the ritual officers, so (in the case of the *egitsu*) do the ritual performances occur more and more within the central plaza, and the participants in both *egitsu* and *undufe* are more numerous. Sometimes there is obvious movement from house circle to plaza, as in the case of the Egitsu performances. Similarly, the ritual becomes more complex. Earlier performances, led by a few undecorated and poorly rehearsed song leaders (*igiñoto*), are followed by larger, more spontaneously formed, and more elaborately decorated groups; in the final performances masks are sometimes used, portraying the faces of the *itseke* inventors of the music. This intensification and compression of ritual time and space and of the unity of the community seems to be felt by the performers through the cumulative effects of their dance movements, repeated costuming of their bodies, and increasing satisfaction resulting from greater performative success. In other words, an intensification of feeling occurs, not about a ritual object but about the ritual experience. In particular, it is the experience of a wonderful power of community emerging from group performance, with a concomitant deemphasis on the inner self and the problems of individuals that is the Kalapalo sense of their ritual musicality.

Let us consider first the "tone" aspect of the performance. A curious aspect of most Kalapalo ritual music is that with the exception of the *itolotepe* and songs associated with the Kwambï, it is rarely accompanied by intelligible words; it consists either of the playing of flutes unaccompanied by songs or of virtually meaningless song texts. Songs are sometimes said to be in another of the local Upper Xingu languages or in a language identified as Kalapalo but unintelligible to current speakers (the Yamurikumalu songs, for example, some of which are in Arawak—a fact the Kalapalo singers deny). Some are in effect tone syllables (similar to our "do re mi") that repeatedly assert a tone center (in Kalapalo, *igitomi*, "in order to sing it"). When songs are sung in Kalapalo the texts consist of seemingly banal descriptions of the beings represented by the performers or very brief descriptions of mythological events, such as "Anteater, the long-nosed one," "Look, look, I'm wearing *itali* paint, I'm wearing red paint," or of repetitive metaphorically constructed lines, such as "the Other Parrot's mouth is opened." To interpret the latter, one must know the story behind the song, that is, the situation in which the song was invented. Few people (mainly older song leaders) know these stories, and those who do not know them claim to be unable to interpret the songs though they know the words. For these people, these words have no signification.

How, then, are we to interpret these "meaningless" songs? My answer is that the specifically musical nature of the performance is the symbolic medium out of which ritual communication is fashioned. With several important exceptions that I will examine later in this chapter, all Kalapalo songs approach "pure" singing and focus the efforts of the singer on the experience of musicality. Thus the performers are afforded a privileged relationship with the special temporal-spatial frame of myth, "the Beginning," the time when human beings could "approach" *itseke* and gain firsthand an experience of their musicality.

Musical performance is associated with powerful beings and is a means of communicating with them although it is not directly addressed to them. The apparently banal and repetitive nature of the lexically meaningful songs emphasizes the crucial objects and attributes that make them distinctive, which the singers need to focus on during the performance—the powerful beings such as Anteater or Ulejalu. Communication may be said to occur not by singing *to* a powerful being but by singing it *into being*. Highly focused mental images of the powerful being are created in the minds of the performers by means of the performance, an act of magic. There is a consequent merging of the self with what is sung about; just as in myth powerful beings participate in human speech, so in ritual humans participate in *itseke* musicality and thereby temporarily achieve some of their transformative power. In public ritual, this is power of community. Rather than implying danger and ambivalence, however, it is collective solidarity emerging out of a performative experience of social restructuring and communal labor, representing a transformative power with markedly creative effects, including the ability to create its own social organization and to help cure the most seriously ill.

In a masterful exposition of the meaning of musical experience, Victor Zuckerkandl writes of the function of singing to create "an enlargement, an enhancement of the self, a breaking down of the barriers separating the self from things, subject from object, agent from action, contemplator from what is contemplated: it is a transcending of this separation, its transformation into a togetherness." In situations without singing "self and object are sharply distinguished." Zuckerkandl continues, "Thus music is appropriate, even helpful, where self-abandon is intended or required—where the self goes beyond itself, where subject and object come together."[11] In choral singing, as often occurs among the Kalapalo during their rituals, the roles of singer and listener are combined, resulting in a person's feeling at one with the group through what (s)he/they are producing and which (s)he/they listen to. In such situations, a person feels, first, at one with the group, and second, an awareness as a musical performer of the concreteness of objects, their exteriority, while experiencing their essential unity with the self, and finally, there is a sense of "space without distinction of places" and "time in which past and future coexist within the present," that is, of the movement of tones which is music itself.[12]

We can now begin to think of the musical aspect of Kalapalo rituals as liminal in many of the senses of the term that Turner developed for it[13] because, through the unification of space and time on the one hand and of persons on the other, Kalapalo musicality enhances among both performers and observers an awareness of the possibility of communitas. This result is achieved by concretely effecting that experience. The economic, instrumental events in Kalapalo ritual which parallel these musical performances also exhibit qualities of communitas in that ordinary relations between the residents of a settlement which tend to divide households, promote jealousies, and prevent group unity are transcended, overcome temporarily by means of the enactment of ritual office and communal labor. Although liminality is usually treated as an anti-structural vision that is at once opposed to but a commentary upon the structure of social life, Kalapalo rituals of the sort I have been describing are, like Turner's "normative communitas," liminal events that periodically emerge from the experience of one kind of social structure—of hierarchically defined obligation and hierarchically framed speaking whose contexts are precisely defined and bounded—to create, by means of the generalization of those same obligations and ways of speaking, a temporary experience of the communal whole, of equality of person and of feeling.

The Kalapalo speak of their experience of communal performance, especially in a ritual context, by means of the verb -ail-. This verb is most often used to speak of rituals in which several types of musical performances occur simultaneously, as during the Egitsu or the Kaŋa Undufegï, when flute playing and several types of communal singing occur at once. The word is also used to refer to a sense of satisfaction resulting from the resolution of a group problem or the accomplishment of a difficult task by a group. Finally, the word is often used to describe a group of people cheering as a sign of that collective feeling of satisfaction. In each usage, the term refers to a collective feeling or its manifestation resulting from a group effort; for this reason I have translated it "feeling harmony," in the sense of "agreement in feeling," or "appropriate combination of elements in a whole" (following *Webster's*). I do not think it would be going too far to call this a South American version of the experience of communitas. Turner's use of this term emphasizes a process of homogenization or equalization of personal qualities and of structurally pertinent differences that characterize social life, whereas the Kalapalo are inclined to use differences among individuals within their aesthetic of repetition that is both experiential and performative. For the Kalapalo (and perhaps other central Brazilian peoples who devote much of their lives to collectively performing musical ritual) it is music as an enacted symbol that communicates and at the same time creates an experience of communitas. Applied to musical ritual, *-ail-* expresses the joy of experiencing communal action.

Instrumental Events of a Kalapalo Ritual

While the musical performances of the *egitsu* are being held, another series of events is taking place, the two sequences paralleling one another in that each instance of one must accompany an instance of the other. The nonmusical events involve principally economic and scheduling tasks, events with clear instrumental goals which together constitute a community project. The community at large (called *sandagï*, which I call "followers") is led by special hereditary ritual officers known collectively as *anetaü* (singular, *anetu*) who manage, organize, and plan the ritual process. Roughly half of the population of the community receives this designation, including persons of both sexes and all ages, but only the oldest and most experienced consistently hold office.[14] Lesser tasks are generally allocated among the younger *anetaü* when an event is sufficiently complex to warrant the use of more than two or three organizers. In the case of the *egitsu*, when as many as five other settlements are invited, each is assigned a leader who serves as messenger (*tiñï*, or "getter") and who is responsible for seeing that his guests are well cared for. He expects payment (normally in the form of shell ornaments or a large Waura pottery vessel) from the visiting group. In the context of these role enactments, the leaders are referred to as *taiyope* ("associated with conversation") or *tagioto* ("conversation masters"). As planners of the complex project, ritual officers schedule and coordinate the public works projects: cleaning up the public space of the settlement, especially the *fugombo* or central plaza, the formal entrance path, and that leading to the bathing place; arranging the collecting, processing, and distributing of food that will be used to pay the participants by the sponsor or to feed the guests later on; collecting raw materials for the manufacture of costumes. These activities must be coordinated with the specific tasks associated with the sending of invitations to other settlements, the preparation of campgrounds outside the settlement, and the collecting and processing of food and firewood that will be given to the visitors upon their arrival.

During much of their public activities, the *anetaü* use a special oratorical style that marks their speech as truthful by means of the repetition of sentences using emphatic-imperative modes of verbs, modes that, rather than implying that demands are being made, are forms that allow a speaker to assert that the activity in question is "good to perform," that it "should be done."

This special way of speaking associated with *tagioto* and the manner of separating themselves spatially from their followers during such oratory marks them as formally distinct through the content of their very utterances: they have the right to urge assistance from the others, to direct the others to do certain collective work. Yet, although these *anetaū* have a certain authority, their decisions are supposed to be formed after opinions have been received from all the adults in the community; their organization of collective work represents community consensus and is motivated by community rather than personal goals.

In nonritual contexts Kalapalo social life tends to be organized around household groups and networks of relatives. The *anetaū* play no role outside of ritual life (except when they are called upon to distribute presents from outsiders), and collective economic activities are organized only within such frameworks. Economic activity associated with ritual life requires a different set of productive relations than those of nonritual economic life. Also, the productive forces are more complex in ritual contexts; more efficient technology is used, resulting in greater productivity, a need for more, and more greatly intensified, labor than normally occurs in kinship and household contexts. Hence the organization, coordination, and scheduling of labor become more complex, making the hereditary officialdom/follower contrast an especially appropriate form of organizing people through application of a principle of social personhood that is different from that of kinship and affinity. Ritual social organization transcends that of kinship and affinity.

In thinking about this reordering of social structure and its essential liminal aspects, I have been concerned about how this symbolic mode and communitas, the feeling engendered by a ritual experience constructed by means of symbols of liminality, could possibly contribute to an understanding of motivation and action oriented toward concrete goals. Turner discusses the dissolution of normal social boundaries and the unification of persons principally in terms of their affectual consequences. He thus leaves open the question of what happens as a consequence of such changes in feeling. How, then, does the experience of communitas concretely affect motivation and subsequent action toward the achievement of goals?

One possibility is to think of communitas as involving a redefinition of the connections between self-identity, moral representations, and the extension of a field of ethical judgments. In the case of self-identity, Turner claims that participants in a liminal process have effectively effaced the "normal" components of their culturally constructed personae, to have redefined their ties to one another so as to appeal to their common humanity, experienced through the enactment of meaning particular to the liminal symbols of the culture in question. (For the Kalapalo, "common humanity" is common membership in the community, which is almost the same as being human because it means adopting the most fundamental moral representations concerning personal conduct; this unity can at best be extended only to other Upper Xingu residents and to the rare foreigner who resides among them. Hence for them it is as important for such outsiders to want to participate in their ritual life as to follow their dietary practices and ideas about *ifutisu*-generated behavior.)

What does this new "self-identity" ("I am Kalapalo" as opposed to "I am Kambe's daughter-in-law," for example) imply about moral representations and ethical judgments, about the ideas concerning how people are expected to conduct themselves toward one another, and how that behavior is evaluated? Clearly, and still within Turner's model, it implies equality or more exactly, identity of participation. Economically, it means that everyone is obligated to participate, but everyone receives regardless of contribution. *Ifutisu*, the most basic value of Kalapalo life (subsuming the notions of generosity, modesty, flexibility, and equanimity in facing unusual social difficulties, and respect for others) is extended beyond the domain of the family to all people in the community. Furthermore, this is not a vague sense of solidarity but is concretely realized through the delineation of peoples' duties during ritual processes. In nonritual contexts, *ifutisu* is expected among persons linked by kinship and affinal ties, particularly among people who live in the same household. But people who share outside their network are suspect: if someone has unexpectedly accumulated a large amount of food (a bounty of fish or an unexpectedly large harvest of melons) a *taiyope* is appointed to effect a communal distribution in the plaza. In ritual life the value of generosity is generalized or universalized to incorporate everyone in ordered relations of mutual sharing and reciprocity. Showing one's generosity has multiple applications in ritual contexts, many more than in nonritual ones; this may be why the effect is said to be "communal joy." Kalapalo seem to enjoy having a chance to share with those they normally do not or cannot share with, and they can do so in many ways: by giving away food, pooling raw materials, helping to process and store food, redistributing food, dividing one's own portion even further, participating in the musical performances, contributing expertise (as songmaster, maskmaker, herbalist, or medical specialist), lending ornaments and sharing paints and dyes, agreeing to plan and organize the entire process, to serve as *taiyope*. As Turner points out in considering the experience of communitas, "Communitas does not merge identities; it liberates them from conformity to general norms."[15]

Kalapalo communitas is a temporary state of being, but rather than antistructural or counterstructural, I prefer to think of it as the consequence of a structured order that reorganizes people according to special principles of classification and relationship, and that reorganizes the specific motives and goals they enact. The appropriate attitudes underlying and creating effective collective work are communicated by collective, repeated, patterned musical performance, in which the joy of communal experience is realized. This collective musical performance allows the economic events to be successful, indeed, to occur. If among the Kalapalo productive relations need to be reordered to take advantage of different productive forces that occur because of changing seasonal conditions, there must be some way of creating temporarily new ego identities, social personages that nonetheless remain meaningfully tied to the dominant moral values of the community. This linking of the new components of role seems to effect concretely motivated goals. Kalapalo collective musical ritual not only serves as a model for this collective productive order; in a truly performative manner it makes it exist.

Insofar as Kalapalo ritual life takes up so much time and is directly correlated with major collective subsistence efforts, it is best thought of not so much in contrast with routine, technological existence, as an unusual or special situation of crisis in which "ordinary life" is suspended, but as a mode of constituting life that complements that of the nonritual rainy season. A cyclical reordering of the community's social structure is made possible by the natural seasonal shifts between heavy, continual rainfall and lengthy drought, between a time when food is scarce and public performance nearly impossible and another time when food is amazingly abundant and diverse and environmental conditions are perfect for public performance.

Rituals of Antagonism

The pleasant, efficient forms of restructuring society that occur during the *egitsu* and *undufe* processes are the most common but not the only forms of ritual experience the Kalapalo create for themselves. In fact, the experience of collective solidarity that occurs during such events may not extend beyond the particular group of performers, especially when these are marked by gender identity, or during events that are collective but that paradoxically emphasize the individual character of the performers. In the case of the two complementary gender-marked musical rituals, the Yamurikumalu and the Kagutu, collective solidarity is experienced by members of each gender category within a context of sexual antagonism and is less an experience that permeates the entire community. During yet another ritual called Kwambï, the effective structure of social life is gradually eroded by the conditions of a performative process that ends in a remarkable display of anarchic chaos. It is to these rituals that I now turn.

Kwambï

The name for this ritual is identical with that given to a water being whose mask was created by Taugi as a protective device; this personage is a powerful being represented by a masked performance which is held separately from but in connection with the events presently under consideration. The Kalapalo were not able to explain to me the relationship between this being named Kwambï and the ritual I will describe, nor does there seem to be any connection between the attributes of the powerful being and the peculiar character of the Kwambï performance. Nonetheless, the same person sponsors each ritual, and the occasion for displaying the masks is also the occasion for performing the distinctively "personal" Kwambï songs.

The Kwambï performances with which I am concerned stand in marked contrast with all other Kalapalo public rituals, for they emphasize the individuality of each performer and personal antagonisms revealed by gossip. Rather than creating a collectively uniform performance, each participant sings as an individual, and the songs are equally distinctive.[16] Each day a number of people one-by-one (but often simultaneously) perform these songs, some of which are traditional, others made up for the occasion. Each is associated with someone—often a recent ancestor whose name is remembered. Kwambï songs center on pieces of gossip the singers or original composers once heard about themselves. The gossip is sung back to the community in these songs, as the performers move from house to house, singing before the members of each household (other than the ones to which the singers belong). If the singer knows exactly who invented the "bad words," the performance will be pointedly directed at whomever is concerned.

The form the songs take is simple: lines of gossip punctuated by the comment "the women" or "someone like me." These are generalized references to the original gossipers, whom men say were usually older women, but whom women (more accurately) consider to have been both men and women:

[tone center hummed]
uwiŋguiŋatikiŋaluake, amañufeke itaū
uwiŋguiŋatikiŋaluake, apadyufeke itaū
uwiŋguiŋatikiŋaluake, apadyufeke itaū
uwiŋguiŋatikiŋaluake, amañufeke itaū

efiñanoiŋo akago, eiŋadyamo atofoi, etidyipïgï
      apadyu kigatafo ufeke wāke
efiñanoiŋo akago, eiŋadyamo atofoi
      amañu kigatafo ufeke, itaū-ni

uwiŋguiŋatikiŋaluake, amañufeke itaū. . . .

My dear mother is surely betraying me, the women
My dear father is surely betraying me, the women
My dear father is surely betraying me, the women
My dear mother is surely betraying me, the women

Your own brothers are the ones who will do that,
your own brothers' friends, the offspring,
      My dear father was saying about me, the women
Your own brothers are the ones who will do that,
your own brothers' friends

      My dear mother was saying about me, the women
My dear mother is surely betraying me, the women. . . .
[repeated three times]

Appendix 2 includes a number of other Kwambï songs, which reveal the poignancy of accusations made about a person's alleged witchcraft, stinginess, and antagonistic speech, and how disturbing are leadership claims made when a person is not a hereditary *anetu*. (Such claims seem to have occurred with some frequency because of the death of many older *anetaū* in the measles and influenza epidemics of the 1940s and 1950s.)

A Kwambï performer dresses in an idiosyncratic costume that is put together from personal possessions whose display in some way makes mocking reference to the wearer. A man whose brother had been accused of witchcraft and who was subsequently hounded out of the community dressed himself in bits and pieces of a soldier's uniform and danced with a revolver pointing at the occupants of the houses he entered. A woman who had been accused of stinginess took all her pieces of cloth and tied them haphazardly around her body and head. Similarly, a man tied together pieces of soap and hung them like a flag from an arrow he carried over his shoulder. Although people paint themselves on the final, climactic day of performance, there is no attempt to make oneself a beautiful ritual object (as is done during other rituals). During the Kwambï, people try to embarrass the gossipers by appearing as innocently absurd as possible. Yet each dancer carries something—a manioc grater, an arrow, an unloaded revolver or shotgun, or a bow—that is a reminder to the listeners of the seriousness of the situation, for these objects, though not actually serving as weapons, could easily be turned into such in the event of a serious fight.

The Kwambï process is structured like other rituals in that the first few performances are held by only a few people, generally the song leaders (in this case, men and women who are experts in traditional Kwambï songs) and anyone they can persuade to join them. After several days, however, more and more people join in, the younger people having carefully memorized several songs they will sing each day, others having secretly invented new ones. Some people, hearing songs against them, decide to make up others that will effect revenge. For example, E. declared in a song that he was the lover of "a woman with many lovers," (referring to W.) and this woman in turn reminded him (also obliquely, as if she had heard gossip about it) that her deceased husband once fought E. during a quarrel over the dead man's wife (whom he later divorced to remarry W.). This fight took place eight years ago!

For people like W. and E. the ritual provides an opportunity to jokingly rebuke in public their lovers and friends. Others use the songs of their ancestors, and try to invent costumes people will laugh at and try to imitate. But some Kalapalo find the affair embarrassing and perform reluctantly. And others are embarrassed because their songs refer to former enemies who died long ago; people say they regret these songs because they have outlived the accused witches to whom they were originally addressed. For yet other Kalapalo the event is deadly serious. When the wife of an accused witch heard another woman singing a statement the wife had made about the accusers, the words were so "painful" to her that she rose to strike the singer, and it was only because her brother was able to restrain her in time that a serious fight did not erupt. The accused witch and his wife soon left the community for another settlement.

The final, climactic performance occurs after the sponsor has finally gone fishing "for the masks," when the masking performance itself is held. Then virtually every adult in the community dances from house to house, as before, performing solo rather than in unison. The effect of such individualized, discontinuous performance is cacaphonous chaos. The people who have stopped performing to rest in their houses become more and more agitated as the level of repeated gossip and the pointed antagonism of the singers increase. In particular, the constant accusation of female gossip by male singers develops into a tension between members of the opposite sex, occasionally erupting into minor fights between the women of a particular household and a group of men who bombard them with sung gossip in a group. When Afualu and Ambo were sung to by their male cousins, for example, they suddenly found their own "bad words" too embarrassing to bear, and to stop the singers they threw ashes and piqui mash over them until the men ran out the front door. To effect so intense a level of embarrassment, the Kwambï songs are virtually shouted by the performers, so that there will be no question as to the gossip that is being repeated or who are the sources. Hence unlike much of Kalapalo ritual music that is referentially meaningless, and in which clear emphasis is placed upon tonality and rhythm at the expense of the verbal, Kwambï music has the opposite effect: the songs have words that not only are understood but are personally meaningful to the listeners as well as the singers. To emphasize the verbal attribute of the music, rhythm and tone are subverted by individual performances that when heard simultaneously conflict with one another and disrupt the effects of rhythm and tonality. People further emphasize the words by shouting them, making little effort to sing well. It is only the song leader's performances of traditional songs that are supposed to be especially interesting and tonally beautiful because of the glissando that the singer can effect, which are performed with an emphasis on the musical features. These performances, though solo, are held in such a way that nothing conflicts with them. In such instances, as when a song leader performs alone at night at the onset of the Kwambï, and again the day before the sponsor's fishing for the ritual, people listen carefully and hear some of the particularly beautiful songs. Virtuosity is displayed to the singer's utmost abilities, and the effect is that of a concert rather than a ritual performance.

The Yamurikumalu and Kagutu Rituals: Music and Sexuality

I will discuss in detail two specific *egitsu* rituals, the women's Yamurikumalu and the men's Kagutu. These are distinctive because they involve musical statements about sexuality, statements that are antagonistic if not actually violent in their expression. The Yamurikumalu features collective performances by the women of a variety of songs, whereas during the Kagutu men (normally in groups of three) play on large flutelike instruments of the same name. Each musical performance is prohibited to members of the opposite sex. Women must not see the flutes or the men playing them; men can observe the women singing during Yamurikumalu, but they are supposed to keep a respectful distance. This time social structure is reordered with respect to gender identity. In each instance musical performance is associated symbolically with gender identity and expresses ideas of feeling about members of the gender opposite to that of the performers. In both cases, several types of music that parallel each other in form and content are performed; they are listed and briefly described in Appendices 2 and 3. One can see from this list that in some songs persons of one gender mock those of the opposite, others comment on the ceremony itself, and yet others are associated with the performers' opposite gender.

Yamurikumalu

The myth of the Monstrous Women persented below thematically focuses upon the nature of gender identity and sex role and plays with various transformations of these ideas: how people of one gender might acquire the physical and characterological attributes of the other; how the merging of these characteristics within a single person is associated with the transformation of the individual into a powerful being; how gender identity is associated with particular attributes of human musicality. Another theme that is developed has to do with how collective solidarity among members of the same gender can become so exclusive as to imply the groups' rejection of normal social roles. The myth implies that collective solidarity of one gender of persons is antithetical to social life and motivates behavior that is in violation of the normal bonds of kinship.

The Monstrous Women
Told by Kambe and Kofoño at Aifa, July 24, 1980

They were Monstrous Women.

This is how it happened that they came into existence,
    the Monstrous Women came into existence.
    Others have informed us they are near Cuiaba.
        Far from here, on this side of Cuiaba,   5
            on this side.
    The Christians know nothing about them,
        nothing.
    Now, when someone comes across them they shoot at him.
    They have arrows, think of it,   10
        and they shoot them to kill their food.

Listen. Their sons' ears had just been pierced.
    It all began with their ear-piercing.
        They were already pierced.
    You've seen the ear-piercing,   15
        it was the same event.
    Following that their sons remained lying in their hammocks.
        This was Kamatafigagi.
        He was Ulejalu's son.
        She was their leader.   20

She was their older sister,
 Ulejalu.
Her younger sister was Isa,
 who is still alive at her settlement,
  her body is there.   25
 She is still at Aŋambïtï.
 She has been buried.
We twitch when she sings.
We never see her when she sings there.
She is still alive at her settlement.   30
There are many followers of hers,
 there are still many of her followers.
 They make themselves invisible, *buuk*! like that.
  Their dangerous body paint has made them invisible,
   their dangerous body paint.   35
The boys had remained lying in their hammocks
 and finally they took stomach-cleansing medicine,
  they regurgitated the stomach-cleansing medicine.
   They were regurgitating the stomach-cleansing
   medicine.
Their parents still slept,   40
 they were there still.

The following day at dawn,
 Their mothers made manioc bread,
  so they could break their fast.
   Cold manioc soup was next to it.   45
They went at dawn to the seclusion house.
 Their parents did so from their own houses,
  the parents went to their sons.
   So many of the followers did so.
You've seen the pierced ones.   50
 These people were members of Aŋambïtï Community.
  Monstrous Women,
   those of the Dawn Time a long time ago.
This account of it was told by my grandfathers,
 our distant grandfathers a long time ago.   55
 More recently—look—it was Grandmother who taught it to me,
  it was Grandfather who told it to me.
   Now it continues with me telling it to you.
   That's how it's been done.

They distributed fish, after one month had passed.   60
 When they had finished distributing the fish,
  "Let's go now so our offspring can break their fast."
   He spoke that way.

Her husband spoke to them.
    Ulejalu's husband spoke.   65
        I really don't know who her husband was.
            Her son was Kamatafigagi.
                He himself had just been pierced.
    The women went to make manioc bread.
        The men's spouses prepared their provisions for them.   70
            They went on through the grasslands,
                through the grasslands a long long way.
When the sun was here,
    they came to a place called Ugatsi.
        They had gone to Ugatsi.   75
It's an oxbow lake like this one here.
        They were going to stupefy the fish with fish-poison vine.
        For their sponsor's presentation food.
    They were setting up camp there,
        they were tying up their hammocks.   80
            They did that among the trees.
    Bah ha ah! there were so many people,
            only men were doing that.
                There were no women.
        They had to present food for their offspring,   85
            to have presentation food for their sons.
Then they began to crush fish poison,
        it was crushed.
            You have already seen fish-poison vine being crushed.
    Next they began to muddy the water,   90
        tuh they went on muddying the water,
            and they muddied the water.
    That having been done many *itañe* fish appeared,
        that having been done many *sahundu* fish appeared.
Then they grilled them.   95
    They had already prepared a grill.
        Only the *itañe* heads were split open.
The men were supposed to return in three days.
        They still remained normal.
    "On this very day we will return.   100
        You must go get manioc," they had told their wives.
So they are still not wild, not wild.
    The women are still normal,
        not wild, without dangerous body paint.
            They prepared hot manioc soup.   105
The sun was like this when they went to do that and while they continued
to wait after they were finished, it set.
    What they had just made was going to be used when they ate fish.
        They hadn't eaten any fish for awhile.

They were waiting far too long.
"Surely tomorrow they will come," they said to each other.   110
    "These three days have been completed,
        have been completed,
            on this fourth day they will arrive."
However, the others still slept on.
    They still hadn't come back.   115
The women waited to distribute the hot manioc soup they were
keeping for their spouses.
    Their pubic ornaments *teh he* their pubic ornaments were
    beautiful,
        and their spouses' belts.
They had divided the hot manioc soup.
    They had done all this for their spouses.   120
        They had done all this for the arrival.
        That was why they did it.
They made manioc bread,
    while they were waiting they did that.
        They still remained content.   125
            It was fish for which they were doing all that,
            joyously.
Listen. When the sun was here the others were going to arrive,
    that is why they had done all that.
The women waited,   130
    they waited,
        they waited as the sun set.
Manioc bread had been made,
    in each house that had been done.
        For what the others should have been doing,   135
        for their final arrival.
Then the sun went on,
        but nothing happened.
The sun had set while they were still awaiting the others.
    "Tomorrow it will probably happen," they went,   140
        "Perhaps they don't have enough fish," they told one
        another.
But the others had already done something.
    They had eaten *asasë* fruit, *ku ku ku*,
        they had done that with *asasë*.
They washed themselves with *itali* fruit,   145
    that was done with *iñandzi*.
They put medicine in their eyes *tik*, *tik*,
    they put medicine in their eyes.
        They wanted to be furred.
The next day as well the women threw out their manioc soup which had   150
become bitter.

It had become bitter so they did that.
  "Our pubic ornaments are premature."
    Their pubic ornaments were premature.

The next day they were still waiting at dawn.
  The sun came here, but nothing happened.   155
    "Another day has passed," it was said.
      This one had passed, look.
        Their third day had already passed.
        Their fourth day had also passed.
          But nothing happened!   160
  "What could have happened to them there?
    What could have happened to our children's parents?"
    What could have happened to our children's parents?"
  "My sisters," she told them, Ulejalu said,
    "What could have happened to them?" she asked.   165
  Their children remained enclosed by their seclusion chamber
    while the others were doing as I described.
      In all the houses.
        Their seclusion chambers had been doing that to
        them.
          That was how they were.   170
  A nearly ripened one was scheduled,
    a beautiful person.
  He was Kamatafigagi.
    Her son was the one to whom that was being done.
      Ulejalu's son was the one to whom that was being   175
      done.
  So they remained there.
Very late in the day when the sun was here,
  "Mother," he said.
    (When that was done to them, they were very hungry.
      Those same people, the pierced ones.   180
      Her son.
        He was Kamatafigagi.
          Teh, he was beautiful!)
Next, he came beside her.
  "Mother," he said,   185
    "What could have happened to Father and his companions,
    what?"
  "I don't know," his mother replied.
    "I don't know. I have no idea of what happened to your
    parents.
      Your heartless parents, your heartless parents."
  "Tomorrow I'll go see them,   190
    I'll go see,

I'll go see them," he told her.
"Certainly you must go as you wish."
They went to sleep while it was still early evening.

At the beginning of the next day,   195
    "Mother, I'm going right now."
He took his *kuluta* flute
    and "Na na na" he went away.
        He went to them,
            to see them,   200
                to see his older relatives
He approached a long way through the grasslands called Këape,
    he approached through the grasslands.
        Look, that's very very far from here.
By morning he was still in the grasslands,   205
    during the morning.
The sun had already awakened,
    the sun had already awakened when he was very far away.
He walked on *ti ti ti* toward Agañe.
    At Agañe is water flowing through the grasslands.   210
        It's called Agañe.
It's a creek,
    a creek that flows through the grasslands.
He had passed by it,
    going through the grasslands.   215
He continued to go toward that place,
    toward Ugatsi.
        You see, he had gone very far.
On the horizon we see it, very far away in the distance we see
Ugatsi.
    From where we are in the grasslands.   220
Then he approached *tititi*,
    no longer playing his flute,
        not doing so.
He went on,
    he went on,   225
    he went on,
    he went on,
        and he came there.
He had come to the forest,
    to the cerrado forest.   230
        To the *iñandzi* trees.
Chew chew chew chew he saw them.
    There they were clearing brush,
        chew chew chew to watch for any people coming.
    Brush was being cleared,   235

chew chew chew chew.

Teh he he! they had made a beautifully cleared line of sight.

As he kept coming,

    as he went on he could see them, near their camp.

Then he approached them.   240

    "Our son is right here!" someone said,

      "Here is our son."

        He could see them.

    Then they filled their carrying baskets *pok, pok, pok* with fish,

    and they hid them,   245

      they hid all their fish.

        Pok pok pok pok.

They had really transformed themselves.

    Here on their chests fur had grown,

      on their faces fur had grown,   250

        on their faces fur had grown.

    They had almost become furred animals.

    They had transformed themselves.

    They were to be the ancestors of this,

      they were to be the ancestors of Yamurikumalu.   255

Then he went on.

    "Our son is right here," someone said.

      "Here is our son," someone said to his father.

    "Very well," he replied.

    "We have nothing, my child," he told him. "It's strange we've   260

been unsuccessful."

    They had already hidden their carrying baskets far away.

      They were by the very border of the camp.

    "Very well," he answered.

      All the time he was there he remained seated on the edge of

      a hammock.

While the sun moved over there,   265

    he had been looking around him.

    Their fish grills were nearby,

      looking peculiar.

    They had been emptied,

      that was what had been done to the grills.   270

        (Just as mine was, *hi hi*.)

So, having stayed there awhile,

    "I'm leaving right now," he said.

      "I'm leaving right now, Father."

    "Go then.   275

      It's strange we've been so unsuccessful."

Here on their faces was fur,

      on their foreheads.

    "Well," he said to himself,

"What could have happened to Father and his
    companions?   280
    What could have happened to them here?
        How strange they look."
They had hidden their fish.
    That was done by placing them inside the carrying baskets.
        Bah ah, they had a lot of fish!   285
Perhaps he only took one away.
    Perhaps he only took away two.
        Ndii, he slipped them inside his flute.
It seems to be somebody's mistake.
    How could he have put them inside his *kuluta* flute?   290
    Some have mistakenly said a *kuluta* flute.
        Two were what he carried away, two *itañe*.

He ran all the way back until he arrived when the sun was here.
    To his parent,
    to the woman,   295
    to his mother.
He came back on the trail behind the houses.
    Since he was still secluded people never saw him.
        He only gave the fish to his parent.
He went into his seclusion chamber by piercing through it.   300
    He pierced through the house wall,
        into his seclusion chamber.
Tiki he entered while his mother sat right there.
    She was processing manioc when he did that.
He came to her.   305
    "Dear child," she said,
        "You have just come back again," she said,
            "You have just come back again."
    "Yes, I have just come back again," he replied.
    "Wherever are those strange parents of yours?   310
        Where are your foolish parents?"
    "Mother," he told her,
        "Father and his companions are no longer right."
    "What is wrong?"
    "They are furred all over, their faces and their arms are furred.   315
        Here as well, their legs are furred."
    "What strange thing have they done?"
        His mother was angry when he told her about them.
    "Father and his companions hid their fish from me," he went,
        "They hid it.   320
           When they saw me they hid it.
'We've really been unsuccessful,' it's strange they kept telling
me that.

They hid their fish in the cerrado nearby.
    Here take these,"
        he gave her the *itañe*.   325
She didn't eat it at all.
    She was really angry,
        Ulejalu was angry.
    She was an old woman then.
        Teh, but still very beautiful,   330
            although she was already an old woman.
    Teh, her younger sister was just the same.
        still very beautiful.
    She still remains at her settlement, at Aŋambïtï,
        having become a monstrous vision.   335
When people go there looking for land snails she's the one who
answers them,
        who answers them.
    She is covered with dangerous body paint.
    Her dangerous body paint is there,
        "Mouse's pubic ornament" is her dangerous body paint.   340
            People never touch it so as to remain normal.
    When people go to touch it,
        itsak, they become deranged,
            "*Waa aa*," like that.
                That is how it is.   345

Next she brought out a large cooking pot because there were two *itañe*.
    She ate none of it,
        none.
    Her son ate none of it either because he was still fasting,
        he was still a faster.   350
    She continued to be angry,
        his mother continued to be angry.
    His mother wanted to break his fast,
        her son's fast-breaking.
The fish boiled in the cooking pot *kududu*, *kududu*,   355
        with a fire that had been built beneath it.
            Kudu, kudu, it went.
    She wanted to bring it outside to her younger sisters.
        Bah ha, there were so many Monstrous Women!
She took it off when it was cooked.   360
    Then she mashed it up, *tuk tuk tuk* with her pestle.
    She put it back on the fire.
Then she mixed manioc starch into it.
    She had already made some manioc bread.
"I'll take this to our relatives,   365
    I'll take this to our relatives."

She went to do that.
　　She was angry.
　　She was annoyed that her son was still fasting.
　　　"All right," she said.
So, "My younger sisters, my younger sisters," she said.
　　"My younger sisters, come outside here.
　　Our son has just gone to see our children's heartless parents,
　　　　to see our children's parents.
　　'I don't know what is happening to them there, Mother,'
　　　　our son just told me.
　　'It's strange. They're furred here,
　　　　they're furred here,'" she told them.
"What could be the matter with them?" the others said.
　　The women came outside,
　　　　they were her younger sisters,
　　　　　　all the women.
　　　　　　　　To the plaza.
　　　　　　　　　　They saw her and came after that happened.
　　　　　　　　　　　Angrily they came.
Ulejalu had gone to bring out food to her followers,
　　so they ate then,
　　　　her followers did.
　　She herself did not eat at all.
　　　She was angry.
　　　　Then she stayed there.

At dusk,
　　"My younger sisters, my younger sisters, come.
　　　So we can decorate ourselves,
　　　　so we can decorate ourselves.
　　I don't know what is happening to our children's parents,
　　　I don't know.
　　　　Come,
　　　　　So we can decorate ourselves."
They painted themselves with *ondo*,
　　they painted themselves with *ondo*.
　　"All right, come here."
　　　They painted each other's foreheads, like that.
When that was finished and the sun was here,
　　they ate *itali* fruit, *kuok kuok kuok*,
　　　in order to transform themselves,
　　　　in order to poison themselves with it.
And *iñandzi* fruit,
　　and *asasë*,
　　　you probably don't know about *asasë*.
　　　Tah haa, its fragrance!

370

375

380

385

390

395

400

405

410

Tah, that's a stomach medicine of ours,
> *asasë.*
Its settlement is far from here.
> Its settlement is Oŋupe.   415
Teh, that's a fragrant one!
> *Tah haa*, its fragrance!
>> A medicine,
>>> a stomach medicine of ours.
>>>> Belonging to the Kalapalo.   420
They were eating that, *kouk kouk kouk*,
> and they rubbed it into their hair *tsik tsik tsik*,
> and put it into their eyes.
Iñandzi fruit with "Mouse's pubic ornament,"
> in order for them to fully transform their eyes.   425

At the beginning of the next day,
> "My younger sisters, my younger sisters," she said.
>> "Come here all of you.
>>> Come now, we're ready," she called them out of their
>>> houses.
All right, Kofoño, sing.   430
> Kofoño will sing for you.
The other was about to sing for the *first time*.
> This was the true beginning of Yamurikumalu.
She sang.
> No one knew Yamurikumalu as yet,   435
>> no one.
>>> It was still that way.

[*Kofoño—Kambe's oldest wife—narrates*]
Listen.
[*Sings*]
> "*Heyjawaajaa*," she said.
>> "What could have happened to cause our husbands to remain   440
>> there?
>> Wherever will we go so as to leave our husbands behind, my
>> younger sisters?"
>>> their older sister said.
>>>> "We will do the same as they,
>>>>> we will do the same as they.
>> For some strange reason they don't want us any longer,   445
>>> So our husbands will remain as they are
>>>> Go ahead, go away," she told them,
>>>>> Ulejulu did.
>>>>>> "Very well."

Then at dawn, 450
        at dawn it happened.
At the beginning of the day she climbed on top of the ceremonial
house,
        she was on the ceremonial house.
      There she remained,
        singing. 455
      They had all put on their pubic ornaments,
        hot manioc soup had been poured out,
          and manioc bread had been made.
      They had completely transformed themselves
        by painting themselves with *itali* resin. 460
Her younger sister was beside her, also on top,
        also on top of the house.
      That one, Isa,
        did this:
[*Sings*]
        "Nugiki'iju nugikiju'u nugikijukijuu 465
        nugiki'iku nugikiju'u nugikijukijuu
        uwafaginawifame' nukajafinjunitahafame'
        nugiki'iju nugikiju'u nugikijukijuum.
        uwafaginawifame' nukajafijunitahafame'
        nugiki'iju'u nugikiju'u nugikijukijuu." 470
She was calling them all out from atop the ceremonial house as they
all came.
      It was manioc bread that she referred to as "nugikiju,"
      it was hot manioc soup that she referred to as "nukaijafinunitsa."
        She did it that way because they were transformed.
        The way they were singing, that is. 475
Ulejalu was the ancestor of Yamurikumalu.
This is how it went:
[*Sings*]
        "kuakutigikufajijaha kuakutigikufajijaha
        ulewi jawagi kafatafigi nukutege ifigi ja'aha
        jahahujaha jahahujaha
        jahaha' ahuu. 480

        kuakutigikufajijaha kuakutigikufajijaha
        ulewijawagi kafatafigi nukutege ifigi ja'aha
        jahahujaha jahajujaha
        jahaha ahuu,"
        she told them, 485
          she told them.
She was Ulejalu.
      She was fully transformed.

She was using different words when she did that.
>They had all just been transformed. 490

[*Sings*]

>"Agigijaka ine gigijoko negigijaka negii
>ewenikunii afutakanii
>jahaahujahaa jahaahujahaa
>jahaha'ahuu."

>Look, she was painted all over with *itali*. 495
>That was Ulejalu.

[*Kambe resumes the narrative*]
Listen. That is what she told them.
>This is used for calling the people out.
>Then this became another settlement's song.
>>No longer is it still as it was. 500
>>>No.
>Since then it is wrong.
When those of the Beginning had them they were still correct.
>But now that our people use the songs of other settlements,
>>what they have are wrong. 505

By late afternoon,
>"Let's all go, let's all go," she said.
>>"Let's all go."
>They had wrapped their husbands' knee bindings on their knees,
>>the men's knee bindings. 510
>They wore their husbands' macaw feather arm ornaments,
>>and their oropendola feather headdresses.
Their son Kamatafigagi was with them.
>All her followers were there,
>>They remained there. 515
>He didn't eat any fish,
>>he hadn't yet broken his fast.
"Let's all go now, my younger sisters," she said,
>>"Let's all go now," she said.
>Then, "Heyjawaajaa." 520
And once again she did that,
>and once again, *hm hm hm*! they were all there,
>>so many Monstrous Women were there!
>Then they all continued singing,
>>they all continued singing Yamurikumalu. 525
>*Pidu pidu pidu*, they stamped in time to the song,
>>on toward the others,
>>>to them.
One of their large basketry mats,
>one like this one, look . . . 530

they wrapped one of their large basketry mats around someone to
make him their leader,
>to make Aguga the Giant Armadillo,
>>so they could go underground,
>>>underground.
>>Giant Armadillo.   535
He was a member of Aŋambïtï Community.
>He had been a person,
>>a very old man whom the others had left behind.
>They wrapped a basketry mat around him,
>>so they could go away.   540
Something else was placed on their son after they did that,
>a beautiful macaw feather headdress was on him.
>*Teh he he he*! this most beautiful thing had been placed on him.
They all continued to go on as before,
>*teh he* beautifully as before!   545
>As they came closer their husbands heard them,
>>as they came closer.
>>>There at the oxbow lake,
>>>>at Ugatsi.
"What could ours be doing, what could ours be doing, what could   550
ours be doing, what could ours be doing?
>Perhaps they want to make love to Isafugiku Community, to
Oŋupe Community," they told each other.
>"Perhaps they want to make love to Oŋupe Community, to
Isafugiku Community."

Then the others came, doing as before *pidu*, *pidu*, *pidu*
gesticulating energetically in the Yamurikumalu dance.
>On their arms were ornaments of macaw breast feathers.   555
>>All of them came that way.
>A stick of *atafi* was their dancing pole,
>>one this size.
>They had made a large tunnel at Aŋambïtï.
>>They went far away doing that!   560
They went on tunneling that way,
>dancing all the while.
Indeed that is how they went,
>they went.
In that manner they approached their husbands.   565
>All of them approached,
>>their arms linked together as they came,
>>>their foreheads having been painted earlier,
>>>>and they still wore their pubic ornaments.
Our people don't have pubic ornaments any longer,   570
>no.

Their vulvas are ugly without them.

"Here is your food, here is your food."
The men brought their fish catch to them.
As they came, the women went past them to grab some of their 575
own.
There was a pond there used for catching fish,
used for catching fish.
There are *fesoko* there *bah haa*,
a great many of them,
which they began to grab. 580
While their husbands watched,
bu bu bu bu they grabbed the *fesoko*,
they grabbed the *fesoko*!
"Look," to their husbands,
"Look how I kill my food. Look now," *ku ku ku ku*. 585
they were still raw while the women ate them.
"Very well," the others said.
The women showed them how they had taken the fish with their
hands.
Here from the corner of their mouths blood kept dripping down,
kept dripping down. 590
"Look," they said to their husbands,
"Look at how I kill my food, this is what
all of you denied us."
Ku ku ku still raw,
as they went on. 595
Their husbands followed behind them,
still foolishly carrying their fish on their backs.
The fish were in their carrying baskets,
on their backs.
They still had a great deal of fish which they had
caught. 600
The others were returning as energetically as before,
coming back as they had been doing earlier with Giant
Armadillo.
Giant Armadillo was taking them,
he was the first in line.
Their son was still in the center of them all as he had been 605
earlier,
Kamatafigagi was that way.
Only one son.
His followers were still at their settlement,
still secluded.
The others were all lined up as before, 610
see, as they come back.

There as before,
>> like that as before at Agañe.
Adyua the Bat is there underground where they had put him earlier,
>> to bite their husbands.   615
Still there are their dancing sticks, this size,
>> they were tall sticks.
>>>> This thick.
They had leaned them up against something *buk buk*,
>> and since then they are there to be used as witches' darts.   620
>>>> (I'm connecting it with my worthless cousin.)
There at Ugatsi,
>> far way at Agañe, it's probably a place you don't know
>> about.
>>>> It's near Aŋambïtï.
They went underground.   625
>> They were all underground,
>>>> as they went on to distant places.
They came to their settlement,
>> to Aŋambïtï.
Many of their husbands were still with them.   630
>> As before, they still kept offering their wives the fish.
>> They had already been completely transformed.
We don't ever touch any wild plants there.
>> *Mïfeipe* is never touched.
>>>> *Iñandzi* is never touched, we never touch *iñandzi*.   635
>> *Mïfeipe* is never touched,
>>>> and we don't touch *iñandzi*.
>>>> *Iñandzi* isn't touched by us.
With *iñandzi* we could paint ourselves,
>> but it isn't touched by us.   640
Because if we ever touched it, even slightly,
>> *buk* our eyes would roll.
We would wander off far away.
>> That's how it is.

Finally for the last time they came,   645
>> once more they were underground,
>>>> they were.
That way they came to the water's edge as before,
>> that was their bathing place to which they went,
>> a creek in the forest to which they went was Aŋambïtï's bathing   650
place.
From there they went on,
>> leaving that place.
>> In this direction,
>>>> still underground.

Their husbands behind them.   655
    "Here is your food," they said,
        but there was no reply.
The others encircled their settlement.
    Like this they all went,
        surrounding the house circle.   660
            A deep tunnel resulted.
They went on,
        by means of the tunnel they went on.
    Still dancing,
        they went on.   665
"All of you go on now," they told their children,
        their children.
    His followers, look, her son's followers—the pierced ones—
    wore earrings.
        they all wore their earrings.
They did that there,   670
        for their fast-breaking.
They were seated here by the doorway
        in order to break their fast.
    Their earrings,
        their armbands,   675
    their shell collars,
    their knee-bands,
    their belts,
        so they could break their fast.
They ate the fish,   680
    and she gave their earrings to them with a spell so that all of
    them became transformed right then,
        her son and his companions,
            her followers' children.
    Only one of this group was to go away with them.
        He himself, Kamatafigagi her son.   685
Someone else was first in line.
    He went with that one,
        with Giant Armadillo.
            The first in line.
He was cherished,   690
        his mother cherished him.
            She didn't want to leave him behind.
Following that what they had done ended.

Listen. By early morning, when the sun was here,
    "Go far away from here,"   695
        to their children whom they didn't want to accompany them.
The women had all been transformed.

None of the men were together with them.
Only one remained together with them,
    their son Kamatafigagi remained.   700
        They didn't want him to be sent off with the others.
    He was wearing his dance headdress.
        "All right," the other boys said.
By dawn . . . right there see,
    since then they are still there,   705
        still at Aŋambïtï.
    Ugigi trees,
        this size.
            Since then.
Since then, sẹe,   710
        nearby is "Mouse's pubic ornament."
            Also this size.
It's a dangerous herb for us if we touch it *tsaki, tsaki.*
    It's Aŋambïtï Community's dangerous herb.
They used to extract the sap and mix it into, "*Ha ha ha ha, ha*   715
ha ha ha" they mixed it into something,
    while they kept laughing about it.
It's a magical herb.
    It's for making love to women.
When someone touches it,
    it enters her eyes *buuk teh he he* then he seems to be a very   720
beautiful man!
It stays in her eyes.
    It's for a man.
        Then she makes love to him.
Following that they went on and their sons *pu pu pu.*
There were a great many of his followers.   725
    They wore their earrings and their belts, *pu pu pu.*
After that they climbed onto those others,
    onto the magical plants *tik tik* they became monkeys as they
went on,
        monstrous howler monkeys as they went on.
            They became monstrous howler monkeys.   730
        Far away at Idyate.
        There they all are.
We came across them in the forest when we go there.
    Another time, I'll teach you.
So they went away,   735
    all of them went away,
        still wearing their earrings,
            still wearing *teh* their beautiful earrings.
Those people had become furred animals,
    they became monkeys.   740

This part of them is monkey while their earrings are still human.
>   *Puu huu*, they grew very tall!

They kept going on after that happened,
>   the young men went on.
>>   They filed off far away into the forest.   745

There in the forest is their settlement,
>   at Idyate.
>>   A distant place beyond Aŋambïtï.

Idyate is a creek.
>   They were all there,   750
>>   they were all there.
>>>   Their sons.
>>>>   Only one was still with the others.

"Let's go now," she said.
>   They kept coming toward their settlement,   755
>>   their husbands as well.
>>>   Fish were still on their husbands' backs.
>>>>   "Here is your food, here is your food."

"Let's go!" she said,
>   "Let's go!"   760

They kept coming toward distant places,
>   *pu pu* they came dancing toward Oŋupe.
>>   Toward Oŋupe.
>>>   There was a settlement called Oŋupe.

The next day, "Let's all go now."   765

They continued dancing at Oŋupe, at Oŋupe.
>   The people of the community all came to the plaza and the
>   unmarried women went on,
>>   following the others.
>>>   It was the dangerous body paint of the others which
>>>   carried them off.

Those who had husbands were held securely by their spouses.   770
>   They had lain down together with them.
>>   They lay down with their wives because they didn't
>>   want them to see the others.

However those who were without husbands saw them,
>   *teh he* they were so beautiful when they were dancing!

That happened when they saw the others,   775
>   they all went on in order to join them,
>>   they went on in order to join them.

They all came,
>   just as they had continued to do before,
>>   with their husbands following behind them,   780
>>>   following behind them,
>>>>   the fish still on their backs,

                    yes, inside their carrying baskets.

Then they all went on
      having left their settlements behind.   785
   "So they will remain, my younger sisters," she said,
      "So what are on us now will remain.
   They haven't even made our spouses cherish us,
      they haven't even made our spouses cherish us, our pubic
      ornaments."
So *tsiu tsiu* they ripped them off,   790
     and *tom! tom!* threw them into the water.
         They went on naked.
Those same things became *ulugi* fish
     tah ha! very tasty when we eat them.
The small children whom they carried,   795
     were too heavy to carry,
   "So they will remain," she said.
     "They're too heavy for us to carry further."
So *tom tom tom* they threw them into the water.
     They became *gïgïŋgïgï* catfish,   800
       large ones like this, look.
        There at Oŋupe.
The smallest nursing children were the ones thrown away,
     those who were still of this small size.
       Those who were somewhat larger became larger fish.   805
They all went on without their children.
     They no longer had their children with them.
   Pu pu pu pu they all went away,
     far away toward Tïpa.

Then they came there.   810
They came to Tïpa.
     to Tïpa.
There is a deep pool there,
     a bottomless one,
       a deep pool.   815
        This is Aŋafuku.
"Go ahead," she said,
   "My younger sisters," she went.
     "Let's look right now for something to eat, our meal."
       "All right."   820
Tom! tom! tom! they went underwater after she said that,
     swimming beneath the surface.
     Tuh! Sahundu were caught that way.
"Look," their husbands were still following behind them,
   "Look, look how I kill my food.   825
     Once you denied me what I'm eating now."

Ku ku ku ku, still raw.
 Doing that while the tails still flapping about.
Ku ku ku, that was done to *afi* fish,
  ku ku ku that was done to *itañe*!   830
Now they were on Afuafïtï Community's trail.
They went on Igisa Trail . . . far away!
  they were passing through a creek in the forest.
 They passed through a creek in the forest,
  in order to be on the other side.   835
They went on from there singing in another way.
 They had changed their song to that of another settlement
 On this side their song had been good,
  one way of singing.
 Because of what they did other settlements have it,   840
  we can't understand any of them.
 Different settlements have other ways of singing.
 This different settlement has another way of singing,
  that different settlement has another way of singing, like
  that.
   This is how it has been.   845
It is still correct here,
 as their songs once were.
  Still right.
The people of an earlier time had them perfectly. Now it's become
ugly here.
  ugly.   850
It's no longer right here,
  no.
Once it was performed properly,
  now it's incorrect.
There at that place they changed it,   855
  there at another place they changed it,
   they sang that way.
 They thought up their songs as they went on,
  so it became incorrect.

They came farther, far away!   860
 Without stopping their husbands still followed them,
  their husbands.
 They went on still with the others,
  with the singers.
 Far away, they all went on for a long way,   865
  far far away!
"Let's stop here, my younger sisters."
 They were on this side of Cuiaba.
  (Cuiaba is very far from here!)

                on the other side of a tunnel.   870
                        Christians haven't seen them.
If a man should go there they would shoot him.
        They have made a lake,
                a large one.
        This was done for their bathing place,   875
                their bathing place.
Their husbands are still on the far opposite side of it where they have
made their own settlement.
        It was done,
                they stay there.
        They are all there,   880
                still all there.
        They are all there,
                still all there.
        They have large gourds,
                this kind.   885
                        Somewhere nearby still.
        Black ones.
                They became black.
                        They are not in the least bit red.
"We will stay here."   890
        They all stopped.
The *kagutu* flutes . . .
        very early in the morning,
                the *kagutu* flutes are played.
                        They perform *kagutu*.   895
                                They have the *kagutu*.
        They play the *kuluta* flutes,
                they perform *kagutu*.
                        Ulejalu is the song leader.
                                Their older sister, Ulejalu.   900

Listen.
        Teh, she was so beautiful when she did all that!

Excerpt from Monstrous Women
Told by Muluku at Aifa, February 13, 1979

"My young sisters. We will make our lake right here, here."
        "Very well," they replied.
        "So we can listen to the others.
                So we can listen to the others."
                        "Very well."   5
        "Go ahead now, go ahead, do it well."

They put a lake there.
    The Monstrous Women made a lake,
        a large one.
"Go ahead now,"   10
    someone wrestled their son.
      Someone wrestled their son.
        Ijalikuegï wrestled Kamatafigagi.
"Go ahead," Taugi said.
      "Go wrestle the Monstrous Women's son right now."   15
      "All right," he answered
Then they wrestled each other,
    Kamatafigagi with Ijalikuegï.

While they were doing that Taugi went to tip over their drinking water,
    while they were doing that he went to tip over their drinking   20
water.
      In each house.
"That's enough," he said.
    The others came to the houses.
"I really want to drink something right away," he went,
    Ijalikuegï said,   25
      as he came into the house *tikii*.
"Is there any water here?"
    There was none.
"I'll go next door."
    Next door,   30
    and next door,
      but there was nothing.
"Go to the water's edge.
      Go drink at the water's edge," Taugi said.
    Then he ran there *pupupu*.   35
Next he was by the lake.
Teh, there was a beautiful beach there at the lake,
    the Monstrous Women's lake.
Then *ku ku ku* he drank, Ijalikuegï drank.
He drank *ku ku ku*, and the lake died.   40
    "There's nothing left at all of our lake," the Monstrous Women
said.
    "Ijalikuegï drank it all up.
So, it will remain as it is
    what we used for listening to the others.
What he has done will remain that way.   45
    We won't stay here any longer.
      Not here."
        "All right."
"Go ahead now."

Then they pounded piqui bark, 50
    the Monstrous Women did.
        Piqui, *tuk!*
Then they sprinkled it into the water
    and it became the irritating mud called *oŋu*.
      "Their *oŋu*," that's "Oŋupe." 55

Notes to Monstrous Women

4   Cuiaba formerly was the capital of the state of Mato Grosso, now of the state called Mato Grosso do Norte. It is located to the southwest of the Upper Xingu Basin.

100   Kambe pointed to his middle finger, to indicate the third day.

129   Kambe pointed low on the western horizon to indicate dusk.

264   He remained seated on the edge of the hammock so as not to be entranced into staying with the men.

265   Kambe pointed slightly to the west of the sun's zenith.

271   Kambe was joking about his fish-smoking grills, which were entirely empty at the time, although he had recently gone fishing.

300   As in the story of Agakuni, the secluded youth leaves and enters his house through the housewall, going directly into (or out from) his seclusion chamber, rather than using the public doorways.

329–31   Ulejalu is beautiful and ageless (see also the story of Sakatsuegï, Chapter 6).

340   *Umbewigï*, "mouse's pubic ornament," comes from the shape of the seed(?) of this very large tree.

344   Kambe rolled his head from side to side.

489   "Speaking falsely" means words were changed from Kalapalo to another language.

499ff.   Kambe asserts that the singing of Yamurikumalu is not the original.

559   The result is the ditches frequently found near settlements, probably formed by old watercourses that drained nearby lakes.

578   *Fesoko* is a common Characin, *Hoplias malabaricus*.

713   *Kugitse* means "dangerous herb." None of the several plants named should be touched for fear of causing madness.

731   Idyate is a place near the former settlement of Jagamï.

793   *Ulugi* is a small (4–5-inch) *Cichlidae* (Portuguese: *acará*).

800   Gïgiŋgïgi is a small (6–7-inch) brown catfish, possibly belonging to the *Pimelodidae* family. It is found inside submerged logs.

809   Tïpa is another site in the ancestral region of the Jagamï, near the upper Tamitatalo River.

816   Aŋafuku is an ancestral settlement of the Jagamï people, located on the upper Tamitatalo River.

831   Afuafïtï is an ancestral settlement of the Jagamï.

884   "Large gourds" refers to gourds being found to the far south.

Muluku's Version

3–4   The water would serve as a sounding board, so they could hear if others were following them.

A Yamurikumalu ritual process begins when a sponsor is selected by the community. As with all ceremonial sponsorship, this person must have had some experience with the ritual in question, either through having been cured during severe illness by the performance of the music (which enticed the relevant powerful being to help return the victim's *akūa*) or by having dreamed of a deceased sponsor. In the following account a middle-aged shaman recalls the circumstances under which he became the sponsor of the Yamurikumalu ritual after his epileptic predecessor drowned while fishing

> I saw him sitting down, very sadly, and then I left.
> Later he came to me on his way back home,
>> it was still very early in the day.
>> "You're really leaving now?" I said.
>> "Yes, I'm leaving," he answered.
>> "You're not going to fish any more?"
>> "No, I want to go back right away."
> I think he was sad because he had dreamed badly, but he still went out fishing when he shouldn't have.
> Later, I returned and forgot about him.
> Then, after it had become dark, his wife began to weep for him.
> We [meaning the shamans of the community] began to smoke and his
>> *akūa* came to me.
> He said, "If A. [the deceased's wife] had sent someone along with me I would have returned.
>> But since she didn't do that, I died."
> Then I told the others he was already dead.
> Then everyone started to cry.
> Later some men went looking for him and found his body at the bottom of the lake.
> Sometime later the people wanted a Yamurikumalu sponsor and sent *taiyope* to ask me to be the sponsor.
>> My father-in-law agreed that I should be the sponsor,
>>> and so that is what happened.
> When I agreed all the women cheered and they were dancing for a long time.

When the new sponsor is declared, people begin to think of an appropriate time for a performance, which is said to be given "for the sponsor." Normally other rituals that have already been planned for will take precedence, so it may be several years before the new sponsor has a chance to be commemorated. The best time is when there is no need to hold a memorial Egitsu for a recently deceased *anetu*, for this ritual takes precedence over the others in the *egitsu* category.

When there is no other ritual scheduled, then, the *tagioto* are selected from among the *anetaū* and formally visit the sponsor to suggest that the ritual process begin. If the sponsor agrees (if he or she has no other important ritual obligation), the *tagioto* return to the plaza and declare that fact. When the women hear this news, they cheer in unison, intoning the Yamurikumalu declaration: "Heyjawajaaah, Yamurikumaah." Then there is a brief performance of several songs that are used to delineate the time as Yamurikumalu ritual time and the space of the settlement as Yamurikumalu ritual space. These songs are called *oh-ho-me* after the most frequently repeated line of words.

As with other *egitsu* planning, the Yamurikumalu sponsor's agreement to hold the ritual usually occurs at the time of Kofoŋo (the "Duck," the stars Procyon and Canopus), which is the end of the dry season, when another ritual process has usually just ended. The announcement is timed so that *sandagï* can collect piqui fruit (which ripens during the months of September, October, and November) for processing and storing underwater during the rainy season. A sponsor uses this processed piqui pulp throughout the months of the dry season to pay the ritual performers. (Piqui, rich in vitamin A, iodine, and oils, is an important dietary supplement during those months, when very little ripened fruit is available.) After the *oh-ho-me* singing that occurs virtually every day during the harvesting of the piqui for the sponsor (some days are set aside for harvesting piqui for household use), there will be no more Yamurikumalu singing until the time of Tute (the "Hawk"; two clusters of stars: Altair, Beta, and Gamma Aquilla; and Fomalhaut, Al Na'ir, and Beta Grus) during April or May, when the rains begin to end. During the time of Ogo ("Storage Platform," the Square of Pegasus) and of Tõ ("Ema," the Pleiades) the sponsor begins more seriously to collect food from the women, especially processed manioc starch from a specially prepared field of his. A substantial amount of this manioc starch will be used from time to time to make cold manioc drink and manioc bread accompanying the fish the sponsor gives in payment for the women's musical performances. It will also be used to feed the visitors from other settlements, but the bulk of all food collected during this ritual process is consumed by the hosts before the visitors arrive. Only a few of his closest relatives accompany the sponsor or her husband on his first fishing trips, but just before the climactic events centering around the ultimate appearance of the guests, nearly all the men (led by the *taiyope*) leave to fish at oxbow lakes, where they spend several days using special nets, weirs, and fish poison. During this more active dry-season stage of the Yamurikumalu, pairs of women decorated with ornaments normally worn by men dance from house to house in the fashion of the men's *ataŋa* playing, this form of musical performance being directly associated with the time of *egitsu* preparations for the benefit of the guests.

On occasions when the sponsor brings out to the plaza boiled or dried fish or manioc soup flavored with preserved piqui pulp (a delicious food that tastes startlingly like Wheatena) the women perform a category of songs directly associated with the myth of the Monstrous Women. These are called *kagutukuegï*, the "other *kagutu*" (monstrosity is implied by the suffix meaning "other"). Women who are songmasters dress in men's feather ornaments and perform in the plaza before the rest of their sex, the sponsor, and *taiyope*. The women as a whole have now taken over the settlement's most important ritual space, a space that is normally occupied in non-ritual contexts by men. The Kalapalo explain this change by saying that women are avoiding the forbidden *kagutu* that are kept inside the *kuakutu*; during the Yamurikumalu, the *kagutu* are taken to the flute sponsor's house, and women frequently enter the *kuakutu* to relax and drink cold manioc soup after a collective effort.

A number of verses in this set of *kagutukuegï* songs have words intelligible to the Kalapalo. They describe in a perfunctory fashion the climactic events in the story of the ritual's origin, when the women decorate themselves like men, transform themselves, and later throw away their children. These songs are performed in the afternoon by a pair of women, decorated with men's ornaments—parrot and toucan feather headdresses, parrot feather armbands, piqui shell ankle rattles. Their ornamentation parallels that of the men during the *kagutu egitsu*. Here again, the structure of the musical themes and the manner of dancing are virtually identical to the *kagutu* playing, with the chief exception being that whereas the *kagutu* are played in unison and in groups of three or in pairs of groups of three alternating their playing, these "other *kagutu*" songs are sung by a single pair of women, each taking her turn with a single verse.

Yet another set of songs called *kagutukuegï* is performed later on in the season, when the women begin to prepare for the arrival of their guests. This performance occurs after the major fishing trip has taken place and dried fish have been stored on grills in each of the messengers' houses. The selection of these messengers from among the *taiyope* at large dramatically fixes the attention of the hosts upon the imminent appearance of people from other settlements. The wrestling practices that have taken place from time to time since the first *ataŋa* performances now become more intense and are led by the songmasters. The women begin to practice the dances that are associated with the entrance of the guests. Now the best wrestlers from among the female *anetaü* are formally recognized, and they are asked by the song leaders and the sponsor to lead the line of dancers during the entry dance on the climactic day.

The musical structure of this second set of "other *kagutu*" songs closely resembles that of the *kagutu* songs. Several hours before dawn, a song leader begins to call out the rest of the women by singing the "calling out" song, a very slow solo performance in oratorical style, which is repeated until she is joined by the other song leader. As more and more women join the pair, the songs increase in tempo. The concluding song in this set is performed just before dawn, when the performers go together to bathe and draw water. This womens' *kagutukuegï* performance (which in the myth is replicated by Kofoño's singing) exactly parallels the men's *kagutu* predawn performances. The songs are in what appears to be Mehinaku, a local Arawak language; none of the singers was able to translate them for me, although Kofoño supplied a few words in translation and claimed that the original is a language invented by the Monstrous Women, a sign of their demonic transformation. (It is another case of the creative powers of invention associated with powerful beings.)

So far all the Yamurikumalu songs I have discussed can be correlated with relative degrees of ritual intensification, more elaborate collective efforts, and a heightening of interest in the meaning of the event as a process involving virtually everyone in the settlement. These performances are designed to create a special effect: to have women perform ritual activities that are more typically associated with men, to manifest the abilities of organization, collective effort, and especially collective musical performance that are usually attributed to men and rarely seen among Kalapalo women. Women's music and women's appearance during Yamurikumalu musical performances are closely identified with the decorative, social, and psychological attributes of men, which were adopted by the original Monstrous Women.

There are yet other songs that construct another, perhaps more explicit vision of the relations between the sexes in Kalapalo society. More shouted than sung, these are mocking songs that (following a standard form) women fit to their knowledge of the foibles of each man in the settlement. The chief theme of these songs is the men's aggressive sexual desire that causes them to follow women even to the latrine areas, to awaken them in the middle of the night, and to pay for something that women consider unworthy of such obsessive desire:

> Tupaga is filled with desire
> For example, at the place where we drink hot manioc soup [that is, in the rear of the house]
> For example, at the place where we bathe ourselves
> For example, at the place where we relieve ourselves!
> [this last line was shouted out by one of a man's lovers]
> [or]
> Desire my vulva, land snail vulva, water snail vulva"

The ironic message of the latter song is that men foolishly desire a part of the women's body that they believe closely resembles the repulsive bodies of these large molluscs.

In all these songs, the men's affairs (which they desperately and unsuccessfully try to conceal from their wives) are revealed in detail. These songs are clearly understood by the Kalapalo and are said to be excruciatingly embarrassing to the men. Because the words are intended to be clearly heard by the men, like the Kwambï their performance is characterized by much less emphasis on the music than on the words; the effect is considerably like American children's chanting games than actual singing. And like the Kwambï, which shows that everyone is the subject of gossip (in which everyone engages with equal fervor), the universality of the lover's foibles is made clear when the women sing to the men this way.

After months of these ritual performances and the collective labor accompanying them, the day finally comes when the guests are camped outside the settlement. At night the song leaders from each group are asked to enter the hosts' plaza to perform *kagutukuegï*. Through the rest of the night the wrestlers among the women remain awake singing and dancing so they will not dream "badly," while the men wrestlers sit in the plaza with the sponsor watching them for as long as everyone can remain awake. The next day begins with the women dancing the opening line dance that is usually performed by men at the start of any *egitsu*. This time the women are fully decorated, the first in line painted like a jaguar (a sign that they are both leaders and wrestling champions), followed by their *sandagï*, not as "beautiful" but nonetheless still strong, nubile women. The older song leaders direct the dancers, but, considering themselves weak and physically unattractive, these grandmothers do not actually participate in the dramatic display of feminine strength and beauty.

These host dancers are eventually joined by groups of visiting women, who are similarly decorated. Hosts and guests dance aggressively toward one another (these "confronting" dances must be carefully coordinated by the *taiyope* and sponsor lest the women crash into each other) and are finally separated and led to their assigned places, each settlement group sitting before the house of its messenger. Then the sponsor calls out his female wrestling champions. They wrestle the champions of the guests, causing great excitement because aside from the earlier practice sessions this is the only time women wrestle one another. Parents have an opportunity to judge the relative success of the puberty seclusion practices they have imposed on their daughters. After the champions wrestle, all the young women participate. When the female wrestling ends, the men follow in their stead.[17] When the wrestling is over, the *taiyope* bring food and drink to their guests. If there is a maiden in seclusion, she is brought out by the sponsor, laden with a variety of ornaments. As she is led before the *anetaū* from each visiting group, these ornaments—feather earrings and shells tied in her hair, cotton wrappings wound around her knees—are removed and kept as gifts by each of the visiting leaders. Later the *masope* dances, a significant act for the men of her settlement, for this means that her parents deem her "ready" (that is, grown enough) for sexual relations. She may marry, thus formally exiting seclusion, but if she is still young, she will return to seclusion. During this "coming out" ritual, male *ataŋa* dancers from the visiting communities perform for their hosts. After their dancers have circled the settlement several times, all the visitors leave their hosts in a decidedly unceremonious manner, packing up their belongings and walking off toward the visitors' path, followed by the sounds of their hosts' cries of farewell.

On the following day, the women perform once more for the sponsor, dancing before his house with songs that resemble the *oh-ho-me* type and thus, like that song, seem to have a bracketing function that serves to mark the conclusion of ritual time and space.

Kagutu

Unlike the story of the Monstrous Women, the origin of the *kagutu* flutes is described in a myth that is unusually brief considering their ritual importance. Nonetheless, this story emphasizes the attributes of the musical instruments that make their ritual performance by men so interesting and important: they are identified as essentially female, with respect to their gender, sexuality, and original state of existence as powerful beings who lived underwater and were caught in traps and nets like fish.

Kafunetiga Found Musical Instruments
Told by Muluku, February 13, 1979

Listen.
    Kafunetiga went fishing with his *ofo* bark weir,
      he went with his bark weir,
        and he waited on top of the weir.
          Kafunetiga was catching fish.   5
    At night he was doing the same thing,
      at night he was shooting at the fish.
    Early in the morning something came,
      the *kagutu* came.
        The *kagutu* came very early in the morning,   10
          it came.
    Then the *kuluta*,
      the very first one was caught.
        It stopped singing when it went inside the *ofo* trap,
          a net.   15
    Then Kafunetiga caught the *kuluta*.
      "Well, what is this thing here, this white thing?"
        Teh it was beautifully painted.
    Then I'm told something else came toward him.
      This was the *kagutu*.   20
      Then I'm told, he caught it.
      "Here is my musical instrument," Kafunetiga said.
    The next was *meneuga*.
      It went inside the net,
        inside the *ekiŋo* net.   25
    That was all.
      "That's all."
    It was daytime now,
      very early in the morning.
      "I'll go now,"   30
        so he went away,
          and he came home,
            Kafunetiga came home.
    Kafunetiga captured it,
      he captured the *kagutu*.   35
        From that time all our people have this thing,
          since then.

Kafunetiga said,
    "What is this wild thing I have?
      This wild thing?   40
    I don't know.
    "Look at it right now."

"All right, as you wish."
Kagutu meneuga kuluta.
Taugi knew nothing about them,   45
    nothing.
"Now, what will I do with them?
    Although there's no reason,
        such as they are I'll take my possessions away with
        me."
Taugi then went to him.   50
    "Well, Kafunetiga, where have these things come from?
    From what place?"
"From beneath the water."
    "I see," he answered.
"Keep examining them, do something for me, look at them.   55
    Keep examining them, do something for me, Taugi."
        "All right," he answered.
"This one here is *kagutu*, *kagutu*," Taugi declared.
"This one is *kuluta*,
    this one is the older sister, *kuluta*.   60
    But the *kagutu* is the younger sister.
This one is female,
    kagutu."
It was held in the water.
What he had caught was a powerful being.   65
    Kafunetiga had caught it with a weir at night.
Since that time this thing is the *kagutu*.
"This is a good thing you caught, Kafunetiga."
    Since that time all our people have it.
        Since that time.   70
While Taugi was the knower of the songs,
    Taugi,
    Taugi was the knower of the *fesofo*,
    Kafunetiga was the owner,
        the owner.   75
Afterward all our people knew about it.

That's all.

A second, more lengthy story describes in detail an ancient *kagutu egitsu* hosted by Kafunetiga, to which the trickster twins Taugi and Aulukuma are invited. In this story, the dueling between hosts and guests is intertwined with a theme about virility and magical power, the *kagutu* playing being the context for liaisons and commentary thereon between host women and guest men and also for displays of bravado after the hosts are defeated in their attempts to choke and poison the guests.

Kafunetiga Tried to Poison Taugi
Told by Kudyu at Aifa, September 11, 1979

Listen.
    This is what is told,
        now this is the truth.
Buh! A crowd of people were cheering,
        all of them were cheering.   5
    "We will go far away,
        we will go far away where we will eat,
            where we will be feasting,"
            that was what he said.
    Very clearly Kafunetiga heard this.   10
        He was a powerful being.
        Taugi was speaking to his followers about him.
Kafunetiga's grandfather spoke,
        Kaŋinditsugu spoke.
    "Grandson," he told him,   15
        "Your grandfather Taugi is surely coming here to make you
        hungry.
            to make you hungry.
        Your grandfather is coming to you to perform for us."
    "Very well," he answered,
        "So he will remain as he is then,   20
        he will remain as he is."
Taugi heard him very clearly,
        Taugi did.
    "He will remain as he is.
        Now, 'Taugi' will no longer be said," Kafunetiga told his   25
        grandfather.
        That is what he said.
    "He always makes us hungry.
        All our ceremonies have been like that.
        He always makes us hungry.
When we made some food,   30
        'The manioc starch is ready now,'
            and it was taken outside after all our things
            were used to pay for it."
            (That was why Taugi did that.
                That was why he did that.)   35
The others traveled on while Kafunetiga said,
    "'Taugi' will no longer be said."
Soon after Kafunetiga began to cook poison.
    Anetufe, the same thing we use now to poison dogs.
        Kafunetiga cooked *anetufe* in order to kill Taugi,   40

in order to kill Taugi.
Listen. Inside a large cooking pot.
So, he told the others to boil it.
Even though the smell should never go inside the top of our heads,
the pungent odor. 45
He wanted Taugi to drink it.
He had heard very clearly what Taugi told his followers.
Then after that happened they slept, they slept,
after they had slept a long time,
they all left. 50
He himself was seated on his stool,
Taugi was seated on his leader's stool.
He was with his younger brother, he was with Aulukuma.
On the other side was the son of a wild creature.
I'm told there were three of them. 55
Kafunetiga spoke to them.
The others had brought macaw tail feathers.
Macaw tail feathers were used for the seating of leaders.
Since then they are at the oxbow lakes and look,
even here in our own lake. 60
Macaw tail feathers.
They are "Taugi's feather headdress,
Taugi's feather headdress."
His younger brother had eagle tail feathers.
Teh he he, those were magnificent things! 65
The one on the other side had large gourd bowls called *kuaŋo*.
Teh he he, those were magnificent things!
There aren't any here,
no longer
since now the people here have metal pots. 70
Inside one this size the *kagutu* drink used to be carried outside.
However, in the past when it was brought outside from the house
someone would throw it *bah*, into the water.
Really.
It was inside gourd vessels. 75
A long time ago it was done with gourd vessels.

Then he slept.
The next day as they went on they slept.
With his hooked tool Taugi pulled.
He dropped his hooked tool and searched about, 80
searched about for the first time.
It was on a rafter of Kafunetiga's house.
Gï gï gï,
he pulled it closer.
Really! 85

That was what happened.
This is the story about it.
　　Now it's our laziness.
　　It's not for listening,
　　　　it makes us lazy.　　　　　　　　　　　　　90
　　　　　It's a dangerous thing.
Listen.
　　They arrived at dusk.
　　　Buh! there were many people there who were Kafunetiga's
　　followers,
　　　　　who were Storm's followers.　　　　　　95
　　　　　　That was who those people were.
　　　　　　　That is what has been said.
　　However, this is what happened next.
　　　"What will we do now, my older brother?" Aulukuma asked.
　　　"Let's go outside the ceremonial house.　　　　100
　　　　We'll stay there."
　　Having done that they all greeted one another.
　　　Then Kafunetiga brought them some cold manioc soup,
　　　　some cold manioc soup which was still safe.
　　　　　Bok bok.　　　　　　　　　　　　　105
　　　"Here, Children," was what he told them.
　　　　"Here, Children."
　　　"Very well," he replied,
　　　　Taugi said.
　　　"Here, Children," his younger brother said,　　　110
　　　　"Here, Children."
　　　　　Then they all drank it *ku ku*.
　　There was fish as well.
　　　"All right everyone," Kafunetiga said.
　　　　Food for distribution,　　　　　　　　115
　　　　　boiled *pasïï*.
　　　There were too many bones in it.
　　　And *kagikagi* with its fin spines,
　　　　in order to have Taugi catch a bone in his throat.
　　　He didn't.　　　　　　　　　　　　　　　120
　　　　He saw them.
　　The *kagutu* flutes were taken to them.
　　　"All right, go on," Taugi said.
　　　　"Go ahead," he said to Pïdyëi.
　　　　"Go ahead," he said to Dyofi.　　　　　　125
　　　　"All right, you go on," to Kadyagima.
　　　　　Those Fish People are really *kagutu* that were made by
　　　　　Taugi.
　　They began to play *amamai* songs.
　　　Amamai.

On one side was Dyofi. 130
He was much taller than the others.
On the other side was Kadyagima.
Those creatures were *kagutu* flutes.
They came to the doors of the houses.
Taugi's followers came there. 135
The poison had begun to steam in order to destroy them.
It was *anetufe*.
Listen.
Then they stopped so Kafunetiga could come to speak to them.
He was the *kagutu* sponsor. 140
They talked with each other about their food.
"Unfortunately I've only been able to make just a little
food," he told them,
while they talked with each other.
Then once again they danced,
they went on. 145

Once again they came toward him,
the *kagutu* did,
once again.
However, Kafunetiga was ready just then to bring out their food.
When he came toward them they went on again, 150
and they returned.
This was the crying song.
They were crying now.
Then they went on,
and they stopped. 155
Then they began again.
"Hoh hua!"
at "Taugi's Campground."
That was how it was done.
This is a story about it. 160
However, this is what happened.
Fish was brought out.
A great deal, just as he had done before,
made from *kagikagi*,
made from *pasïtï*. 165
He gave it to them so that the bones which were mixed
into it would catch in their throats.
"All right now," Taugi said,
"What are you trying to do to me?
I want to show you, Children, that their brother just
tried to kill us with this.
The one who is your grandfather," Taugi said. 170
Then he crumbled the bones and mixed them into the fish,

pu pu pu and right away the bones became very soft.
    Really!
        He's a powerful being.
            He, Taugi, is a powerful being.   175
Then, to the one whose face is painted,
    Agafafa the Anhinga,
        "Go ahead, eat this here,
            eat this for your grandchildren."
    "All right," he went,   180
        "*Kwi kwi kwi*," *mbisuk* it was all gone!
Because of that the anhinga eats *kagikagi*.
        Because of that.
    It dives down inside a rock and *kwiki*! swallows one.
        Taugi had made its food.   185
"All right everyone, go ahead," he said.
    The fish bones were now very small and had become soft,
        so Taugi ate after that.
    The bones had become soft, just like your hair.
        "Kwi kwi."   190
He had eaten all the *pasïtï*.
    Taugi had finished eating,
        Taugi had.
    He said, "Mortals will never eat this because it will always be
the same as it is,   195
        no."
    When someone else is pregnant we don't eat it.
    Nor do we eat *kagikagi*.
        Its fin spines are dangerous.
    It's the creature who holds fast with its spines.   200
    Taugi declared it to be so.
        Taugi prohibited it to us.
Then when it was late at night he played the flutes,
        at night.
While it was just beginning to dawn   205
        the first one was set in order.
    Dogfish began.
        Early in the morning.
             The first one.
[*Kudyu hums the song*]
This one was invented by Taugi for us.   210
    For we people.
    That is what they play first since it's used to introduce the flutes
when presents are given to the sponsor.
    This is a *kagutu* song.
        This is the first one.
He was the leader,   215

Dogfish is the leader.
  The very first one.
 It changes back and forth.
  There are two.
   When they were done they danced with the *kagutu*.   220
When Dogfish was finished he was removed.
  "Go ahead, you go to it,"
   Taugi said to Utigi Fish,
    to him.
 Taugi said to him,   225
  "Go back and finish it this way:
[*Kudyu hums the song*]
   I mean it's about you," he told him.
  "Always say it this way, listen."
   He sang it.
    Three of them.   230
When he finished,
  "All right, you go to it."
 Someone else came.
  Someone else came,
  someone else came,   235
   someone else came.
 That's the way they were,
  that's the way they were.
When they were finished,
  then Akutsagï the Boat-Billed Heron,   240
   then Itsëgi the Sunbittern,
   he himself came.
And Agitaidyua the Great Blue Heron did what the others had done.
  He himself came.
  And . . . that was all.   245
"So, I want to do it now," someone else said.
  Nzueŋi the Cicada.
 He performed alone.
 "Go ahead," Taugi said.
There was a woman inside her house,   250
  a beautiful woman who didn't like men.
 She didn't like men at all,
  not at all.
When someone would go to her she would reject him,
  When another person would go to her she would reject him.   255
  And when another person would go to her.
However, Taugi spoke to someone.
  "Grandson," he said to Tsikigi the Black Ibis.
   That man was very ugly.
To that woman over there,   260

to the woman who didn't like men,
    the ugly one became her husband.
But someone who was attractive, never,
    so Taugi put an ugly one with her.
        That is what happened.   265
        Because she refused Taugi's followers.
            The ugly one came together with the woman who
        didn't like men.
Then they were together.
    She made love to Black Ibis.
    Black Ibis was ugly.   270
        He was a follower of Taugi.
        Tsikigi the Black Ibis.
"Go ahead, Grandson," he said to him.
    It was Black Ibis who came to her in his usual way.
    Tikii he came inside the house,   275
        to that same woman I spoke of earlier.
        She,
            the one who disliked men.
Then he went to see her.
    "Hi hi," was what Black Ibis said.   280
    Black Ibis was looking at the woman.
    She saw him,
        "Hi hi."
    Buh!
        "Why are you here?"   285
        "To see you."
        "All right."
Then he spread open her legs and he made love to her.
    Black Ibis the ugly one,
        the ugly one.   290
    In the darkness he did that,
        he made love to her.
            He came.
    "I'll leave now."
        "Go then."   295
He returned.
    "It's done," he said.
    "Hoh hoh!"
        Still another one went to do as he had done.
Listen to that!   300
    Taugi had told him to do it.
    Because Taugi sent him he went.
        Taugi was the one who had been telling them what to do.
        Taugi was the one.
This is what he said,   305

Taugi said,
"Hoh hoh hoh hoooh!" he went,
"Black Ibis was made love to,
Black Ibis was made love to,"
        he told everyone.   310
The woman spoke.
   "How disgusting.
      It must have been Black Ibis!"
         That was what she said.
She made a song about it,   315
     the woman made a song about it
        when Taugi spoke about it.
           When he spoke about Black Ibis.

[*Sings*]
     "Look, look, someone has made love to your daughter.
     It was Black Ibis who made love to your daughter.   320
     Ajanawagi."
She was Ajanawagi's daughter.
     She was the woman who despised men.
        Ajanawagi was her father.

[*Kudyu hums the tune*]
That is just how it goes.   325
     "That was the one I made love to."
     "Yes," they said.
So this became something for lovemaking.
     If we go with a woman,
        teh he, a very beautiful one like the one Black Ibis made   330
     love to,
        we make love with it.
          It's a spell,
           a spell.
We put it on our penises.
     "Fuh!" we blow it on,   335
        "Fuh!" we go.
Finally,
     "You must go to me,
        to me."
     A beautiful woman comes to make love to us,   340
        and so we clear the ground of leaves.
     There we stay,
        placing it on our penises.
          This is the song spell of Black Ibis.
          The spell of Black Ibis.   345
She comes,
     the woman comes to sit on our thighs,
        and she is made love to.

After that happens one sleeps,
    look, the next day is slept.   350
        Then it becomes small again.
        That is just what happens.

At dawn,
    very early what had been done before was still being done.
        The *anetufe* was still being heated so it would boil.   355
        Kafunetiga wanted to carry it out so Taugi would drink it.
            He wanted Taugi to drink it so that something would
            happen.
    It was so strong
        Taugi smelled it.
        "We'll really die now with this, Children," he went.   360
            "Our grandfather will certainly kill us now.
                I'll go look right now."
    Taugi went inside a *ŋïndi* cricket,
        inside a cricket.
        Again *tutik! tutik!*   365
            he came inside the house.
                This was Taugi.
                    He looked around him.
    Then he kept going as a *kapiñakagï* lightning bug.
        The lightning bug is a tiny thing,   370
            glowing beautifully at night.
                He was inside that same creature,
                    inside a lightning bug.
    Then he came toward the poison *tuuu,*
        very close.   375
            Nearby was some *kofï* fruit.
    As he came toward it he threw some inside the cooking pot,
        and *kuaaa* the water stopped boiling.
    Kafunetiga came to see what had happened.
        The fire still surrounded the pot.   380
        "This was Taugi, this was Taugi's doing.
            It's dead," he went.
                The other was once again inside the cricket.
    "Has it been taken care of?"
        "Yes."   385
    "Huhu!" they all cheered with joy.
    Following that the *kagutu* were played.
        "Go ahead," Taugi said,
            "Play!
    All right, Children, go ahead, play!"   390
        so they played.
    Tugeŋgi the Bushmaster continued.

[*Kudyu hums the tune*]

        That's called *tigata*.

        "Hoh hoaah!"

        "More, more!" Taugi told him.   395

            "More, more! Go on, go on, try to poison me!"

Listen carefully now!

He spoke to him,

        to Kafunetiga.

        "He's bringing out *anetufe*," he told the others,   400

        he told the others.

        "Go on, go on, try to poison me!"

        "Hoh hoh!" his followers said.

            "Taugi is speaking to me right now,"

                so Kafunetiga removed his cooking pot from the fire.   405

Fish.

        Fish were then brought out.

        This time they were safe.

        Kafunetiga wanted the others to eat them.

        Teh with delicious salt mixed in.   410

        Pepper as well.

A pot of cold manioc soup was brought out,

        and another pot of cold manioc soup was brought out.

At that time the manioc starch replenished itself.

        Kafunetiga's wife's manioc starch replenished itself.   415

        When it reached a very low level,

        by dawn.

        So manioc bread was always brought out.

        The manioc starch silo was this large,

        the manioc starch silo.   420

Then he spoke this way to Agaka the Jay.

        Taugi spoke.

"Go, Grandfather.

        Go ahead, Grandfather, and look at our grandfather's food,"

        Taugi said.

Then the other approached as jays do.   425

    Bok, he perched on top of the house.

        "It seems to be still full."

While he remained perched there he placed a spell on it.

        This was Taugi himself.

        "Taugi, you look this time at how the manioc starch is."   430

        The manioc starch silo was very tall.

Then Taugi wanted to eat all of that.

        Taugi was truly envious of that other thing,

        I mean the manioc starch.

        A dry season of his passed,   435

a dry season of his passed,
        like that.
                His envy never ended.
"Here is some cold manioc soup," someone went to him.
"Here is some cold manioc soup," someone else went to him.   440
"The Mortals' food will always be used up," he declared,
        he then declared.
                Taugi had spoken.
Because that was done manioc starch has to be made.
After the rainy season,   445
        pisuk, pisuk
                it's processed.
Fish went to him.
        Just that way someone places it before us.
        The same is done when we go to a trading ceremony.   450
                Fish is brought out at night.
                Hot manioc soup is brought out.
                Cold manioc soup is brought out.
                        That is how we are when we eat in another settlement.
                        That is how it's done.   455
Now I've got to go. They're calling me to do just that!

Notes to Kafunetiga Tries to Poison Taugi

16   Like all flute sponsors, Kafunetiga must feed his visitors during the period they have come to play his flutes. Taugi visits Kafunetiga for this purpose because he is envious of Kafunetiga's ability to feed his guests no matter how often they visit him. Only at the end of the story does he realize there is a manioc silo that is never depleted.

54   "Son of a wild creature" is a being who was not human.

57–58   Macaw feathers "for the seating of leaders" refers to gifts that are given by the guest leaders to their hosts. These particular ornaments of Taugi changed the following day into plants; when their owners discovered this they were thrown into the water, from which came the water plants called "Taugi's feather headdresses."

72–74   Food is offered to the *kagutu* powerful being who lives underwater.

88–91   Kudyu emphasizes that long stories put people to sleep—sometimes for longer periods of time than are necessary or normal. This story is dangerous because of the spells that are mentioned and the references to poisonous substances.

110   After receiving the drink from Kafunetiga, Aulukuma gave it to his followers.

116   *Pasïtï* is a small brownish-black member of the *Apteronotidae*.

118   *Kagikagi* is a small member of the *Pimelodidae* that has dangerous barbs on its fins and tail.

124   *Pïdyëi* is a medium-sized (16–17-inch) catfish of the *Pimelodidae* family (Portuguese, *barbado*).

125   *Dyofi* is one of the larger characins in the Upper Xingu region (about two feet in length when mature), *Boulengerella cuvieri* (Portuguese, *bicudo*).

126   *Kadyagima* is a medium-sized (about 12–15 inches) catfish characterized by a markedly shorter lower jaw, *Platistoncatichthys sturio* (Portuguese, *pirapeuaua*).

128   *Amamai songs*. A collection of songs associated with various creatures. In addi-

tion to the players named, Tsikigi the Black Ibis, Kusu the Bare-faced Currasow, Akaga the Jay, Aguga the Fly, and Fifutu the Least Catfish played.

142   This line is a polite deception.

152   The "crying song" indicates to the sponsor that he has to bring out more food; if he does not do so he will dream badly and die.

158   "Taugi's campground," now called "*kagutu* campground," is the site in the plaza where the men gather to play the *kagutu*.

177   Agafafa the Anhinga is *Anhinga anhinga*.

212   This was the origin of the playing that is performed when the *taiyope* give presents to the sponsor.

223   Utigi is a small (2–3-inch) characin, unidentified.

227   The three-note tune replicates the name of the fish.

240   Akutsagï the Boat-billed Heron; *Cochlearius cochlearius*.

241   Itsëgi the Sunbittern; *Eurypyga helias*.

243   Agitaidyua the Great Blue Heron; *Ardea herodias*.

247   Nzueŋi the Cicada is a general term for cicadas, of which the Kalapalo name at least eight different types.

258   Tsikigi the Black Ibis may be the bare-faced (or whispering) ibis, *Phimosus infuscatus*. The Kalapalo name for this species is *kogokogoti*.

335–36   *Tsikigi kefegegï*, "Tsikigi's song spell," is applied together with a mixture of *itali* resin and semen.

392   Tugeŋgi the Bushmaster, *Lachesis muta*.

393   The tune replicates the snake's name.

421   Akaga the Jay; *Cyanocorax* sp.

446   This is the sound of manioc mash being squeezed by a woman.

456   Kudyu, a *kagutu ifï* or "knower," was called out during the last few minutes of the story to participate in a food distribution.

The language used by the Kalapalo to talk about the *kagutu* is characterized by metaphors of female sexuality. The shape and appearance of these large, tubular instruments, rather than seeming phallic to them, are likened to the female sexual organ: the mouth of this flute is called its "vagina" (*igïgï*), and when the set of *kagutu* is stored high in the rafters of the sponsor's house during periods when it is not played, the instruments are said to be "menstruating."[18] During this time the sponsor, like a husband avoiding his menstruating wife, is not supposed to fish for the players, nor are the flute players supposed to eat fish given them by the sponsor. Yet when the flutes are played, women must avoid seeing them lest they be gang-raped, and they are also supposed to avoid seeing the men prepare the flute-sponsor's manioc field (from which food will be made to pay the players and feed guests at the *kagutu egitsu*). Sometimes, as in the preceding myth, the manner of playing the flutes suggests they are used to express this potentially violent potency, as when the players beat them against the closed doors of the houses, allegedly so as to frighten the women inside. I never saw adult women reacting in fright, but younger girls were markedly affected, and in calming them, the older women did not laugh as they would on other occasions when children became frightened; there is no doubt that they view the threat as serious. Some men, however, seemed unsure of their capacity for such violence when I questioned them about the threat of rape.

The *kagutu* songs are of several types, and some seem to parallel those of the Yamurikumalu. Others, however, are distinctive to the *kagutu*. One aspect of the *kagutu* ritual music I did not observe in the Yamurikumalu are what I call oratorical songs. After the flutes have been played for several hours, a song-master will sing out in a falsetto voice combining oratorical and musical styles, asking the sponsor (*oto*) for food and drink to be given to the players. Two of these oratorical songs follow. Unmeasured, they are sung in falsetto, which indicates that the singer has taken on the role of a powerful being.

a. *Ohsi tuikefa kagifagu fomisu baba baba*
   "You should go pick Bull Frog's chili pepper, baba baba."
b. *Ande wokiŋo timbukugu wokiŋo*
   "Here's my future meal of manioc starch, my future meal."

As in the first story, the *kagutu* sponsor is identified with *kagutu oto*, who are powerful beings that live in the water, such as Bull Frog and Shrimp. Some *kagutu* music is identical to songs performed by the women during their ritual (as I have already described and as Kudyu quotes in his story of the flute ritual sponsored by Kafunetiga, the original owner and sponsor). But in addition to these forms of music, the men play other songs which women sing in contexts other than the Yamurikumalu process. These are called *itolotepe*, "birding," and several are given in Appendix 3. These songs are said to have been composed by women, and they clearly reflect a woman's point of view for they refer to food taboos women should follow when their children are sick, the relations between women and their lovers and husbands, and female rivalries. The songs are commentary upon past incidents involving known and frequently named ancestors, but most people were not able to describe these incidents to me, and none could provide any detail.

Women are interested in the music played on the *kagutu* flutes, particularly the women's songs, some of which they may not know as well as the Kagutu ritual performers. During a Kagutu ritual in 1979, Ambo, a young leader and song authority always ready to learn new music, called Kudyu, who was visiting in her house, to sit by her hammock so he could sing for her some of the songs that were being played outside. She also asked him who was playing. Indeed, many women are aware of which men are playing the *kagutu*, perhaps because they remember having heard certain individuals practicing on their *ku-luta* flutes.

In the Kagutu and Yamurikumalu rituals people play songs that refer to members of the gender opposite to that of the performers. Some of this music is said to have been originally "pieced together" by persons of the opposite sex. Other songs, composed by persons of the same sex as the performers, explicitly refer to commonly held images of the typical sociosexual behavior of members of the opposite sex. Furthermore, the symbols—forms of performance, costumes, instruments—used in each ritual carry sexual meanings that concern the opposite gender. In the Yamurikumalu, the women perform and behave aggressively like men. As the story describes so well, they adopt this role because the original female inventors of the Yamurikumalu acquired masculine characteristics by applying substances used only by men: *itali* resin, whose "pungency" is dangerous to women and which is worn by men during wrestling because it is supposed to impart physical strength; chili peppers (that originally swelled the women's genitalia into those of men) that are associated with a man's potential ability to control and use hyperanimate (*itseke*) power;[19] *kugitse* or love medicine that is supposed to attract women fatally to men and thus represents the sexual desire that men can generate in women. I have already shown that the men are handling a powerful symbol of female sexuality when they play the *kagutu*.

The men literally handle a representation of female sexuality when, at the time the sponsor receives payment from the *taiyope*, they flourish before the women large gourds upon which beeswax vaginas are modeled.[20] During this phase of the Kagutu ritual women and men engage in dances that end in debris-throwing brawls between *ifandaū*.

But the particular sexual attributes that are referred to in these rituals are precisely those that are considered repellent and pose the most danger to persons of the opposite sex. For the men, these are the insatiable female vaginal mouth and its mysterious and fearful menstrual processes. For the women, masculine dangers are ever-present in the form of potentially dangerous seminal substance (an excessive quantity from a number of men can rot inside a woman and make her seriously ill, for it cannot agglutinate to form a child), and even worse, the aggressive sexual passion of men that constantly threatens to turn into rape.

Yet despite these references to what persons of each gender understand to be the most difficult and threatening aspects of sexuality, during their rituals they enact those very qualities of sexual being. When people of one sex are performing, they are associating themselves with and even adopting qualities of feeling that are part of the imagined model of the opposite sex. These feelings include those that are directly linked to gender identity (uncontrollable sexual feelings, dangerous sexual substances) and others that emerge in the course of social life (jealousy, excessive modesty, fear of the opposite sex, absurd passions). Music is the enacted metaphor in each case.

Let us look more closely at that exceptionally violent (for the Kalapalo) and therefore strange injunction: women must not watch the flutes being played lest they be gang-raped, being taken, some men told me, to a place where a hornets' nest had been found so that the insects would later sting the victim to death.[21] This might appear to be a punishment, and women are not afraid of the flutes but of the men raping them.[22] This rape is described as if it were a reaction men have if they see women watching them play the flutes, and the Kalapalo suggest that this reaction is a consequence of the flutes' temporary association with female sexual parts and qualities of sexual passion. The men are, in fact, combining their own sexual feelings (aggression, initiating relations before women) with a particularly intense form of female sexual feeling that comes from their contact with the powerful beings that most clearly manifest those feelings, the *kagutu*. In combination with that of men, this female sexuality becomes violent and aggressive, marked by antipathy toward the victim. So rape may not be so much a punishment, something that men do to "get back" at women who have violated a serious injunction, as it is considered a compulsive effect of performance observed.

Regarding the Yamurikumalu rituals, we learned in the myth that the Aŋambïtï women's acquisition of male sexual feeling results in their seduction of women from other settlements, which is effected by the plants they rub over their bodies, being in contemporary life the fatal attractants called *kugitse*, which are said to cause madness. The women who hear the Yamurikumalu performers as they travel from settlement to settlement cannot resist following the Monstrous Women into a life that is the antithesis of settled, familial existence. In this myth the Monstrous Women have acquired the aggressive sexuality and fatal attractiveness of men, which results in their disruption of social life by drawing women away from men. In the story, the men are not attacked sexually but find themselves repellent to their women, who in various ways show that they are capable of living independently of their husbands (they can fish for themselves, for example). In another version of the same story, the women create male genitalia for themselves by tying up their labia, rubbing them with a mixture of *itali* resin and chili peppers, and then exposing them to the stings of spiders, venomous caterpillars, and stinging ants. These horrid body techniques result in the distinctly male musicality and unfemininely vigorous singing and dancing of the Monstrous Women. A concomitant loss of female emotions and capacities is associated with female sexuality that is later made clear in the story when the women relinquish the role of seducers of men, childbearers, and guardians and nurses of infants. The Monstrous Women are portrayed in the story of Sakatsuegï as women whose roles are those of men: they play the forbidden *kagutu*, and their sexual activities are aggressively masculine rather than passively feminine.

During the time of year when the Yamurikumalu ritual is held, women attack and beat up any man other than the sponsor who dares to enter the plaza. A visitor from the nearby settlement of Aŋafutu was so upset by the violence of their attack on a relative that he likened them to men clubbing to death an accused witch. As the women pound on the man's body with their fists and pull his hair, they smear him with *ondo*, the variety of red paint that only women use and that, when mixed with the resin called *tifa*, some men liken to menstrual blood. This symbolizes the dangers to men of sexual contact with women. Yet, a man who suffers this ordeal has the right to ask his female cousins for sexual relations, as if in defiance of the women's counterpart to the men's threat of rape that is ever present during the Kagutu. In the Yamurikumalu, the women violently repel men by means of a symbol of what seems to provoke the greatest overt anxiety in men concerning their relations with women. In both Kagutu and Yamurikumalu, neither male sexuality nor female sexuality alone is inherently violent or merely aggressive, but in conjunction they become seriously threatening. As the myths propose and the Kalapalo enact during their musical rituals, this combination is socially lethal, and it can be extremely dangerous—even fatal—to a member of the opposite sex.

What of the other musical instruments discovered by Kafunetiga? The *me-*

neuga was described to me as an instrument resembling the *kuluta* but no longer made. The *kuluta*, on the other hand, is still important, and its manner of use seems to represent an aspect of male sexuality that markedly contrasts with what is expressed through the *kagutu* playing. Whereas the *kagutu* flute performances suggest the aggressive and violent aspects of male sexuality, the older *kuluta* sister suggests what is charming and seductive in Kalapalo masculine behavior. This flute, being older, is less powerful, less beautiful, and hence not forbidden to women. On the contrary, men play the *itolotepe* songs on their *kuluta* to charm and seduce women, to let their lovers know they are approaching as they walk along the paths that wind among the manioc fields. And there are other flutes—the *ataŋa* and the *takwaga*—which are not associated with Kafunetiga and played by men who are dancing with women in highly positive erotic contexts.

A possible female counterpart to the *kuluta* is not a musical instrument but the distinctive female pubic ornament known as *uwigï*. This ornament is an erotic one that calls attention to a woman's vulva but at the same time makes intercourse impossible as long as it is worn. Kalapalo women do not now wear this ornament unless they are decorated for dancing. Their explanation is that the men decided they did not like them because the cord that was worn between a woman's legs in order to anchor the object to her belt could come in contact with feces. The owner might then contaminate food she is preparing.

So we return once more to the ambiguity that is inherent in Kalapalo conceptions and experiences of sexuality. Although I—and the Kalapalo—emphasize the dangers and difficulties through a focus on certain rituals and myths, there is always also present the pleasurable, erotic feelings (described in the same, as well as other myths) that draw men and women to each other and that are the very basis for continued human existence.

Conclusion

In the Yamurikumalu and Kagutu ritual processes, the performance of music effects a paradoxical relationship between the two categories of gender. First, the symbols it calls to mind emphasize the differences and antagonisms between the sexes through their reference to the dangerous powers inherent in human sexuality. Yet at the same time the music effects communication between the performers (of one sex) and the listeners (who are of the opposite sex), a situation of communicative control over those dangerous powers. Just as music is defined within narrative art as both the manifestation of transformative and aggressive attributes of powerful beings and a means available to people for controlling these forces, so Kalapalo use music ritually as a means of communicating between what they define as insurmountably separated or grossly unequal categories of beings.

This communication is effected not so much by establishing a mood of sympathy as by entrancing the listeners through explicit reference to their own power, using the powers of the listeners to disarm them temporarily. Such control cannot be effected through language, which obliquely deceives by creating mental illusions. It is true that Kalapalo music—like their speech—can emphasize boundaries and create antagonisms, as we see during the Kwambï, Kagutu, and Yamurikumalu rituals. But music has as well the paradoxical effect of simultaneously transcending boundaries, allowing people to communicate across the formidable divisions they create among and between themselves and the rest of their concerned existence. What is most successfully expressed in the environment of music paradoxically emphasizes formally opposed categories of being by bridging the chasms that separate them.

There is, however, at least a parallel, if not a true relation of identity, between Kalapalo ideas of language and Kalapalo ideas of music. Just as mythical discourse (speech unmarked for truth) is presented assertively by the speaker and received doubtfully by the Kalapalo listener, so in music there is a contrast between the psychological stance of the performer that occurs as a consequence of how that music is understood and that of the listener. These musical events may be either verbally messageless (as with most of Kalapalo collective ritual) or heavily laden with verbal messages (as in the Kwambï), but the experience of the performer and the listener are essentially different. Both are aware that the event is a communicative one, but each interprets the situation somewhat differently. The performers try to create an illocutionary effect, to move the listener, to create a feeling about the performative situation, to effect a shared feeling. The mode of their communicative act is assertive. The nonperforming listener, however, wishes to give meaning to the event, but, not being fully convinced of the validity of the message and needing to evaluate it and compare it with others, receives the music in a psychological state of doubt or even (as in the Kwambï) a state of disbelief. Yet the listener, who is also a participant some other time, has a double experience of assertion and doubt. As a result, performative participation offers simultaneously multiple interpretations to the listener. Kalapalo ritual music thus effects another paradox, that of combined assertiveness and doubt. Given this distinction in the roles of performer and listener, the culturally asserted differences between men and women, between human being and powerful being, do not pose the problems they do when language is the means of communication, when there is, in other words, a need for sharing the meaning of what is being said. Since music is multiply interpretable, it is effective when there is need for communication between beings who cannot, or will not, bring to a communicative event the same presuppositions about the truth of what is being said. This multiplicity of interpretation and distinction between performer and listener emphasizes boundaries created by classification and opposition, while at the same time paradoxically fusing the bounded and opposed into a unity of performative discourse, a domain of discourse which the Kalapalo represent by their ideas about powerful beings.

In the "Finale" to *Mythologiques*, in which ritual is set far apart from myth because of what he takes to be its essentially "meaningless" constitutive symbols, Lévi-Strauss—in strong opposition to Victor Turner—considers ritual exegesis as a mode of representation that is different from ritual but of the same order as mythology; he refers to it as "implicit mythology." For Lévi-Strauss, a "pure state of ritual" would have "no connection with language because it would consist of sacred words—meaningless to the ordinary person, or belonging to an archaic language no one can understand, or even formulaic expressions denuded of intrinsic meaning as one often finds in magic, in bodily gestures and in various selected and manipulated objects. At this moment, ritual like music at the other side of the system, passes definitely beyond language" (1981: 600).

Furthermore, citing a piece first published twenty-six years before, Lévi-Strauss reasserts that performance and discourse are not significant phenomena for the study of myth: "The substance of a myth is not found in its style, not in its mode of telling [in the English text "its original music"], nor in its syntax, but in the history ["the story"] that is told therein."[23] But we have come far from the position that there is no logic or continuity in a myth, that "everything is possible." Paying attention to performance and to discourse structure has allowed us to enhance the proposition that myth and music are opposed and correlated terms in a formal structure. Furthermore, we have been able to do this ethnographically, so as to contribute to an understanding of a specific South American set of ideas about music and language and specific South American performances of musical ritual and verbal art. The Kalapalo interpret these by means of a genealogical image of the emergence of human life from powerful beings· through the cumulative force of specific powerful processes, and this genealogical image is dependent upon their simultaneously linear and cumulative understanding of time. The emergence of humanity as a distinct category of being then allows for a contrast between human and powerful beings, a contrast that is psychological in its configuration, concerned with motivation and action, and sonorous in its expression. There is thus a conceptual tension between a genealogical, continuative idea of the relations between human beings and powerful beings and the idea of a contrast of feeling occurring between them. Hence language and music are the symbolic forms that most completely and fully express the powers and motives attributed to each class of entity, and as signifying structures these forms participate in this tension. When people perform music, they have the ability to move powerful beings because the latter can thereby most clearly recognize something of themselves in humanity.[24] Human beings, on the other hand, discover their pedigree through music.

The formal parallels between the myths of the New World and Western music that Lévi-Strauss understood so clearly may indeed be a consequence of how experience is created, organized, and interpreted by the indigenous inhabitants of the Americas, where not only are mythological genres complex poetic performed processes, but ritual is essentially a series of musical events. For the Kalapalo, the two are linked, first, by a sound symbolism that gives meaning to language and to music as signifying forms implying feelings and relations between entities, and second, by a performative frame that dissolves social and personal differences so as to create an experience of unity that is simultaneously physical and mental and therefore has deep moral significance. In Kalapalo verbal art, the performance of sound creates a sense of multiple presences through shifts in rhythm, tempo, tonality, contouring, and timbre—a musical process, though it need not always incorporate music per se. In Kalapalo mythic discourse, unity of participants occurs by means of mental imagining; hearing leads to "seeing" and understanding, and the meanings of words are taken to be shaped by illusionary images. In ritual performance, the unity of persons is effected through musical expression, wherein the body is an important musical instrument that helps to create a feeling about the motion of sounds in space, an understanding of a particular sense of time and of the most intense expression of life itself, which is the experience—however transient—that one is indeed a powerful being.

The mingling of different sounds in various situations of performed Kalapalo art is therefore a truly ecological representation of the universe. Through sound symbols, ideas about relationships, activities, causalities, processes, goals, consequences, and states of mind are conceived, represented, and rendered apparent to the world. It is through sound that cosmic entities are rendered into being and represented by the Kalapalo—not as object-types but as beings causing and experiencing action in a veritable musical ecology of spirit.

Appendix 1

Transcribing and Translating

Most Kalapalo stories require no more than half an hour to an hour for their telling, but the longest may take as long as several hours and are typically broken into separate storytelling sessions that occur over many days. In my experience, these longer stories are so truncated in their telling that a person may learn the complete story only after many days or even weeks or months if intervening events prevent a telling from being finished. Some people told me they had to piece together an entire myth from incomplete tellings of several different narrators, and they were consequently extremely keen on hearing a full account.

The stories included in this book were transcribed from taped performances, a procedure that influenced markedly the amount of detail I was able to obtain from narrators, who normally would have truncated the most lengthy story lines. They regarded the taped versions as definitive and realized that other Kalapalo would listen critically to their performances when I began to translate them. The longest story (called "Kwätïnï," not included in this book) was told over the course of four days. Kambe used his previously taped text as a guide to remembering what to say next, and the fact that his story was so detailed was surely an artifact of the methods of recording. Normally such a long story would be condensed to a few episodes, with subsequent tellings highlighting other episodes.

The tape recorder influenced narratives in another important way. Aware that their performances would be heard by many people outside their own household, narrators were concerned to display a degree of virtuosity they might not have otherwise, aiming at an impossibly perfect way of speaking. No Kalapalo performer was ever fully acceptable to the entire community, and even close relatives gently criticized a speaker's performance because each person's narrative style was considered imperfect. One man's children said he spoke so fast that even they could hardly understand him at times. Another spoke too repetitively for some and was thought to speak too slowly in his care to make his words understood by the tape recorder. Yet another storymaster was thought to be too imaginatively (and deceptively) flamboyant: "He makes up too much of the story," people said. Some others were thought to speak well, but their versions "weren't Kalapalo" because the tellers had originally lived in other settlements. In this highly critical climate, people would often introduce disclaimers, telling me they themselves did not know the "true" Kalapalo version but only that of the Jagamï or Wagif'ïtï or Kuikuru people. The speech of the rapidly speaking man became noticeably clearer after he listened to several of his own tapes, though he still transported himself with the excitement of his subsequent tellings. The second narrator became less repetitive and more detailed in response to his wife's ridicule.

Although the majority of stories were told because I happened to be present with a tape recorder, the selection was up to the narrators and quite often people present in the house made suggestions. The "what-sayers" were an extremely varied lot and included myself on many occasions when the narrators were concerned specifically to convey to me some particular knowledge. Knowing that a certain person was the possessor of an unusual story or knew one especially well, people often advised me to ask for a specific performance from that man or woman. The seeming capriciousness of the storytelling motive, depending on a teller's mood and the presence of the right audience, and the considerable variation in performances because of the personal qualities of a narrator and the expertise that seemed to be related to the particular narrators to whom they had listened in the past gave me cause to live in a number of different houses in the Kalapalo settlement over the time I taped these performances.

My method of preparing these texts in the field was to transcribe from the tapes with the help of three constant assistants, Madyuta, Faidyufi, and Ausuki. My transcriptions were checked with them with the help of the original tellers when possible. My assistants were valuable not only for their interest and pleasure in the stories but for their ability to clarify obscurities (that is, to provide information narrators had assumed I already possessed), identify natural species, and provide exemplifications of concepts labeled by words I did not immediately understand. Everyone involved in the project was concerned that the texts were correctly transcribed, and it was to this end (and also as a way of learning the stories) that volunteers spent extraordinary amounts of time seeing that I got them right.

Kwambï *Songs*
(as sung by Kambe)

1. Apuŋu, apuŋufa itau, itau
   Apuŋu, apuŋufa itau, itau
   Apuŋu, apuŋufa itau, itau
   Apuŋu, apuŋufa itau, itau
   Itau-ni, itau-ni
   Eitalufekegufa akanepui
   Apanufekegufa akanepui
   Andapepoŋu apuŋui
   Itaū-ni, itaū-ni

   Once and for all, once and for all the women, the women
   Once and for all, once and for all the women, the women
   Once and for all, once and for all the women, the women
   Once and for all, once and for all the women, the women
   Because of your constant arguing you shouldn't seat yourself
   Because of your constant gossip you shouldn't seat yourself
   You should remain like someone's follower once and for all
   The women, the women

   (invented by a man named Manua)

2. Idyatsi, dyatsi, dyatsi
   Isike atinïmiŋo witsigote fetsaŋe itaū
   Taidyoko atinïmiŋo witsiga fetsaŋe itaū
   Kapafu atani
   Doŋafu atani
   Isike atinïmiŋo witsiga fetsaŋe, itaū
   Taidyoko atinïmiŋo witsiga fetsaŋe, itaū

   Alas, alas, alas
   The stinging ant will bite me when I am to finally die, the women
   The stinging caterpillar will bite me when I am to finally die, the women
   He will be in the sky
   He will be underground

The stinging ant will bite me when I am to finally die, the women
The stinging caterpillar will bite me when I am to finally die, the women

(invented by a man named Kamani,
killed by snakebite)

3. Tïkinawakiñalï efeke, itaū-ni
   Tïkinawakiñalï efeke, itaū-ni
   Tïkinawakiñalï efeke, itaū-ni
   Tïkinawakiñalï efeke, itaū-ni
   Tila (ko)su uwipi tafandene ïŋï
   Ñatuisu uwipi augene ïŋï

   How many stories do I tell about you? the women
   How many stories do I tell about you? the women
   How many stories do I tell about you? the women
   How many stories do I tell about you? the women
   I have three disreputable containers of gossip
   I have five disreputable containers of lies

(Source not given)

4. Utepetuiŋofa agofeke ukilï
   Utuiluiŋofa agofeke ukilï
   Kuaku otoi uwinïmiŋoigey
   Tajofe otoi uwinïmiŋoigey

   I will declare myself later before all the people,
   I will display myself before all the people, the women (say)
   I'm planning to become the ceremonial house owner,
   I'm planning to become the owner of the big house

(invented by a man named Janukene)

5. Tsatue tepegani
   Ditue tepegani
   Itsatue tepegani
   Ditue tepegani
   Wifuŋupetale ugetatega ifeke, itaū
   Anatugofopetale ugetatega, itaū
   Anatugofo fumanikale nombesu, itaū
   Uwifuŋupetale ugey, itaū

   Listen to him lying
   Look at him lying

Listen to him lying
Look at him lying
Not he, but someone like me should be seated on the leader's seat, the women
Not he, but a prepared one such as myself should be seated on the leader's seat,
    the women
A prepared one just exactly like me, not someone spoiled by the disreputable
    thing he has been doing, the women
Not he, but someone like me should be seated on the leader's seat, the women

                    (invented by Manua)

6. Tïfekena ufiñandeŋalï itau-ni
   Fogoñafekefa ugepïlenïmiŋo tufïgeki figey
   Domiŋofekefa ugepïlenïmiŋo tufïgeki figey

   Who will cause me to be the last of my line? the women
   It will be Fogona who will shoot me directly with his revolver
   It will be Domingo who will shoot me directly with his revolver

                (about some Brazilians
                at an old Indian Service
                post called Batovi)

7. Aŋifale aŋoloiŋo uwagiŋo, uwagiŋo-ni
   Kanalufale aŋoloiŋo uwagiŋo
   Kaitefifale aŋoloiŋo uwagiŋo

   But there is someone who will be killed by you, those like me say,
       those like me say
   But Kanalu will be killed by you, those like me say
   But Kaitefi will be killed by you, those like me say

                (invented by a man named Kafigï)

8. Unde Tsimanage ufiñafono enimbïgï, itau-ni
   Uwotïf'iŋïitï futegatomi aka-ni

   Where is Tsimanage, my late older brother, the women
   I no longer want to have any parents

              (invented by Kadyua, Kambe's father)

9. Yatsiuitsu witsiluiŋo itaū-ni
   Taili titikana witsiluiŋo

Ago tegofoiŋo witsiluiŋo
Itau tegofoiŋo witsiluiŋo

Alas for me, I am going to die, the women
Everyone must be happy because I am going to die
My relatives will smile when I die
The women will smile when I die

> (invented by a man named Ugisapa, a leader
> of Lahatua Community, a former
> Kuikuro settlement)

10. Kukwifini kukwifini
    Ifisuagï tagofïŋī
    Ekegefeke ukweneluiŋo
    Nofakefeke ukweneluiŋo

Let's flee right away, let's flee right away.
His brother isn't any relative of ours
The jaguar will eat us.
The puma will eat us.

> (an accused witch sings about himself)

11. Tufefofa ekege anïgïufeke tapifofa ekege anïgïufeke
    Tufefofa nofake anïgïufeke
    Itaūfekelefa itafakuwi ifenïgï wake fugeni
    Ufïgifenïgï tufenui ufeke

Once a jaguar was almost killed by me, once a jaguar was almost shot by me
Once a puma was almost killed by me.
So I remember how the woman grabbed my bow as I was about to kill him.
As I was about to kill him she grabbed my arrow.

> (invented by a man whose
> wife prevented him from
> shooting an accused witch)

12. Ago tafandofati uge-ni
    Tufeke itau fandofati uge-ni
    Tafandofatifa uge
    Atofoki uge tiŋapale
    Kugife oto-i wataniti
    Oiñi oto-i watani

People gossiping about me
The women like to gossip about me
They like to gossip about me
But I don't have anything to do them in with
I want to own witches' darts
I want to be the owner of the tied-up things

(Source not given)

13. Tifenimbïgï inate wagiŋo
    Tiketinimbïgï inate wagiŋo
    Tuwakagatïnda itaũfeke tindapïgï tifati

    You're a person without any cleared fields around here, those like me
    You're a person without anything planted around here, those like me
    After the woman went to the water's edge she told what she had heard

(invented by Yanukula, leader
of the Aŋagafïtï Community,
now extinct)

14. Ete otuŋupa legey ukifiti ukwelïti
    Ufugogo otuŋupa
    Ete otoŋo ukwelïti
    Agakipïnegï ukifitsi
    Egealaŋipa, otolaŋipa etagiñunake
    Otoŋo ukifitsi.

    The people of this settlement want to have me dead, they want to club me
    The people of my plaza
    The people of this settlement want to have me dead
    They want to have me killed by a revenger
    This very one, another one are discussing it
    They want someone else to kill me.

(invented by Kumatsi, leader
of the former Kalapalo
community called Kanugidyafïtï)

15. Tufani itsomi uwelïti einïgï wagiŋo
    Tefuwi katofa tsagatega-ni
    Tuwai katofa tsagatega-ni

Why do you always want to kill me?, those like me
Are you an enduring rock?
Are you enduring water?

(Source not given)

Appendix 3

Songs Called "Birding"
(itolotepe)
(as sung by Kudyu, Ugaki, Tsaŋaku)

1. *Anetufo*
   Fadyanualu
   Etinageifalei eniñunake
   Emukufitsu fïŋïnefeke

   The leader:
   Fadyanualu
   Even though you try not to be jealous
   You're just like your own son's wife

2. *Isiŋina, anetufo otohoŋo*:
   Kukwiŋike Sanuku
   I ho ho, ku fe he

   The next one, another leader:
   Look at us all together, Sanuku
   I ho ho, ku fe he

3. Inafefa tisuake
   Ufisufeke ukilu
   Kuakukuegïfefale tïndagï afikini

   Walk quickly by us
   I said to my younger brother
   Even though Other Parrot's mouth is
   opened wide

4. Aŋitsale iñoiŋo anïgï
   Agifisu apogofotse
   Faŋanu apogofotse

   Here comes my future husband
   Decorated with painted hair
   Decorated with parrot feathers in his ears

5. Keyfatigo fetsaŋe
   Anukufa inigote
   Afinakemaŋa

   Try not to go outdoors
   Since Anukufa might see you
   Or even Afinake

6. Kudyagi tufa tugufa
   Kïŋafïŋa otofeke
   Ulefineti

   Kudyagi truly is the one I mean
   The owner is like a oropendola
   Doing like that other one

7. Tapogiŋotse Katudyigi
   Aŋifilake
   Enfiñano anïgï
   Asoti tentïfïgïa fïŋï

   Beautiful is Katudyigi
   But here
   Is his older brother
   Curled up like a roasted frog

8. *itaũ igisu fegey*
   Aŋitsufa Kaŋaŋakaga tepïgï
   Aŋadyuafeke anakaga
   Isogufeke nakaga tepïgï
   Yanuafeke nakaga tepïgï

This is a woman's song:
It was just now that Aŋadyua went
   To lie down with Kaŋaŋakaga
Her uncle went to lie down with her
Yanua went to lie down with her

9. Egipageginipa tuikeni

   Luwadyakana
   Apogofonipa tuikeni.

He'll certainly put on his ankle
   wrappings
Luwadyakana
He'll certainly put on his beautifiers

10. Enunduke
   Ugake fenunduke
   Opekugu maŋeley
   Kaŋakuegï eŋune

You should eat it
You should eat electric eel
It's really good despite what you say
Eat some giant catfish

11. Undema kupisu anïgï iniñui kupehe

   Undenialini
   Tufakandofoteni
   Ituga ŋonindïfïgï-na
   Ndïtï ŋonindïfïgï-na

Where is our younger brother, we're
   watching for him
Where could he be?
He must be seated by someone
He must be seated by Kingfisher
He must be seated by Motmot

12. Nikefinekefa uño atsaga tepïgï

   Iñafïgïkue
   Apïŋïfegey tuñokilu figey
   Iñafïgïkue

Look, look my husband stands
   motionless
By Ñafïgï
Our husband is dead once and for all
By Ñafïgï

13. Ikulufïŋï segey-ni
   Safisugu seley-ni
   Umïŋiusu segey-ni
   Safisugu segey-ini
   Afiti usu eley

This woman here must have made love
That's someone's design on her
This is his red paint
This is his design
This is urucu plant paint

14. Tëgano wake enitu
   Igey iga Kafokiŋalu wenitu

   Isilutalï ufeke
   Fitsaguta ufeke
   Ina nakatani fitsalufeke

Of Black Caracara I was once dreaming
While I dreamed Kafokiŋalu was over
   there
The thunder called to me
I became angry with it
I was angry with it because I woke up to
   her

15. Kigefetsaŋe uwake fagito-i
   Ufisu kilufeke, ufisu kilufeke

You should come with me to the *egitsu*
My younger brother said to me, my
   younger brother said to me

Uwikinduni faiŋitomi fagito-i
Ufisukilufeke
Utsakili nifainitomi fagito-i
Ufisukilufeke.

I want you to see me wrestle at the *egitsu*
My younger brother said to me
I want you to see me race at the *egitsu*
My younger brother said to me

Notes

Chapter 1: Introduction: Meaning Constructed Through Performance

1. In Geertz's words, we are "incomplete or unfinished animals who complete or finish ourselves through culture" (1965: 113).
2. Richard Bauman's succinct description of performance (building upon Hymes, 1975), although restricted to verbal communication, has useful implications for understanding other forms of symbolic action: "Fundamentally, performance as a mode of spoken verbal communication consists in the assumption of responsibility to an audience for a display of communicative competence. This competence rests on the knowledge and ability to speak in socially appropriate ways. Performance involves on the part of the performer an assumption of accountability to an audience for the way in which communication is carried out, above and beyond its referential content. From the point of view of the audience, the act of expression on the part of the performer is thus marked as subject to evaluation for the way it is done, for the relative skill and effectiveness of the performer's display of competence. Additionally, it is marked as available for the enhancement of experience, through the present enjoyment of the intrinsic qualities of the act of expression itself. Performance thus calls forth special attention to and heightened awareness of the act of expression and gives license to the audience to regard the act of expression and the performer with special intensity" (Bauman, 1977: 11; footnotes deleted).
3. Dell Hymes suggests that "in an oral tradition performance is a mode of existence and realization that is partly *constitutive* of what the tradition is. The tradition itself exists partly for the sake of performance; performance is itself partly an end. And while there are cases analogous to the prima donna who cannot go on if any detail is not right, more often the performers of tradition are masters of adaptation to situation" (1981: 86).
4. Abrahams, 1972; Bauman, 1972, 1975.
5. Such studies sometimes lead to precise substantive statements about the intermedial properties of a culture, as in Armstrong's admirable analysis of Yoruba affecting works and Witherspoon's study of Navajo art (Armstrong, 1971; Witherspoon, 1977).
6. Bauman, 1975: 292.

7. Langer, 1957: 42.
8. "In the first place he [the artist] knows how to work over his day dreams in such a way as to make them lose what is too personal about them and repels strangers, and to make it possible for others to share in the enjoyment of them. He understands, too, how to tone them down so that they do not easily betray their origin from proscribed sources. Furthermore, he possesses the mysterious power of shaping some particular material until it has become a faithful image of his phantasy; and he knows moreover, how to link so large a yield to pleasure this representation of this unconscious phantasy that, for the time being at least repressions are outweighed and lifted by it. If he is able to accomplish all this, he makes it possible for other people once more to derive the consolation and alleviation from their own sources of pleasure in their unconscious which have become inaccessible to them" (Freud, 1966: 377). My use of the word "fantasy" refers to imaginative activity in which thoughts and feelings concerning the self dominate, but in contrast with the psychoanalytical implications present in Freud's text I do not wish to imply that such daydreams are necessarily "neurotic."
9. "Cet appetit de connaissance objective" (Lévi-Strauss, 1962: 5).
10. Blacking, 1981: 596–603.
11. This notion was stated as early as 1953 by Suzanne Langer and discussed by Jakobson in a lecture given in 1968 (Langer, 1953: 31; Jakobson, 1971: 704; see also Zuckerkandl, 1976).
12. Lévi-Strauss, 1981: 596–603.
13. Lévi-Strauss, 1981: 654.
14. Zuckerkandl, 1956: 374.

Chapter 2: Narrative Performances and Discourse Structures

1. Described well by Casagrande, 1954.
2. Tedlock, 1972a, 1972b; Jakobson, 1960.
3. Hymes, 1981.
4. Labov, 1972.
5. The brilliant writings of Kenneth Burke on rhetoric and the representation of human motives provide an important framework for understanding symbolic action and its description in literature (Burke, 1961, 1962, 1966). That good stories are psychologically pleasing has been frequently noted and correlated with the different processes by which narratives give meaning to experience. In addition to Hymes and Labov, authors who have commented upon this idea in particularly interesting ways are Fowler, 1981; Wagner, 1975; and Wright, 1975.
6. Goffman, 1974: 43–44.
7. Intransitive subjects precede the verb, as do those of question and imperative sentences. Speech act verbs indicate the agent who causes the speech act. This agent is not necessarily the speaker. For example, *Maiki kilï*, "Maiki said," (*ki* = conversational speech act + *lï* = unmarked punctuate reportive tense, singular subject), but *kitse ufeke*, "Say it to me" (*ki* = conversational speech act + *tse* = imperative singular subject, *u* = first person singular + *feke* = causative) and *taifeke isifeke*, "He answered (told) his mother" (*ta* = nonconversational speech act + *i* = third person singular + *feke* = causative; *isi* = mother of a third person

+ *feke* = causative). Focalization is a special type of "topicalization" wherein any noun or adverbial phrase is shifted from its normal position in a sentence to the beginning of a sentence. An example of nonfocalized topicalization occurs in line 8, when Ulutsi makes reference to the *kaŋaŋatï* arrows in order to explain what they were. Because arrows, as inanimate objects, cannot serve as agents of transitive verbs, they are not marked by *-feke*.

8. I call these purposive, negative purposive, inceptive, negative inceptive, completive, repeative, negative repeative, conjunctive, oppositive, customary, malefactive, benefactive, unexpected, disjunctive, emphatic, durative, negative, necessary, frustrated, conforming, acceptable or valued, unacceptable or devalued, unwished for, unexpected, desired, metonymic.

9. Austin, 1962; Searle, 1979.

10. This novelistic device seems to be important in many South American mythologies. See, for example, Larsen, 1977, and Sherzer, 1983.

Chapter 3: Myth as an Explanatory Mode

1. This word has clear spatial significance as well, and implies a traveling motion. To explain the temporal idea, some people said it was like the road from Brasilia to Saõ Paulo, stretching off on the horizon apparently without end. Others likened it to a rash spreading over a person's entire body. Another use of *tïtehemi* is to refer to the dancing that occurs "all over" the settlement (that is, it moves from house to house).

2. Although he emphasized the role of precedent in myth, Malinowski saw it as a model for ritual action (1948). At the same time, his rejection of the etiological role of myth reinforced what he considered the theoretical importance of myth's psychological function: myth strengthens faith through a description of the "miracle" demonstrating ritual's efficacy. There are several reasons why this model of the homologous connection between myth and ritual falls short in the Kalapalo case. Kalapalo rituals of the sort I will be concerned with in this book do not serve to effect instrumental ends, nor is instrumentality normally mentioned in descriptions of the first performances. In myth, music has no instrumental function but is a manifestation of feelings and moods of powerful beings. Messages of etiology and of precedent are clearly present in these myths, but they are not stated as they would be in Western scientific explanatory contexts. Might not Malinowski's refusal to accept this function of myth have had to do with his implicit application of Western standards of explanation (especially, how causal statements must be framed and linguistically constructed) to Trobriand utterances? Might not these assumptions have misled Malinowski into believing that Trobriand myths do not contain such statements? (It is difficult to answer these questions because he published only one full text and translation of a Trobriand myth; Malinowski, 1961).

3. Eggan, 1967.

4. Evans-Pritchard, 1962: 174.

5. Lévi-Strauss, 1979.

6. See, for example, De Civrieux, 1970.

7. On three occasions Muluku refers to the deep sadness of a person in response to another character's death or disappearance: Saganafa's father and grandparents (after Saganafa has been taken away) and Kagayfuku after Paypegï has died. The

expression used is *ñalï ekugu*, accompanied by a special intonational contour (initial high pitch descending to low pitch) that emphasizes the intensity (the *ñalï*) of the feeling. This expression is abstract (a literal translation into English sounds odd: "doesn't much!"). It contrasts in form and meaning with the labels Muluku uses to characterize feelings, which are discrete verbal lexemes.

Chapter 4: Sound as Symbol: Orders of Animacy

1. The same word is used to refer to certain dangerous substances such as unboiled manioc juice that contains dangerous amounts of prussic acid and *itali* resin that is supposed to be dangerous to women and fatal to children.
2. Described further in Basso, forthcoming.

Chapter 5: The Government of Grief

1. According to Melatti (1978: chap. 2) the Ge-speaking Kraho are concerned with virtually identical matters during their mourning of the recently dead.

Chapter 6: Fantasies of Erotic Aggression

1. This aspect of the myths is reminiscent of the contrast once made by Victor Turner between structured and liminal social modes, exemplified by the differences between patrilineal and matrilateral relations in Tallensi society (1967).
2. These herbal teas have been incorrectly termed "emetics" in the literature on the Upper Xingu Basin; they do not spontaneously induce vomiting.
3. I have described Kalapalo affinity in Basso, 1975.
4. *Pseudoplatystoma fasciatum* L. (Port. "pintado," or "surubim"). The Kalapalo think of this species as especially strong because it can escape capture easily even when wounded by twisting its body out of the hands of people trying to grab it.
5. In a story of two men who make themselves invisible by using ear plugs made from the bones of the cannibal forest monster Afasa, the friend who engages in sexual intercourse with a woman under such circumstances is turned into an Afasa at the moment of ejaculation.
6. Other common species of native bees in the Upper Xingu Basin nest in amorphous or extremely elongated cavities within rotting trunks of trees. Lévi-Strauss makes much of an equation between menstrual blood and honey, but this is not an equation made by the Kalapalo, being a violation of their distinction between "fishy" (*üegï*) and "sweet" (*tatitsui*) substances; this is why I have not used it in referring to the *aga* nest as womb (see Lévi-Strauss, 1973). A viscous substance that is both a food and poison, honey much resembles semen, which the Kalapalo understand to be both the source of conception and of danger for women (Lévi-Strauss, 1978: 412). Another Amazonian people—the Tupi-speaking Kagwahiv—are reported to link pregnancy and bees in dream symbolism (Kracke, 1979).
7. Lévi-Strauss views the clinging motif in South American myths as a metaphor for copulation (1978: 33), more generally concluding that such myths proclaim the

suitability of all women for wifehood, though not all women are equally desirable (1978: 76). In the present case the female aspect of the clinging figure is only part of the entire image, who is sexually ambiguous because he continues to speak of his human victim, the tapir, and even the demoness Ñafïgï as his "brother-in-law." Aulati is thus classed (and classes himself) into one gender—the male—but monstrously adopts the characteristics of the other. It is Aulati who does the eating, and this reinforces my sense that he is monstrously female in his emotions because for the Kalapalo listener eating fish (an act recalling for them the female role in sexual intercourse and one of the things women wish for in exchange for sex) is treated here in its most voracious extreme. Some people thought Aulati was finally transformed by castration into Akugefe, the imprisoned servant of the sexually ambiguous demoness. Their household is a bizarre travesty of human domesticity.

8. People who are excessively *üegï* (menstruating women, boys whose ears have not healed after ear-piercing, children who have not yet been fully weaned and their parents) must refrain from eating (in the first two cases) any fish or (in the third instance) those that are considered—for reasons of taste but congruent with extremely large or small size—to be too "fishy."

9. Kofi told me: "When Ñafïgï desires a woman, she becomes a man. When she desires a man, she becomes a woman. When a person with children thinks about them, she appears as a child, embraces the parent and runs away. Because she does that the parent dies." Ñafïgï has the ability—apparently unique among powerful beings—to move through virtually every element in the environment: she can travel through the air, underground, through trees, rocks, and water. A river that she creates in another story is the only one that can flow in both directions, another suggestion of her pervasive powers of destructive transformation.

10. An evaluative judgment is implied by the caricaturing of compulsiveness and by the comments of other characters in the story. In this aspect Kalapalo myths may function in a way similar to Labov's description of Black English narratives, in which judgments are expressed by means of a third party's quoted speech, thus (according to Labov) carrying a special authoritative force that opinions expressed directly by the speaker would not carry (1972).

11. Spiro, 1979: 11.

Chapter 7: Saturated with Music, Submerged in Sense

1. Turner, 1967, 1969, 1974.
2. Geertz, 1973.
3. Fernandez, 1972, 1974, 1977.
4. Unlike potblack, the paint made from juice of unripe genipapa fruit (*Genipa americana*) does not wash off; it wears off after several days. The Kalapalo do not attribute any significance to this property, the gleaming black color seeming to be of most importance.
5. *Mïŋi* and *ondo* are the two varieties of red paint made from the widely cultivated *Bixa orellana*, known as *ururu* in Brazil and *achiote* or *onoto* in Spanish-speaking countries. Mixed with piqui oil, the pulp of the *urucu* seeds forms a "fragrant" (*sikegï*) glossy paint that is used not only during ritual adornment but occasionally on nonritual occasions when people want to beautify themselves. Kalapalo paint

themselves with *urucu* after eating large amounts of fish, for they feel that the fragrance of it will overcome the excessive and potentially harmful "fishyness" in their bodies. Painting also precedes sexual advances. One important sign of mourning is the refusal to be painted with *mïŋi*.

6. Lévi-Strauss's discussion of the relation between polychromaticism, confusion, and differentiation in South American myths is pertinent here (1969: 324–25).

7. I have described the nonmusical details of the Ifagaka, Egitsu, and boys' ear-piercing at some length in detail in an earlier work and will therefore not repeat that material here; see Basso, 1973, especially chapter 8.

8. When visitors come to trade (*uluki*) they are asked to perform whatever *undufe* music their hosts are engaged in and are joined by the host women.

9. Zuckerkandl, 1956: 219.

10. According to Robert P. Morgan, in tonal music the tonal system—the octave—constitutes the basic structure for musical space. But the less emphasis placed upon tonality to structure space, the more a composer uses performance space (and even visual space as represented by the score) to do so. In this connection, "A weakening of one kind of musical space was countered by a strengthening of another, more literal one. Indeed, the more removed a composition is from the older conventions the more likely it is that the performance space will be incorporated into its overall conception" (1980: 577).

11. Zuckerkandl 1976: 24–25.

12. Ibid. p. 374.

13. See especially Turner, 1967.

14. Although approximately a third of the adult population of the settlement is designated *anetaü*, only a relatively small number ever participate actively in an official capacity for affinal and political reasons that I discuss in Basso, 1973. In 1979, fifteen adults were sponsors, of whom six were *anetaü*. The others were closely allied with prominent leaders.

15. 1974: 274.

16. Seeger (1977) describes a similar ritual event among the Ge-speaking Suya, emphasizing the connection between individual song and communication across social and psychological distance.

17. This wrestling is described in detail in Basso, 1973.

18. According to Rafael de Menezes Bastos (1978: 175), among the neighboring Tupi-speaking Kamaiura, men paint themselves with designs they call "menstruation" when they play the *kagutu* (called *jaku'i* in their language). Christine and Steven Hugh-Jones's interpretation of the Tukanoan Barasana *He* House rituals as "symbolic menstruation" is a fascinating counterpart to the present discussion of the representation of human sexual processes through musical ritual performance (C. Hugh-Jones, 1979; S. Hugh-Jones, 1979). Menezes Bastos (1978: 171–72) finds their argument applicable to Kamaiura ideas about male and female musical rituals.

19. Sauces made with hot chili peppers are customarily used as ceremonial food when men are working together independently of women.

20. According to Steven Hugh-Jones, beeswax is possibly identified with menstrual blood by the Barasana. The Kalapalo do not so identify it, as far as I know.

21. This seems to be yet another important instance of associating stinging insects with the violence of male sexuality. The sexually ambiguous demoness Nafïgï is also associated with stinging insects: the biting flies called *tugeŋgi* are her nail parings, and, as Muluku described in a story about her, her vagina originally held a stinging

ant, poisonous caterpillar, and tiny piranha. Now, as Kambe reiterated many times in his own story, she is dangerous because of her genitals' "poisonous pungency" (*piŋegï*), also a masculine trait.

22. An exact counterpart is described by Steven Hugh-Jones concerning the Barasana *He* flutes (1979: 129).

23. 1981: 577; originally published in 1955 and reprinted with some modifications 1963: 210.

24. Other American instances of music that moves powerful beings come to mind: the Inuit shaman who by singing to the life-controlling water demoness Sedna revives the dead; the Navajo Night Chant hero myth, in which figure the maimed twins, who—by song—finally move the gods into curing them, after speech, prayers, payment, and weeping each fails in turn. Only when their weeping turns to song are the gods moved by the yearnings of human beings for the beauty that comes with health, strength, and order.

Bibliography

Abrahams, Roger
    1972   "Personal Power and Social Restraint in the Definition of Folklore." In *Towards New Perspectives in Folklore*, edited by Americo Paredes and Richard Bauman, pp. 16–30. Austin: University of Texas Press.

Agostinho, Pedro
    1974   *Kwarìp. Mito e Ritual no Alto Xingu*. São Paulo: Editora da Universidade de São Paulo.
    1978   *Mitos e Outras Narrativas Kamayurá*. Bahia: Universidade Federal da Bahia (Colecão Ciencia e Homem).

Armstrong, Robert Plant
    1971   *The Affecting Presence: An Essay in Humanistic Anthropology*. Urbana: University of Illinois Press.

Austin, J. L.
    1962   *How to Do Things with Words*. Oxford: Oxford University Press.

Basso, Ellen B.
    1973   *The Kalapalo Indians of Central Brazil*. New York: Holt, Rinehart and Winston.
    1975   "Kalapalo Affinity: Its Social and Cultural Contexts." *American Ethnologist* 2:207–237.
           "The Implications of a 'Progressive' Theory of Dreaming." In *Dreaming in Cross-Cultural Perspective*, edited by Barbara Tedlock. Albuquerque: University of New Mexico Press, forthcoming.

Bastos, Rafael José De Menezes
    1978   *A Musicológica Kamaiurá*. Brasilia: FUNAI.

Bauman, Richard
    1972   "Differential Identity and the Social Base of Folklore." In *Towards New Perspectives in Folklore*, edited by Americo Paredes and Richard Bauman, pp. 31–41. Austin: University of Texas Press.
    1975   "Verbal Art as Performance." *American Anthropologist* 77:290–311.
    1977   "Verbal Art as Performance." In *Verbal Art as Performance*, pp. 3–58. Rowley, Mass.: Newbury House. (Reprint, Waveland Press.)

Blacking, John
    1981   "The Problem of 'Ethnic' Perceptions in the Semiotics of Music." In *The Sign in Music and Literature*, edited by Wendy Steiner, pp. 184–94. Austin: University of Texas Press.

Cemeu, Helza
    1977   *Introducão ao Estudo da Musica Indigena Brasileira*. Rio de Janeiro (?):
           Conselho Federal de Cultura e Departamento de Assuntos Culturais.

Casagrande, Joseph
    1954   "The Ends of Translation." *International Journal of American Linguistics*
           20:335–40.

De Civrieux, Marc
    1970   *Watunna: Mitología Makiritare*. Caracas: Monte Avila Editores.

Eggan, Fred
    1967   "From History to Myth: A Hopi Example." In *Studies in Southwestern
           Ethnolinguistics*, edited by Dell Hymes, pp. 33–53. The Hague: Mouton.

Evans-Pritchard, E. E.
    1962   "Anthropology and History." In *Social Anthropology and Other Essays*,
           pp. 172–91. New York: Free Press.

Fernandez, James W.
    1972   "Persuasions and Performances: Of the Beast in Every Body and the
           Metaphors of Everyman." *Daedalus* 101 (1):39–60.
    1974   "The Mission of Metaphors in Expressive Culture." *Current Anthropology*
           15:119–45.
    1977   "The Performance of Ritual Metaphors." In *The Social Use of Metaphor:
           Essays on the Anthropology of Rhetoric*, edited by J. David Sapir and J.
           Christopher Crocker, pp. 100–131. Philadelphia: University of Pennsyl-
           vania Press.

Fowler, Roger
    1981   *Literature as Social Discourse*. London: Batsford Academic and Educa-
           tional Ltd.

Freud, Sigmund
    1966   "Lecture XXIII: The Paths to the Formation of Symptoms." In *The Com-
           plete Introductory Lectures on Psychoanalysis*, translated and edited by
           James Strachey, pp. 358–77. New York: W. W. Norton.

Geertz, Clifford
    1965   "The Impact of the Concept of Culture on the Concept of Man." In *New
           Views of the Nature of Man*, edited by John R. Platt, pp. 93–118. Chi-
           cago: University of Chicago Press.
    1973   *The Interpretation of Cultures*. New York: Basic Books.

Goffman, Erving
    1974   *Frame Analysis*. New York: Harper & Row.

Hugh-Jones, Christine
    1979   *From the Milk River*. Cambridge: Cambridge University Press.

Hugh-Jones, Stephen
    1979   *The Palm and the Pleiades*. Cambridge: Cambridge University Press.

Hymes, Dell
    1975   "Breakthrough into Performance." In *Folklore: Performance and Com-
           munication*, edited by Kenneth S. Goldstein and Dan Ben-Amos, pp. 11–
           74. The Hague: Mouton.
    1981   *"In Vain I Tried to Tell You"*: Essays in Native American Ethnopoetics.
           Philadelphia: University of Pennsylvania Press.

Jakobson, Roman
    1960   "Concluding Statement: Linguistics and Poetics." In *Style in Language*,
           edited by Thomas A. Sebeok, pp. 350–77. Cambridge, Mass.: MIT
           Press.

1971 "Language in Relation to Other Communication Systems." In *Selected Writings* 2:695–708. The Hague: Mouton.

Kracke, Waud
1979 "Dreaming in Kagwahiv: Dream Beliefs and Their Psychic Uses in an Amazonian Indian Culture." In *The Psychoanalytic Study of Society*, edited by Warner Muensterberger and L. Bryce Boyer, 8:119–71.

Labov, William
1972 "The Transformation of Experience in Narrative Syntax." In *Language in the Inner City*, pp. 354–96. Philadelphia: University of Pennsylvania Press.

Langer, Susanne
1953 *Feeling and Form*. New York: Charles Scribner's Sons.
1957 *Problems of Art*. New York: Charles Scribner's Sons.

Laraia, Roque de Barros
1967 "O Sol e a Lua na mitologia Xinguana." *Revista do Museu Paulista* n.s. 17: 7–46.

Larsen, Mildred
1977 *The Functions of Reported Speech in Discourse*. Norman, Okla.: Summer Institute of Linguistics.

Lévi-Strauss, Claude
1962 "The Structural Study of Myth." In *Structural Anthropology*, translated by Claire Jacobson and Brooke Grundfest Schoepf, pp. 206–31. New York: Basic Books.
1963 *La pensée sauvage*. Paris: Librarie Plon.
1969 *The Raw and the Cooked*. Vol. 1 of Introduction to a Science of Mythology, translated by John and Doreen Weightman. New York: Harper & Row.
1973 *From Honey to Ashes*. Vol. 2 of Introduction to a Science of Mythology, translated by John and Doreen Weightman. New York: Harper & Row.
1978 *The Origin of Table Manners*. Vol. 3 of Introduction to a Science of Mythology, translated by John and Doreen Weightman. London: Jonathan Cape.
1979 *Myth and Meaning*. New York: Schocken Books.
1981 *The Naked Man*. Vol. 4 of Introduction to a Science of Mythology, translated by John and Doreen Weightman. New York: Harper & Row.

Malinowski, Bronislaw
1948 "Myth in Primitive Psychology." In *Magic, Science and Religion*, pp. 93–148. Garden City: Doubleday.
1961 *Argonauts of the Western Pacific*. New York: E. P. Dutton.

Melatti, Julio Cezar
1978 *Ritos de Uma Tribo Timbira*. São Paulo: Editora Atica.

Monod-Becquelin, Aurore
1975 *La pratique linquistique des Indiens Trumai. Vol. 2, Mythes trumai (Haut-Xingu, Mato Grosso, Bresil)*. Languages et Civilizations à Tradition Orale, 10. Paris: Société d'études Linguistiques et Anthropologiques de France.

Morgan, Robert P.
1980 "Musical Time/Musical Space," *Critical Inquiry* 6 (3):527–38.

Searle, John R.
1979 "A Taxonomy of Illocutionary Acts." In *Expression and Meaning*, pp. 1–29. Cambridge: Cambridge University Press.

Seeger, Anthony
    1977   "Por que os Indios Suya Cantam para as suas Irmas?" *Arte e Sociedade*, pp. 39–63. Rio de Janeiro: Zahar Ed.

Sherzer, Joel
    1983   *Kuna Ways of Speaking*. Austin: University of Texas Press.

Spiro, Melford E.
    1979   "What Ever Happened to the Id?" *American Anthropologist* 81:5–13.

Stevens, Wallace
    1951   *The Necessary Angel*. New York: Vintage Books.

Tedlock, Dennis
    1972a   *Finding the Center*. New York: Dial Press.
    1972b   "On the Translation of Style in Oral Narrative." In *Towards New Perspectives in Folklore*, edited by Americo Paredes and Richard Bauman, pp. 114–33. Austin: University of Texas Press.

Turner, Victor
    1967   "Symbols in Ndembu Ritual." In *The Forest of Symbols*, edited by Victor Turner, pp. 19–47. Ithaca: Cornell University Press.
    1969   *The Ritual Process*. Ithaca: Cornell University Press.
    1974   "Metaphors of Anti-structure in Religious Culture." In *Dramas, Fields, and Metaphors: Symbolic Action in Human Society*, pp. 272–99. Ithaca: Cornell University Press.

Villas Boas, Orlando and Claudio Villas Boas
    1970   *Xingu: Os Indios Seus Mitos*. Rio de Janeiro: Zahar Editores. English translation: *Xingu: The Indians, Their Myths*. New York: Farrar, Straus, and Giroux, 1973.

Wagner, Roy
    1975   *The Invention of Culture*. Englewood Cliffs, N.J.: Prentice-Hall.

Willie, A. and O. D. Michener
    1973   *The Nest Architecture of Stingless Bees with Special Reference to those of Costa Rica* (Hymenoptera, Apidae). *Revista de Biologia Tropical*, vol. 21, suppl. 1. San Jose, Costa Rica: Editorial Universitaria.

Witherspoon, Gary
    1977   *Language and Art in the Navajo Universe*. Ann Arbor: University of Michigan Press.

Wright, Will
    1975   *Sixguns and Society: A Structural Study of the Western*. Berkeley and Los Angeles: University of California Press.

Zuckerkandl, Victor
    1956   *Sound and Symbol*. Princeton: Princeton University Press.
    1976   *Man the Musician*. 2d ed. Princeton: Princeton University Press.

Index

adolescence, Kalapalo, 9, 167–70: puberty seclusion, 14, 34–35, 56–57, 106, 142, 167–70, 290

Afasa (cannibal forest monster), 328 (chap. 6, n. 5)

affines, relations among, 68–69, 166 with notes to ll. 30–32, l. 58, l. 134, 170, 207. *See also* In-law speech

Agakuni (Kalapalo songmaster and storyteller), 74, photo. no. 8

akūa (interactive self), 30, 72–73, 105, 107, 246

Akwakaŋa, discussion of story, 170

Alamigi, discussion of story, 32, 74, 81 (table 9)

anaphora, 27, 32

animacy orders, 65 (table 7), 66, 70–71, 73

anthropology, 1–4, 37, 62, 244

Arawak language, Kalapalo songs in, 108, 124 with note to l. 250, 288

Armstrong, Robert Plant, 2–3, 325 (chap. 1, n. 5)

art, 3–6: among Kalapalo, 6–10

asceticism, 106, 169

ataŋa players, 139, 287, 290, 308, photo. nos. 8, 11. *See also* Ritual processes, *egitsu*

audience (listeners), 7, 13, 15, 208, 309. *See also* What-sayer

Aulati, discussion of story, 207–8, 212–13

Austin, J. L., 35, 71

auūgufi performance, 126, 251, photo. no. 3. *See also* Ritual processes, memorial

Barasana Indians, 330 (chap. 7, nn. 18, 20), 331 (chap. 7, n. 22)

Bastos, Rafael de Menezes, 330 (chap. 7, n. 18)

Bat, discussion of story, 108, 125–26

Bat's Song, 108, 125

Bauman, Richard, 4, 325 (chap. 1, nn. 2, 6)

bees, symbolic use of, 212–13, 328 (chap. 6, n. 6)

beeswax equated with menstrual blood, 330 (chap. 7, n. 20). *See also* Barasana Indians; Hugh-Jones, Steven

birth order and personal attributes, 58, 142, 308

Black English narratives, 329 (chap. 6, n. 10)

Blacking, John, 8

body parts, organs: sounds made by, 66–67; as sources of feeling, 65–66, 169ff.

body techniques, 9, 106, 141, 169–70, 208, 307

Bororo Indians, 241

bowmasters (*tafaku oto*), 167–68

burial, 89, 105

Burke, Kenneth, 326 (chap. 2, n. 5)

calls, animal and bird (*itsu*), 63ff.

cannibalism, 59

caricature, 209, 240, 329 (chap. 6, n. 10)

Casagrande, Joseph, 326 (chap. 2, n. 1)

ceremonial house (*kuakutu*), 13–14, 125, 247, 251, 287–8

characters in Kalapalo myths, 36, 54, 61, 208; physical distinctiveness and attitudes, 61–62, 210–11; references to moods of, 56 (table 6), 60; relations among, 36, 67–71, 207; and sound symbols, 73–74. *See also* Myths

childbirth, 106, 211, 213

children and storytelling, 17, 38

chili pepper sauce (men's ceremonial food), 330 (chap. 7, n. 19)

337

Index of Myths

University of Pennsylvania Publications in Conduct and Communication

Erving Goffman and Dell Hymes, Founding Editors
Dell Hymes, Gillian Sankoff, and Henry Glassie, General Editors

Erving Goffman, *Strategic Interaction*
Ray L. Birdwhistell, *Kinesics and Context: Essays on Body Motion Communication*
William Labov, *Language in the Inner City: Studies in the Black English Vernacular*
William Labov, *Sociolinguistic Patterns*
Dell Hymes, *Foundations in Sociolinguistics: An Ethnographic Approach*
Barbara Kirshenblatt-Gimblett, editor, *Speech Play: Research and Resources for the Study of Linguistic Creativity*
Gillian Sankoff, *The Social Life of Language*
Erving Goffman, *Forms of Talk*
Sol Worth, *Studying Visual Communication*, edited by Larry Gross
Dell Hymes, *"In Vain I Tried to Tell You"*
Dennis Tedlock, *The Spoken Word and the Work of Interpretation*
Ellen B. Basso, *A Musical View of the Universe: Kalapalo Myth and Ritual Performances*

Kalapalo Myth and Ritual Performances

University of Pennsylvania Press
Philadelphia
1985

A Musical View of the Universe